MASS MEDIA LAW

This book is part of the Peter Lang Media and Communication list.
Every volume is peer reviewed and meets
the highest quality standards for content and production.

PETER LANG
New York • Washington, D.C./Baltimore • Bern
Frankfurt • Berlin • Brussels • Vienna • Oxford

ARTHUR S. HAYES

MASS MEDIA LAW

The Printing Press to the Internet

PETER LANG
New York • Washington, D.C./Baltimore • Bern
Frankfurt • Berlin • Brussels • Vienna • Oxford

Library of Congress Cataloging-in-Publication Data

Hayes, Arthur S.
Mass media law: the printing press to the Internet / Arthur S. Hayes.
pages cm
Includes bibliographical references and index.
1. Mass media—Law and legislation—United States. 2. Press law—United States.
3. Internet—Law and legislation—United States. I. Title.
KF2750.H39   343.7309"9—dc23   2013003331
ISBN 978-1-4331-0756-6 (paperback)
ISBN 978-1-4539-1043-6 (e-book)

Bibliographic information published by **Die Deutsche Nationalbibliothek**.
Die Deutsche Nationalbibliothek lists this publication in the "Deutsche
Nationalbibliografie"; detailed bibliographic data is available
on the Internet at http://dnb.d-nb.de/.

Contents

Preface

Mass Media Law: The Printing Press to the Internet is a different kind of media law textbook in many respects. When the mold was cast for the communications media law subgenre in the late 1960s, departments and schools devoted to communication and media studies were new, and the World Wide Web did not exist. The traditional communications media law text targeted journalism and political science majors and emphasized First Amendment case law stemming mostly from journalism and print media controversies. That approach, some might say, is so 20th century.

This communications media law text targets mostly communications and media studies majors. It emphasizes the interaction between law and media technologies. First Amendment case law still is paramount, but the dynamic legal territory is digital media law. Legal controversies stemming from digital software and hardware, and Internet use have thrust copyright, common carriage, and invasion of privacy law to the forefront, and also have made foreign media law difficult to ignore. And media abundance and convergence call into question the diminished First Amendment status of broadcasting. Some, such as Harvard Law professor Lawrence Lessig, contend computer code—the text of a computer program—is a law that regulates cyberspace as much as traditional brick-and-mortar laws.

It follows then that an introduction to media law doctrines and principles should underscore communication and media studies education and introduce students to the panoply of legal theories raised by the Internet revolution, as well as those supporting traditional media. Chapter 2, "History and Impact of Media Law," for example, covers cases, controversies, and concepts that traditionally are not included in communications media law texts: cyber libertarianism, cyber-collectivism, First Amendment media-specific analysis, common carriage law, the Postal Service Act of 1792 and 1794, and universal service obligation.

The link between the law and the development of mass media technologies is explored in the obvious chapters: Chapter 3, "Cyberspace & Free Expression," Chapter 11, "Broadcast & Cable

Television Regulation," and Chapter 14, "Copyright, New Technologies & Trademark." Also, law and media technologies are central in the less obvious ones: Chapter 5, "Defamation: Constitutional and Cyber Law," Chapter 6, "Privacy," and Chapter 10, "Fair Trial/Free Press."

There is another feature that sets this book apart from other communications media law texts. At the end of each chapter, the reader will find questions in the form of legal hypotheticals. The hypotheticals will give students the opportunity to put the principles of legal precedent, and the analytical skills of analogy and distinguishing, discussed in Chapter 1, "Principles of Reasoning and First Amendment Theory," to work. Each chapter identifies and explains the doctrinal tests students need to apply to the hypotheticals. The author of this book has used many of the hypotheticals published here to spark in-class discussion and as questions on midterm and final exams. Furthermore, Web addresses to online media law sources are provided at the end of each chapter. The Web provides a great deal of authoritative information that can enliven any discussion of media law, sometimes found in the unlikeliest of places. Chapter 13, "Copyright Law," for example, identifies a YouTube webpage where students can better understand the copyright doctrines of infringement and substantial similarity at issue in *Bright Tunes Music v. Harrisongs Music*, 420 F. Supp. 177 (S.D.N.Y. 1976) by listening to the pop hits "He's So Fine," and "My Sweet Lord" layered on top of each other. Additionally, www.scholar.google.com provides a gateway to a trove of federal and state judicial rulings and scholarly articles.

Finally, this book is different because each of the fifteen chapters opens with "Controversy" anecdotes. Their purpose is to make the mysterious and abstract familiar and concrete. For example, Chapter 2 discusses, among other concepts, the immunity from certain civil actions that online intermediaries enjoy under Section 230 of the Communications Decency Act (CDA). In the abstract, that might mean little or nothing to the average undergraduate. But consider the chapter's introduction, which tells how that the federal statute shields the owners of RateMyProfessors.com from certain civil actions, including libel, and that the First Amendment makes it extremely difficult for angry professors to learn the identities of students who use the social media site. Through this real-world vignette, the significance of CDA § 230 and the First Amendment becomes fathomable and relevant.

Mass Media Law: The Printing Press to the Internet, however, is not a radical departure from the subgenre. It covers traditional subjects and doctrines, as the chapter descriptions below make clear.

Chapter 1, "Principles of Legal Reasoning and First Amendment Theory," opens with a capsulized summary of *Brown v. Entertainment Merchants Association*, 131 S. Ct. 2729 (2011). In *Entertainment Merchants Association*, a landmark ruling, the U.S. Supreme Court said video games were fully protected under the First Amendment. The chapter uses the ruling, its path to the high court, and its impact on media law as a way of introducing students to core litigation principles, the structure of our state and federal court systems, and the basics of legal and judicial analysis. The chapter also covers traditional and recently formulated First Amendment theories: the marketplace of ideas, civic courage, self-government, individual self-fulfillment and autonomy, checking the abuse of official power, the safety value function, absolutism, tolerance, sponsoring of nonconformity, the constitutional concept of public discourse, and the theory of democratic culture.

Chapter 2, "History and Impact of Media Law," traces the U.S. approach to regulating mass media technologies for the purpose of facilitating the flow of information to promote national unity, economic growth, cultural development, democratic participation, and individual freedom. The chapter covers the U.S. Constitution's First Amendment free press and free speech clauses (1787), the Constitution's Article I, Section 8, known as the Copyright Clause, which authorized the Copyright Act of 1790, and the Postal Service Act of 1792 and 1794. The chapter also explains the Court's First Amendment media-specific analysis, now under attack by free marketers and First Amendment advocates.

Chapter 3, "Cyberspace & the Free Expression," examines efforts in the U.S. and abroad to regulate online speech. In the U.S., congressional campaigns to protect children from the alleged harms of sexually explicit content on the Internet produced the Communications Decency Act of 1996, Child Online Protection Act (COPA) of 1999, and the Children's Internet Protection Act (CIPA) of 2000. Only the CIPA survived constitutional scrutiny. The chapter also discusses two types of legal controversies labeled as cyberbullying. One category involves efforts by public schools to punish students for things they say online. It's a controversy that the Court declined to resolve in 2012. The other form of cyberbullying does not implicate public school authority and has involved adults as well as minors. So far, anticyberbulling efforts have not passed constitutional scrutiny. The chapter continues with a discussion of Internet governance issues, including kill-switch authority, censorship by foreign nations, and the network neutrality and Internet exceptionalism policy debates.

Chapters 4 and 5 cover libel law. Chapter 4, "Defamation: Common Law Elements," discusses the elements of a cause of action for libel that a plaintiff is required to establish to get a case before a trier of fact, a judge or jury, developed through the state common law and statutory process. It also discusses common law and statutory defenses and privileges that can defeat a libel action before and during trial.

Chapter 5, "Defamation: Constitutional and Cyber Law," discusses *New York Times Co. v. Sullivan*, 376 U.S. 254 (1964), the Court ruling that gave libel defendants, particularly journalists, strong First Amendment protections. It also examines *Sullivan*'s impact on state libel law, as well as legal controversies stemming from libel law and cyberspace, particularly the impact of the Communication Decency Act § 230, which immunizes Internet service providers from libel actions originating from third-party comments.

Chapter 6, "Privacy," looks at two categories of privacy protection theories: (i) invasion of privacy torts, which are statutory protections, allowing individuals to bring claims against nongovernment defendants, and (ii) the Fourth Amendment, which prohibits unreasonable search and seizure by government officials. The chapter also covers invasion of privacy controversies related to, and the statutes affecting, online activity—particularly the use of individuals' personal data stored on social media sites and collected by search engines.

Chapter 7, "Prior Restraints & Subsequent Punishment," examines how the Court has sought to balance the free expression rights of the news and entertainment industries with the right of the government and individuals to prevent harm to national security, domestic safety, and individual well-being. This chapter also examines how the Court can punish individuals after speech has caused harm or death. Government has tried to prevent the press from publishing certain content—a prior restraint. Individuals have sued authors, filmmakers, and music artists, claiming that what they published caused anguish, injury, and death. Such actions are subsequent punishment in the form of lawsuits. *U.S. v. Alvarez*, 132 S.Ct. 2537 (2012), the ruling in which the Court struck down the federal Stolen Valor Act, is discussed as a subsequent punishment that "chills" speech.

Chapter 8, "Reporter's Privilege," looks at the statutes and judge-made law affecting a newsgatherer's privilege to defy a prosecutor or judge's demand to testify about confidential information or sources. It is widely recognized that to protect the public's right to know, a reporter must be able to withhold information given in confidence. At the same time, the information the reporter holds may be relevant to the fair administration of justice. Thirty-nine states and the District of Columbia balance those interests in the form of statutory protection for the reporter's privilege, commonly called shield laws. The federal government, however, does not have a shield law, though U.S. Court of Appeals Circuits have created similar protections.

Chapter 9, "Access to Government Records, Property and Services," introduces students to federal and state open records and meetings laws and the First Amendment public forum doctrine. The statutes and the doctrine recognize the public's right to obtain government-held public records and to use government-controlled spaces and services for expressive activities such as information gathering, assembly, and discussion. The U.S. Supreme Court's ruling in *Milner v. U.S. Department of the Navy*, No. 09–1163 (2011), which makes it harder for the federal government to withhold records related to agency rules and practices, is discussed.

Chapter 10, "Fair Trial/Free Press," looks at the tension between the First, Sixth, and Seventh Amendments that arises when the news media reports on criminal and civil proceedings. The chapter reviews the U.S. Supreme Court's effort to strike a balance between the interests of the news media, parties to criminal and civil proceedings, and the fair administration of justice. The more than 50-year debate over cameras in federal courtrooms is addressed, including the most recent twist on that issue, rulings on the use of webcasting, cell phones, smartphones, BlackBerrys, iPhones, Palm Pilots, laptop computers, iPads, and other digital technologies in courtrooms.

Chapter 11, "Broadcast & Cable Television Regulation," explains the rationale underpinning the First Amendment broadcast regulatory model that allows Congress and the Federal Communications Commission (FCC) to impose unique content restrictions on radio and television. *FCC v. Fox Television Stations*, 132 S.Ct. 2307 (2012), the U.S. Supreme Court ruling in which the constitutionality of broadcast's unique First Amendment status was challenged, is discussed. The chapter also covers cable TV laws and regulations by providing a brief examination of how the industry went from an unregulated mass medium with undefined First Amendment rights to one regulated by the FCC within a 50-year span.

Chapter 12, "Sexual Expression & the First Amendment," considers the leading cases in the U.S. involving the clash between individual freedom of expression and thought, and society's interest in policing alleged pornography-linked harm, antisocial conduct, and offensiveness. Case law and controversies regarding child pornography convictions are given special attention, including the unique case of teenagers sextexting. Should the law treat a minor, who texts sexually explicit images of themselves to friends, like a child pornographer? The campaign to decriminalize sextexting is examined.

Chapters 13 and 14 address media-related intellectual property law: copyright and trademark. Copyright protects a copyright holder's right to control creativity fixed in a tangible form—e.g, books, photographs, and compact discs—for a limited time. In other words, it gives a holder the right to prevent others from making copies of an original work. Trademark protects brand names, logos, color designs, and symbols that identify commercial products and services.

Chapter 13, "Copyright Law," introduces students to the key sections of Title 17 of the U.S. Code covering a copyright holder's rights and the elements of an infringement action. The chapter looks at judge-made doctrines of merger and substantial similarity and the critical role they play in determining whether impermissible copying has occurred. It also covers the key limitations the law imposes on a holder's right to prevent others from copying his or her work, including the fair use doctrine.

Chapter 14, "Copyright, New Technologies & Trademark" continues with an examination of the fair use doctrine and its relationship to new mass media copying technologies. It examines the connection between the doctrine and photocopying, audio-visual taping, and digital technologies such as MP3 peer-to-peer file sharing, search engines, YouTube, and the Google Books settlement. The Digital Millennium Copyright Act (DMCA) also is addressed.

Chapter 15, "Commercial Speech," focuses on our First Amendment and regulatory approach to speech that does "no more than propose a commercial transaction"—specifically advertising and marketing. The commercial speech doctrine seeks to strike a balance between the free expression rights of advertisers, marketers, and consumers with the state's interest in protecting consumers from false, deceptive, or misleading advertising, and those promoting unlawful activities and vice.

There is a great deal of material covered in this book—material that law school curricula typically treat in as many as four separate courses. It is suggested, then, that it makes perfect sense to devote a semester's course to portions of this text.

Finally, the author hopes that readers find this book beneficial and would appreciate hearing your comments, criticisms, and suggestions. Please email me at ahayes@Fordham.edu.

Acknowledgments

I am deeply grateful to the law professors who made a difference years ago and to this day: New York Law School Professor Michael Botein, and Quinnipiac University School of Law Professor Marilyn J. Ford and Professor Emeritus of Law Martin B. Margulies. I also wish to thank Fordham University School of Law Associate Professor Olivier Sylvain for reviewing parts of this text.

CHAPTER ONE

Principles of Legal Reasoning and First Amendment Theory

CONTROVERSY: It wasn't California Senator Leland Yee's intention to trigger a catalyst that would change First Amendment media law. But when he introduced a bill banning the sale or rental of violent video games to minors in 2005, the final outcome would be the landmark ruling *Brown v. Entertainment Merchants Association*, 131 S. Ct. 2729 (2011). A landmark ruling creates a new and significant principle in a particular area of the law; such a ruling alters the legal landscape. *Brown v. Entertainment Merchants* is landmark because the Court said the First Amendment gives full protection to the video gaming medium. That declaration also set a legal precedent—a standard that lower courts must apply to cases raising the same legal questions. (All landmark rulings set precedents, though all legal precedents are not landmark rulings.) Now, because the U.S. Supreme Court is the highest judicial authority in the U.S., federal and state laws banning the sale of violent video games to minors are presumed to infringe upon video game merchants' and minors' First Amendment free speech rights. It's a presumption only because there is a remote chance that a legislature could craft a law restricting the sale or rental of violent video games to minors that would pass the Court's toughest level of constitutional review, strict scrutiny.

In reaching its decision to strike down the California law, the Court relied on precedent, too. About 14 months before, the Court ruled that the First Amendment prohibited legislatures from banning videos depicting deadly violence committed against animals in *U.S. v. Stevens*, 130 S. Ct. 1577 (2010).

Chapter's Scope

Landmark rulings, precedent, and strict scrutiny are concepts essential to understanding how our American common law system of judicial review operates, how judges reason in general, and how they analyze First Amendment free speech and press cases in particular. Because the U.S. Supreme Court's interpretation of the First Amendment's free speech, press, and assembly clauses shapes the contours of all media law, regulations, and policy in the U.S., a basic understanding of the Amendment's purpose is essential. To that end, this chapter (i) identifies the most significant laws and regulations affecting media use; (ii) provides an outline of the hierarchical structure of our state and federal court systems; (iii) summarizes how civil actions proceed through those systems, from filing a lawsuit, trial, appeal, to resolution; (iv) acquaints students with the basics of legal reasoning—the analytical rules judges abide by when deciding cases; and (v) discusses classic and recently devised First Amendment theories that attempt to explain why society's benefits from the protection of free expression rights may trump other fundamental societal interests such as national security, civility, and fair trial rights.

Primary Sources of Media Law

The U.S. Constitution

The preemption doctrine, which derives from the U.S. Constitution's Supreme Clause, Article VI, holds that the "Constitution, and the Laws of the United States which shall be made in Pursuance thereof…shall be the supreme Law of the Land." Thus, it follows that the Constitution's First Amendment free speech and press clauses—Article I, Section 8, known as the Copyright Clause—are the ultimate media laws in the U.S. Those two clauses, the Copyright Act of 1790 and the Postal Service Act of 1792 and 1794 (now the Postal Reorganization Act of 1970) are the nation's first media laws. The Copyright Act gives individuals or corporations who own the copyrights to books, movies, plays, photographs and other creative works a right to bring a lawsuit in federal court against those who have used their works without permission. The First Amendment's free speech and press clauses, however, constitute the most wide-ranging media law in the U.S. The First Amendment is implicated when a plaintiff sues for copyright infringement, libel, or invasion of privacy, or when a defendant fights off an obscenity charge, or a ban on video games, or when a public school student argues that school authorities have no right to punish her for the disparaging comments she posted about her principal on a social networking site. States also have constitutions and many provide free expression guarantees similar to the First Amendment's. Some provide more. But they cannot provide fewer free expression guarantees than the federal Constitution's First Amendment.

Federal and State Statutes

The U.S. Constitution is the nation's ultimate statute. Additionally, there are hundreds of federal statutes affecting free expression and individuals' and corporations' use of mass media technologies. In our legal system, legislative bodies create statutes to target a specific problem or set of problems, or to expand individuals' rights. Generally, a statute sets boundaries for future conduct. Typically, Congress enacts statutes to address national or regional issues.

The reach of state statutes, which are typically preempted by federal laws, is limited to a state's borders. The First Amendment limits the scope of federal and state laws affecting free expression and mass media. This book devotes substantial space to the following federal statutes that either protect or limit free expression and media use: Section 230 of the Telecommunications Act, the Communications Act of 1934, Freedom of Information Act, the Copyright Act, Cable Television Consumer Protection and Competition Act (1992 Cable Act), the Lanham (Trademark) Act, the Espionage Act, and the Digital Millennium Copyright Act.

Regulatory Law

What is the difference between a statute and a regulation? Legislative bodies create statutes targeting national, regional, and international circumstances. Government agencies, departments, and commissions create regulations to carry out their missions, which are defined by statutes. The Federal Communication Commission (FCC) and the Federal Trade Commission (FTC) are the most powerful media regulatory bodies in the U.S. The FTC regulates advertising. The FCC, however, has a far wider purview. It regulates interstate and international telecommunications transmitted by television, radio, telephone, cable, and satellite. Its regulations are called rules. The FCC makes rules to carry out a Congressional mandate, or in response to a petition for rulemaking. FCC rules regulate corporations' ownership and operation of telecommunications as well as the public's use of them. For instance, the FCC created a "fleeting expletive" rule in 2004, based on its authority under federal law, to ban the airing of indecent content or profane language during certain hours. The U.S. Supreme Court upheld the fleeting expletive rule as constitutional in June 2012.[1]

Federal and State Common Law

Legislators make statutes. Bureaucrats make regulations. Judges make common law on a case-by-case basis. In the U.S., we inherited our common law tradition from British common law, which started in the Middle Ages. The overwhelming majority of mass media law covered in these pages is common law, rulings handed down by mostly federal judges at the district (trial), and intermediate appeals (circuit courts of appeals) levels, and by the U.S. Supreme Court. Unlike statutes or rules that regulate future conduct, common law resolves a specific legal conflict of a case before a judge or a panel of judges. As the brief discussion of *Brown v. Entertainment Merchants* shows, when circumstances present an issue never before addressed by a court, a judge's ruling creates a legal precedent—an authoritative ruling for subsequent similar cases implicating the same legal questions—and all courts in the same jurisdiction are bound by the ruling. The binding principle is called stare decisis—"to stand by that which is decided."

Here is how it works. In *New York Times v. Sullivan*, 376 U.S. 254 (1964), a landmark First Amendment case, the U.S. Supreme Court created a test for judging when a news outlet would be held responsible in libel cases for reputation-damaging comments it published about the public conduct of government officials. In 1960, Montgomery, Alabama, Public Safety Commissioner L. B. Sullivan brought a libel action against the *New York Times* for publishing an op-ed political advertisement that criticized the Montgomery police authorities' handling of civil rights demonstrations. Though the gist of the accusations against the police in the ad was true, several factual assertions were inaccurate. Under the libel law in Alabama, as well as many other states, even minor factual inaccuracies were sufficient to hold a defendant culpable for making false statements that damage a plaintiff's reputation.

In a 9–0 ruling, the Court overturned the verdict and rewrote libel law in the U.S. News outlets, the Court said, will be held culpable only when they publish statements they know to be false, or when they do so with reckless disregard for the truth. (See Chapter 5 for more on the problematic meaning of "actual malice.")Hence, *New York Times v. Sullivan* established a common law precedent for every court in the U.S. Today, whether you are mayor of Miami, Florida, Alaska's public safety commissioner, or a U.S. senator from Maine, when you sue a news outlet for reputation-damaging statements, judges must require that you prove that the news outlet made the statements with either reckless disregard for the truth or knowing falsity.

Recall that the U.S. Constitution is the supreme law of the land. Recall also that our common law includes precedents from British law because, as former British colonies, we adopted much of British common law. Those two distinctions are important in media law because much of the U.S. Supreme Court's free expression and media law rulings result from balancing First Amendment interests against other important societal interests that the government seeks to protect, such as national security, public safety, fair trial rights, and reputational rights.

Balancing Societal Interests

Courts engage in three types of balancing approaches: ad hoc, preferred, and categorical. Under the ad hoc theory or approach, judges assign a preference to either free expression or other societal values by considering the individual circumstances of each case. Under the preferred approach, courts tip the scales toward free expression and place the burden of proof on government to show why its restriction is valid. Under the categorical approach, the Court has ruled that certain types of speech—libel, obscenity, incitement, fighting words, true threats, and child pornography—fall outside of First Amendment protection. It is important to keep in mind that speech can be relegated to this unprotected status only after a ruling or verdict has been made. For example, pornography is protected speech unless a judge or jury finds it to be obscene. Libel, obscenity, incitement, fighting words, true threats, and child pornography are, as Justice Antonin Scalia explained in *U.S. v. Stevens*, 130 S. Ct. 1577, 1585–1586 (2011), "of such slight social value as a step to truth that any benefit that may be derived from them is clearly outweighed by the social interest in order and morality...that no process of case-by-case adjudication is required, because the balance of competing interests is clearly struck."

What does this have to do with common law? There are also non-speech interests that the Court has recognized that are generally equal to free speech interests such as the right of an individual to bring an action against someone whose speech has ruined his or her reputation because that right, adopted from British common law, predates the First Amendment. Consequently, the Court in *New York Times v. Sullivan* found a way to balance the right of individuals to sue media outlets for libel while protecting the First Amendment right of individuals to vigorously criticize government, a fundamental principle of the American form of government. It carved out a special category of protected speech—speech concerning the public conduct of government officials. By requiring public officials to meet the tough standard of proving that statements were reckless or false, the Court intentionally made it difficult for public officials to win in libel actions brought against media outlets. In contrast, the Court retained the common law standard for private individuals. They did not have to prove falsity or recklessness, but a lower standard of culpability, typically negligence. The Court, however, tipped the balance further toward free speech in *Philadelphia Newspapers, Inc. v. Hepps*, 475 U.S. 767 (1986), where it ruled that private figures suing media outlets for libel have the burden of proving the statements false. Once a trier-of-fact, either judge or jury, finds expression to be libelous, that expression falls into the historically unprotected categories of speech.

The Increasing Importance of International Law

In 1988, Congress enacted the Berne Implementation Act, making the U.S. a party to the Berne Convention for Protection of Literary and Artistic Works. Nations that sign on to the Berne Convention agree that their courts will recognize the copyrights of authors and artists whose works are published in any of the 147 member nations. As discussed in Chapter 13 , generally that means the owner of a copyright granted in a foreign country can sue an alleged copyright violator (called infringer) in U.S. courts and vice versa. The adverse impact of globalization on U.S. copyright holders compelled the U.S. to join the Berne Convention. By the second half of the 20th-century, quick and efficient air transportation, improved roads, and satellite transmission made it easier for foreign individuals to produce unauthorized copies or adaptations of American-made media content and redistribute them as originals. Now, U.S. membership in the Berne Convention gives U.S. copyright holders the right to sue foreign copyright infringers in their nation's courts under mutually agreed-upon legal standards.

The international use of the World Wide Web during the last 15 years or so has forced American lawmakers, regulators, courts, and scholars to be more mindful of foreign and international media laws and regulations. Often, it has placed the U.S. in opposition to European laws and regulatory efforts. Congress, for instance, enacted the Securing the Protection of our Enduring and Established Constitutional Heritage (SPEECH) Act in 2010 to protect U.S. citizens who are sued for libel in foreign nations. The SPEECH Act renders foreign libel judgments against U.S. plaintiffs unenforceable if the foreign nation's laws are inconsistent with U.S. libel protections. (See Chapter 5.)

International law also affects U.S. oversight of Internet governance. As discussed in Chapter 3, the U.S. government has delegated authority via contract to the Internet Corporation for Assigned Names and Numbers (ICANN), a private corporation, to coordinate the Internet's unique identifier system, which allows information to flow across the Web. But U.S. law does not control ICANN. Under Article 4 of its Articles of Incorporation, ICANN must operate in conformity with international law and applicable international conventions.[2] As of early 2012, the U.S. had chosen not to endorse the European Union's proposed General Data Protection Regulation. The regulation, expected to go into effect by 2014, would harmonize the laws of 27 EU nations and recognize privacy rights and legal remedies for individuals who transmit personal data via the Internet and impose privacy obligations on social media sites and other Internet Service Providers. (See Chapter 6.)

SUMMARY: The First Amendment's free speech and press clauses define the scope of all media laws in the U.S. The First Amendment is part of the U.S. Constitution, our system's ultimate statutory law. The U.S. Supreme Court, however, creates the highest level of common law in our system. Common law is judge-made law; the law handed down by judges in the Anglo-American system since the Middle Ages, and the principle of stare decisis—"to stand by that which is decided"—is at its core. Federal and state statutory and regulatory laws also play a major role in regulating free expression and our use of mass media technologies. Federal and state legislative bodies create statutes. Government agencies, departments, and commissions create regulations and rules to carry out their missions, which are defined by statutes. The FCC is the most powerful media regulatory body in the U.S. It regulates interstate and international telecommunications transmitted by television, radio, telephone, cable, and satellite, and corporations' ownership and operation of telecommunications, as well as the public's use of them.

Recently developed media technologies have created tensions between U.S. law and foreign and international agreements. While the U.S. has resolved or reduced such differences in areas of copyright and Internet governance, its First Amendment principles put it at opposition with libel laws of some nations, notably Britain, and with the European Union's efforts to protect personal data on the Internet.

The Federal Judicial System

Article III Courts

Article III of the U.S. Constitution provides in part, "The judicial power of the United States, shall be vested in one Supreme Court, and in such inferior courts as the Congress may from time to time ordain and establish." Those courts include: the Supreme Court; twelve geography-based U.S. Circuit Courts of Appeals and one for the Federal Circuit; 94 trial-level courts called "district courts" in the fifty states, District of Columbia, and Puerto Rico, and subordinated bankruptcy courts; and a Court of International Trade.

The overwhelming majority of media law cases stem from civil actions. The key distinction between civil and criminal cases is punishment; specifically, a defendant who loses in a civil action cannot be sentenced to serve prison or jail time. The defendant faces fines, injunctions, monetary damages paid to the plaintiff, and injunctions, which are court orders to refrain from engaging in specific conduct. In contrast, a guilty defendant in a criminal case faces fines, and limits on his or her liberties, such as community service, imprisonment, or death.

Under 28 U.S.C. §1331, Congress grants federal district courts the authority to hear federal questions, which are "all civil actions arising under the Constitution, laws, or treaties of the United States." Hence, media lawsuits raising, for example, First Amendment questions, challenging FCC rulemaking, or pertaining to federal statutes like the Freedom of Information Act may be filed with a federal district court pursuant to federal question jurisdiction. According to *Louisville & Nashville Railroad v. Mottley,* 211 U.S. 149, 152 (1908), "a suit arises under the Constitution and laws of the United States only if the original statement of the plaintiff's cause of action shows that it is based on the Constitution or federal statutes."

Under 28 U.S.C. §1332, federal district courts also have diversity jurisdiction, which is authority to hear civil actions between (i) citizens of different states; (ii) state citizens and subjects of foreign nations; (iii) citizens of different states in "which citizens or subjects of a foreign state are additional parties"; and (iv) foreign nations, as plaintiffs and a state of different states. Federal diversity jurisdiction also requires that the plaintiff sue for damages of $75,000 or higher. Class action plaintiffs must seek $5 million or more to qualify under federal diversity jurisdiction.

Making a Federal Case out of a Media Law Dispute

Because the overwhelming majority of the judicial opinions considered in this book are federal appeals court and U.S. Supreme court rulings, we'll trace the path of *Brown v. Entertainment Merchants*, as a way of demonstrating how many media lawsuits flow through the three levels of the federal court system. As discussed at the outset of this chapter, the Entertainment Merchants Association and other plaintiffs challenged a California statute, signed by then-Governor Arnold Schwarzenegger, which would have required violent video games to be labeled and their sale and rental prohibited to minors. The association sued in federal court in San Jose, California, before the law was to go into effect in 2006. The association had the right to bring its case to a federal court, instead of a state court, because its original statement of cause of action was based on the U.S. Constitution.

At the Federal District Court

In *Video Software Dealers Association v. Schwarzenegger*, 401 F. Supp. 2d 1034 (N.D. Cal. 2005), the federal district court judge ruled in the association's favor by granting an injunction, an order preventing California from enforcing the new law. The ruling was issued on December 21, 2005.

At the Intermediate Federal Appeals Level

Losing parties may appeal verdicts, summary judgments, and injunctions to the appeals court situated in the same federal circuit. Thus, California, the losing party, filed an appeal with the U.S. Court of Appeals for the Ninth Circuit. The Ninth Circuit includes Arizona, California, Hawaii, Guam, Idaho, Montana, Oregon, and Washington, and has 28 judgeships. Federal circuit court judges hear appeals in panels of three. In special cases, a circuit will rehear a case **en banc**, meaning the entire bench rules.

On October 29, 2008, lawyers for the parties argued before a three-judge panel. The three-judge panel filed its ruling on February 20, 2009. In *Video Software Dealers Association v. Schwarzenegger*, 556 F.3d 950 (9th Cir. 2009), it affirmed the district court's ruling. The panel's ruling was binding in the circuit's seven states and Guam.

Filing for Certiorari

On May 19, 2009, California filed a Petition for a Writ of Certiorari asking the U.S. Supreme Court to overturn the Ninth Circuit's ruling. Unlike all the other federal and state courts, the U.S. Supreme Court hears only the cases it wishes to review, and four of its nine justices must agree to grant **certiorari**. (The Court also has original jurisdiction over cases involving ambassadors, as well as those involving two or more states.) When certiorari is granted, the petitioner's name comes first in the citation and so the surname of Jerry Brown, the new California governor, became the party listed in *Brown v. Entertainment Merchants*. The Court granted certiorari on April 26, 2010. The Court grants certiorari in about only 100 of the more than 10,000 petitions filed each term.

Often, other interested parties file **amicus curiae** (friends of the court) legal briefs in hopes of persuading the justices to rule in favor of the petitioner or the respondent. Amicus curiae briefs are hardly pro forma, as justices often paraphrase the parties' arguments or cite the legal precedents from some of the briefs in their own opinions. Starting in June 22, 2009, and ending in September 17, 2010, entities and persons such as Eagle Forum Education and Legal Defense, Common Sense Media,

California State Senator Leland Y. Yee, Marion B. Brechner First Amendment Project, the ACLU, Microsoft Corporation, and the Entertainment Consumers Association were among the many to file amicus curiae briefs.

Before the High Court

The Court convenes starting the first Monday in October to hear one-hour arguments from the parties who have been granted review. On November 2, 2010, lawyers representing California and the video game industry stood before the Court's nine justices. On June 27, 2011, the Court handed down its opinion. Seven of the nine justices voted to strike down the California statute as unconstitutional because video games, like books, plays, and movies, qualify for First Amendment protection. Typically, one justice writes the majority opinion; this time, it was Justice Antonin Scalia. As often is the case, one or more justices joining the majority write a concurring opinion in which they agree with the judgment but use alternative legal theories to reach the same result.

For example, in *Brown v. Entertainment Merchants*, Justice Samuel Alito, filed a concurrence in which Justice John Roberts joined. Justices Clarence Thomas and Stephen Breyer, however, filed separate dissenting opinions setting forth their reasons for why they believed the majority's opinion was wrong. Sometimes, opinions are delivered in the name of the Court and credited to no particular judge. These are per curiam decisions and do not necessarily reflect a majority consensus. Per curiam and slim majority decisions, typically 5–4, are the most vulnerable to being overturned by subsequent Supreme Court panels.

A Supreme Court ruling binds all the nation's courts. Like all federal and state legislative bodies which have had the Court strike down one of their statutes, the California legislature may seek to rehabilitate its failed law regulating violent video games by revising its language to address the Court's concerns. If it does so, and if it passes constitutional muster at the circuit court level, it might end up before the U.S. Supreme Court again. If, on the other hand, the Ninth Circuit were to strike the revised statute, the Court would likely let the ruling stand by not granting certiorari. The other way to challenge a U.S. Supreme Court ruling is to overturn it by passing a constitutional amendment. A congressional proposal for an amendment may be made either by a two-thirds majority vote in Congress or by a constitutional convention called by two-thirds of state legislatures.

Legal Reasoning: "Tests," Analogy, the Practice of Distinguishing, and Policy

At the end of each chapter in this book, you will find questions, and many of those questions take the form of a legal hypothetical. The hypothetical is the professor's pet pedagogical tool for teaching how to reason like a lawyer. The hypothetical is a set of facts designed to test a student's ability to apply a legal doctrine to a set of facts that are similar in many aspects to cases already decided by the courts.

A legal **doctrine** is part of common law. Doctrine comprises the rules and tests that judges create to resolve future legal disputes implicating the same statutes or substantive areas of law. The fundamental rules of legal analysis require identifying the substantive area of law, precedent, and doctrine that should be applied to the facts of a new dispute. Then, the judge makes a determination that the facts of the new case are significantly similar, or dissimilar, to the facts of precedential cases. This analytical practice is called analogizing and distinguishing cases. According to UCLA School of Law Professor Eugene Volokh:

> To distinguish cases, you need to (1) identify the differences between the cases, and (2) explain why the differences should be legally significant. The explanations called for in step 2 are often based on (3) particular policy arguments that point in different directions for the two cases and (4) analogies to other legal rules in which a similar distinction is drawn....To analogize cases, you need to (1) identify the cases to which you want to analogize, (2) point to the similarities and explain why they should be legally significant, and (3) explain why the differences should not be legally significant.[3]

If the case before the court is significantly similar to the early case, then the doctrine of stare decisis requires that a judge apply the same doctrinal tests to reach a decision, called the holding. Precedent, it is said, controls. Lawyers also make **policy arguments**, as Volokh notes. In other words, they ask a court to consider, in addition to, or in spite of, precedent, how its ruling will promote a doctrine's underlying societal values. If the facts of the two cases are reasonably dissimilar, a judge may break from precedent and apply a different doctrinal rule or test.

Let's apply those analytic tools to the following brief hypothetical. Gabriel Hounds, a municipal dogcatcher, sues a local newspaper for allegedly defaming him, disparaging his good reputation by saying he abuses dogs and maintains a filthy dog pound. Does the ruling in *New York Times v. Sullivan* control? In other words, should a court require him to show that the newspaper knew the statements were false or made them with reckless disregard for the truth because he is a public employee? First, we analogize, as much as we can, given the limited facts. Sullivan was a Montgomery commissioner whose public responsibilities included supervising the police department. As a municipal dogcatcher, Hounds does not appear to hold a position of authority comparable to Sullivan. Therefore, the cases might be distinguishable based on those facts.

The Court actually took up the issue raised by our hypothetical in *Rosenblatt v. Baer*, 383 U.S. 75 (1966). Baer was a public employee in charge of supervising a public recreational facility. He answered to commissioners. Thus, Baer's status was more like Hounds' than Sullivan's. Was Baer a public official for defamation purposes? The Court did not say. Baer's libel case was decided before the Court handed down its ruling in *Sullivan*. For that reason, the Court remanded the case for retrial. But the Court established a test for determining when a government employee is a public official under *Sullivan*: "It is clear, therefore, that the 'public official' designation applies at the very least to those among the hierarchy of government employees who have, or appear to the public to have, substantial responsibility for or control over the conduct of governmental affairs" and when their positions have "such apparent importance that the public has an independent interest in the qualifications and performance of the person who holds it, beyond the general public interest in the qualifications and performance of all government employees."[4] Does Hounds fit the above description? Like the Court in *Baer*, we would need to know more about his responsibilities and his prominence in the community to make such a determination.

SUMMARY: The overwhelming majority of media law cases stem from lawsuits filed in federal courts. The 94 federal district, or trial-level, courts have original jurisdictional authority to hear lawsuits that raise federal questions. For instance, a plaintiff alleging that a state statute infringes First Amendment free expression rights raises a federal question.

Federal district courts also have diversity jurisdiction authority to hear cases in which the litigants are citizens of different states or citizens of foreign nations. The federal system has twelve geography-based circuits and one for the Federal Circuit. A losing party may appeal to the U.S. Court of Appeals situated in the same circuit. Under the doctrine of stare decisis, a ruling by a federal circuit court three-judge panel binds all the courts in the circuit's geographical jurisdiction.

The party that loses at the circuit level may file a Petition for a Writ of Certiorari asking the U.S. Supreme Court to overturn the lower court ruling, but the Supreme Court does not have to hear the case. The Court grants certiorari in about 100 of the more than 10,000 petitions filed with the Court each term. Under the doctrine of stare decisis, a Supreme Court ruling binds all the nation's courts, federal and state.

The principle of stare decisis—the common law notion that precedent, a higher court's ruling, binds future rulings—is at the core of legal reasoning. The other fundamental legal analytical tools are: analogy, the application of judge-made standards and tests; the process of distinguishing; and the consideration of the underlying policies of legal doctrines. Lawyers and judges apply those analytical tools to determine when precedent controls the outcome of a new case.

First Amendment Theories of Free Expression

Imagine the following: You and your family are reeling from the emotional turmoil of burying a loved one who died in combat and, as your funeral procession approaches the church, you're confronted by a phalanx of protesters. The protesters are spiteful. They yell that God killed your spouse, sibling, child, parent, or cousin as punishment for fighting for a military that allows homosexuals to serve. They carry signs proclaiming, "America is doomed," "You're going to hell," "God hates you," "Fag troops," "Semper fi fags," and "Thank God for dead soldiers." Albert Snyder, of Westminster, Maryland, does not have to imagine such a painful scenario. He lived it. Pastor Fred Phelps and members of his Topeka, Kansas, Westboro Baptist Church engaged in such a protest when Snyder buried his son, Marine Lance Corporal Matthew Snyder, in 2006. Snyder believed that no one had the right to speak and behave in such a vile manner, and he sued Phelps and his church. A jury found for Snyder on intentional infliction of emotional distress, intrusion upon seclusion, and civil conspiracy claims, and held the church liable for $10.9 million in damages.

The U.S. Supreme Court, however, said Snyder and the jury were wrong. In its 8–1 ruling in *Snyder v. Phelps*, 131 S. Ct. 1207 (2011), the Court said the church engaged in speech about a matter of public concern—gays in the military—and at a public place. Accordingly, the church's protest was entitled to special treatment under the First Amendment. "Such speech cannot be restricted simply because it is upsetting or arouses contempt," the Court explained. The Court continued, "If there is a bedrock principle underlying the First Amendment, it is that the government may not prohibit the expression of an idea simply because society finds the idea itself offensive or disagreeable."[5]

Snyder v. Phelps, however, did not play well in the court of public opinion. Legal scholar Stanley Fish expressed the thoughts of many when he remarked, "Normally' (one hopes) you won't be at your young son's funeral, and if you are, is it really your obligation to react coolly to malevolent strangers who are doing their best (or, rather their worst) to add injury to injury? Give me a break! The Court certainly didn't give Snyder one." In effect, Fish and others were asking: Why should a private individual such as Snyder, who had taken no public stance on the issue of gays in the military, have to put up with such abuse and have no legal recourse for his suffering? How does society benefit from giving Phelps and his followers a license to exceed near-globally agreed upon boundaries of common decency, respect, and privacy?

This section seeks to provide answers to those questions by exploring core First Amendment free expression theories: (i) the **marketplace of ideas**, (ii) civic courage, (iii) self-government, (iv) individual self-fulfillment/autonomy, (v) checking the abuse of official power, (vi) the safety value function, and (vii) absolutism. Scholars developed these classic First Amendment theories as the Court developed its First Amendment doctrines after the end of World War I and into the 1990s, attempting to flesh out what the Constitutional framers and sometimes the Court has failed to do: Explain how a democratic republic benefits by valuing free speech, press, and assembly rights over other core societal and individual interests.

The philosophical inquiry appears unending, as leading scholars continue to rethink the First Amendment's purpose in the context of our use of broadcast and digital media. Consequently, this chapter also looks at more recently developed First Amendment theories: dissent, tolerance, public discourse, and democratic culture.

In their original form, First Amendment theories are hardly the voluminous tomes typically produced by political philosophers. Rather, they are the products of common-law adjudication. The Court developed them as it developed various First Amendment doctrines such as **prior restraint**, incitement, or **obscenity**. And in their rulings, justices often reached back to borrow from free expression and democratic theorists of the Age of Enlightenment such as John Milton and John Locke. As you will see below, justices often allude to these theories using the judicial shorthand of citing an earlier ruling and quoting key language from the decision. The Court has never published a systematic study of all or any of its First Amendment theories. That task has been left to scholars, most notably Zechariah Chafee Jr., Thomas I. Emerson, Alexander Meiklejohn, and Vincent Blasi.

The First Amendment's Origins

There is no single First Amendment theory. The absence of one commonly held theory is largely attributable to the impossibility of citing any definitive document that clarifies "exactly what the colonists had in mind, or just what they expected from the guarantee of freedom of speech, press, assembly, and petition."[6] What is more, shortly after the colonists became self-governing, Congress enacted the Alien and Sedition Acts of 1789. The statutes were ostensibly subsequent punishment statutes but had the effect of a prior restraint, or censorship. By criminalizing dissent, Congress intimidated individuals from criticizing the federal government. For those who argue that the founders, framers, and ratifiers understood that the First Amendment meant government could not censor political speech—prior restraint—the Alien and Sedition Acts are troubling. Then again, many in the new nation questioned the constitutionality of the laws. Thomas Jefferson, his Democrat-Republicans, and many newspaper publishers vigorously denounced the laws imposed by the Federalist Party majority.

Nevertheless, Adams and Jefferson shared with their literate new Americans a common grounding in the writings of John Milton (1608–74), John Locke (1632–1704), and John Trenchard and

Thomas Gordon, who, through their *Cato's Letters* (1720–1723), spread Locke's theories championing free expression as a core principle of self-governance. Virtually all of our First Amendment jurisprudence was fashioned in the 20th century, and U.S. Supreme Court Justices Oliver Wendell Holmes and Louis Brandeis played a seminal role in that effort. They and legal scholars have drawn upon Milton, Locke, Trenchard, and Gordon, as well as Thomas Jefferson, James Madison, and the 19th-century British philosopher John Stuart Mill to justify why other important societal values may be of less priority than free expression.

The Marketplace of Ideas

This theory argues that society benefits when government allows all ideas to be exchanged among its citizenry because truth will emerge from the unfettered discussion. In *Areopagitica* (1644)—Milton's second-best known work, the other being *Paradise Lost*—the poet penned an ode to the virtues of free expression and the disadvantages of government censorship: "And though all the winds of doctrine were let loose to play upon the earth, so Truth be in the field, we do injuriously by licensing and prohibiting to misdoubt her strength. Let her and Falsehood grapple; who ever knew Truth put to the worse in a free and open encounter?"[7]

In *On Liberty* (1859), the utilitarian philosopher Mill asserted, "We can never be sure that the opinion we are endeavoring to stifle is a false opinion; and if we were sure, stifling it would be an evil still.[8]"

In a dissenting opinion in *U.S. v. Abrams*, 250 US 616 (1919), Justice Oliver Wendell Holmes wrote,

> If you have no doubt of your premises or your power and want a certain result with all your heart, you naturally express your wishes in law and sweep away all opposition…But when men have realized that time has upset many fighting faiths, they may come to believe even more than they believe the very foundations of their own conduct that the ultimate good desired is better reached by free trade in ideas—that the best test of truth is the power of the thought to get itself accepted in the competition of the market, and that truth is the only ground upon which their wishes safely can be carried out.

Justices and judges have invoked the "marketplace of ideas" metaphor repeatedly to prevent government from curtailing freedom of expression.[9] In *Lamont v. Postmaster General*, 381 US 301, 308 (1965), Justice Brennan actually used the term: "The dissemination of ideas can accomplish nothing if otherwise willing addressees are not free to receive and consider them. It would be a barren marketplace of ideas that had only sellers and no buyers."

And the Court has used the theory to support what some see as the opposing proposition: that government has authority to impose licensing and editorial requirements on broadcasters to ensure that the public receives a diversity of opinions over the airwaves. Take, for example, *Red Lion Broadcasting v. FCC*, 395 U.S. 367 (1969). There, the Court used the theory to justify the government's control of broadcasting to preserve "an uninhibited [marketplace] of ideas in which truth will ultimately prevail, rather than to countenance monopolization of that market, whether it be by the Government itself or a private licensee."

Political economists, agenda-setting and public-sphere theorists and others, however, say the marketplace of ideas model is a flawed and an inadequate justification for prizing free expression over other important societal interests. It is flawed, they say, because it is premised on a false assumption: that the public will reject falsehoods over truthful ideas. Public debate doesn't necessarily produce the truth, certainly not in the short term, as illustrated by the Nazi Party's ability to gain control of the Reichstag by election in 1933, or the U.S.'s inability to end slavery through peaceful means in 1861. (That's assuming one believes that no ethnic group is inferior, and that slavery is morally wrong.) History also shows that demagogues and marketers can manipulate public opinion to persuade majorities to accept pernicious ideas. Reliance on the marketplace of ideas also does not take into account corporate media's power to set the agenda of topics discussed in the public arena, and the inability of disadvantaged groups to get their voices heard, critics say.[10]

Civic Courage

Project Marriage Washington, an anti-gay group, spearheaded a campaign in Washington to have voters determine whether to extend domestic partnership rights to gays in 2009. Project Marriage got the referendum they sought, but not the result. Voters approved the bill. Meanwhile, gay-rights backers sought the names of individuals who had signed the Project's petition calling for the referendum under the state's open-records law. The Project and others sought to block disclosure.

The dispute made its way to the Supreme Court, and on April 28, 2010, James Bopp, arguing for the Project, butted heads with Justice Antonin Scalia during oral arguments. Bopp contended that a First Amendment right to privacy gave petition signees a right to remain anonymous to avoid public criticism. Incredulous, Scalia talked about civic courage: "And in light of the fact that for the first century of our existence, even voting was public…the fact is that running a democracy takes a certain amount of civic courage. And the First Amendment does not protect you from criticism or even nasty phone calls when you exercise your political rights to legislate or to take part in the legislative process."[11] The Project lost its case in *Doe vs. Reed*, 130 S. Ct. 2811 (2010), in which the Court ruled that disclosure of referendum petitions does not, as a general matter, violate the First Amendment. (See Chapter 9.)

The idea that the First Amendment supports the proposition that government, organizations, and individuals should not be shielded from disturbing unorthodox and obnoxious speech and that public discussion of such views is essential to democracy and progress stems mostly from Justice Louis Brandeis's majority opinion in *Whitney v. California*, 274 U.S. 357 (1927). Renowned First Amendment scholar Vincent Blasi ranks Whitney as "arguably the most important essay ever written, on or off the bench, on the meaning of the first amendment."[12]

> Those who won our independence believed that the final end of the State was to make men free to develop their faculties; and that in its government the deliberative forces should prevail over the arbitrary. They valued liberty both as an end and as a means. They believed liberty to be the secret of happiness and *courage* [emphasis added] to be the secret of liberty. They believed that freedom to think as you will and to speak as you think are means indispensable to the discovery and spread of political truth; that without free speech and assembly discussion would be futile; that with them, discussion affords ordinarily adequate protection against the dissemination of noxious doctrine; that the greatest menace to freedom is an inert people; that public discussion is a political duty; and that this should be a fundamental principle of the American government.[13]

The Court has returned to the idea that free expression and civic courage are intrinsically linked, most notably in *Kingsley Int'l Pictures Corp. v. Regents of the Univ. of the State of New York*, 360 U.S. 684, 689 (1959); *Cohen v. California*, 403 U.S. 15, 24 (1971); *New York Times Co. v. Sullivan*, 376 U.S. 254, 270 (1964); and most recently in *Snyder v. Phelps. Snyder* is premised on at least two other First Amendment theories. *Snyder* cites *Sullivan* for the proposition that the First Amendment reflects "a profound national commitment to the principle that debate on public issues should be uninhibited, robust, and wide-open." It also relies on Alexander Meiklejohn's theory that the First Amendment protects speech so that citizens can govern themselves by citing *Garrison v. Louisiana*, 379 U.S. 64, 74–75 (1964), for the concept that "speech concerning public affairs is more than self-expression; it is the essence of self-government."

Self-Government

Meiklejohn, a philosophy professor, university president, and author of *Free Speech and Its Relation to Self-Government* (1948), was the foremost advocate for the proposition that the First Amendment's only purpose was to protect a collective, not individual, interest in engaging in political speech, that is, speech relevant to the democratic process. He believed that political speech was entitled to absolute protection under the First Amendment because it is indispensable to the democratic process.

In *Free Speech and Its Relation to Self-Government* (1948), Meiklejohn used the town meeting as his metaphor for defining the scope of free expression provided by the First Amendment: "These speech-abridging activities of the town meeting indicate what the First Amendment to the Constitution does not forbid. When self-governing men demand freedom of speech they are not saying that every individual has an unalienable right to speak whenever, wherever, however he chooses."[14] Thus, self-restraint and adherence to rules of civility and order are required in public democratic discussion, he contended.

Though the Court has justified many of its free expression rulings on the self-government theory and gives political speech more protection than artistic self-expression or commercial speech, it does not adhere to Meiklejohn's belief that the First Amendment protects *only* speech that benefits the collective good in the political context, as the following discussion below on the First Amendment's purpose of promoting individual self-fulfillment and autonomy explains.

One of the key flaws of Meiklejohn's theory is his reliance on the metaphor of the New England town hall meeting. Simply put, if speech in the public arenas of the street, the political rally, or the Internet had to adhere to the rules of civility and order of the town hall meeting, as Meiklejohn argued, there would be no First Amendment free speech right to hold rowdy protest rallies such as those conducted by the Tea Party and Occupy Wall Street movements, no First Amendment protection against flooding the Internet with invectives against Presidents George W. Bush or Barack Obama, and no First Amendment protection for those engaged in civil disobedience.

Individual Self-Fulfillment/Individual Autonomy

Counterpoised to Meiklejohn's assertions stands the belief that free expression is justified as a right of an individual to form and express one's beliefs. It includes freedom from certain government restrictions on accessing ideas and content or expressing ideas that the majority might find unacceptable, and limits the state's ability to impose ideas on private individuals or groups. Though it is often associated with the Court's rulings on sexual expression, the justices also have invoked it to protect political speech.

Dissenters in *Branzburg v. Hayes*, 408 U.S. 665, 725–726 (1972), referenced self-fulfillment, the marketplace, and self-government theories, arguing for recognition that reporters have a First Amendment right to keep a source confidential: "Enlightened choice by an informed citizenry is the basic ideal upon which an open society is premised, and a free press is thus indispensable to a free society. Not only does the press enhance personal self-fulfillment by providing the people with the widest possible range of fact and opinion, but it also is an incontestable precondition of self-government."

In *Young v. American Mini Theaters, Inc.*, 427 U.S. 50, 64 (1976), the Court said, "To permit the continued building of our politics and culture, and to assure self-fulfillment for each individual, our people are guaranteed the right to express any thought, free from government censorship."

In *Hurley v. Irish–American Gay, Lesbian and Bisexual Group of Boston, Inc.*, 515 U.S. 557, 573–74 (1995), the Court said to allow Massachusetts to order a privately organized St. Patrick Day's parade to include homosexuals would alter the expressive content of the parade which is a "use of the state's power" that "violates the fundamental rule of protection under the First Amendment, that a speaker has the autonomy to choose the content of his own message."

Checking the Abuse of Official Power

Legal scholar Vincent Blasi argued in "The Checking Value in First Amendment Theory" (1988) that the Court needed to add to its free expression theories a rationale recognizing the role that tactics such as sit-ins, mass demonstrations, and the news media's publication of classified documents and exposés (such as Watergate) play in checking the abuse of official power. Blasi traced the concept to John Locke's *Second Treatise on Civil Government* (1690), the writings of the English Levellers, a 17th-century British political movement, and the *Cato's Letters* (1720–1723), among other sources. Blasi identified Justice Hugo Black's opinion in the Pentagon Papers case as one significant application of his theory:

> The Government's power to censor the press was abolished so that the press would remain forever free to censure the Government. The press was protected so that it could bare the secrets of government and inform the people. Only a free and unrestrained press can effectively expose deception in government. And paramount among the responsibilities of a free press is the duty to prevent any part of the government from deceiving the people and sending them off to distant lands to die of foreign fevers and foreign shot and shell.[15]

Safety Valve Function

This theory argues that society benefits when the disaffected and angry vent orally and verbally, rather than through violence. Emerson wrote in his article "Toward a General Theory of the First Amendment," "The classic example is the Hyde Park meeting where any person is permitted to say anything he wishes to whatever audience he can assemble. This results in a release of energy, a lessening of frustration, and a channeling of resistance into courses consistent with law and order. It operates, in short, as a catharsis throughout the body politic."[16]

In *Whitney v. California*, Brandeis said the founding fathers knew that "order cannot be secured merely through fear of punishment for its infraction; that it is hazardous to discourage thought, hope and imagination; that fear breeds repression; that repression breeds hate; that hate menaces stable government; that the path of safety lies in the opportunity to discuss freely supposed grievances and proposed Remedies."

Dissent, Tolerance, Public Discourse Speech, and Democratic Culture

Perhaps it is merely coincidental that three legal scholars published new interpretations of the First Amendment meanings in 1990. Whatever the reason for the timing, that year Steven H. Shiffrin,

Lee Bollinger, and Robert C. Post published writings on First Amendment theories which, they contended, the older theories dismissed or treated inadequately.

The marketplace of ideas, safety valve, self-fulfillment, and checking theories acknowledge that society and individuals benefit from dissent. But in *The First Amendment, Democracy and Romance* (1990), Shiffren argued that a major purpose of the First Amendment is to protect "the romantics—those who would break out of classical forms: the dissenters, the unorthodox, the outcasts" and "to sponsor the individualism, the rebelliousness, the antiauthoritarianism, the spirit of nonconformity within us all."[17]

In *The Tolerant Society*, Bollinger concluded that the First Amendment's major purpose is to teach self-restraint. Society is strengthened, Lee Bollinger argued, when it must find a nonviolent response to antisocial behavior:

> Every individual and group must decide again and again how much they will permit society to be structured along lines of thought differing from their own. When we speak of this we speak in terms of being 'tolerant,' of tolerating a wide diversity of viewpoints and life styles and choices. What ought to interest us about our extraordinary self-restraint in the realm of speech acts is that it may serve to emphasize the cultural importance not just of tolerating the expression of attitudes and ideas, but also their implementation—of allowing the world to be shaped in ways of which we might disapprove.[18]

Lastly, Post argued that one function of the First Amendment is to prevent communities with a certain set of values from punishing speakers engaging in public discourse whose tone, choice of language, and presentation does not conform to a community's values of decency, so that all may contribute to the public discourse in our culturally heterogeneous society. Post crafted his theory based on an analysis of *Hustler Magazine v. Falwell*, 485 U.S. 770 (1984), and its antecedents. In *Hustler v. Falwell*, the Court ruled that under the First Amendment a public figure could not recover damages for emotional harm caused by an offensive parody of him that was gross and repugnant in the eyes of most. "If the state were to enforce the civility rules of one community, say those of Catholics, as against those of another, say Jehovah's Witnesses, the state would in effect be using its power and authority to support some communities and repress others," explained Post in "The Constitutional Concept of Public Discourse: Outrageous Opinion, Democratic Deliberation, and *Hustler Magazine v. Falwell*."[19] Post concludes, "But the First Amendment forbids the state from doing this, in order that 'many types of life, character, opinion and belief can develop unmolested and unobstructed.'"[20]

Does the Internet change some tenets of First Amendment free speech theory? In a 2004 publication, "Digital Speech and Democratic Culture: A Theory of Freedom of Expression for the Information Society," Harvard Law School Professor Jack Balkin argued that free speech theory should focus on the ability the Internet gives ordinary individuals "to speak, to create, to participate in the creation of culture, and to distribute their ideas and innovations around the world."[21] Balkin argued that protecting and promoting individuals' right to create and participate in shaping culture is as important as protecting and promoting their right to create and participate in political discourse. He argued that under the First Amendment, individuals have a right to access the basic elements of culture. His theory calls into question one of the oft-quoted principles of the Meikeljohnian theory: "What is essential is not that everyone shall speak, but that everything worth saying shall be said." Balkin wrote,

> A theory of democratic culture, by contrast, argues that what is important is that everyone gets a chance to say it. Freedom arises out of participation in culture, and so the point of a system of freedom of expression is to facilitate this participation. That is why a focus on democratic culture places a greater emphasis than

the Meiklejohnian approach on how people appropriate popular culture and make it their own; it values interactivity, creativity and the ability of ordinary people to route around and glom on.[22]

Balkin's First Amendment theory of democratic culture also challenges the rights and privileges online service providers now enjoy under the First Amendment and copyright law to control end users' ability to access distribution networks, such as broadband, and post, download, share, and alter copyrighted content.

SUMMARY: No single theory or philosophy adequately explains the benefits individuals and society derive from the protections the U.S. Supreme Court has accorded speech that, for example, inflicts emotional harm, violates commonly held notions of civility, decency, morality, or allows for news organizations to publish stolen government documents. Instead, scholars have identified what have become known as "classic" First Amendment free expression theories by analyzing Court rulings: (i) marketplace of ideas, (ii) civic courage, (iii) self-government, (iv) individual self-fulfillment/autonomy, (v) checking the abuse of official power, and (vi) the safety value function. Though most justices have invoked the marketplace of ideas theory, typically justices call upon more than one of the theories to justify why free expression warrants constitutional protection, often at the expense of other important societal values. Since the 1990s, legal scholars, arguing that the classic theories collectively or individually do not fully take into account the significance of the full range of free expression individuals engage in, have devised new conceptions. Chief among them are the dissent, tolerance, public discourse, and democratic culture theories.

ONLINE RESOURCES

1. Vincent Blasi, "The First Amendment and the Ideal of Civic Courage: The Brandeis Opinion in *Whitney v. California*," 29 *William. & Mary Law Review*, 653, 668 (1988), http://scholarship.law.wm.edu/wmlr/vol29/iss4/2

2. Vincent Blasi, *Ideas of the First Amendment*, http://www.blasi-first-amendment.com/, http://www.blasi-first-amendment.com/display.asp?displayID=preface.pdf; http://www.blasi-first-amendment.com/display.asp?displayID=chapter4.pdf; http://www.blasi-first-amendment.com/display.asp?displayID=chapter8.pdf

3. Citizen Media Law Project, CMLP International Blog, http://www.citmedialaw.org/international/blog

4. Mark F. Radcliffe and Diane Brinson, "The U.S. Legal System," *FindLaw* (2012), http://library.findlaw.com/1999/Jan/1/241487.html

5. Antonin Scalia, "Common Law Courts in a Civil-Law System: The Role of U.S. Federal Courts in Interpreting the Constitution and the Laws," The Tanner Lectures on Human Values delivered at Princeton University, March 8 & 9, 1995. Tanner Lectures, The University of Utah, http://www.tannerlectures.utah.edu/lectures/documents/scalia97.pdf

6. Supreme Court of the United States Blog, http://www.scotusblog.com/

QUESTIONS

Identify the First Amendment theory or theories that might justify protecting the following expressive activities.

1. A high school student uses her Facebook page to say that her school principal is a mean SOB who is going to get what he deserves some day.
2. A seller of marijuana operating in a state where the use and sale of marijuana for medical purposes is legal advertises his low prices on the Internet, making the ad accessible to residents of states where the sale of marijuana for any purpose is criminalized.
3. Wikileaks' publication of stolen classified U.S. documents.
4. A gay rights group changes some of the words of the Martin Luther King Jr. "I have a Dream" speech to promote gay rights. The group does not obtain permission from the Estate of Dr. Martin Luther King, Jr., which owns the copyright to the speech, and posts the modified text on its web site, where it is downloaded by millions.

ENDNOTES

1. *FCC v. Fox Television Stations*, 132 S.Ct. 2307 (2012)
2. Articles of Incorporation for Assigned Names and Numbers, Internet Corporation for Assigned Names and Numbers, http://www.icann.org/en/general/articles.htm
3. Eugene Volokh. "Analogizing and Distinguishing Cases," August 10, 2009, http://www.volokh.com/posts/1249928819.shtml
4. *Rosenblatt v. Baer*, 383 U.S. 75, 85–86 (1966).
5. *Snyder v. Phelps*, 131 S. Ct. 1207, 1219 (2011).
6. Thomas I. Emerson. "Colonial Intentions and Current Realities of the First Amendment" (1977). *Faculty Scholarship Series*. Paper 2774, http://digitalcommons.law.yale.edu/fss_papers/2774
7. John Milton. *Areopagitica*. London: Oxford University Press (1932), 51, http://www.archive.org/stream/areopagitica00miltuoft/areopagitica00miltuoft_djvu.txt
8. John Stuart Mill. *On Liberty*. Boston: Ticknor and Fields (1863), 36.
9. See W. WatHopkins. "The Supreme Court Defines the Marketplace of Ideas," *Journalism and Mass Communication Quarterly*, 73(1), 40–52 (1996).
10. See Paul H. Brietzke. "How and Why the Marketplace of Ideas Fails," 31 *Valparaiso University Law Review* 951 (1997).
11. *Doe v. Reed*, 09–559 (April 28, 2010), http://www.supremecourt.gov/oral_arguments/argument_transcripts/09-559.pdf
12. Vincent Blasi. "The First Amendment and the Ideal of Civic Courage: The Brandeis Opinion in *Whitney v. California*," 29 *William. & Mary Law Review* 653, 668 (1988), http://scholarship.law.wm.edu/wmlr/vol29/iss4/2
13. *Whitney v. California*, 274 US 357, 375 (1927).
14. Alexander Meiklejohn. *Free Speech and Its Relation to Self-government*. New York: Harper & Brothers (1948), 24.
15. *New York Times Co. v. United States*, 403 U.S. 713, 717 (1971).
16. Thomas I. Emerson. "Toward a General Theory of the First Amendment," 72 *Yale Law Journal*, 877, 885 (1963).
17. Steven H. Shiffrin. *The First Amendment, Democracy and Romance*. Boston, MA: Harvard University Press (1990), 5.
18. Lee C. Bollinger. "Commentaries: The Tolerant Society: A Response to Critics," 90 *Columbia Law Review* 979, 986 (1990).
19. Robert C. Post. "The Constitutional Concept of Public Discourse: Outrageous Opinion, Democratic Deliberation, and *Hustler Magazine v. Falwell*," 103 *Harvard Law Review* 602, 630 (1989–1990), http://digitalcommons.law.yale.edu/cgi/viewcontent.cgi?article=1209&context=fss_papers&sei-redir=1#search=%22post%20constitutional%20public%20discourse%22

20. Ibid.
21. Jack Balkin. "Digital Speech and Democratic Culture: A Theory of Freedom of Expression for the Information Society," 79 *New York University Law Review* 1, 14 (2004).
22. Jack Balkin. "How Rights Change: Freedom of Speech in the Digital Era," 26 *Sydney Law Review* 5, 11 (2004), http://www.yale.edu/lawweb/jbalkin/articles/howrightschange1.pdf

CHAPTER TWO

History and Impact of Media Law

CONTROVERSY: After you receive your semester grades, many of you are likely to grade your professors on the wildly popular RateMyProfessor.com. Some of you might post unfavorable—possibly false and reputation-damaging—comments about professors. You might say something similar to the following, a slightly revised version of a real student posting taken from RateMyProfessor.com: "Socrates is a lousy teacher and probably would be fired. But these professor dudes have tenure and are untouchable. He has an ego-centric, pompous personality. He is rude, mean, disrespectful, all of which take away from any teaching ability he may have. Other profs don't like him." You are likely to post such comments anonymously and, generally, the law will protect your anonymity. As Justice Hugo Black explained, under the First Amendment, "Anonymous pamphlets, leaflets, brochures and even books have played an important role in the progress of mankind…the Federalist Papers, written in favor of the adoption of our Constitution, were published under fictitious names. It is plain that anonymity has sometimes been assumed for the most constructive purposes."[1]

Moreover, a federal statute provides immunity from liability to the owners of RateMyProfessor.com for student postings. That's why the social media site works so well, at least in the eyes of students and the website owners.

In contrast, a sensible newspaper publisher would not provide such a forum in its pages because no law shields print publishers from the defamatory and false comments of anonymous speakers. Thus, an angry professor wouldn't bother suing the anonymous student. He or she would sue the newspaper publisher.

Chapter's Scope

Since the late 1780s, Congress has crafted hundreds of laws covering mass media use and development. Those laws, or the absence of them, can make a world of difference. For example, the owners of RateMyProfessors.com, MTV Networks, and other Internet service providers (ISP), or intermediaries, enjoy immunity from defamation, privacy, intentional infliction of emotional harm, misappropriation, and negligence claims, state-law intellectual property claims, including unfair competition, false advertising, and right of publicity[2] resulting from the conduct of online users under Section 230 of the Communications Decency Act of 1996. Though many question the wisdom of protecting ISPs from such legal liability, the U.S. Court of Appeals for the Second Circuit concluded that without such protection,

> it would be impossible for service providers to screen each of their millions of postings for possible problems. Faced with potential liability for each message republished by their services, interactive computer service providers might choose to severely restrict the number and type of messages posted. Congress considered the weight of the speech interest implicated and chose to immunize service providers to avoid any such restrictive effect.[3]

This chapter's central purpose is to aid you in understanding the law's impact on the corporate development, individual use, and government control and regulation of mass media in the U.S. We will (i) discuss how media law shapes media technological development, use, and content; (ii) identify the leading media policy theories and their advocates; (iii) analyze the role the First Amendment free speech and press clauses, the Copyright Clause, and Postal Service Act played in establishing our nation's original media policy; and (iv) examine the U.S. Supreme Court's **medium-specific First Amendment analysis** approach to mass media technologies.

Why the Law's Impact on Media Matters

Many of you have chosen to study a field that examines mass media production, content, and audiences. Since its origins in the 1920s, most mass communication and media studies scholars have examined how media affect individual behavior, communities' cultural behavior and beliefs, institutions, and how audiences use media. In contrast, this chapter looks at the impact legislation, regulation, and judge-made law have had in shaping the development of mass media technologies, industries, content and individual use of mass media. Why this approach? Because the legal and legislative systems have played an important, sometimes pivotal role in tailoring the development of mass media industries, their related technologies, and the content they allow businesses and individuals to disseminate and use. In other words, your ability to download music from the Web, to record TiVo television programs using a remote storage digital video recorder (RS-DVR), or to watch TV-MA-rated cable programming is not dictated solely by the architecture of those technologies that allow you to access or copy content. For a few years—June 1999 to July 2001—anyone could download music from the Web free of charge thanks to the technology of Napster, an online file-sharing service. But Napster lost a copyright lawsuit to A&M records in 2001, *A&M v. Napster, Inc.*, 284 F.3d 1091 (9th Cir. 2002). Now you have to pay to download music (see Chapter 14). So far, your freedom to "TiVo" is protected under the court's ruling in *Sony Corp. of America vs. Universal City Studios*, 464 U.S. 417 (1984), stating that users of home recording devices were allowed to time shift programming under the fair use doctrine of copyright law, and the U.S. Court of Appeals for the Second Circuit, in *Cable News Network, Inc., et al. v. CSC Holdings, Inc., et al.* 536 F.3d 121 (2d Cir. 2008), cert. denied 129 S. Ct. 2890 (2009), ruled that the distribution and use of RS-DVR technology is similarly protected.

As you will see later in this chapter and in Chapter 12, you can watch sexually explicit content on a cable television channel that you cannot find on a broadcast channel because the former technology enjoys greater First Amendment protection than the latter. About that TV-MA rating? Well, that's self-imposed. The National Cable Television Association (NCTA) has pledged to adhere to voluntary ratings guidelines regarding mature programming (see Chapter 11).

Technology is not determinative. Law, economics, culture, and technology are central forces that, according to Georgetown University Law Professor Rebecca Tushnet, "help to constitute the audience for speech, shaping what speech reaches an audience and what that audience can do in response."[4] Law, for example, can promote the use of mass media technologies with the goal of nurturing a highly informed, civically engaged citizenry, or promote scientific and artistic innovation and commercial growth. It can give a mass media industry economic incentives to expand and take risks. Conversely, law has the power to slow, sometimes cripple mass media technologies' impact on society by, for example, favoring established industries over new ones. For about 10 years, the free culture movement has made such an argument. Its motto: "information wants to be free." Among other concerns, the free culture movement fears that current copyright law restricts the creativity that digital technology can unleash.

William Shakespeare famously said, "What's past is prologue." That phrase has come to mean that history repeats itself, influencing the present and future. After reading this chapter, you will see that the axiom rings true in the law and media technology arena. Today, legislators, lawyers, scholars, and advocacy groups debate the merits of regulating the Internet and other digital technologies. Some argue that in the current era of converging telecommunications and computing technologies, traditional legal approaches should not apply. Yet, many of the contemporary arguments about regulating the Internet and cell phones, for example, echo disputes waged decades ago over Industrial Revolution-age mass media technologies such as telegraphy, photography cameras, and the player piano.

Mass Media Policy Advocates

Generally, **mass media policy** refers to the principles that governments use to guide them in establishing goals, methods, and laws affecting media ownership, technological development, and the public's use of those media technologies. How is mass media policy created? Generally, organized groups, corporations, think tanks, scholars, economists, bureaucrats, regulators, legislators, judges and others cooperate and compete in an effort to establish values, goals, and methods for the use of public expression and media technologies to benefit the public good. Traditionally, media policy advocates fall into two ideological camps—those who favor regulation and those who do not. These two camps represent the polar opposites of media policy approaches in the U.S. Both camps argue that their approaches toward regulation protect and foster free expression interests. Such interests include individual ability to exchange ideas and information for the purposes of self-governance, political dissent, self-fulfillment, commercial exchange, artistic creativity, and scientific development.

Since the mid-1980s, deregulation advocates, or neo-liberals, have contended that our free expression interests are best served by allowing the economic marketplace to function with as little interference from government as possible. This stance developed during a time of abundant media choices created by the growth of cable and satellite television, and by the consumer's ability, starting in the late 1990s, to easily receive and, most importantly, post their own content on the Internet. They attracted ideological kin among cyber libertarians and **cyber exceptionalists**. Generally, these two media policy advocates argue that the Internet is a unique mass media technology, one designed to promote free expression and egalitarian values. Thus, the libertarians say, laws targeting brick-and-mortar media concerns do not apply to cyberspace.

Here is how John Perry Barlow, the father of cyber libertarianism, put in his "Declaration of Independence of Cyberspace: "We are creating a world that all may enter without privilege or prejudice accorded by race, economic power, military force, or station of birth…Your legal concepts of property, expression, identity, movement, and context do not apply to us. They are all based on matter, and there is no matter here."[5]

Then, there are those, mostly law professors such as Lawrence Lessig, who some label as "cyber collectivists" or "information commons adherents." Broadly, they argue that media policy and lawmakers must recognize that the architecture of the Internet is a law itself, and must be part of the legal calculus. As Lessig puts it, "The single most significant change in the politics of cyberspace is the coming of age of this simple idea: The code is law. The architectures of cyberspace are as important as the law in defining and defeating the liberties of the Net."[6]

Public interest or pluralist media policy advocates stand at the opposite end of the ideological spectrum from the neo-liberals. They are mostly organized in groups such as Free Press, the Media Access Project, and the Center for Digital Democracy. Such advocates contend that neither the abundance, the design of media technology, or the economic marketplace guarantees that free expression interests—or, for that matter, other civil liberties such as privacy—will be protected. Consequently, they argue that government intervention through law, subsidies, and regulation are necessary to promote the free flow of information, diversity of opinions, and participation in the democratic process, and to protect other fundamental rights.

The Founding Fathers and Mass Media Technology

In 1970, the poet Gil Scott-Heron proclaimed famously, "The Revolution Will Not Be Televised." Ever since, individuals have argued the contrary, asserting that a mass medium played a critical role in rousing revolt. In 2009, some insisted the revolution would be tweeted in Iran. Iranians tweeted, but no revolution followed. In 2011, pundits argued heatedly over the role that social networking sites played in sparking and organizing the rebellion in Egypt. But one can make a compelling case, without exaggeration, that the American Revolution was published; that is, that printing press-produced materials such as *Cato's Letters* and Thomas Paine's *Common Sense* played an indispensable role in inciting colonists to rebel against the British crown.[7]

But tools are neutral. A knife can kill. A knife can cut out cancer. And when the ex-rebels met at the Constitutional Convention in 1787, they understood that the mass media tool that helped them overthrow a king could also play a central role in helping them grow the former colonies into a highly productive and unified republic. Their view is evident in the Constitution's First Amendment free press and speech clauses (1787), the Constitution's Article I, Section 8, known as the Copyright

Clause, which authorized the Copyright Act of 1790, and the Postal Service Act of 1792 and 1794. Collectively, these three constitutional clauses incorporate the seemingly contradictory approaches used in U.S. law to promote our policy goal of facilitating the flow of information to promote national unity, economic growth, cultural development, democratic participation, and individual freedom. The three clauses show that at the nation's inception we chose to limit government's reach over individuals' use of mass media with the First Amendment, while extending government's reach under the Copyright Act and Postal Service Acts, all to reach the same goals.

> SUMMARY: Alone, technology is not determinative. The mass media policy and legal choices legislatures, courts, and regulators make—along with economic and cultural determinants—play a major role in shaping how corporations and the public use mass media technologies. From our nation's inception, legislators and policy makers used the law—First Amendment free press and speech clauses (1787), the Constitution's Article I, Section 8, known as the Copyright Clause, which authorized the Copyright Act of 1790, and the Postal Service Act of 1792 and 1794—to promote national unity, economic growth, cultural development, democratic participation and individual freedom.

The First Amendment's Free Press Clause

"Congress shall make no law respecting an establishment of religion, or prohibiting the free exercise thereof; or abridging the freedom of speech, or of the press . . ."

We do not know precisely what the 39 signatories of the Constitution in 1787 intended, or what state ratifying conventions had in mind when they voted to incorporate the First Amendment's free press clause as part of the Constitution by 1790. Though some, notably U.S. Supreme Court Justice Stewart Potter, have argued that the clause protects the institutional press, that position is not widely held.[8] The majority view is that the clause protects an individual's right to publish. Edward S. Lee of Ohio State University, who has written extensively about the Constitution framers' understanding of the free press clause, adds that in the colonial period, when "the 'press' referred to the technology of the printing press or, more generally, the publishing of any material by the printing press...It marked a sentiment that government should not be allowed to control or interfere with the public's ability to use the technology that enabled the mass production of speech."[9]

Accordingly, neither federal nor local laws in the U.S. have targeted the use of the printing press machinery as British law did under the Licensing Order of 1643, which John Milton protested in *Areopagitica*, and under the Licensing of the Press Act of 1662. There have been occasions when states have tried to tax the ink and paper used by a newspaper, similar to the approach the British took under the Stamp Act of 1765. This act, as every school child learns, riled the Colonists, who rallied behind the call, "No taxation without representation." The U.S. Supreme Court, however, has found laws that impose a special tax on the use of paper and ink to be an impermissible violation of freedom of the press.[10] No other medium enjoys a similar First Amendment protection. Under *Leathers v. Medlock*, 499 U.S. (1991), states may tax cable television. Government-regulated radio, television, telephone, cell phone, satellite media pay license and other fees. The Internet's protection against specially targeted taxes is similar to print's, but it is only guaranteed under a federal law, the Internet Tax Freedom Act, which imposes a temporary moratorium that Congress has extended three times since 1998.

Because legislatures in the U.S. have refrained from limiting individuals' use of the printing press technologies, battles over press clause liberties have focused on content. Within a mere eight years of the press clause's adoption, Congress passed the Alien & Sedition Acts of 1799. Signed by President John Adams, these federal laws targeted mainly the opposition party, the Democratic-Republicans, and their backers. Simply put, criticism of the government and its policies amounted to a criminal offense, **seditious libel**. Under the acts, which expired in 1801, 25 newspaper editors and publishers were arrested.[11] Thomas Jefferson, the subsequent president and leader of the Democratic-Republicans, declared the acts unconstitutional, but his action held no legal authority.

Was Jefferson wrong? More than 100 years would pass before the Court embarked upon an answer. It handed down a landmark ruling on prior restraints in *Near v. Minnesota*, 238 U.S. 697 (1931). And, though the Court never explicitly declared the Alien & Sedition Acts unconstitutional, in *New York Times v. Sullivan*, 376 U.S. 254 (1964), its landmark ruling on libel, the Court noted that, "Although the Sedition Act was never tested in this Court, the attack upon its validity has carried the day in the court of history."[12]

Technology and the First Amendment

In the U.S., media policy is as old as the U.S. Constitution's First Amendment speech and press clauses, adopted December 15, 1791, along with the other nine amendments of the Bill of Rights. As Philip Napoli notes in *Foundations of Communications Policy: Principles and Process in the Regulation of Electronic Media*, the First Amendment is the "boundary-setting foundation principle of [electronic media] communications policy."[13] It also serves the same function for all mass media policy, as all other laws affecting media must conform to First Amendment-imposed limitations on government interference with free expression. The amendment is 220 years old. The U.S. Supreme Court's earliest efforts to explain its meaning, however, started only during the second decade of the 20th century; thus, our understanding of the First Amendment's scope and purpose is less than 100 years old.

The printing press was the only mass medium in existence at the time of the nation's founding, and one of only two technologies explicitly identified in the Bill of Rights. The other is the gun, identified in the Second Amendment. Oral, written, and printed forms of expression were the only means for transmitting ideas through language. Thus, the Constitution protects freedom "of speech or the press."[14]

Since then, technological innovations have spawned the telegraph, photography camera, telephone, sound recording, motion picture recording, radio, television, cable television, satellite transmission, cell phone, video game, Internet, digital video disc, broadband transmission, and sound and image recording devices. The Constitution's framers did not contemplate such media; they only knew of the printing press and the post office. Consequently, the Court has devised a medium-specific approach to determine how much First Amendment protection it will grant to speech conveyed by different media because, as Justice Robert H. Jackson reasoned, "[t]the moving picture screen, the radio, the newspaper, the handbill, the sound truck and the street orator have differing natures, values, abuses and dangers. Each…is a law unto itself."[15]

First Amendment Medium-Specific Analysis

Here is how the Court applies its First Amendment medium-specific analysis . The Court examines the characteristics of the medium when deciding cases involving content-based restrictions. (The Court has said that when a government regulation seeks to limit or ban speech because of its message, then it is a "content-based" restriction. When judging the constitutionality of such restrictions, the Court applies what is known as "strict scrutiny" analysis, asking whether the restriction serves a compelling state interest and whether there is not a less speech-restrictive way to achieve that goal.[16] The Court considers four characteristics. (I) The Court looks to see whether the owners and users of a technology use it to facilitate the dissemination of news and opinion about civic affairs. (II) Because precedent binds judges, the Court considers how the law has treated an older mode of expression that may be similar to the emerging one in question.[17] (III) It also examines whether the medium allows for individuals to control reception of content into the home, or in legal jargon, it asks whether the medium is "invasive," transmitted into private spaces without an individual's ability to know when a sexually offensive or profane message might occur.[18] (IV) The Court asks whether the technology allows for simultaneous transmission by multitudes, or is it a "scarce" expression commodity that needs government oversight to insure widespread use.[19] Typically, the Court will confer full First Amendment protection on an emerging media technology when the medium plays a major role in allowing citizens to share news and ideas, is not invasive, and is not a scarce commodity.

Now, in the second decade of the 21st century, increasing numbers of academics and lawyers are reevaluating the legitimacy of the Court's medium-specific approach.[20] Critics say medium-specific classifications make little sense in a digital world in which, for example, a telephone company uses its lines to send video programming via broadband or to provide Internet access. In other words, in a digital world there is no such thing as one medium when content is transmitted and received by using combined technologies.

Nevertheless, courts still adhere to the traditional approach. Under this approach, every medium enjoys some degree of First Amendment protection—generally the right to be free from interference from the government and the courts as long as the message conveyed does not harm national security or public safety, or undermine competing social values and other fundamental rights. Keep in mind, however, that even print and online service providers and users are subject to lawsuits claiming harm—libel, incitement, invasion of privacy, contract and antitrust violations, for example. The government can bring criminal actions against service providers and users, charging, among other crimes, obscenity or violation of federal wiretapping laws. As noted earlier, Congress has carved out a major exception for the Internet—§ 230 of the Communications Decency Act shields ISPs from civil actions such as libel, negligence, fraud, and state law false advertising claims[21] stemming from the content posted by users.

> SUMMARY: To confer full First Amendment protection on a new medium, the U.S. Supreme Court asks (i) whether a new medium facilitates the dissemination of news and opinion about civic affairs; (ii) how the law has treated an older mode of expression that may be similar to the emerging one in question; (iii) whether the medium allows for individuals to control reception of content into the home, or, in legal jargon, it asks whether the medium is "invasive;" and (iv) whether the technology allows for simultaneous transmission by many, or is a "scarce" expression commodity that needs government oversight to insure widespread use.

All media are not created equally under the First Amendment. Generally, mass media fall within three types of legal models: print, common carriage, and broadcast. There are also hybrid classifications covering cable, satellite, and cable modem service.

The Print Model

Does a new mass medium benefit the public the way books and newspapers do? Is it used to convey ideas and opinions about civics, culture, the arts, and sciences? That's the core criterion for qualifying under the print model. Today, for example, cinema enjoys full First Amendment protection. But that was not true in the early days of its development as an industry, starting in 1891 when the Edison Laboratories used a Kinetoscope to show *Dickson Greeting*. Local governments passed laws to censor movies over concerns that their treatment of race, sex, and romance posed a serious threat to community morals, culminating in the Court's ruling in *Mutual Film Corporation v. Industrial Commission of Ohio*, which upheld such bans in 1915. In its medium-specific analysis in *Mutual Film*, the Court chose to emphasize the differences between cinema and print media, rather than the host of free expression attributes they share:

> It cannot be put out of view that the exhibition of moving pictures is a business, pure and simple, originated and conducted for profit, like other spectacles, not to be regarded, nor intended to be regarded by the Ohio Constitution, we think, as part of the press of the country, or as organs of public opinion. They are mere representations of events, of ideas and sentiments published and known; vivid, useful, and entertaining, no doubt, but, as we have said, capable of evil, having power for it, the greater because of their attractiveness and manner of exhibition. It was this capability and power, and it may be in experience of them, that induced the state of Ohio, in addition to prescribing penalties for immoral exhibitions, as it does in its Criminal Code, to require censorship before exhibition, as it does by the act under review. We cannot regard this as beyond the power of government. [22]

The flaws in the Court's reasoning should be immediately apparent to a 21st-century teenager. Documentary films, such as Al Gore's Academy Award-winning *An Inconvenient Truth*, provoke civic debate and help shape public opinion worldwide about important topics like global warming. Even movies that are purely fictional, such as *Avatar*, have messages that resound in the public sphere. Aren't the newspapers and publishing industries big businesses like the film industry, producing a great deal of materials primarily for profit? There are no significant First Amendment distinction between print and cinema. Yet, not until its ruling in *Joseph Burstyn, Inc. v. Wilson*, 343 U.S. 495, 501 (1952), did the Court recognize that "motion pictures are a significant medium for the communication of ideas." In the intervening period, the Motion Picture Association of American sought protection from government censorship by imposing its own censorship guidelines, the Motion Picture Production Code of 1934 (Hays Code).

The Court—applying its medium-specific analysis—placed the Internet on the same footing as print the first time it was asked to address the constitutionality of a statute that sought to treat the emerging technology like broadcast, which does not enjoy full First Amendment protection. When you consider that search engines and web browsers became available for widespread public use in 1993, *Reno v. ACLU*, a 1997 ruling, marked the first time in U.S. history the Court accorded a communications technology full First Amendment rights in the initial judicial hearing. Note how the Court distinguishes the Internet's technical operation from broadcasting's and compares its use favorably to the use of the printing press by 18th-century pamphleteers:

> Finally, unlike the conditions that prevailed when Congress first authorized regulation of the broadcast spectrum, the Internet can hardly be considered a "scarce" expressive commodity. It provides relatively unlimited, low-cost capacity for communication of all kinds. The Government estimates that [a]s many as 40 million people use the Internet today, and that figure is expected to grow to 200 million by 1999. This

dynamic, multifaceted category of communication includes not only traditional print and news services, but also audio, video, and still images, as well as interactive, real-time dialogue. Through the use of chat rooms, any person with a phone line can become a town crier with a voice that resonates farther than it could from any soapbox. Through the use of Web pages, mail exploders, and newsgroups, the same individual can become a pamphleteer. As the District Court found, "the content on the Internet is as diverse as human thought."[23]

While the Internet enjoys full First Amendment protection, it is unsettled whether that status should be conferred upon all computer-related technology. For example, federal courts are split on whether computer source code, the human-readable mechanism that allows a computer to operate, is free speech protected under the First Amendment.[24]

Most recently, the Court added video games to the category of mass media technologies that enjoy full First Amendment protection in *Brown v. Entertainment Merchant Association*, 08–1448 (2011). The case was brought by the video game industry to challenge a California statute, which would have required violent video games to be labeled and their rental or sale to minors banned. The Court struck down the statute as an impermissible infringement of the First Amendment. It applied medium-specific analysis, finding significant parallels between video games and books, movies, and plays. "Like the protected books, plays, and movies that preceded them, video games communicate ideas—and even social messages—through many familiar literary devices (such as characters, dialogue, plot, and music) and through features distinctive to the medium (such as the player's interaction with the virtual world). That suffices to confer First Amendment protection."[25]

The Curious Case of the Camera

Courts have not fashioned a First Amendment legal model for image capture technologies such as the photo camera, film, or video cameras.[26] Consequently, over the years judges and lawmakers have used the law to protect individuals from a level of harm they detected in the still or moving image that they do not attribute to the printed word. In doing so, they have limited newsgathering rights in private places, quasi-public places such as courtrooms, and public places such as public streets. The use of photo cameras by news journalists spurred Louis Brandeis and Samuel D. Warrant to pen their *Harvard Law Review* article "The Right of Privacy," in 1890, and also led to the New York case, *Roberson v. Rochester Folding Box Co.*, 171 N.Y. 538 (1902). Today, every state recognizes rights of privacy, stemming from these early efforts (see Chapter 6). Yet, in 1937 the American Bar Association (ABA) adopted Judicial Canon 35 and spurred the federal government and all states to ban cameras and broadcasting equipment from courtroom proceedings. The ABA adopted Canon 35 in response to what many saw as the largely media-created chaos of the Bruno Hauptmann trial of 1937. To protect defendants' Sixth Amendment right to a fair trial, the federal government and the states banned cameras from courtrooms for more than 40 years. Even now, U.S. Supreme Court justices will not allow their proceedings to be televised or photographed (see Chapter 10).

The Broadcast Model and the Federal Communications Commission

While print and the Internet stand atop the First Amendment protective hierarchy, broadcast—radio and television—occupy the lowest rung. For example, one needs a federal license to legally operate radio and television stations. The Federal Communications Commission (FCC) approves the award of licenses to owners. In contrast, requiring a license to print a newspaper, distribute a movie, or post a blog would be deemed an impermissible prior restraint.

Unlike owners of print- and Internet-based media, radio and television owners do not have editorial autonomy. The FCC, for example, has the legal authority to tell its licensees that they have to give time to certain speakers under the Personal Attack Equal Time Rule.[27] Similarly, under the Fairness Doctrine—which the FCC has ceased to enforce, though the U.S. Supreme Court has never ruled the doctrine unconstitutional—licensees are required to present controversial public issues in an honest and balanced manner.[28] It's also a violation of federal law for radio or television to air indecent sexual content or profane content. In contrast, print, Internet, cable and cinema publishers, and producers are subject only to laws banning obscene sexual content. Consequently, broadcasters face the possibility of being prosecuted for obscenity as well as indecency and profanity. In contrast, the Internet, cinema, and print media are only subject to laws forbidding sexually obscene content.

The FCC also has the authority under its News Distortion Rule to penalize a licensee for rigging, slanting, or falsifying the news. The FCC also can limit broadcasters' freedom to buy other media companies under its Broadcast Ownership Rules.[29] In practice, that means the FCC can limit the ability of newspaper, cinema, and Internet owners from owning radio and television stations, though it has no direct authority over those industries. Nevertheless, broadcasting still enjoys some First Amendment protection, as the Court stressed in *Turner Broadcasting System v. FCC*, 512 U.S. 622, 650 (1994), noting that "the FCC's oversight responsibilities do not grant it the power to ordain any particular type of programming that must be offered by broadcast stations."

The broadcast regulatory model has been under attack as unconstitutional since the 1960s, but particularly since the emergence of the cable TV industry in the 1980s. Its detractors contend that the legal doctrines supporting government authority to regulate broadcasting in a unique fashion—**spectrum scarcity**, pervasiveness, and accessibility to children—are illogical. Those who want to see the end of the over-the-airwaves broadcast regulatory regime argue: (i) the electromagnetic spectrum is no more scarce than the trees that make newspapers; (ii) now with cable TV, the Internet, satellite, and cell phone transmission, an abundance of media exist, undercutting the suitability of scarcity; and (iii) radio and television are no more pervasive and accessible than the Internet, and parents can acquire filtering technologies to screen out harmful content from televisions. Moreover, with the advent of media convergence, the Court's medium-specific classifications and the treatment of broadcast content differently from print, Internet, and movie content under the law makes little sense. Why does it make sense to treat the broadcast content one way when it is transmitted over the airwaves, and another way when the same content is watched via the Internet or cable TV? As the discussion in Chapter 11 makes plain, the U.S. Supreme Court recently had three opportunities to abandon the broadcast regulatory model—*FCC v. Fox Television Stations*, 132 S.Ct. 2307 (2012), *Media General v. FCC*, No. 11–691 (2012), *Tribune Co. v. FCC*, No. 11–696 (2012)—and chose not to.

The Common Carriage Model

In between the fully protected and least protected media, fall a number of technologies that the law classifies as **common carriers**—postal service, telegraphy, and telephone or telephony, and direct broadcast satellite providers (DBS). The origin of common carrier law stems from mass media used to transport people and cargo, for the most part, ships and railroads. Under the U.S. legal media regime, mail, telegraphy, and telephony are viewed as operating in two fundamentally different ways from print publishing. First, they are natural monopolies, meaning that where one system operates it is physically or technologically impossible, or economically inefficient, for another system to provide the same service to the public. Public supplies of water and electricity, for example, are usually considered natural monopolies. Second, there is the rationale that these services are using public property to operate and, therefore, must make some concessions for the public good. Common carriers owe a duty of nondiscrimination. They must offer service on a nondiscriminatory basis, charge just and reasonable rates, and must be designed so that other carriers can interconnect with them.

Traditionally, courts analyze First Amendment rights from the perspective of "speakers," those who disseminate content, and not from the perspective of the owners of that technology, although "speakers" can be owners, too. Consider how our society has used telephones for more than a century. The telephone company did not use its system to send its own content to the public; rather, individuals used it to talk to other individuals. In other words, traditional common carriers do not exercise editorial control, identified by the Court in *CBS, Inc. v. Democratic National Committee*, 412 U.S. 94, 124 (1973) as "selection and control of material."

The advent of converged mass media technologies has raised questions about the First Amendment rights of cable companies that use their technologies to send content of their own choosing. In the mid-1990s, cable companies challenged a cable-telecommunications cross-ownership ban blocking local telephone companies from owning cable companies on First Amendment free speech grounds. In one such case, *Chesapeake & Potomac Telephone Co. v. United States*, 42 F.3d 181 (4th Cir. 1994), the Fourth Circuit Court of Appeals held that the ban violated telephone companies' free speech rights. The federal appeals court said, "[r]egulations that discriminate among media, or among different speakers within a single medium, often present serious First Amendment concerns."[30] The court chose to impose **intermediate scrutiny** to determine whether the content-neutral ban was constitutional, asserting that the ban must be narrowly tailored to serve a significant governmental interest, while leaving open ample alternative channels for communication of information.[31] The issue became moot under the Telecommunications Act of 1996, which removed the cable-telecommunications cross-ownership ban and allowed local telephone companies to offer video programming.[32]

In contrast, by mid-2012, Google's First Amendment status was far from clear. Whether Google qualifies under the law as a common carrier or a publisher may make all the difference in its defense against the antitrust investigations it was expected to face in the U.S. The European Commission, India, and Korea also were investigating the search engine company for antitrust violations stemming from its search selection process and related advertising business. But under U.S. law, if Google's search engine selections are deemed the product of editorial decision making, the company would have a plausible First Amendment defense against antitrust charges that it misused the process to favor itself and its advertisers. At least that is the position asserted in Eugene Volokh and Donald M. Falk's white paper "First Amendment Protection for Search Engine Results."[33] The Google-commissioned paper relies in part on two precedents: *Search King, Inc. v. Google Technology, Inc.*, No. Civ-02–1457-M (W.D. Oklahoma, 2003) and *Langdon v. Google, Inc.*, 474 F. Supp. 2d 622 (D. Del. 2007).

In *Search King*, a federal judge ruled that Google's PageRank, which ranks the importance of sites based on link popularity, was First Amendment-protected opinion. In *Langdon*, a case involving Google, Yahoo, and Microsoft, a federal judge held that the First Amendment barred actions against search engine companies that refused to run ads promoting a certain website on their search engines. The plaintiff asked the court to order the online companies to place ads for his websites in prominent places on their search engines and "honestly" rank them. The judge, however, said such an order would violate the First Amendment right of editorial autonomy: "(Court cannot compel the publisher of a private daily newspaper to accept and print advertising in the exact form submitted based upon the freedom to exercise subjective editorial discretion in rejecting a proffered article.) Accordingly, the Court will grant Google's and Microsoft's Motion to Dismiss the Amended Complaint on the basis that Plaintiff seeks relief precluded by their First Amendment rights."[34]

University of California, Los Angeles, Law Professor Eugene Volokh, a co-author of "First Amendment Protection for Search Engine Results," points to federal statute 47 U.S.C. §230 to argue that intermediaries, such as Google, can simultaneously invoke First Amendment publisher and common carrier status:

> Indeed, § 230 was enacted in response to a court decision (*Stratton Oakmont v. Prodigy*) that concluded that online organizations had to choose whether to be (1) common carriers, immune from liability but barred from making editorial judgments, or (2) publishers, entitled to make editorial judgment but subject to liability for others' speech. Congress specifically intended to overrule that decision, and to make it easier for content providers—such as search engines—to both make editing judgments of their own, and avoid civil liability for the speech of others.[35]

Additionally, as the Court held in *National Cable & Telecommunications Association v. Brand X Internet Services*, 545 U.S. 967 (2005), the FCC may classify cable operators that provide broadband as an "information service," and not a "telecommunications service." In contrast, when cable TV operators transmit via cable and satellite they are telecommunications services or common carriers.

Law professors Frank A. Pasquale III and Oren Bracha, however, argue that the First Amendment allows for government regulation of search engines under a common carrier theory.[36] The reasoning in *Search King* and *Langdon* is flawed, they contend. The speech that search engines produce is not analogous to the speech that a bond ranking or newspaper produces. A listing of websites does not assert an opinion or an idea in the First Amendment sense of the word, and traditionally only media—and content for that matter (see commercial speech chapter)—that provide ideas, opinions, and news about civic affairs is entitled to full First Amendment protection, according to Pasquale and Bracha.

Google or other intermediaries do not contend that the first result is better or worse than the 10th result on the listing produced by the search engine; that the content of the Web page in the first result is more informative, more reliable, or better written than the 10th result. Thus, the search engine "ranking" does not produce an assertion that can be proven true or false. In contrast, when a company ranks bonds, it asserts that the first bond is superior to the 10th bond, an assertion that can be proved true or false, Pasquale and Bracha argue.

Newspapers endorse their content. Editors and publishers, for example, implicitly claim that their news accounts can be relied on for accuracy. Search engine companies make no such claims about the reliability of any of the hundreds of websites that appear in search engine results. Therefore, search engine companies are not analogous to newspapers, books, or cinema, Pasquale and Bracha contend:

> It is highly questionable that search results constitute the kind of speech recognized to be within the ambit of the First Amendment according to either existing doctrine or any of the common normative theories in the field. While having an undeniable expressive element, the prevailing character of such speech is performative rather than propositional. Its dominant function is not to express meaning but rather to "do things in the world"; namely, channel users to websites.[37]

The Cable TV Hybrid Model and the Federal Communications Commission

The Court has fashioned a hybrid First Amendment status for cable television. Originally, cable TV technology acted merely as a conduit or passive carrier for television signals. Accordingly, a cable operator could reasonably be regulated as a common carrier. But that wasn't the regulatory framework adopted by the FCC. Starting in the 1960s, the FCC, noting that cable operators had the potential to transmit their own content as well as television-produced content, created a legal framework that mixed common carrier with broadcast law. Under this framework, operators must obtain franchise licenses—a type of prior restraint that could not be legitimately imposed on a newspaper—from local governments to lay cable under streets. Under such local laws, they are treated not quite like common carriers because local franchising authorities have adopted laws and regulations covering public access requirements, for example.

The Communications Policy Act of 1984 grants the FCC authority to regulate cable nationwide. The Court upheld the FCC's authority mostly because the vast majority of Americans get broadcast television via cable. Consequently, cable service operators are subject to "must carry" rules, mandating that cable companies carry local and public television stations within a cable provider's service area.[38] (See Chapter 11.) Cable operators also are subject to, among other rules and regulations, "original cablecasting" rules that place limits on an operator's editorial autonomy similar to broadcast equal time rules.[39] As the law has developed during the last 30 years, though, cable has come to enjoy increased First Amendment protection.

Additionally, as the Court in *National Cable & Telecommunications Association v. Brand X Internet Services*, 545 U.S. 967 (2005), held, the FCC may classify cable operators that provide broadband service via modem and then by telephone, cable, and wireless as "information services" under Title I of the Communications Act. In contrast, when cable operators transmit television programming via cable lines and satellite they are classified as telecommunications services or common carriers under Title II of the Act. Under the act, as amended by the Telecommunications Act of 1996, an "information service involves the capacity to generate, store, interact with, or otherwise manipulate information via telecommunications." In turn, "telecommunications" is defined as "the transmission, between or among points specified by the user, of information of the user's choosing, without change in the form or content of the information as sent and received."[40] The result of *Brand X* is that cable companies providing broadband service do not have to allow companies providing slower dial-up Internet service to link with them. If the Court had ruled that cable operators providing broadband were telecommunications services or common carriers, they would not have had the right to deny other Internet service providers access.

SUMMARY: Print, cinema, video games, and the Internet enjoy the most protection from government interference under the First Amendment. Government cannot require those who operate media enjoying full First Amendment protection to obtain a license to operate or interfere with their editorial autonomy. In contrast, the Court does not accord broadcast—radio and television—full First Amendment rights. Broadcasters must obtain licenses to operate and the FCC imposes restrictions on their editorial autonomy. Cable operators enjoy slightly greater First Amendment protection than broadcasters. Under a hybrid regime of law and regulations, cable television operators are subject to local and federal regulations requiring that they obtain licenses to operate locally, mandate that they carry local and public television stations, and are subject to rules that limit their editorial autonomy.

Constitution's Article I, Section 8, Known as the Copyright Clause

After the First Amendment, the Copyright Act, which has been amended several times since its inception, is, arguably, the second most significant media statute in the U.S. The founders adopted a concept of copyright law that was a direct response to the introduction of Johannes Gutenberg's printing press in England around 1475. Copyright law protects an author's right to control the copying of his expression when it is in tangible form. It is a concept nearly 1,000 years old. But Gutenberg's printing press threatened to undermine that age-old approach because once the original author circulated his book, the printing press enabled others to reproduce it at such speed and quantity as to make it impossible sometimes to determine who was the original author. The British Crown intervened. By creating the Stationers' Company in 1556, it used copyright law as a form of licensing to prevent certain works from getting into print. In 1710, Parliament passed the Statute of Anne, the first law to recognize author's rights. It stripped the Crown of its censorship authority via copyright law. The first U.S. Copyright Act of May 31, 1790, was fashioned with the terms of the Statute of Anne in mind.

The U.S. Copyright Act struck a balance between the author's and the public's interests. An author need not fear that he or she would be deprived of an opportunity to win recognition and financial gain by sharing works with the public, even when someone else, claiming originality, copies and distributes the work faster than the original author. Under copyright law, the true author or copyright owner can sue to remove the copies from the public and be compensated for losses. But the monopoly over that work is limited—14 years under the 1790 Act. Currently, under the Copyright Extension Act of 1998, that period has been extended to the life of the author plus 70 years and for works of corporate authorship to 120 years after creation or 95 years after publication, whichever comes first.[41] Once the copyright expires, the work passes into the public domain and anyone can use it, for example, to create parodies, sequels, works that use famous fictional characters in unanticipated settings and genres, or to rework a string of well-known musical notes.

According to U.S. Supreme Court Justice Ruth Bader Ginsberg, writing for the majority in *Harper and Row v. Nation Enterprises*, 471 U.S. 539 (1985), the goals of the Copyright Clause and the First Amendment free speech and free press clauses are mutually reinforcing: "…it should not be forgotten that the framers intended copyright itself to be the engine of free expression. By establishing a marketable right to the use of one's expression, copyright supplies the economic incentive to create and disseminate ideas."[42] She cautioned, however, that the engine does not work properly when courts allow a copyright owner's monopoly to "choke off multifarious indirect uses and consequent broad dissemination of information and ideas."[43]

New Media Responsive

Generally, copyright law has been responsive to emerging media; Congress and the courts have not interpreted copyright law in a medium-specific manner. It is widely believed that Congress and judges should know when, and when not, to extend copyright's control to emerging media technologies that allow others to infringe—to copy without permission—on copyrighted content. Columbia University Law Professor Jane C. Ginsburg has identified a pattern: When a copyright owner seeks to "eliminate a new kind of dissemination, and when courts do not deem that dissemination harmful to copyright owners, courts decline to find infringement, even though the legal and economic analyses that support those determinations often seem strained, not to say disingenuous."[44]

Courts and Congress tend to side with copyright owners who only seek to take advantage of a new market created by the new technology, rather than to "prevent these new means from becoming available to the public."[45] In other words, copyright law should seek to strike a balance between the economic interests of the author/owner, on one hand, and the public benefit the new technology provides to the educational, cultural, creative, and informational interests of the public, including other authors and artists, on the other.

Over the years, Congress has revised copyright law to cover new media technologies, as the Court noted in *Sony Corp. of America v. Universal City Studios, Inc.*, 464 U.S. 417, 430–431 (1984), when it ruled that Betamax video tape recorders did not violate the copyright of film and television studios:

> From its beginning, the law of copyright has developed in response to significant changes in technology. Indeed, it was the invention of a new form of copying equipment, the printing press, that gave rise to the original need for copyright protection. Repeatedly, as new developments have occurred in this country, it has been the Congress that has fashioned the new rules that new technology made necessary.

In one of those responses to emerging mass media technologies, Congress began a major reassessment of copyright law in 1955 culminating in a major reform, the 1976 Act, which took effect in 1978. It dealt with, among other concerns, motion pictures and other audiovisual works, sound recordings, electronic broadcasting, photocopy machines, and cable television.

Just as important, Congress wrote it in anticipation of new technologies: "Copyright protection subsists…in original works of authorship fixed in any tangible medium of expression, *now known or later developed* [emphasis added], from which they can be perceived, reproduced, or otherwise communicated, either or with the aid of a machine or device."[46] From 1978 to 2009, Congress amended the 1976 Act seventy times, often in response to new technologies, including semiconductor chips, satellite transmission to homes, computer software, digital audio recording equipment, online copying, and web casting.[47]

The U.S. Postal Service: Constitution's Article I, Section 8, 1790: "The Congress shall have the power to establish post offices and post roads . . ."

Why do so many in the U.S. presume that government is inherently hostile to free expression? Most Americans, it seems, could not imagine that the federal government could own and operate the Internet, for instance, without massive infringement on users' free expression rights. Well, the federal government has owned and operated a mass communication system that is something like the Internet for more than 200 years, the U.S. postal system—the information network of the Enlightenment era. And, by any objective measure, the federal government has done an outstanding job of protecting and promoting free expression interests under its ownership and management of the postal system. Consider that in 2008, the U.S. Postal Service processed 203 billion pieces of mail, delivering more mail "to more addresses in a larger geographical area than any other post in the world."[48] The system's establishment and the early decades of its operation are inextricably tied to facilitating national distribution of newspapers, books, magazines, and information about government, the arts, and science.

The postal system—the network of regular mail delivery, you know, "snail mail"—is the oldest mass communication system we have. Its successors are the telegraph, telephone networks, and the Internet. For decades, particularly during the 19th century, it served as the primary and most dependable means by which an intellectual in Massachusetts could exchange ideas with his counterpart in Virginia, a merchant in New York could conduct business with a business partner in South Carolina, a newspaper publisher in Washington, D.C., could get the local news from Vermont, or a citizen in Philadelphia could obtain timely federal government documents.

A Unique Media Law Statute

The Postal Service Act of 1792 and 1794 and its current incarnation, the Postal Reorganization Act of 1970 (PRA), are unique among U.S. mass media laws. The PRA is the only law authorizing the U.S. government to own and operate a mass medium with the obligation "to bind the Nation together through the personal, educational, literary, and business correspondence of the people." [49] Congress could have chosen to allow private interests to run the postal system and regulate the system the way it did newspapers. That is, it could have taken a hands-off approach under the First Amendment. But it did not. Congress could have chosen to allow private interests to run the postal system under common carrier law. It did not. Instead, Congress chose to allow the federal government to run the postal system as a monopoly and regulate it under a common carrier approach. It chose that path principally to ease the distribution of newspapers and magazines nationwide. What better way to build national unity, Congress believed, than to make it easier for each citizen to keep abreast of what their representatives were doing in New York and Washington, D.C.

Universal Service

The policy concept of making a mass medium accessible to all citizens, now referred to as the Postal Service's "universal service obligation (USO), is embedded in the U.S. Constitution" and though "not explicitly defined, the Postal Service's universal service obligation (USO) is broadly outlined in multiple statutes and encompasses multiple dimensions: geographic scope, range of products, access to services and facilities, delivery frequency, affordable and uniform pricing, service quality, and security of the mail." [50] Regulated as a common carrier, the postal service may not examine or read the content of the mail it carries. It cannot charge different rates based on the quality or nature of the information it carries, though it can charge different rates for the weight and form of the mail. It must serve all parties.

Universal service—the idea that a long-distance communication service should be affordable and available to even the most economical poor and geographically remote segments of a nation—is a media policy goal followed by many nations. In the U.S., the FCC created the Universal Service Fund, which relies on corporations for funding, to meet universal service goals mandated by the Telecommunications Act of 1996, and the focus has been on broadband service. But the U.S. has lagged behind many other developing nations—United Kingdom, Germany, France, Denmark and Canada—in providing widespread and affordable broadband service. By mid-2012, the commission's plans to devise a universal broadband service remained moored in dry dock. Might a government-owned and operated broadband service provide an alternative way to obtain universal service? After all, the government financed the creation and development of the Internet.

The first Congressional generation was not troubled that, on one hand, it passed a First Amendment protecting the press from government, while on the other hand, it passed a Postal Service Act empowering government to take affirmative actions to help bind the nation, help the press, and own and run our first long-distance communication service. According to MIT's Ithiel de Sola Pool, "The twentieth century notion that the proper relation between government and the press is one of arm's-length adversaries has no roots in the thinking of the founding fathers. Their belief in the importance of the press not only led them to insist that Congress pass no law 'abridging the freedom of…press' but also persuaded them to subsidize that press."[51]

> SUMMARY: The Postal Service Act of 1792 and 1794 and its current incarnation, the Postal Reorganization Act of 1970 (PRA), are unique among U.S. laws regulating expressive media. No other law authorizes the U.S. government to own and operate a mass medium with "the obligation to provide postal services to bind the Nation together through the personal, educational, literary, and business correspondence of the people."

First Amendment and the Mail

The postal service's mandated public-service mission did not eliminate the possibility of abuse by its postmaster general, who has the authority to balance the free expression and privacy concerns of those who use the mail against other society needs, such as public safety. Clearly, the postal service should have the authority to exclude certain items from the mail, particularly if they pose health or safety threats. Yet, the Court noted in *Ex Parte Jackson*, 96 U.S. 727 (1878), that such authority should not "interfere with the freedom of the press, or with any other rights of the people, but to refuse its facilities for the distribution of matter deemed injurious to the public morals."[52]

But is the use of the mail system merely a privilege, rather than a right? That's what Postmaster General Frank Walker maintained in *Hannegan v. Esquire, Inc.*, 327 U.S. 146 (1946). Walker argued that he had the authority to revoke *Esquire* magazine's second-class mailing status because he found its content "indecent, vulgar, and risqué,"[53] though the statute in question required that material be obscene before being banned from the mail. Until *Hannegan*, the Supreme Court allowed the Postmaster General wide discretion in determining access to the mail system. But in *Hannegan*, the Court took another direction, one consistent with its overall newly emerging First Amendment analysis. (Recall, that the Court's current First Amendment doctrine emerged after World War I.) The Court ruled for *Esquire*, concluding that the mail system played an essential role in facilitating free expression guaranteed under the Constitution. In *Lamont v. Postmaster General*, 381 U.S. 301 (1965), the Court recognized that the right to receive mail is protected under the First Amendment right to receive information. But the free expression rights of mail senders does not trump the postal service's monopoly on access to letterboxes; it is illegal for non-postal service employees to place mail in letterboxes, the Court ruled in *U.S. Postal Service v. Council of Greenburgh Civic Associations*, 453 U.S. 114 (1981).

Telegraph: A Major Shift in Media Policy

By the 1840s, the political zeitgeist in the U.S. had changed dramatically from the time of the first Congressional generation of the 1790s. The first Congressional generation was comfortable with the federal government's control and operation of a mass communication network, the postal service. Fifty years later, however, the Jacksonian Democrats were not; they did not want the federal government to own and operate an electric telegraph system, the second mass communication network in the U.S.

The federal government had a number of opportunities to own and run the emerging technology of electronic telegraphy. In 1843, Congress gave telegraph inventor Samuel Morse $30,000 in funding to build an experimental telegraph line from Washington to Baltimore. Morse offered to sell the rights to the system to Congress in December 1844.[54] Morse had urged Congress to make his system part of the Post Office. He was not alone. Penny press innovator James Gordon Bennett "spoke for the dominant view among the nation's editors when he wrote in the *New York Herald* that 'government must be impelled to take hold' of the telegraph and develop it as part of the Post Office."[55] Still, Congress refused to have the post office take over a telegraph system. Instead, Congress passed the Pacific Telegraph Act of 1860, eventually awarding a $40,000 contract to the sole bidder, the Western Union Telegraph Company, to construct a transcontinental telegraph line.

The significance of the Pacific Telegraph Act is widely overlooked, though it marks a critical turning point in U.S. media law and policy. In *Prologue to a Farce: Communication and Democracy in America*, Mark Lloyd argues that the act marks the first time the federal government used public money to subsidize a private company's ability to allow businesses to share information, noting that "businesses were the primary telegraph company customers."[56] In contrast, the Postal Service Act of 1792 and 1794 used public money to enable privately owned newspapers and magazines to allow the public to share information.

In Lloyd's view, the act was the start of a pattern: "important policy decisions that veered away from the course set by the founders…(1) early investment in development of the technology; (2) abandonment of control of that technology to private industry, except for military purposes; (3) continuing subsidy of the industry; and (4) a weak response to the emergence of private monopoly or oligopoly control over national communications."[57] As Lloyd documents in *Prologue to a Farce*, Congress has provided early support for the telegraph, telephone, broadcast, satellite, and Internet industries.

The Rise of Private Monopoly Control of Mass Media

By abandoning the Founders' approach of government control of mass communication networks, Congress also created ripe conditions for the rise of private monopoly control of mass communications in the U.S. From 1866 to 1900, many in Congress voiced fears about private monopoly or oligopoly control of the flow of information, specifically Western Union's monopoly control over the national telegraph system and, with it, control over commercial information and political news, and later the Associated Press's control over news transmitted via the telegraph. In "Rehearsal for Media Regulation: Congress Versus the Telegraph News Monopoly, 1866–1900," Menahem Blondheim counted "ninety-six bills and resolutions brought before Congress that addressed the problem of Western Union."[58] The FCC's current media ownership rules are a regulatory response to similar concerns about concentration of ownership of news, knowledge, and information.[59] Meanwhile, several states—New York was the first in 1848—passed laws regulating telegraph lines based on common carrier principles.

Regulation of interstate telegraphy was finally resolved under the Mann-Elkins Act of 1910. Today, most of the act's language makes up Title II of the Communications Act of 1934, which gives the FCC broad authority to regulate interstate common carriers to prevent discriminatory pricing, quality, or service. In the Mann-Elkins Act, Congress classified interstate telegraph and telephone systems as common carriers, obligating them "to provide service on request at just and reasonable rates, without unjust discrimination or undue preference."[60] Congress gave the Interstate Commerce Commission, originally established in 1887 to regulate railroads, authority to regulate the two electronic mass communication systems. The ICC was terminated in 1995. By the early 21st century, electric telegraphy no longer served as a mass communication network; Western Union's business is now electronic money transfer.

> SUMMARY: Media regulated as common carriers—postal service, telegraphy, and telephone or telephony, and direct broadcast satellite providers—must serve as neutral conduits for users' content and under the policy of universal service must offer their services to everyone in a fair and nondiscriminatory manner.

Broadcast: The Communications Act of 1934

By the 1920s, radio transmission posed a challenge previously unknown to media law and regulators—physical scarcity. Radio signals, first in the form of a telegraph's dot-dash signal and then later full conversations, are sent through the air from a transmitting antenna using the electromagnetic spectrum as a channel. Then, millions of receiving antennae pick up the signal and decode it into sound and, by the late 1930s, video images or television. That's broadcasting: one-to-many transmission. The problem, however, is that our technological ability to make full use of the electromagnetic spectrum is limited. When more than one signal is sent on the same frequency at the same time, no message can be discerned.

The limitations of transmission via the electronic spectrum were well known by 1912. That's when the *Titanic* sank in the North Atlantic Ocean. While the *Titanic* and potential rescue ships attempted to communicate they were interrupted by frivolous and erroneous messages. Amateur, or ham operators, for example, claimed the *Titanic* was safe and on its way to Halifax, Nova Scotia. Congress responded with the passage of the Radio Act of 1912, requiring broadcasters to obtain a federal license to operate.

By the 1920s, the U.S. Navy, which controlled ship-to-shore transmitters, found itself competing with more than 1,000 commercial radio stations. Interference on the radio spectrum intensified. Enter Congress, which passed the Radio Act of 1927. The Act declared that the government owned the electromagnetic spectrum, held in public trust, and that it would license the spectrum to private entities to promote the "public interest, convenience or necessity," a phrase that has never been clearly defined. It also gave the Federal Radio Commission (FRC) regulatory authority of the airwaves. Soon after, Congress passed the Communications Act of 1934, which created the Federal Communications Commission (FCC). Under the Act, the FCC gained the authority to regulate common carriage and subsumed the regulatory authority of the FRC.

Early on, broadcasters challenged the authority of the FRC and then the FCC on First Amendment grounds. Both times the broadcasters lost. In *Trinity Methodist Church v. South v. Federal Radio Commission*, 62 F.2d 850 (D.C. Cir 1932), the U.S. Circuit Court of Appeals for the District of Columbia upheld the FRC's authority to revoke a radio station's license. It ruled that the Commission's licensing authority "was neither censorship nor previous restraint, nor is it a whittling away of the rights guaranteed by the First Amendment, or an impairment of their free exercise."[61] The appeals court, however, did not confer full First Amendment protection on radio, rather it describes radio as merely "an instrumentality of commerce."[62] In a case brought in 1941, NBC and others challenged the new FCC, arguing, in part, that its licensing authority infringed applicants' free speech rights. In *NBC v. U.S.*, 319 U.S. 190 (1943), NBC lost as the U.S. Supreme Court upheld the FCC's authority under the Communications Act of 1934.

The Court's ruling in *Red Lion Broadcasting Co. v. FCC*, 395 U.S. 367 (1969), expanded on its *NBC v. U.S.* rationale that government may regulate broadcast in ways that would be unconstitutional for print. And the Court addressed the growing chorus of critics who argued that advances in technology have made "spectrum scarcity" an untenable rationale for denying radio and television full First Amendment status: "Nothing in this record, or in our own researches, convinces us that the resource is no longer one for which there are more immediate and potential uses than can be accommodated, and for which wise planning is essential."[63] Even today, with the availability of other electronic media such as cable and the Internet, the U.S. Supreme Court has not budged from its position in *Red Lion*. And because Congress charged the FCC with regulating interstate and international communications, the agency's regulatory authority covers radio, television, wire, satellite, and cable.

> SUMMARY: The FCC's authority to regulate broadcast, cable television, telephones, and satellite transmission stems largely from the Communications Act of 1934, the Cable Acts of 1984 and 1992, and the Telecommunications Act of 1996. The U.S. Supreme Court has upheld the FCC's authority to regulate based on three rationales: spectrum scarcity, electronic broadcasting's invasive nature, and Congress's authority to regulate interstate commerce under the Constitution's Commerce Clause (Article I, Section 8, Clause 3). Today, however, technological advances—the invasive nature of cable and the Internet—make the scarcity and invasiveness rationales less defensible, many argue.

ONLINE RESOURCES.

1. "Connecting the Globe: A Regulator's Guide to Building a Global Information Community," http://transition.fcc.gov/connectglobe/welcome.html
2. "Copyright Basics," http://www.copyright.gov/circs/circ1.pdf
3. "Common Carriers," CyberTelecom Federal Internet Law & Policy: An Educational Project, http://www.cybertelecom.org/notes/common_carrier.htm
4. Lawrence Lessig, http://www.lessig.org/
5. Media & Communications Policy: Issues & Developments in the Realm of Communications and Media Policy and the First Amendment, http://www.mediacom policy.org/
6. Philip M. Napoli, "Media Policy: An Overview of the Field" (2007). *McGannon Center Working Paper Series.* Paper 19, http://fordham.bepress.com/mcgannon_working_papers /19
7. Russell L. Weaver and Donald E. Lively, "The Origins and Nature of the First Amendment." *Understanding the First Amendment.* New York: LexisNexis (2003). http://www.lexisnexis.com/lawschool/study/understanding/pdf/FirstAmendCh1.pdf

8. "Section 230 of the Communications Decency Act," Citizen Media Law Project, http://www.citmedialaw.org/section-230

9. "Universal Service and the Postal Monopoly: A Brief History," United States Postal Service, http://about.usps.com/who-we-are/postal-history/universal-service-postal-monopoly-history.pdf

Questions

1. While all media corporations operating in the U.S. enjoy First Amendment free expression protections, some corporations are accountable to more media laws and regulations than others. Based on the outlets they own, what type of media law and regulation can Google (http://www.google.com/corporate/) afford to ignore that Walt Disney (http://www.cjr.org/resources/?c=disney) cannot?

2. As discussed in this chapter, John Perry Barlow, the father of cyber libertarianism, declared, "We are creating a world that all may enter without privilege or prejudice accorded by race, economic power, military force, or station of birth…Your legal concepts of property, expression, identity, movement, and context do not apply to us. They are all based on matter, and there is no matter here." Do you agree with Barlow? Before you answer, does it bother you that a social network can sell your personal information to others? Do you believe that the search engine you use finds the best sites or the ones that are "search engine friendly"? Should identity thieves be immune from prosecution?

3. Over the years, the courts seem to continue to fear the harm that still and moving images might do. Even today, the U.S. Supreme Court does not allow cameras into to its proceedings. Do still and moving images have greater power than words to influence human behavior?

ENDNOTES

1. *Talley v. California*, 362 U.S. 60, 65 (1960).
2. *Carafano v. Metrosplash*, 339 F.3d 1122, 1125 (9th Circ. 2003); *Perfect 10, Inc. v. CCBill LLC*, 488 F.3d 1102, 1118–19 (9th Cir. 2007).
3. *Carafano v. Metrosplash*, 339 F.3d 1122, 1124 (9th Circ. 2003).
4. Rebecca Tushnet. "Power without Responsibility: Intermediaries and the First Amendment," 76 *George Washington Law Review* 986 (2008).
5. "A Declaration of Independence of Cyberspace," Electronic Frontier Foundation (1996), http://projects.eff.org/~barlow/Declaration-Final.html
6. Lawrence Lessig. "The Code Is Law," *The Industry Standard* (April 9, 1999), http://www.lessig.org/content/standard/0,1902,4165,00.html
7. See Jeffrey A. Smith. *Printers and Press Freedom: The Ideology of Early American Journalism.* New York: Oxford University Press (1988).
8. Stewart Potter. "Or of the Press," 26 *Hastings Law Journal* 631 (1975).
9. Edward Lee. "Freedom of the Press, 2.0," 42 Georgia Law Review 308, 328–29 (2008).
10. *Grosjean v. American Press Co.*, 297 U.S. 233 (1936).
11. John C. Miller. *Crisis in Freedom: The Alien and Sedition Acts.* Boston: Little, Brown and Company (1951).
12. *New York Times v. Sullivan*, 376 U.S. 254, 276 (1964).
13. Philip M. Napoli. *Foundations of Communications Policy: Principles and Process in the Regulation of Electronic Media.* Cresskill, NJ: Hampton Press, Inc. (2001), 29.
14. U.S. Const. amend. I.

15. *Kovacs v. Cooper*, 336 U.S. 77, 97 (1949).

16. See *Austin v. Michigan Chamber of Commerce*, 494 U.S. 652, 655 (1990). The Court has said that when a government regulation seeks to limit or ban speech because of its message, then it is a "content-based" restriction. When judging the constitutionality of such restrictions, the Court applies what is known as "strict scrutiny" analysis, asking whether the restriction serves a compelling state interest and whether there is not a less speech-restrictive way to achieve that goal.

17. *Mutual Film Corporation v. Industrial Commission of Ohio*, 236 U.S. 230 (1915); *Reno v. ACLU*, 521 U.S. 844 (1997).

18. *Sable Communications of Cal., Inc. v. FCC*, 492 U. S. 115, 128 (1989).

19. See *Red Lion Broadcasting Co. v. FCC*, 395 U.S. 367, 386 (1969); *Reno v. ACLU*, 521 U.S. 844 (1997).

20. See Christopher S. Yoo. "The Rise and Demise of the Technology-Specific Approach to the First Amendment," 91 *Georgetown Law Journal* 245 (2003).

21. See *Perfect 10, Inc. v. CCBill LLC*, 488 F.3d 1102 (9th Cir. 2007).

22. *Mutual Film Corporation v. Industrial Commission of Ohio*, 236 U.S. 244–245 (1915).

23. *Reno v. ACLU*, 521 U.S. at 870 (1997).

24. See *Bernstein v. USDOJ*, 176 F.3d 1132 (9th Cir.1999); *Junger v. Daley*, 209 F.3d 481 (6th Cir. 2000); *Karn v. USDOJ*, 107 F.3d 923 (D.C. Cir. 1997).

25. *Brown v. Entertainment Merchant Association*, 08–1448, *2 (2011).

26. For further discussion on image-capturing technology and the First Amendment see: Seth F. Kreimer. "Pervasive Image Capture and the First Amendment: Memory, Discourse, and the Right to Record," 159 *University of Pennsylvania Law Review (January 26, 2011). University of Pennsylvania Law Review,* (2011), http://ssrn.com/abstract=1553920

27. Sec. 312 of the Communications Act of 1934, as amended, 47 U.S.C § 312; See Communications Act of 1934, § 315; codified at 47 U.S.C. § 315.

28. *Red Lion Broadcasting Co. v. FCC* ; *NBC v. FCC*, 319 U.S. 190 (1949); *FCC v. Pacifica*, 438 U.S. 726 (1978).

29. Federal Communications Commission. "Review of the Broadcast Ownership Rules." (June 23, 2008), http://www.fcc.gov/cgb/consumerfacts/reviewrules.html

30. *Chesapeake & Potomac Telephone Co. v. United States*, 42 F.3d 181, 196 (1994).

31. Ibid., 198.

32. 47 U.S.C. § 571: Regulatory treatment of video programming services.

33. Donald M. Falk and Eugene Volokh. "First Amendment Protection for Search Engine Results" [White Paper] (2012), http://www.volokh.com/wp-content/uploads/2012/05/SearchEngineFirstAmendment.pdf

34. *Langdon v. Google, Inc.*, 474 F. Supp. 2d 622, 630 (D. Del. 2007).

35. Eugene Volokh. "Is Search Protected by the First Amendment? Comments by Eugene Volokh" [Web log post] (May 22, 2012), http://lawprofessors.typepad.com/antitrustprof_blog/2012/05/is-search-protected-by-the-first-amendment-comments-by-eugene-volokh.html

36. Frank A. Pascale III & Oren Bracha. "Federal Search Commission? Access, Fairness and Accountability in the Law of Search," *Cornell Law Review* 93 (September 2008): 1149, http://www.lawschool.cornell.edu/research/cornell-law-review/upload/Bracha-Pasquale-Final.pdf

37. Ibid. 1193.

38. *Turner Broadcasting System v. FCC*, 520 U.S. 180 (1997).

39. "Cable Television Fact Sheet Program Content Regulations," Federal Communications Commission (October 1995), http://www.fcc.gov/Bureaus/Cable/Informal/pcontent.txt

40. *National Cable & Telecommunications Association et al. v. Brand X Internet Services et al.*, 545 U.S. 967, 1006 (2005).

41. "Copyright Basics," *Copyright Law.* Washington, D.C.: U.S. Copyright Office (2010), 5–6, http://www.copyright.gov/circs/circ01.pdf

42. *Harper and Row v. Nation Enterprises*, 471 U.S. 539, 558 (1985).

43. Ibid. 589.

44. Jane C. Ginsburg. "Copyright and Control over New Technologies of Dissemination," 101 *Columbia Law Review* 613, 617 (2001).

45. Ibid,.619.

46. 17 U.S.C 102. Subject matter of copyright: In general. Legal Information Institute, Cornell University Law School, http://www.law.cornell.edu/uscode/text/17/102

47. U.S. Copyright Office. "Copyright Law of the United States of America and Related Laws Contained in Title 17 of the United States Code" [Circular 92]. (October 2009), http://www.copyright.gov/title17/92preface.html

48. "Post Office Facts," Merrimack College, http://www.merrimack.edu/about/offices_services/postoffice/Pages/PostOfficeFacts.aspx

49. Title 39, Section 101.1; United States Postal Service, "Universal Service and the Postal Monopoly: A Brief History," (October 2008), http://about.usps.com/who-we-are/postal-history/universal-service-postal-monopoly-history.pdf

50. United States Postal Service, "Report On Universal Postal Service and The Postal Monopoly," (October 2008), http://about.usps.com/universal-postal-service/usps-uso-report.txt http://www.usps.com/postallaw/_pdf/USPSUSOReport.pdf

51. Ithiel de Sola Pool. *Technologies of Freedom.* Boston: Harvard University Press, (1992), 78.

52. *Ex Parte Jackson*, 96 U.S. 727, 736 (1878).

53. *Hannegan v. Esquire, Inc.*, 327 U.S. 146, 149 (1946).

54. Paul Starr. *The Creation of the Media: Political Origins of Modern Communications* New York: Perseus Books Group (2004), 163.

55. Ibid. See also *Hannegan v. Esquire, Inc.*, 327 U.S. 146 (1946).

56. Mark Lloyd. *Prologue to a Farce: Communication and Democracy in America.* Urbana: University of Illinois Press (2006), 51.

57. Ibid. 41.

58. Menahem Blondheim. "Rehearsal for Media Regulation: Congress Versus the Telegraph-News Monopoly," 56 *Federal Communications Law Journal* 299 (2004).

59. Section 202(h) of the Telecommunications Act of 1996.

60. *Essential Communications Systems, Inc. v. American Telephone & Telegraph Co.*, 610 F.2d 1114, 1118 (1979).

61. *Trinity Methodist Church v. South v. Federal Radio Commission*, 62 F.2d 850, 853 (D.C. Cir 1932).

62. Ibid.

63. *Red Lion Broadcasting Co. v. FCC*, 395 U.S 399 (1969).

CHAPTER THREE

Cyberspace & the Free Expression

CONTROVERSY: When J. Snyder and "K.L." were eighth graders attending Blue Mountain Middle School in Orwigsburg, Pennsylvania, in 2007, they created a MySpace parody profile of their school principal. Some of the least offensive text read as following: "HELLO CHILDREN yes. it's your oh so wonderful, hairy, expressionless, sex addict, fagass, put on this world with a small...PRINCIPAL I have come to myspace so i can pervert the minds of other principal's [sic] to be just like me."[1] The students used their home computers to create the site. They were suspended for 10 days. J.Snyder's parents sued, arguing that the suspension violated their daughter's First Amendment free speech and state and federal due process rights. In *Snyder v. Blue Mountain School District*, 593 F.3d. 286 (3d Cir. 2010), the U.S. Court of Appeals for the Third Circuit, 2–1, ruled that the school district did not violate J. Snyder's First Amendment free speech rights by suspending her for statements she attributed to her principal on the MySpace profile. On the same day, another Third Circuit three-judge panel drew the opposite conclusion in a case involving a student who used an off-campus computer to create a vulgar, fictitious MySpace parody profile of his principal. In *Layshock v. Hermitage School District*, 593 F.3d 249, 263 (2010), the panel ruled, 3–0, that, "the District is not empowered to punish [the student's] out of school expressive conduct under the circumstances here." Precedent requires that cases implicating the same laws with similar facts produce similar legal results. The disturbing inconsistency between the two rulings was not resolved until June 2011 when a majority of the full Third Circuit held that school authorities had violated Snyder's First Amendment rights.

Chapter's Scope

The current legal battles stemming from public school students' use of the Internet are yet another front in the more than 15-year effort to prevent minors from using the Internet to access and engage in what some see as harmful speech. At first, parents and legislators targeted pornography. That campaign led to the U.S. Supreme Court's landmark ruling *Reno v. ACLU,* 521 U.S. 844 (1997), a decisive victory for civil libertarians, Internet operators, and users. In this chapter's first section, we consider *Reno v. ACLU* and its aftermath: (i) Congress's largely unsuccessful efforts to restrict minors' access to sexually explicit material on the Internet, and (ii) the role the First Amendment plays in limiting government and individuals from punishing cyberbullies. The chapter continues with an examination of the laws and policy debates over Internet regulation: (I) Internet governance: the international debate over which nation, group of nations, or nongovernment organizations will control the Internet. (II) Network neutrality: The debates in the U.S. over whether the president has the right to shut down the Internet and whether the FCC has authority to prevent telephone, cable companies, and Internet companies from favoring certain users over others or limiting how some individuals use cyberspace. (III) Internet exceptionalism: the contention that laws designed with offline media in mind, such as libel and copyright, should not be applied to curtail online activity. The overarching inquiry here is: who should control the Internet? Please note that while foreign legislatures and policymakers also are engaged in their own disputes over network neutrality, Internet governance, and exceptionalism, this chapter focuses on how those disputes are playing out in the U.S.

The Highest Level of Constitutional Scrutiny

As U.S. use of the World Wide Web boomed by the mid-1990s, Congress tacked on two statutory provisions to the Telecommunications Act of 1996 to protect minors from sexually explicit materials accessible on the Internet. The indecency transmission and patently offensive display provisions were contained in Title V of the Telecommunications Act, known as the Communications Decency Act of 1996 (CDA). In *Reno v. ACLU,* the Court, however, struck down the CDA's indecency and patently offensive provisions by applying strict scrutiny analysis, and declared them vague and overbroad content restrictions. The Court declared there was no "basis for qualifying the level of First Amendment scrutiny that should be applied to this medium."[2] In other words, the Court said that the Internet enjoyed full First Amendment protection like print and cinema. Strict scrutiny gives enhanced protection to fundamental rights, such as First Amendment free speech, from government actions that seek to restrict such rights.

Under the strict scrutiny test, the Court will uphold a speech restriction only if it is necessary to promote a *compelling* government interest and is *the least restrictive alternative.* In contrast, under the less speech-protective intermediate-level scrutiny applied to broadcast, a content-based restriction need only promote a *substantial* government interest and be *narrowly tailored to achieve that interest.* The **overbreadth doctrine** and **vagueness doctrine** also provide fundamental rights with heightened protection. A statute that is substantially overbroad has a substantial chilling effect on protected speech. For example, adults enjoy a First Amendment right to consume sexually explicit content, provided a court or jury has not found the material obscene. Yet, the terms of the CDA, the Court said, would deprive adults of their right to access sexually explicit material that is not obscene.

Adhering both to the overbroad doctrine and applying strict scrutiny, the *Reno* court explained that, in an attempt to "deny minors access to potentially harmful speech, the CDA effectively suppresses a large amount of speech that adults have a constitutional right to receive and to address to one another. That burden on adult speech is unacceptable if less restrictive alternatives would be at least as effective in achieving the legitimate purpose that the statute was enacted to serve."[3]

Under the due process vagueness concept, the Court can strike down a statute because a reasonable person could not determine whether his or her conduct falls within the prohibition. The CDA failed to define the terms "indecent" or "patently offensive." The Court asked rhetorically, "Could a speaker confidently assume that a serious discussion about birth control practices, homosexuality, the First Amendment issues raised by the Appendix to our *Pacifica* opinion, or the consequences of prison rape would not violate the CDA? This uncertainty undermines the likelihood that the CDA has been carefully tailored to the congressional goal of protecting minors from potentially harmful materials."[4]

The government argued that the CDA justified the validity of its compelling interest to protect children and to foster the growth of the Internet, claiming that countless consumers avoided using the Internet out of fear of exposing themselves and their children to sexually explicit material. With the CDA in place, they argued, children would be protected and parental fears would be allayed, leading to increased usage of the Internet. The Court rejected the government's contention, finding that,

> The dramatic expansion of this new marketplace of ideas contradicts the factual basis of this contention. The record demonstrates that the growth of the Internet has been and continues to be phenomenal. As a matter of constitutional tradition, in the absence of evidence to the contrary, we presume that governmental regulation of the content of speech is more likely to interfere with the free exchange of ideas than to encourage it. The interest in encouraging freedom of expression in a democratic society outweighs any theoretical but unproven benefit of censorship.[5]

Coping with Copa

A statute struck down as unconstitutional can be revised and considered again. Accordingly, Congress sought to cure the ills of the CDA with the Child Online Protection Act (COPA), passed in October 1999. Unlike the CDA, the Child Online Protection Act banned material harmful to minors and applied only to commercial communications on the World Wide Web. Nevertheless, the ACLU, representing a diverse group of website owners, challenged COPA. The plaintiffs contended that, "although they believed that the material on their Web sites was valuable for adults, they feared that they would be prosecuted under COPA because some of that material 'could be construed as 'harmful to minors' in some communities."[6]

The ACLU won a preliminary injunction against enforcement of COPA at the federal district court level, which said the new law was unlikely to survive strict scrutiny analysis.[7] The federal judge, however, underestimated the number of constitutional flaws in the statute. Ten years later—after two U.S. Supreme Court rulings, three rulings by the U.S. Court of Appeals for the Third Circuit, another by a federal district court and two changes of U.S. Attorneys General—COPA's saga ended with a whimper. In *ACLU v. Murkasey*, 534 F. 181, 207 (2008), the Third Circuit rejected the government's case, concluding, "In sum, COPA cannot withstand a strict scrutiny, vagueness, or overbreadth analysis and thus is unconstitutional." The U.S. Supreme Court declined to hear the case for a third time.[8]

Filtering Software at Public Institutions

About the same time that Congress tried to tackle the problems it associated with minors' easy access to sexually explicit content on the Internet with COPA, it opened another flank in December 2000:

the Children's Internet Protection Act (CIPA). Under the CIPA, a public library may not receive federal assistance to provide Internet access unless it installs software to block material that is harmful to minors, including child pornography and other obscene materials. The American Library Association challenged CIPA on First Amendment free speech grounds. In *American Library Association, Inc. v. U.S.*, 201 F. Supp. 2d 401 (2002), a federal district court judge in Pennsylvania held that the CIPA filtering software was an unconstitutional content-based restriction on access to a public forum and, therefore, subject to strict scrutiny. Under the **public forum doctrine**, government may not restrict speech based on content unless it can show that its restriction meets the strict scrutiny test. Public forums include public streets, parks, and sidewalks and limited or designated public forums, which the state has opened for use by the public as a place for expressive activity (See Chapter 9).[9] The judge held that the CIPA failed the strict scrutiny test because software filters were not a narrowly tailored use for preventing minors from accessing the targeted harmful materials.

But in *U.S., v. American Library Association, Inc.*, 539 U.S. 194 (2003), the U.S. Supreme Court upheld CIPA. It said that, "The public forum principles on which the District Court relied…are out of place in the context of this case. Internet access in public libraries is neither a 'traditional' nor a 'designated' public forum."[10] Rather, the Court said, "because public libraries' use of Internet filtering software does not violate their patrons' First Amendment rights, CIPA does not induce libraries to violate the Constitution, and is a valid exercise of Congress' spending power."[11]

SUMMARY: The U.S. Supreme Court's landmark ruling in *Reno v. ACLU*, 521 U.S. 844 (1997), opened the door to a new era of First Amendment free speech doctrine. The Court ruled that government efforts to regulate cyberspace to protect minors from sexually explicit content is subject to the highest form of judicial scrutiny to protect adults' rights to access pornography on the Internet. Thus, *Reno* established the First Amendment boundaries for laws pertaining to Internet content. Congress, however, continued to test those boundaries in its effort to protect minors from online pornography with the Child Online Protection Act (COPA) and the Children's Internet Protection Act (CIPA). Only CIPA withstood constitutional scrutiny. Now, public libraries receiving federal assistance to provide Internet access must install software to block material that is harmful to minors, including child pornography and other obscene materials.

Student Speech and Cyberspace

Public school students have First Amendment free speech rights. Those rights, however, can be checked by a school's need to maintain discipline, order, and safety. In *Tinker v. Des Moines School District*, 393 U.S. 503, 513 (1969), the U.S. Supreme Court ruled that it was an unconstitutional abridgement of a public school student's First Amendment free speech right to ban student speech, "if it could not be justified by a showing that the students' activities would materially and substantially disrupt the work and discipline of the school."

The First Amendment also permits schools to ban lewd, indecent, and offensive speech. In *Bethel School District No. 403 v. Fraser*, 478 U.S. 675, 683 (1986), the Court said, "The schools, as instruments of the state, may determine that the essential lessons of civil, mature conduct cannot be conveyed in a school that tolerates lewd, indecent, or offensive speech and conduct . . ." *Fraser* also asserted that the First Amendment rights of public school students "are not automatically coextensive with the rights of adults in other settings."[12]

In *Hazelwood v. Kuhlmeier*, 484 U.S. 260 (1988), the Court held that "educators do not offend the First Amendment by exercising editorial control over the style and content of student speech in school-sponsored expressive activities so long as their actions are reasonably related to legitimate pedagogical concerns."

Those rulings, however, concerned student speech conveyed on public school property. In contrast, in *Morse v. Frederick*, 551 U.S. 393 (2007), a student was suspended for holding up a sign that a principal said was pro-drug—"Bong Hits 4 JESUS"—at a school-supervised public event held on a public street. The Court upheld the suspension, ruling that the school could ban speech advocating drug use conveyed at school events that were not held on public school property. Yet, the Court noted that "had [the student] delivered the same speech in a public forum outside the school context, it would have been protected."[13] Moreover, *Morse v. Frederick* is widely viewed as having a narrow application to speech involving the promotion of illegal drug use. In his concurrence, Justice Samuel Alito stressed that the ban on such student speech stands "at the far reaches of what the First Amendment permits."[14]

In the absence of U.S. Supreme Court guidance, many plaintiffs have argued that *Tinker* should not control cases concerning student speech made in cyberspace off school grounds. Rather, such school students should be accorded adult free speech protection, requiring the school to show that a restriction is necessary to promote a compelling government interest and is the least restrictive way to do so. Some take the position that the incitement or true threats doctrines are the appropriate tests to regulate threatening online and off school property student speech (see Chapter 7).

Lower courts, however, have clung to *Tinker* and its progeny to resolve such controversies. Under *Fraser*, courts have ruled that off-school-grounds cyberspace speech is not protected by the First Amendment when it is lewd, vulgar, or profane. In most rulings, when off-school-grounds cyberspace speech falls outside the *Fraser* category, courts have applied *Tinker*'s substantiality test to determine whether off-school-grounds student speech posed a reasonably foreseeable risk of substantial disruption of the school environment. Sometimes, however, courts do not make a distinction between the two tests. Instead, some courts consider the offensiveness of language in determining whether the speech posed a risk of a substantial disruption to the order and safety of the school.

For example, the U.S. Court of Appeals for the Second Circuit applied the *Tinker* standard in *Doninger v. Niehoff*, 527 F.3d 41, 51 (2d Cir. 2008), interpreting it as requiring the plaintiff to show that off-school-grounds speech posed a reasonably foreseeable risk of disrupting the school environment. In *Doninger v. Niehoff*, a school disqualified a student, Avery Doninger, from running for senior class secretary after administrators determined that her blog's message was inconsistent with the school's student government policy of good citizenship. The Second Circuit said the blog posed a reasonably foreseeable risk of disrupting the work and discipline of the school because it contained false charges, offensive language, and encouraged students to engage in disruptive conduct.

In Pennsylvania, inconsistent judicial application and interpretation of the two tests lay at the core of the contrasting rulings in *Layshock v. Hermitage School District* and *Snyder. v. Blue Mountain School District*. For the three judges ruling in *Layshock*, the student's lewd, profane, and sexually inappropriate speech was irrelevant. The judges rejected the school district's argument that *Doninger v. Niehoff* and two other rulings were authority enough to support the proposition that schools are allowed "to respond to a student's vulgar speech when that speech is posted on the Internet."[15] All that mattered to the *Layshock* panel was that the student's words did not affect in-school activities and that his downloading of an image from the school website did not constitute entering the school.[16]

The in-school effect of the student's false MySpace parody of her principal in *Snyder v. Blue Mountain School District* was largely attributed to the principal who, not finding the MySpace profile online because the student had limited its accessibility, asked someone to bring a printed copy of the profile to school. Nevertheless, the 2–1 majority adopted an elastic interpretation of foreseeable school disruption to support the school district's punishment of the student mostly because the student's post, which implied that the principal engaged in illegal sexual conduct, was viewed by at least twenty students.

The conflicting rulings were extremely problematic. In March 2010, the Third Circuit granted the plaintiffs' request to have the two rulings reheard en banc, by the circuit's 14 judges, which took place June 3 of that year.[17] A little more than a year after, the Circuit ruled 8–6 in *Snyder v. Blue Mountain School District*, 08–4138 (3d Cir. 2011), that under the First Amendment the Pennsylvania public schools cannot discipline students for their MySpace parodies of their principals created on their off-campus computers, however lewd or offensive the language of the postings, because they were not likely to cause significant disruptions at school. *Fraser,* the court said, does not apply to off-campus speech, and "because J.S. was suspended from school for speech that indisputably caused no substantial disruption in school and that could not reasonably have led school officials to forecast substantial disruption in school, the School District's actions violated J.S.'s First Amendment free speech rights."[18]

The Third Circuit's ruling puts it at odds with the Second Circuit's ruling in *Doninger v. Niehoff,* 09–1452-cv (L) (2d Cir. 2011). In that case, the parties from the 2008 ruling were back in court. The judges said that the school's principal and superintendent were entitled to qualified immunity from Avery Doninger's First Amendment and equal protection claims. Doninger argued that the school authorities violated her rights by preventing her from running for senior class secretary and prohibiting her from wearing a homemade printed t-shirt at a school assembly as a direct consequence of her off-school-ground cyberspace speech. In essence, Doninger's argument was that the 2008 ruling was wrongly decided. Doninger claimed that under *Tinker* and its progeny, including *Thomas v. Board of Education,* 607 F.2d 1043 (2d Cir. 1979), "it *was* clearly established at the time [of the events in this case] that offcampus speech could not be the subject of school discipline."[19]

Rejecting her argument, the Second Circuit court said that because the U.S. Supreme Court has not ruled on the matter, "it is thus incorrect to urge, as Doninger does, that Supreme Court precedent necessarily insulates students from discipline for speech-related activity occurring away from school property, no matter its relation to school affairs or its likelihood of having effects—even substantial and disruptive effects—in school."[20]

The Second Circuit court said *Thomas v. Board of Education* did not eliminate school authority to discipline speech made off school grounds. It pointed out that one judge's concurrence, "explicitly noted that '[s]chool authorities ought to be accorded some latitude to regulate student activity that affects matters of legitimate concern to the school community, and territoriality is not necessarily a useful concept in determining the limit of their authority.'"[21]

In a surprising acknowledgment, the judges said that one reason the school officials should not face liability for punishing Doninger is because First Amendment law on off-school-grounds student speech confuses even the experts: "The law governing restrictions on student speech can be difficult and confusing, even for lawyers, law professors, and judges. The relevant Supreme Court cases can be hard to reconcile, and courts often struggle to determine which standard applies in any particular case."[22]

Student online speech cases *Snyder v. Blue Mountain School District*, *Layshock v. Hermitage School District*, and *Kowalski v. Berkeley*, 652 F.3d 565 (4th Cir. 2011), were appealed to the Supreme Court. In 2012, the Court declined to review them, leaving school administrations to look to their state or federal district or appeals courts for guidance.

Non-School-Related Cyberbullying

Tinker and its progeny do not control in cases stemming from cyberbullying that has nothing to do with schools or their personnel. Typically, such online speech threatens or disparages. The typical scenario involves adults or minors who carry on campaigns of verbal harassment against a specific individual. The targets of this harassment and their families claim that the harassment caused severe emotional distress—in some cases to the point of suicide. The victims and their families have sued based on several theories and prosecutors have brought criminal charges against such cyberbullies. But well-settled First Amendment and Constitutional principles of intent, causality, overbreadth, and vagueness pose huge hurdles for successfully bringing civil or criminal actions against such cyberbullies. The case of *U.S. v. Drew*, 259 F.R.D. 449 (C.D. Cal. 2009), epitomizes the difficulty the First Amendment poses in prosecuting such cyberbullies.

U.S. v. Drew stems from the suicide of 13-year-old Megan Meier, whose death in 2006 drew national attention to cyberbullying. Meier, who had been under the care of a psychiatrist, hung herself after a "boyfriend" she knew only from contact on MySpace broke up with her. The "boyfriend" was not real; he was Lori Drew, a 49-year-old mother and neighbor of the Meiers. Drew's daughter had been friendly with Meier, but Drew and her daughter came to believe that Meier had spread rumors about the daughter. They created the MySpace account to get information about Meier and to humiliate her. Federal prosecutors indicted Drew in California, where MySpace is headquartered, on charges of co-conspiracy to inflict emotional distress in violation of the Criminal Fraud and Abuse Act (CFAA). A jury found Drew guilty of a misdemeanor violation of the CFAA. But a judge overturned the verdict in 2009 because the statute's language was unconstitutionally vague. The judge noted that, among other shortcomings, the law did not give fair warning to individuals of "common intelligence" that violating the terms of their contracts with a social networking site to provide truthful information would be criminal, as opposed to a mere breach of contract.

Congress's attempt to rein in non-school-related cyberbullying, the Megan Meier Cyberbullying Prevention Act, first introduced in 2009, stalled over concerns that the law would not withstand constitutional scrutiny. The proposed law would have amended "the federal criminal code to impose criminal penalties on anyone who transmits in interstate or foreign commerce a communication intended to coerce, intimidate, harass, or cause substantial emotional distress to another person, using electronic means to support severe, repeated, and hostile behavior." Its critics said that it would have punished a great deal of protected online speech, and thus be unconstitutionally overbroad. University of California, Los Angeles, Law Professor Eugene Volokh offered several such scenarios, including:

> A company delivers me shoddy goods, and refuses to refund my money. I e-mail it several times, threatening to sue if they don't give me a refund, and I use 'hostile' language. I am transmitting a communication with the intent to coerce, using electronic means 'to support severe, repeated, and hostile behavior.' Result: I am a felon, if my behavior is 'severe.' [23]

The U.S. Supreme Court has not weighed in on this type of cyberbullying, either. But any legal actions and new laws designed to attack cyberbullying cannot ignore the limits imposed by defamation,[24] incitement, true threats, and intentional infliction of emotional harm doctrines on efforts to punish hostile speech. Defamation is discussed in Chapters 4 and 5; incitement, true threats, and intentional infliction of emotional harm are discussed in Chapter 7.

SUMMARY: Public school students who have sent lewd, offensive, and profane messages about school personnel and policy in emails, blogs, and on social networking sites from their home computers have had difficulty in finding refuge in the First Amendment. Schools that have punished students for online speech contend that under the First Amendment, they have authority to regulate student speech that is offensive and poses a threat to the school environment even when it does not occur on school grounds or at a school-sponsored event. Many courts have ruled in their favor, citing *Tinker v. Des Moines School District*, 393 U.S. 503 (1969); *Bethel School District No. 403 v. Fraser*, 478 U.S. 675, 683 (1986); *Hazelwood v. Kuhlmeier*, 484 U.S. 260, (1988); and *Morse v. Frederick*, 551 U.S. 393 (2007). Those rulings stand for the proposition that school authorities may regulate student speech that poses a reasonably foreseeable risk of substantial disruption of the school environment, uses offensive language, or promotes illegal drug use. Those precedents, however, do not address whether the heightened free speech protection resulting from *Reno v. ACLU* applies to student speech made off school grounds in cyberspace.

Who Has Legal Authority to Control the Internet? No Easy Answers

Egyptian President Hosni Mubarak pulled the plug on the Internet in late January 2011, leaving millions of Egyptians without access to the World Wide Web for several days. Meanwhile, about 5,600 miles away, Americans asked, "Does the U.S. president have authority to shut down the Internet?" Not yet, but he will, some observers say, under the terms of the Cybersecurity and Internet Freedom Act of 2011—an amendment to the Homeland Security Act of 2002—which reached the U.S. Senate Committee on Homeland Security and Governmental Affairs several days after Mubarak left office.

When the proposed law surfaced in 2010, it was labeled "Protecting Cyberspace as a National Asset Act." But free expression, privacy, and Internet deregulation advocates dubbed it the "Internet Kill Switch" because, they said, it could be reasonably read to allow the president to shut down the Internet for national security reasons without obtaining a court order. The 2011 revision did not assuage their fears.

The bill's sponsors, however, make a surprising argument to support their claim that the proposed law does not give the president kill-switch authority. According to the sponsors, the president already possesses such authority under Section 706 of the Communications Act of 1934. They argued that Section 706 grants the president nearly unchecked authority to invoke special war emergency powers to suspend electronic communications by proclaiming a state or threat of war. Their law checks that authority by, among other restrictions, requiring the president to give Congress advanced notice to declare a national cyber emergency. They contend: "Rather than granting a 'kill switch,' S. 3480 would make it far less likely for a President to use the broad authority he already has in current law to take over communications networks."[25]

An assertion that the president already possesses the authority to kill the Internet comes as a surprise to most, particularly because the Internet did not exist in 1934 when Congress passed the Communications Act. How could Congress have intended that Section 706 cover a nonexistent communication technology unless Congress explicitly added language to cover a yet-to-be developed telecommunications network? The section has no such language. Rather, Section 706 can reasonably be read to limit presidential control of broadcast outlets and facilities and not the narrowcast outlets and facilities of the Internet, which are not directly regulated by the Federal Communications Commission. So far, no court has said whether the president's war emergency powers include Internet control. Consequently, there is no explicit legal precedent supporting such alleged presidential authority. In his writings exploring executive authority to shut down the Internet, legal scholar David W. Opderbeck observed, "The Senate Committee on Homeland Security and Government Affairs' conclusion that Section 706 authorizes the president to shut down the Internet, then, represents a dramatic and unprecedented assertion of authority over Internet governance."[26]

Unless, President Barack Obama is challenged in court about kill-switch authority, it appears that he does not need congressional backing to exert it. In July 2012, President Obama signed "Executive Order—Assignment of National Security and Emergency Preparedness Communications Functions." Some have interpreted Section 5.2 of the order as giving the president control over the Internet during emergencies and during peace. Section 5.2 reads, in part,

> The Secretary of Homeland Security shall: (a) oversee the development, testing, implementation, and sustainment of NS/EP communications, including:…infrastructure protection networks; and non-military communications networks, particularly with respect to prioritization and restoration; (b) incorporate, integrate, and ensure interoperability and the necessary combination of hardness, redundancy, mobility, connectivity, interoperability, restorability, and security to obtain, to the maximum extent practicable, the survivability of NS/EP communications defined in section 5.2(a) of this order under *all circumstances, including conditions of crisis or emergency* [emphasis added].[27]

Censoring the Internet Abroad

The Obama administration's claim to exert authority over the Internet for national security purposes is similar to the claims made by many sovereign powers, though many do not have to resort to flipping a kill switch to rein in online content they consider harmful. The OpenNet Initiative, a collaboration of operations at the University of Toronto, Harvard University, and the SecDev Group, identifies 26 nations that routinely filter the Internet, though it acknowledges that the number is increasing.[28] The governments of these nations block websites of political dissidents, insurgents, and terrorists for national security purposes; pornographic, gay, lesbian, and gambling sites for antisocial reasons; and low-cost, foreign-based email and Internet telephone service such as Skype to protect domestic economic interests. China, India, Iran, Pakistan, Saudi Arabia, Singapore, South Korea, Thailand, and Vietnam are among such nations. Clearly, nations that require Internet service providers to block certain sites or filter the Internet by other means believe that the Internet should be regulated like any other medium, and each nation has the authority to regulate it to suit its own political, social, and economic interests.

Though OpenNet has no hard evidence that any European governments are filtering the Internet—it suspects Belarus—the threat is still there, particularly in efforts to protect copyrighted material. But in one such case, the Court of Justice of the European Union ruled that requiring Internet service providers to filter sites is inconsistent with EU law. In its landmark 2011 ruling, C-70/10 *Scarlet Extended SA v. Sociétébelge des auteurs, compositeurs et éditeurs SCRL (SABAM)*, the EU court said such a requirement could lead to blocking lawful as well as unlawful content.

In the U.S., after the battles over CDA, COPA, and CIPA discussed above, it is unlikely that a state-imposed filtering requirement could be imposed on IPs, which, however, does not mean legislatures will refrain from attempting to impose such measures. In *Center for Democracy & Technology v. Pappert*, 337 F.Supp.2d 606, 610 (2004), for example, a federal judge struck down as unconstitutional "the first attempt by a state to impose criminal liability on an ISP which merely provides access to child pornography through its network and has no direct relationship with the source of the content." The attempt, Pennsylvania's Internet Child Pornography Act, was overbroad and an impermissible prior restraint under the First Amendment, and unconstitutional under the Commerce Clause because of its affect on interstate commerce, the judge ruled. Congress shelved the proposed Stop Online Privacy Act (SOPA) in early 2012 after protests, which included a blackout of top websites. A few days before the blackout, SOPA's sponsors removed a provision that would have required Internet service providers to block foreign-operated sites identified as using pirated copyrighted content.

Managing the Internet's "Root"

ICANN is a private corporation contracted by the U.S. government to manage what is referred to as *the root*—"the beginning point in a long chain of contracts and cooperation governing how Internet service providers and end users acquire and utilize the addresses and names that make it possible for information to reach its destination....The security and stability of the root server system is critical to the viability of any service or function that relies on the Internet." [29] The corporation assigns domain names and Transmission Control Protocol/Internet Protocol (TCP/IP) numbers, and each one of the millions of computers connected to the Internet must have a unique domain name and IP address. Without the system, users would have to remember or keep records of the numerical IP addresses assigned to each computer to communicate on the Internet. When you click on a website, for example, a "root server" directs your computer's IP number to the top-level domain zone files such as .com, .net, .org, .edu, .uk, and .us.

In the 1970s, during the Internet's early years, the functions that made up the root were like a little-known frontier town. No one really cared much to ask, "Who is in charge here." But gold was discovered by the early 1990s; the Internet had become a global commercial phenomenon. Because a great deal of money and power, and the future of the Internet's original noncommercial, loosely structured character was at stake, it became vitally important to determine who controlled the root.

The Internet is a global network of millions of private-, government-, and business-owned computer networks. Cyberspace is intangible and transcends national borders. Thus, Internet exceptionalists, globalization advocates, cyber libertarians, and the system's so-called founding fathers, computer scientist and engineers, can be counted among the factions that have argued that no government should control cyberspace. Cyberspace, they argued, "was supposed to allow like-minded people to join communities and govern themselves without respect to geography, without regard to the top-down coercive structures of territorial governmental systems, and without the usual pathologies and corruptions that characterize territorial rule." [30]

The Internet, however, is quite tangible as its routers, cables, servers, and millions of interconnected computers and other transmission infrastructure are located in hundreds of nations. Thus, governments, exercising their authority under traditional notions of sovereign jurisdiction, have enacted laws limiting Internet usage and content, have imposed legal liability on Internet service providers, and, in a minority of nations, have required them to censor certain content. In the U.S., federal laws, for example, criminalize the use of cyberspace for fraud, transmission of child pornography, and software piracy. And in cyberspace, a national government's legal reach may extend far beyond its territorial borders. Consider, for example, a French's judge's ruling that French criminal law could be applied to the American company Yahoo to prevent Nazi memorabilia from being auctioned on its website, even though U.S. law does not criminalize such activity.[31] Some nations, such as China, filter a great deal of foreign information from its Internet users.

In a push back against nations' efforts to make Internet companies comply with the peculiarities of domestic laws, the Internet Governance Forum, a United Nations-affiliated group, proposed in 2010 a treaty "to protect the Internet from political interference and place into international law its founding principles of open standards, network neutrality, freedom of expression and pluralistic governance."[32] Practically speaking, the treaty was little more than a symbolic gesture. Only the **Internet Engineering Task Force (IETF)** and ICANN set global standards for Internet technology and content, and are widely considered authoritative.

Internet Engineering Task Force & Rulemaking Authority

The task force, founded in 1986, "is a loosely self-organized group of people who contribute to the engineering and evolution of Internet technologies. It is the principal body engaged in the development of new Internet standard specifications" and it sets the essential TCP/IP standards.[33] In short, the task force is concerned with the adoption of technical standards to preserve decentralization, user empowerment, and **interoperability**—that all technologies using the Internet can operate with other existing and new technologies in cyberspace. The task force, however, is not a governing or regulatory body in the traditional sense. Yet, its engineers argue that IETF has legitimate authority to fashion rules for the Internet.

Legal scholar Olivier Sylvain explains that some legal scholars, notably A. Michael Froomkin, would have governmental policymakers "defer substantial first-instance rulemaking authority to private self-regulatory organizations, like the Internet Engineering Task Force, for which decentralization, user empowerment, and interoperability are a priority" because its "engineers and application designers…are far better suited than centralized agency bureaucrats to develop the rules for broadband network management…the strongest version of this argument goes, [that] the deliberative processes by which the IETF develops transmission standards are far more transparent and democratic than extant governmental processes."[34]

There is, however, a critical difference between ICANN and the task force. The task force's claim to wield authority to set Internet policy and standards is not grounded in court-made law, legislation, or any action recognized by a sovereign state. Rather, the task force's computer scientists and engineers create standards and policy for Internet-related technology by issuing Request for Comment (RFC) memoranda, something akin to peer-review articles that the task force adopts. RFCs are the law of the Internet. Well, at least to the task force and its members. But RFCs hold no sway in any legal jurisdictions.

In contrast, ICANN derives its authority from a government, the U.S. federal government. In December 1998, the U.S. Department of Commerce, which then controlled the Internet technical management functions known as the Internet Assigned Numbers Authority (IANA), contracted ICANN to oversee the system that links website names and suffixes with Internet protocol numbers assigned to your computer.[35] ICANN's management of the root gives it authority to decide which parties get to use valuable domain names. If you want your website to be named medialawstudent.net, you would register it and renew it annually with ICANN. If someone steals your website name—cyber-squatting or cyber-piracy—ICANN offers an administrative dispute resolution procedure to resolve the dispute. Claimants may also take such disputes to court. Alone, ICANN's contractual authority would not compel global compliance. It works with the Regional Internet Registries in Asia, Latin America, and Europe through mutual agreement. Nevertheless, the U.S. retains a legal claim to some degree of control over the important worldwide domain name system stemming from its seminal role in the Internet's development.

Dominating the Domain Naming System

The U.S. Department of Commerce was in the enviable position in 1998 to award a contract to control the IANA because the U.S. government financed—and with the help of private contractors such as the University of California and the Stanford Research Institute—created, operated, and developed the Advanced Research Projects Agency Network (ARPANET), which evolved into the Internet. ARPANET was a U.S. military project that developed Cold War weapons and secret systems. Because the network's "packet switching" technology allowed a message to find its destination via several routes, it was believed that it would allow the military to continue communications even after a nuclear attack.

In 1983, a Department of Defense project led by Vinton Cerf and Robert E. Kahn created the TCP/IP protocol that allows different networks to connect, forming what is now the Internet. Meanwhile, Jon Postel, the inventor of the e-mail protocol, took over the management of the early Internet domain naming system, then maintained by the Stanford Research Institute under contract with the Defense Department. If one wanted a domain name, Postel was the man to see. Postel, however, lost control of the naming system and the root zone file by 1998, but not without stubborn resistance.

The wrangle over control of the domain naming system started when the Department of Commerce opened the contract to manage the role file and domain name system to bidders. It awarded it to Government Systems Inc. in 1990, which then subcontracted it to Networks Solutions, now Verisign Inc. By the mid-1990s a clash of cultures ensued. For about 20 years, the so-called "Fathers of the Internet" including Postel and Cerf, oversaw a freewheeling, collegial, decentralized, and nonprofit culture of university-affiliated research units. Networks Solutions, however, was an animal of the for-profit corporate culture and started charging a $50 registration fee per domain. Postel, for one, did not protest the $50 fee. Rather, he argued that Network Solutions should reduce the fee when the company earned more collectively from the fees than it cost to run the domain name system. As Jack Goldsmith and Tim Wu noted in *Who Controls the Internet*, Network Solutions collected $200 million in revenues in 1999 and it "realized that it had hit a gold mine and began to see its monopoly over domain-name registration as worth fighting for."[36]

But even before Network Solutions started raking in huge revenues, Cerf founded the Internet Society (ISOC) in January 1992, partly in an effort to claim legal authority to set technical standards and policy for the domain naming system independent of the U.S. Defense Department. In March 1995 the U.S. government, represented by Department of Energy engineer Robert Aiken, sent an email to the ISOC, wanting to know, "Is ISOC claiming that it has jurisdiction and overall responsibility for the top-level address and name space? If yes, how did ISOC obtain this responsibility; if no, then who does own it?"[37]Cerf's email response argued that the U.S. government and other organized Internet groups should reach an agreement on that matter, noting that, "My bias is to try to treat all of this as a global matter and to settle the responsibility on the Internet Society as an non-governmental agent serving the community."[38] Cerf pursued that goal without involvement by any government in an effort that culminated in the signing of the Generic Top-Level Domain Memorandum of Understanding in 1997 declaring the Society's authority to establish Internet policy. Still, the Society had no formal legal authority over the root file and the domain naming system.

The U.S. Government & ICANN

In late January 1998, the power grab by the Internet engineers ended when the U.S. Department of Commerce issued a Statement of Policy on the Management of Internet Names and Addresses or Green Paper. The report said that the U.S. government held authority over the root file, but also said it was committed to a transition that would allow private sector management of the domain name system. The government did not recognize the Internet Society or the Generic Top-Level Domain Memorandum of Understanding.[39]

Since 1998, Commerce has renewed its contract with ICANN with the goal of turning over the operation of the domain name system to private hands. But the terms of the contract gave Commerce the authority to dictate ICANN's governing procedures and control of the important root zone file. In 2009, however, the two parties executed the Affirmation of Commitments with terms that included the U.S.'s acknowledgement that no one entity controls the corporation, that ICANN must remain headquartered in the U.S.—thus, subject to U.S. jurisdiction—and that the corporation no longer has to report separately to the U.S. government.[40] According to legal scholar Froomkin, under the terms of the Affirmation of Commitments, the U.S. retains a small degree of control of the domain name system: "ICANN is now free of U.S. Government control (except perhaps at the extreme margin) and yet still substantially free of real control by other governments."[41]

SUMMARY: Though there has been worldwide debate over who has legitimate authority to control Internet operations and standards since the early 1990s, Internet governance and regulation remains a murky area of law. Internet exceptionalists, globalization advocates, and cyber libertarians argue that no government should control the Internet mostly because cyberspace transcends territorial jurisdictions. Efforts by nongovernmental organizations, such as the Internet Engineering Task Force, to set worldwide Internet technical standards do not have the force of law. Now, only the Internet Corporation for Assigned Names and Numbers (ICANN) has globally recognized authority to control the root, or to assign domain names and computer addresses essential for communication over the Internet. The US, which grants this power to a private company, still appears to hold a legitimate claim to controlling the root function stemming from its role in funding the creation and development of the Internet. Nevertheless, no one nation or organization owns or controls the Internet.

Does the FCC Have Authority to Regulate Network Neutrality?

In 2003, Tim Wu, a law professor and now senior adviser at the Federal Trade Commission, correctly predicted that "communications regulators over the next decade will spend increasing time on conflicts between the private interests of broadband providers and the public's interest in a competitive innovation environment centered on the Internet."[42] Wu was talking about **network neutrality**, a phrase he popularized and a concept he championed. Almost 10 years later, cable companies that provide broadband service and the Federal Communications Commission (FCC) were at odds over whether the commission has the authority to impose network neutrality rules on such media companies.

The principle of network neutrality encompasses all Internet management and use. It is the belief that, as FCC Commissioner Michael Copps said,

> Anyone can access the Internet with any kind of computer, for any type of application, and read or say pretty much what they want. No one can corner control of the Internet for their own limited purposes....From its inception, the Internet was designed, as those present during the course of its creation will tell you, to prevent government or a corporation or anyone else from controlling it. It was designed to defeat discrimination against users, ideas, and technologies.[43]

Keep in mind that companies providing broadband service are analogous to private bus companies or train service. Those companies didn't pave the highways or own all the land upon which their vehicles travel. Similarly, broadband companies did not create the broadband width; they constructed the copper or fiber optic cable through which the high-speed signal travels. Therefore, network neutrality proponents argue that broadband service providers have a duty to the public. As Wu explained, the goal is to

> strike a balance: to forbid broadband operators, absent a showing of harm, from restricting what users do with their Internet connection, while giving the operator general freedom to manage bandwidth consumption and other matters of local concern. The principle achieves this by adopting the basic principle that broadband operators should have full freedom to 'police what they own' (the local network) while restrictions based on inter-network indicia should be viewed with suspicion.[44]

Broadband network neutrality proponents argue that without government intervention, companies providing broadband network service are likely to block or slowdown access to lawful services and applications such as iPhone service, Netflix movies, peer-to-peer file sharing protocol, email, or video games to improve their overall network performance. Proponents also argue that network neutrality restrictions would prevent companies providing Internet service from allowing some content providers to pay more for faster transmission. Network neutrality backers tend to be content providers, including large companies such as Amazon.com, Disney, and Google who are opposed to paying more for preferred service. Free speech activists, such as the American Civil Liberties Union, also support the principle out of concern that broadband providers might discriminate unfairly against lawful content they do not like.

Network neutrality opponents include cable companies providing broadband service and traditional pro-market deregulators. Some argue that broadband service providers must have the right to filter or slow data that consume significant amounts of the bandwidth to insure that all data flows smoothly. Others argue that there is no need for government to impose network neutrality principles because companies do not discriminate, and if they were to, content providers and individual users would abandon them and do business with rivals, encouraging greater marketplace competition instead.

Guidelines, Not Rules

In 2005, the FCC declared that it held the authority under Title I ancillary jurisdiction "to ensure that providers of telecommunications for Internet access or Internet Protocol-enabled (IP-enabled) services are operated in a neutral manner."[45] Title I of the Communications Act of 1934 gives the FCC authority to make regulations "reasonably ancillary to the effective performance of the Commission's various responsibilities" identified elsewhere in the act. Consequently, the following network neutrality rules were merely guidelines: (1) consumers are entitled to access the lawful Internet content of their choice; (2) consumers are entitled to run applications and services of their choice, subject to the needs of law enforcement; (3) consumers are entitled to connect their choice of legal devices that do not harm the network; and (4) consumers are entitled to competition among network providers, application and service providers, and content providers.[46] The FCC invoked Title I ancillary jurisdiction consistent with the Court's ruling in *National Cable & Telecommunications Association v. Brand X Internet Services*, 545 U.S. 967 (2005). In *Brand X*, the Court ruled that the FCC had the authority to classify cable operators that provide broadband service via modem and then by telephone, cable, and wireless as "information services" under Title I. That designation, however, has weakened the FCC's argument that it has authority to impose network neutrality rules on broadband service providers.

Relying on the FCC guidelines, several Comcast broadband subscribers sued the company in 2007 when they discovered that Comcast blocked them from using peer-to-peer networking applications. Comcast responded that it blocked the applications because such applications used large amounts of the company's scarce network capacity. The FCC ruled that Comcast had violated the FCC's network neutrality policy because the company had other ways to manage bandwidth traffic without discriminating against peer-to-peer communications. Comcast challenged the FCC's ruling on several grounds, including jurisdiction. It said the FCC had no authority to exercise jurisdiction over the company's network management practices.

The FCC argued that it derived ancillary jurisdiction—authority to regulate services not specifically identified in the Communications Act—from its general rule-making authority under Title I of the Communications Act and under Section 230(b) of the Communications Act, which states that "it is the policy of the United States…to promote the continued development of the Internet and other interactive computer services [and] to encourage the development of technologies which maximize user control over what information is received by individuals, families, and schools who use the Internet."

In *Comcast Corp v. FCC*, 600 F.3d 642 (2010), the U.S. Court of Appeals for the D.C. Circuit rejected the FCC's claim. The D.C. Circuit said the FCC failed to meet a two-part test for determining when the FCC may exercise ancillary jurisdiction laid down in *American Library Association v. FCC*, 406 F.3d 689, 691–692 (2005): "(1) the Commission's general jurisdictional grant under Title I of the Communications Act covers the regulated subject and (2) the regulations are reasonably ancillary to the Commission's effective performance of its statutorily mandated responsibilities."

The FCC met the first part of the test. But to meet the second part of the test, the FCC argued that the network neutrality policy by itself created "statutorily mandated responsibilities." The D.C. Circuit, however, said that the FCC was required to identify a specific statutory mandate, not a policy, because to do otherwise would allow the commission the power to regulate the Internet as though it were broadcast, cable, or telephone service.

Significantly, the D.C. Circuit identified Section 706 of the Telecommunications Act as "at least arguably" a basis for the FCC's legitimate ancillary authority to regulate network management practices.[47] Taking its cue, the FCC, in a 3–2 vote in December 2010, tethered its network neutrality rules to Section 706. Section 706 contains a direct mandate authorizing it to "encourage the deployment on a reasonable and timely basis of advanced telecommunications capability to all Americans…by utilizing…price cap regulation, regulatory forbearance, measures that promote competition in the local telecommunications market, or other regulating methods that remove barriers to infrastructure investment." The FCC argued that, "under our reading, Section 706(a) authorizes the Commission to address practices, such as blocking VoIP communications, degrading or raising the cost of online video, or denying end users material information about their broadband service, that have the potential to stifle overall investment in Internet infrastructure and limit competition in telecommunications markets."[48] Had the FCC originally classified broadband service under Title II of the Communications Act, it would have had a much stronger argument for the authority to impose nondiscriminatory obligations on broadband service providers. Under Title II, common carriers are also required to provide services without "unjust or unreasonable discrimination in charges, practices, classifications, regulations, facilities, or services."

Verizon Wireless and MetroPCS Communications challenged the FCC's authority to imposed network neutrality rules in accordance with Section 706. In an appeal filed with the D.C. Circuit, the broadband service providers argued that the FCC sought to imposed common-carriage requirements on broadband services based "on a hodgepodge of provisions scattered throughout" the Communications Act and in an arbitrary and unlawful manner. The **appellants** also maintained that the FCC action violated their First Amendment rights "by stripping them of control over the transmission of speech on their networks," and their Fifth Amendment rights by taking away their property without just compensation.[49] Meanwhile, the FCC's chances of prevailing in the legislative branch were difficult to predict as the Obama administration and Democrats, backers of the regulations, and the Republican-dominated House of Representatives, who voted down a proposed legislation in support of the regulations, had reached a stalemate.

SUMMARY: Network neutrality is a principle that holds that companies providing broadband access to customers should not discriminate based on the applications, computers, or software consumers use, or the content other media companies provide via broadband. Broadband network neutrality proponents argue that without government intervention, companies providing broadband network service are likely to block or slow down access to lawful services and applications such as iPhone service, Netflix movies, peer-to-peer file sharing protocol, email, or video games to improve their overall network performance. The FCC has sought to impose network neutrality regulations on broadband service providers. In *Comcast Corp v. FCC*, 600 F.3d 642 (2010), the U.S. Court of Appeals for the D.C. Circuit rejected the FCC's attempt to impose such rules, finding that the FCC failed to identify the specific statutorily mandated responsibility in the Communications Act that would allow it to regulate broadband service providers under its ancillary authority.

Media Policy & Internet Exceptionalism

The shape of Internet law to come may come down to how much legislators, regulators, and judges apply the tenets of Internet exceptionalism media law policy. Cyber libertarian John Perry Barlow and cyber collectivist Lawrence Lessig subscribe to Internet exceptionalism. Internet exceptionalism is predicated on the belief that cyberspace is so radically different from other media that it cannot be regulated, as Barlow contends. Or it requires, as Lessig argues, a unique set of Internet-specific regulations and laws to protect its unique attributes.

Barlow's vision is utopian, romantic, and uncompromising. Lessig's approach is pragmatic; cyberspace needs a legal regime to preserve the equality, freedom, and collectivism that is its architecture naturally provides: "In real space, we recognize how laws regulate—through constitutions, statutes, and other legal codes. In cyberspace we must understand how a different 'code' regulates—how the software and hardware (i.e., the 'code' of cyberspace) that make cyberspace what it is also regulate cyberspace as it is."[50] Lessig, for example, argues that network neutrality is the natural consequence of the "simple but brilliant 'end-to-end' design of the Internet that has made it such a powerful force for economic and social good: All of the intelligence and control is held by producers and users, not the networks that connect them."[51]

Just how is cyberspace so different from the real world of flesh and brick-and-mortar? No other media technology matches the Internet's interactivity combined with its one-to-many communication ability. A phone provides audio interactivity, but not one-to-many communication. The Internet is alone in its ability to allow anyone to send cheap, anonymous communication worldwide and instantaneously. Online technology allows anyone to make multiple and universally downloadable copies of content in print, audio, and video, individually and combined. And software code allows for rapid innovation of online capabilities. All these attributes have led to the development of Twitter, social networking, video- and music-sharing, and online commerce sites. All these attributes, however, have also made it easier for anyone anywhere to steal your identity, money, and intellectual property, sully your reputation; and threaten your safety. Nevertheless, the "Internet's perceived novelty has prompted regulators to engage in 'Internet exceptionalism,' crafting Internet-specific laws that diverge from regulatory precedents in other media," observes Eric Goldman, associate professor of law at Santa Clara University School of Law.[52]

Goldman identifies three waves of Internet exceptionalism. During the first wave, legislators sought to craft laws that "diverge from regulator precedents in other media," and Section 230 of the Communications Decency Act "is a flagship example of mid-1990s efforts to preserve Internet utopianism."[53]As discussed in Chapters 3 and 5, §230 CDA shields online intermediaries from liability from civil actions such as libel, negligence, and fraud stemming from the content posted by users.

During the second wave in the late 1990s, legislators disfavored certain online activity. For example, three dozens states banned Internet hunting though real world hunting was legal in the same states.[54] In the current third wave, "exceptionalism proliferation," the law treats social networking sites differently than blogs, for example:"Rather than regulating these sites like other Web sites, regulators have sought social networking site specific laws, such as requirements to verify users' age, combat sexual predators and suppress content that promotes violence. The result is that the regulation of social networking sites differs not only from offline enterprises but from other websites as well."[55]

Increasingly, judges are rejecting Internet exceptionalism arguments. Those setbacks occurred in copyright cases involving peer-to-peer file-sharing software (P2P), as discussed in Chapter 14, as well as in questions about personal jurisdiction as addressed in *Best Van Lines, Inc. v. Walker*, 490 F.3d 239 (2d Cir. 2007), *Zippo Manufacturing Company v. Zippo Dot Com, Inc.*, 952 F.Supp. 1119 (W.D.Pa.1997), and *In the Matter of Liskula Cohen v. Google, Inc., and Blogger.com*, 887 N.Y.S.2d 424, 428–429 (NY: Supreme Court, Aug. 17, 2009), discussed in Chapter 5.

At least one court, the influential U.S. Court of Appeals for the Ninth Circuit, has rejected the exceptionality of the Internet when determining cases in which plaintiffs seek to pierce the shield of immunity that §230 CDA provides. In *Fair Housing Council of San Fernando Valley v. Roommates.com*, 521 F. 3d 1157 (9th Cir. 2008) (en banc), the Ninth Circuit held that §230 did not bar the claim that Roommates.com, a website designed to match people renting out spare rooms with potential renters, violated the Fair Housing Act by requiring subscribers to create profile pages containing illegal discriminatory information about their sex, sexual orientation, and whether they planned to bring children to the household, information which Roommates.com posted on the site.

Ninth Circuit Chief Judge Alex Kozinski, the author of the *Roommates.com* opinion, is unabashedly opposed to Internet exceptionalism, as evidenced by his co-authored law review article, "A Declaration of the Dependence of Cyberspace," its title clearly mocking Barlow's, "Declaration of Independence of Cyberspace."[56] In *Roommates.com*, Kozinski said, "The court held essentially that an online business had to be held to the same substantive law as businesses in the brick-and-mortar world."[57] He described the dissent as echoing the oft-said exceptionalism prediction that the majority's approach threatened the survival of the Internet.

> **SUMMARY:** Is cyberspace legally different from brick-and-mortal reality? Is it exceptional? No other mass media technology matches the Internet's interactivity combined with its one-to-many communication ability. The Internet also is alone in its ability to allow anyone to send cheap anonymous communication worldwide and instantaneously. Online technology allows anyone to make multiple and universally downloadable copies of content in print, audio, and video, individually and combined. And software code allows for rapid innovation of online capabilities. But do these unique attributes qualify Internet owners, operators, and users for exemption from copyright, libel, and other laws? Increasingly, courts confronted with such arguments are rejecting the argument that the Internet is legally exceptional.

ONLINE RESOURCES

1. Brief History of the Internet, http://www.internetsociety.org/internet/internet-51/history-internet/brief-history-internet
2. Cybersmut: Protecting Kids, Preserving Freedom, http://www.freedomforum.org/packages/first/cybersmut/index.htm
3. Electronic Frontier Foundation, https://www.eff.org/
4. Internet Governance, http://digitalenterprise.org/governance/gov.html
5. Open Internet, http://www.fcc.gov/topic/open-internet
6. *Reno v. ACLU*, http://www.oyez.org/cases/1990–1999/1996/1996_96_511
6. Berin Szoka & Adam Marcus (Eds.), *The Next Digital Decade: Essays on the Future of the Internet*, http://nextdigitaldecade.com/ndd_book.pdf

QUESTIONS

1. Might public school safety and order be at greater risk if off-school cyberspace student speech enjoyed heightened First Amendment protection? Apply the strict scrutiny test to facts of *Doninger v. Niehoff*, 527 F.3d 41 (2d Cir. 2008). The full facts of the case can be found at the following sites: http://www.wneclaw.com/lawed/doninger.pdf; http://caselaw.findlaw.com/us-2nd-circuit/1325010.html

2. & 3. Next, apply the incitement, *Brandenburg v. Ohio*, 395 U.S. 444 (1969), and true threat, *Planned Parenthood of the Columbia/Willamette Inc. v. American Coalition for Life Activists* (2002), tests discussed in chapter 7.

4. Do you believe that the U.S. president should have the authority to kill Internet access in times of emergencies? If so, what circumstances would justify the president taking such action? Should the law require him to seek congressional approval before he pulls the switch?

5. Some, such as legal scholar A. Michael Froomkin, would have governmental policy makers "defer substantial first-instance rule-making authority to private self-regulatory organizations, like the Internet Engineering Task Force (IETF), for which decentralization, user empowerment, and interoperability are a priority" because its "engineers and application designers…are far better suited than centralized agency bureaucrats to develop the rules for broadband network management…the strongest version of this argument goes, [that] the deliberative processes by which the IETF develops transmission standards are far more transparent and democratic than extant governmental processes."[58] But law professor Olivier Sylvain argues, "Communications are too fundamental to democratic self-governance. As such, voters and elected officials ought to be making decisions about communication policy's normative priorities, not outsourcing them, no matter how expert industry standard setters might be or how unnerving democratic governance is."[59] Who do you think is right?

ENDNOTES

1. *Snyder v. Blue Mountain School District*, 593 F.3d. 286, 291 (3d Cir. 2010).
2. *Reno v. ACLU*, 521 U.S. 844, 870 (1997).
3. Ibid. 874.
4. Ibid. 871.
5. Ibid. 885.
6. *Ashcroft v. ACLU*, 535 U.S. 564, 572 (2002).
7. *ACLU v. Reno*, 31 F.Supp.2d 473, 481 (E.D.Pa.1999).
8. *Mukasey v. ACLU*, 555 US 1137 (2009)
9. *Perry Education Association v. Perry Local Educators' Association*, 460 U.S. 37 (1983).
10. *American Library Association v. U.S.*, 539 U.S. 194, 205 (2003).
11. *American Library Association v. U.S.*, 539 U.S. 194, 205, 214 (2003).
12. *Bethel School District No. 403 v. Fraser*, 478 U.S. 675, 682 (1986).
13. *Morse v. Frederick*, 551 U.S. 393, 404 (2007).
14. Ibid. 425.
15. *Layshock v. Hermitage School District*, 593 F.3d 249, 261 (2010).
16. Ibid. 263.
17. *Snyder v. Blue Mountain School District*, 593 F.3d 286, vacated, 2010 BL 80170 (3d Cir. 2010); *Layshock v. Hermitage School District*, 593 F.3d 249, vacated, 2010 BL 80169 (3d Cir. 2010).

18. *Snyder v. Blue Mountain School District*, 08–4138 *3 (3d Cir. 2010).

19. *Doninger v. Niehoff*, 642 F. 3d334,347 (2d Cir. 2011).

20. Ibid. 346.

21. Ibid. 347.

22. Ibid. 353.

23. Eugene Volokh. "Federal Felony to Use Blogs, the Web, Etc. to Cause Substantial Emotional Distress through 'Severe, Repeated, and Hostile' Speech?" [Web log post](April 30, 2009), *The Volokh Conspiracy*, http://volokh.com/posts/1241122059.shtml

24. See *Finkel v. Dauber*, 906 N.Y.S.2d 697 (2010).

25. Senate Committee on Homeland Security & Governmental Affairs, "Myth v. Reality of Cybersecurity Legislation: The Facts About S. 3480, 'Protecting Cyberspace as a National Asset Act of 2010,'" [Press release](June 23, 2010), http://www.hsgac.senate.gov/media/majority-media/myth-v-reality-of-cybersecurity-legislation

26. David W. Opderbeck. "Cybersecurity and Executive Power," *Seton Hall Public Law Research Paper* no. 1788333 (March 16, 2011), 29, http://papers.ssrn.com/sol3/papers.cfm?abstract_id=1788333

27. President Barack Obama. "Executive Order: Assignment of National Security and Emergency Preparedness Communications Functions," (July 6, 2012), http://www.whitehouse.gov/the-press-office/2012/07/06/executive-order-assignment-national-security-and-emergency-preparedness—

28. Robert Faris and Nart Villeneuve. "Measuring Global Internet Filtering." In Ronald Deibert, John Palfrey, Rafal Rohozinski, Jonathan Zittrain (Eds.), *Access Denied: The Practice and Policy of Global Internet Filtering*. Cambridge: MIT Press, (2008), http://access.opennet.net/wp-content/uploads/2011/12/accessdenied-chapter-1.pdf

29. MiltonL. Mueller. *Ruling the Root*. Cambridge, MA: The MIT Press,(2004), 6–7.

30. Jack Goldsmith and Tim Wu. *Who Controls the Internet? Illusions of a Borderless World*. New York: Oxford University Press (2006), 181.

31. *Association Union des EtudiantsJuifs de France v. Yahoo! Inc.* (May 2000), http://www.juriscom.net/txt/jurisfr/cti/yauctions20000522.htm

32. Mark Ballard. "Europe calls for global Internet treaty," *ComputerWeekly.com*, (September 20, 2010), http://benton.org/node/42351

33. Paul Hoffman. "The Tao of IETF: A Novice's Guide to the Internet Engineering Task Force," *The Internet Society* (2006), 4, http://www.rfc-editor.org/rfc/rfc4677.txt

34. Olivier Sylvain."Internet Governance and Democratic Legitimacy," *Federal* 62 *Communications Law Journal* 206–207 (2010).

35. U.S. Department of Commerce, Management of Internet Names and Addresses, "Statement of Policy on the Management of Internet Names and Addresses," Docket Number: 980212036–8146–02 (1998), http://www.ntia.doc.gov/federal-register-notice/1998/statement-policy-management-internet-names-and-addresses

36. Jack Goldsmith and Tim Wu. *Who Controls the Internet? Illusions of a Borderless World*. New York: Oxford University Press (2006), 36.

37. Milton L. Mueller. *Ruling the Root*. Cambridge, MA: The MIT Press, (2004), 136.

38. Ibid.

39. U.S. Department of Commerce, Docket No. 980212036–8146–02, White Paper on Management of Internet Names and Addresses, (1998), http://www.icann.org/general/white-paper-05jun98.htm

40. Affirmation of Commitments by the U.S. Department of Commerce and the Internet Corporation for Assigned Names and Numbers, September 30, 2009, http://www.ntia.doc.gov/ntiahome/domainname/Affirmation_of_Commitments_2009.pdf

41. Michael A. Froomkin. "Almost Free: An Analysis of ICANN's 'Affirmation of Commitments,'" 9 *Journal of Telecommunications and High Technology Law* 223 (2011).

42. Tim Wu. "Network Neutrality, Broadband Discrimination," 2 *Journal of Telecommunications and High Technology Law* 141 (2003).

43. Mark Roy. "Copps: FCC Following 'Ill-Advised' Internet Policy" (October 10, 2003), http://www.internetnews.com/xSP/article.php/3090301

44. Tim Wu, "Network Neutrality, Broadband Discrimination," 2 *Journal of Telecommunications and High Technology Law* 167168 (2003).
45. Federal Communications Commissions. Policy Statement: In the Matters of Appropriate Framework for Broadband Access to Internet Over Wireless Facilities, FCC-05–151A1 (September 23, 2005), http://www.publicknowledge.org/pdf/FCC-05–151A1.pdf
46. Ibid.
47. *Comcast Corp v. FCC*, 600 F.3d 642, 658 (D.C. Cir. 2010).
48. Federal Communications Commissions. Policy Statement: In the Matter of Preserving the Open Internet Broadband Industry Practices, FCC 10–201 *66 (December 21, 2010), http://www.fcc.gov/document/preserving-open-internet-broadband-industry-practices-1
49. In Brief of Appellant-Petitioner, *Verizon Wireless v. FCC*, No. 11–1355 (D.C. Cir. July 2, 2012) *33, http://www.arentfox.com/pdf/NewsletterPDF1forJuly9.pdf
50. Lawrence Lessig. *Code, Version 2.0.* (New York: Basic Book (2006), 5.
51. Lawrence Lessig and Robert W. McChesney. "No Tolls on the Internet," *Washington Post* (June 8, 2006), A23.
52. Eric Goldman. "The Third Wave of Internet Exceptionalism," [Web log post] (March 11, 2009), http://blog.ericgoldman.org/archives/2009/03/the_third_wave.htm
53. Eric Goldman. "The Third Wave of Internet Exceptionalism." In BerinSzoka& Adam Marcus (Eds.), *The Next Digital Decade: Essays on the Future of the Internet.* Washington, D.C.: TechFreedom (2010, 165.
54. Ibid.
55. Ibid. 167.
56. Alex Kozinski and Josh Goldfoot. "A Declaration of the Dependence of Cyberspace," 32 *The Columbia Journal of Law & the Arts* 365(2009).
57. Ibid. 370.
58. Sylvain, "Internet Governance and Democratic Legitimacy," 206.
59. Ibid. 251.

CHAPTER FOUR

Defamation

Common Law Elements

CONTROVERSY: Most likely, the name Richard Jewell means nothing to those under 25, and little to those who are older. In July 1996, however, Jewell became internationally famous overnight. And just as quickly, it seems, internationally infamous. That summer, Jewell, while working as a security guard at Centennial Olympic Park, the site for the 1996 Summer Olympics, found a pipe bomb. He alerted the police, the site was evacuated, and hundreds of lives were saved, though two died in the explosion. He was hailed as a hero. That changed three days later when the *Atlanta Journal-Constitution* reported that the FBI was investigating Jewell as the lead suspect in the bombing. Then, about three months later, authorities cleared Jewell as a suspect. In 2005, Eric Robert Rudolph confessed to the bombing. In January 1997, Jewell sued the newspaper and other news outlets for libel. He won out-of-court settlements from a number of outlets that reported the same accusations originally reported by the *Atlanta Journal*. But the newspaper refused to settle. In January 2012, the Georgia Supreme Court appears to have put an end to Jewell's lawsuit when it upheld a lower court ruling absolving the newspaper of culpability. The *Atlanta Journal* persuaded the Georgia courts that its reporting was substantially true because it relied on a credible source and included in the same story comments from sources who dismissed or cast doubts about the FBI's accusation.[1] Its story was substantially true, and truth, as discussed below, is the best defense a media defendant can raise against an accusation of libel, even though, as the Court of Appeals in Georgia noted, Jewell "and his family suffered tremendously as a result of this ordeal."

Chapter's Scope

In the U.S., there are basically two libel law narratives. One starts in 13th-century England and is reshaped by judges and legislators in each state here. The second story starts with the U.S. Supreme Court and its ruling *New York Times Co. v. Sullivan*, 376 U.S. 254 (1964), and interweaves with the older narrative, creating a complicated area of law something akin to a patchwork quilt. This chapter covers the first narrative, detailing the elements of a cause of action for libel that a plaintiff is required to establish to get a case before a trier of fact, that is, a judge or jury. These elements include defamation, publication, identification, injury, and fault. This libel law narrative was developed by the state common and statutory process. Chapter 5 discusses the second libel law narrative, explaining *Sullivan*'s impact on state libel law, as well as discussing legal controversies stemming from libel law and cyberspace, particularly the impact of the Communication Decency Act § 230.

Before a libel action can go before a jury, all its elements must be satisfied. For example, Jewell established defamation, publication, identification, and injury. But truth is the best defense for a libel defendant. Jewell's family could not persuade the Georgia courts that the *Atlanta Journal* was at fault because the newspaper's statements were substantially true. Consequently, it appears that his family will never get the chance to have a jury or judge decide the merits of his libel action.[2]

In addition to discussing the elements of a cause of action, this chapter also identifies and discusses the most widely applied privileges and defenses available to libel defendants to win a summary judgment or a verdict, or to modify damages. These privileges and defenses include: negating the plaintiff's case, truth, fair comment or criticism, opinion, retraction, statute of limitations, the single publication rule, wire service defense, breaking news defense, anti-SLAPP suits, legislative immunity, consent, fair and neutral reports.

Libel Law's Evolution

If your mother told you "sticks and stones will break your bones, but words will never hurt," she was wrong, well at least in the eyes of the law. Anglo-Saxon law has recognized the right to bring an action against those who would speak ill of others as early as the De Scandalis Magnatum in 1275. That law banned "seditious libel," making it a criminal offense to spread false news that would sow discord between the King and his people. During the following six centuries, four different types of British courts—seigneurial (those run by feudal lords), religious, common law, and the English Court of Star Chamber—held jurisdiction over defamation cases. Ultimately, defamation developed into two forms of legal actions, libel and slander, though the majority of states no longer distinguish between the two. **Libel** refers to defamation fixed in a medium, whereas **slander** covers spoken defamation.

Most of the leading libel rulings stem from plaintiffs displeasure with statements published about them in newspapers. Consequently, newspapers have played a large role in shaping the scope and character of libel law, none with more impact than the *New York Times*. The "Old Gray Lady" was the defendant in an Alabama libel action and ultimately the winning petitioner in the landmark First Amendment and libel ruling *New York Times Co. v. Sullivan*. *Sullivan* reconfigured the libel landscape in the U.S. Before *Sullivan*, defendants in libel cases did not enjoy First Amendment protection, though they may have been able to invoke state-provided free press and free speech guarantees. Though it took 160 years, *Sullivan* repudiated the Sedition Act of 1798, a federal statute that criminalized criticism of government and its officials, or seditious libel. In the wake of *Sullivan*; *Garrison v. Louisiana*, 379 U.S. 64 (1964); and *Brandenburg v. Ohio*, 395 U.S. 444 (1969), most legal scholars argue that seditious libel is unconstitutional.

One of the reasons why it is difficult to say without qualification that seditious libel is unconstitutional is because as of 2003, 17 states and two U.S. territories had laws on their books that allowed for criminal penalties for libel. And according to the Media Law Resource Center, which conducted a study on criminal libel cases, many of those cases "echo prosecutions for seditious libel, which has been rejected as contrary to American principles of free speech and liberty. The MLRC study proves that criminalizing speech about reputation is inherently troublesome even under modern First Amendment principles, since it involves the highly selective determinations of government prosecutors of whose reputation to protect and what speech to punish."[3]

At this point, a pattern should be apparent: libel law lacks uniformity. It varies from the federal to the state level, and from state to state. That means that depending on the jurisdiction, requirements imposed upon the plaintiff to prove liability may differ, the distinction between libel and slander may be significant, or the defendant might not have certain qualified immunities or privileges to invoke, to name only a few variations. But *Sullivan* and its progeny have reined in a great deal of the haphazardness of state libel laws. Now, for example, all states must require that an elected official or public figure prove that defamatory statements about them were made with "actual malice," more easily understood as "reckless disregard for the truth or knowing falsity." That standard applies for both civil and criminal libel. But even U.S. Supreme Court rulings on libel law do not necessarily supersede state law. A recent Massachusetts case, *Noonan v. Staples*, 556 F. 20 (1 Cir. 2009), brought to the forefront yet another inconsistency between federal and state law: truth is *not* an absolute defense in all libel cases, as the overwhelming majority of legal scholars and lawyers had claimed for more than 40 years.

Rather, truth is an absolute defense only in libel cases brought by public persons, or in actions against media defendants when the communication involves matters of public concern. It turns out that Massachusetts is one of a handful of states that allows a "private figure" plaintiff to argue that though the statement is true, the defendant made the comments with a bad motive, or "actual malevolent intent or ill will."

The Elements of a Libel Suit, or How to Get a Libel Case to Trial

Defamation

It is well-established that communication is defamatory if it tends to lower an individual's reputation or deters others from associating with the individual. An individual who believes he or she has been the victim of such language files a complaint with a local court. That action makes the individual a plaintiff. In the complaint, the plaintiff establishes that he or she has the right to sue in the particular jurisdiction, identifies the parties to the suit, and, in a libel action, identifies the alleged defamatory communication. Keep in mind that an alleged defamatory communication may consists of ten, one hundred, or a thousand words. The point is that the plaintiff must identify each word or sentence, photograph, headline, caption, and more that he or she believes is false and defamatory. A plaintiff who fails to identify the appropriate defamatory statements cannot fault a court for failing to analyze them.[4]

Libel Per Se: A Statement That Is Defamatory on Its Face

It is to the plaintiff's advantage to have alleged defamatory statements declared "libelous or defamatory per se." That's because state courts have designated libel per se statements as those that, on their face, cause reputational harm to the plaintiff in question, and, consequently, the plaintiff can win a monetary award without having to show how he or she was harmed. In some states, such plaintiffs can seek punitive damages which may far exceed the real extent of the monetary injury. For example, in Connecticut, juries are told that, "…if the defamatory material is (libel/slander) per se, the plaintiff is entitled to an award of general damages for injury to reputation without proof of monetary loss, and an award of special damages upon proof of actual injury or loss. You may award punitive damages as a matter of discretion."[5] The four widely established libel per se categories are: (i) charging someone with a serious crime; (ii) statements that tend to injure another in his or her trade, business, or profession; (iii) statements that say a plaintiff has a loathsome disease or mental illness; and (iv) imputing unchastity to a woman.

A key point to appreciate about libel per se is that the category is largely the result of judge-made law reflecting the mores of the 19th and early 20th centuries. Consequently, as the moral codes of communities and criminal laws change, libel per se designations may change, accordingly. For example, during the 1940s it was libelous per se to call someone a communist in states such as New York, Oklahoma, California, and Illinois. But the U.S. Supreme Court's ruling in *Brandenburg v. Ohio*, 395 U.S. 444 (1969), invalidated the Smith Act and state sedition laws restricting radical political groups. Consequently, branding someone a communist is no longer libelous per se, but can still be libelous per quod, discussed below. But courts do not always respond quickly to changes in social mores. For instance, in the generally liberal state of New York, not until May 2012 did a court rule that an accusation of homosexuality was not libelous per se.[6]

Libel Per Quod: A Statement That Requires Extrinsic Facts to Understand Its Defamatory Meaning

When the defamatory meaning is not apparent, states categorize the communication as libel per quod—communication capable of two interpretations, one of which is defamatory and the other not, or communications not obviously defamatory until considered with innuendo and "colloquium" by showing its connection to the plaintiff.

A judge decides whether libel per quod statements can be reasonably understood to expose a plaintiff to hatred, ridicule, contempt, scorn, or shame. For instance, *In the Matter of Liskula Cohen v. Google, Inc., and Blogger.com*, 887 N.Y.S. 2d 424 (N.Y. Sup. Ct. 2009), a New York state judge consulted "*The American Heritage Dictionary of the English Language*, 4th Edition 2009, found at www.dictionary.reference.com," to conclude that "skank" and "ho" had well-established defamatory meanings.[7] Illinois applies an "innocent construction rule." Under the rule, courts must give the allegedly defamatory words their natural and obvious meaning.[8]

Defamation by Implication. Some jurisdictions recognize that even accurate, factual information is capable of bearing defamatory meaning. According to the U.S. Court of Appeals for the Fourth Circuit in *White v. Fraternal Order of Police*, 909 F.2d 512, 519 (1990): "The usual test applied to determine the meaning of a defamatory utterance is whether it was reasonably understood by the recipient of the communication to have been intended in the defamatory sense."

Defamatory to Whom?

Words that are defamatory in one community may be praiseworthy in another. Consequently, plaintiffs generally choose the community of relevance by showing that he or she has lost esteem among a specific community defined by geographical, cultural, or professional affiliations. In complaints, plaintiffs often provide quotes from third parties to support their claims of defamatory meaning. Vicki Iseman's complaint filed against the *New York Times*, stemming from a February 21, 2008, front-page story on then-U.S. presidential candidate John McCain, is typical. The complaint quoted leading print journalists and broadcast pundits to support Iseman's contention that many covering politics believed the article insinuated that McCain and Iseman had an affair. Iseman and the *New York Times* settled out of court in February 2009.

The law did not require Iseman to show that all or most pundits and journalists came to the same conclusion about the article. Rather, libel law requires that a plaintiff need only show that the defamatory communication injured his or her reputation among a substantial and respectable group, or "in the eyes of right-thinking men generally"[9]—a community of relevance. If, however, the group is of a blatantly anti-social nature, courts may deny the plaintiff a defamation action. Though courts recognize that a community relevance can extend to an international or nationwide group of professionals or experts, no court has ruled that a relevant community can be nationwide by virtue of the widespread dissemination of the defamatory content by a media outlet.

> SUMMARY: A plaintiff bringing an action in libel must establish that the defendant has made defamatory comments about him or her. The plaintiff must also show that the defendant's statements exposed him or her to hatred, ridicule, contempt, scorn, or shame in a community of relevance. Defamatory statements fall into two main categories: per se and per quod. Libel or defamation per se are statements that courts have deemed to be defamatory without the plaintiff having to show harm. The four widely established libel per se categories are: (i) charging someone with a serious crime; (ii) statements that tend to injure another in his or her trade, business or profession; (iii) statements that say a plaintiff has a loathsome disease or mental illness; and (iv) imputing unchastity to a woman. Once a judge declares a statement libelous per se, a plaintiff can win a monetary award without having to show harm, and, in some states, be allowed to seek punitive damages that may far exceed the real extent of the monetary injury. When the defamatory meaning is not apparent, states categorize the communication as libel per quod and the plaintiff must show evidence, typically testimony or evidence of economic lost, stemming from the comments.

Publication

A plaintiff must establish in his or her complaint that at least one other person in addition to the plaintiff and the defendant was exposed to the allegedly defamatory communication. When a mass media outlet is a defendant, publication is obvious; the date of the newspaper edition or time and date of television broadcast are identified. But publication exists also when a defamatory statement is conveyed over the phone, spoken at a cocktail party, or transmitted by letter. But, as a general rule, when the person defamed voluntarily discloses the contents of a libelous communication to others, the originator of the libel is not responsible for the resulting damage.[10]

Each publication gives rise to a new cause of action for libel. Hence, the **republication rule**: Every repetition of the defamatory statement is a publication, and anyone who repeats the defamatory communication is a publisher of that defamatory statement. Further, "the courts have said many times that the last utterance may do no less harm than the first, and that the wrong of another cannot serve as an excuse to the defendant."[11] Section 230 immunity, however, shields online service providers from the liability of republication.

Identification: "Of and Concerning"

The rule is that there must be "certainty as to the person who is defamed, for no innuendo can render certain that which is uncertain."[12] Accordingly, a plaintiff must establish that he or she was the target of the allegedly defamatory communication, known as "colloquium." The absence of colloquium was one of the bases for the Court's overturning an Alabama libel verdict in *Sullivan*. The Court said that a *New York Times* advertisement never identified L.B. Sullivan by name or referred to his position as a Commissioner of Public Affairs. The ad merely described police activities at the Alabama State College campus. Cloaking defamatory statements and descriptions of someone in a Roman à Clef, a novel describing real events and individuals, will not necessarily protect an author from a libel action. As a New York state judged explained in *Carter-Clark v. Random House*, 196 Misc. 2d 1011, 1014 (2003): "For a depiction of a fictional character to constitute actionable defamation, the description of the fictional character must be so closely akin to the real person claiming to be defamed that a reader of the book, knowing the real person, would have no difficulty linking the two. Superficial similarities are insufficient."

Some plaintiffs are "libel-proof," meaning that courts will not recognize their claim or they ultimately cannot win because they are habitual criminals.[13] Typically, such plaintiffs have been convicted of multiple felonies. For plaintiff's whose reputations are tarnished to a limited degree, courts determine their suitability to bring a libel action based on the relationship between the defamatory statements and the plaintiff's prior bad reputation. If the statement is not substantially related to the prior bad reputation, the court is likely to allow the plaintiff to sue.

Also, you cannot libel the dead. In other words, the law does not permit heirs to bring a defamation suit against someone who has defamed their departed loved one.

Group Libel

As early as 1840, courts recognized an exception to the rule that there must be certainty as to the individual targeted, "if the words may by any reasonable application, import a charge against several individuals under some general description or general name, the plaintiff has the right to go on to trial, and it is for the jury to decide, whether the charge has the personal application averred by the plaintiff."[14]

Corporations May Bring Libel Suits

Thirteen states—Alabama, Arizona, Colorado, Florida, Georgia, Idaho, Louisiana, Mississippi, North Dakota, Ohio, Oklahoma, South Dakota, and Texas—also have "product disparagement" laws on the books. Generally, such laws require the following: that the statement be false; that the defendant knew that such a statement was likely to harm the plaintiff's financial interest; that the defendant was motivated by ill will; and that the defendant intended to interfere with the plaintiff's business interests.[15] Defendant Oprah Winfrey famously prevailed in such a law suit in *Texas Beef Group v. Winfrey*, 11 F. Supp. 2d 858 (N.D. Tex. 1998), affirmed 201 F.3d 680 (5th Cir. 2000).

SUMMARY: A plaintiff must establish that the alleged defamatory was published. Publication means that at least one individual other than the plaintiff and the defendant heard, saw, or read the allegedly defamatory comment. Under the republication rule, each repetition of the defamatory statement is a publication, and anyone who repeats the defamatory communication is a publisher of that defamatory statement. Section 230 immunity, however, shields online service providers from the republication liability. A plaintiff must also establish "identification" that he or she is the target of the statements. Identification becomes an issue when the plaintiff is not identified by name, but rather by status, conduct, or implication.

Fault

A plaintiff deemed a public figure must prove that a defendant made defamatory statements with reckless disregard for the truth or knowing falsity, and private figures must show that a defendant made such statements with negligence or gross negligence. The exeption is a private figure suing media outlets for defamatory statements about matters of public concern. Under such circumstances, a private figure plaintiff must prove falsity and recklessness.

Defamation originates in **tort**, a violation of a noncontractual, legally identified duty owed to a plaintiff. Duty, breach, causation, and injury are the traditional elements of a tort claim, and negligence is the most common type of tort. In a negligence action, a plaintiff argues that the defendant failed to exercise the degree of care appropriate for the circumstance, or which a reasonable person with equal experience would have applied. In the past, ordinary care was judged by the "reasonable man standard"—how the typical middle-class white male ought to behave in circumstances in which there was a potential or actual risk of harm to others. By the late 1980s, that standard was replaced by "the reasonable person" standard, and eventually in cases involving sexual harassment, for example, courts are likely to impose a reasonable woman standard.

Next, the plaintiff shows causation, that is, that the defendant's conduct caused the injury. Typically, that means the plaintiff will show that, but for the defendant's conduct, the harm would not have occurred. In contrast, under the doctrine of strict liability, a defendant's effort to exercise the required degree of care is irrelevant. All that matters is that the defendant's act or omission caused the harm. Strict liability creates an incentive for those engaged in highly dangerous activity to take full precautions to avoid harm.

Traditionally, most states held libel defendants to a strict liability standard. The plaintiff did not have to show that the defendant's communication caused harm, only that the allegedly defamatory statement was about him or her, and in most instances damages were presumed. Also, the defendant had the burden of showing that his or her statement was true.

That changed after *New York Times v. Sullivan* and *Gertz v. Robert Welch, Inc.*, 418 U.S. 323 (1974). Today, plaintiffs must show in their complaint, and prove at trial, some degree of wrongful conduct related to the publication of allegedly false defamation—negligence, gross negligence, recklessness, or knowing falsity.

New York Times v. Sullivan requires that elected and some classifications of public officials suing the news media or individuals for libel must prove that the defendant made the defamatory statement with recklessness or knowing falsity. In *Curtis Publishing Co. v. Butts*, 388 U.S. 130 (1967), the Court extended the *New York Times v. Sullivan* test to include criticism of public figures. *Gertz* ruled that limited purpose public figures—private figures that thrust themselves into the vortex of a public controversy—also must meet the recklessness or knowing falsity standard.

Gertz allows states to define for themselves the appropriate liability standard for private individuals who sue for libel, as long as it is not strict liability. As of 1995, thirty-eight states, the District of Columbia, and three other U.S. jurisdictions required private individuals to show negligence to recover against media defendants. Media industry-friendly jurisdictions are likely to impose the gross negligence standard on private individuals. In New York, for instance, a private individual suing for defamation "must establish, by a preponderance of the evidence, that the publisher acted in a grossly irresponsible manner without due consideration for the standards of information gathering and dissemination ordinarily followed by responsible parties."[16]

But the Court later carved out an exception. Under *Dun & Bradstreet Inc. v. Greenmoss Builders, Inc.*, 472 U.S. 749 (1985), when the false and defamatory statements do not involve matters of public concern, a plaintiff does not have to show reckless or knowing falsity to gain presumed or punitive damages.

Also, in *Hutchinson v. Proxmire*, 443 U.S. 111, 133–34 n. 16 (1979), the U.S. Supreme Court has left it up to states to decide whether to apply the recklessness or knowing falsity standard when a public figure sues a private figure. *Gertz*, however, bars states from imposing strict liability in all defamation actions.

Falsity

A plaintiff must show that the statement taken as a whole is false. If the statement is substantially true, the plaintiff has failed to prove its falsity, even though the plaintiff may have proved it false in insignificant details.[17]

Injury and Damages

Courts award **compensatory or general damages** for harm or injury, though the plaintiff provides no evidence of a specific dollar amount such as bills or receipts. In contrast, **special damages** are based on evidence of a specific dollar amount as evidence in bills or receipts. **Punitive damages** are awarded to punish a defendant for extreme carelessness or maliciousness. Nominal damages are typically awarded when a jury believes the harm is negligible.

Plaintiffs must identify the impact of the allegedly defamatory communication and link the impact to the types of damages recognized in the particular jurisdiction—general or compensatory, special, punitive, or nominal . Typically, plaintiffs describe in their complaints how they suffer emotionally and mentally because their friends and business acquaintances shun them, if, for example, one might show unfavorable quotes posted on the plaintiff's Facebook profile, or chart a precipitous drop off in the number of Facebook friends. Of course, monetary loss is persuasive evidence of harm.[18]

Next, the plaintiff pleads for damages. General or actual damages are those that the plaintiff is presumed to have sustained. As noted earlier, plaintiffs alleging libel per se are entitled to general damages. They do not have to provide evidence or proof of monetary loss. Some states allow such plaintiffs to pursue punitive damages to punish the defendants for serious misconduct by showing monetary loss, or other special damages, that is, injuries traceable to the defendant's defamatory statement. Plaintiffs making a case for libel per quod must prove special damages—evidence of economic loss as no damages are presumed. Juries may also award nominal damages when they believe that the harm to the plaintiff was minimal.

SUMMARY: A plaintiff deemed a public figure must prove that a defendant made defamatory statements with reckless disregard for the truth or knowing falsity with clear and convincing evidence, typically a difficult standard to meet. A private figure's task is easier. In most states, the private figure need only show negligence. Some states require a showing of gross negligence. Private figures suing media outlets for defamatory statements about matters of public concern, however, must prove falsity and recklessness.

Plaintiffs must identify the impact of the allegedly defamatory communication and link the impact to the types of damages recognized in the particular jurisdiction—general, compensatory, special, punitive, or nominal. Courts may award compensatory or general damages for injury though the plaintiff shows no fixed exact harm related to the speech. Special damages are based on evidence of specific economic loss. Punitive damages are awarded to punish a defendant for extreme carelessness or maliciousness. Nominal damages are typically awarded when a jury believes the harm is negligible.

Libel Defenses

Libel defendants can avail themselves of federal constitutional, common law, and state statutory privileges and defenses to persuade a judge to render a summary judgment in their favor, thus preventing the lawsuit from going to trial, or to persuade a judge or jury to find in their favor. Just as the plaintiff must persuade a judge at the pre-trial stage that there is a genuine issue of fact to support a trial by a showing evidence to support a libel claim—defamation, publication, identification, fault, and injury—a defendant need only show that there is insufficient evidence to support one of the elements of a libel case to win a summary judgment and have the case dismissed.

Additionally, since *Gertz*, it has been to a defendant's advantage to persuade a judge to designate the plaintiff as a public or limited-purpose public figure rather than a private one. Such a designation will not necessarily get the case dismissed. But, typically, it increases the load on the plaintiff's burden of proving liability because the public figure recklessness and knowing falsity standard is far more difficult to prove than negligence or gross negligence.

And, for media defendants, it does not matter whether the plaintiff is private or public when the defamatory content is political speech or speech of public concern because under *Philadelphia Newspapers, Inc. v. Hepps*, 475 U.S. 767 (1986), private figures suing media outlets for libel have the burden of proving statements false.

Thus, the logical result of *Sullivan*, *Gertz*, and *Hepps* is that "media defendants win a significant number of cases on pre-trial motions as a matter of law," as the Media Law Resource Center noted.[19] The Center points out that even when plaintiffs suing media win—307 of 506 trials (60.7%) between 1980 and 2004—appeals court judges overturned the judgment or reduced the amount of awards in 25.2 percent of those cases.[20]

Negating the Plaintiff's Case

Judges may come to a decision about which party wins a case before the case goes before a jury by reaching a summary judgment. Such a judgment is a decision made when, taking into account all factual inferences in the favor of the party opposing the motion, there exists no genuine issue as to a material fact such that the party asking for the motion deserves judgment as a matter of law. A material fact is one that tends to prove or disprove an element of the claim, or affects the outcome of the lawsuit.[21] Thus, a defendant may prevail on summary judgment by negating one or more of the essential elements of a plaintiff's case—defamation, publication, identification, fault, or harm. Of course, the same defenses can be used during the trial.

In *Anderson v. Liberty Lobby, Inc.*, 477 U.S. 242 (1986), the U.S. Supreme Court held that "the clear-and-convincing standard of proof should be taken into account in ruling on summary judgment" when public figures, elected officials, and many government figures are plaintiffs in libel cases because that is the standard such plaintiffs would have to meet at trial. There isn't uniformity on this procedural approach among the states, though most have accepted the *Anderson* standard. The Court did not mandate that state courts apply the "clear-and-convincing" standard during the pre-trial phase. Texas, among the minority, requires that defendants obtain summary judgment "only if they conclusively negate one of the elements of the plaintiff's claims," as it explained in *Huckabee v. Time Warner Entertainment Co.*, 18 SW 3d 413, 420 (Tex. Supreme Court 2000).

> SUMMARY: Summary judgment will lie when, taking all factual inferences in the favor of the party opposing the motion, there exists no genuine issue as to a material fact such that the party asking for the motion deserves judgment as a matter of law. Thus, a defendant may prevail on summary judgment by negating one or more of the essential elements of a plaintiff's case—defamation, publication, identification, fault, or harm. Of course, the same elements can be used as defenses during the trial.

Truth

In the overwhelming majority of states, truth is the absolute defense against a libel charge. In jurisdictions where truth is an absolute defense, it is well settled "that a defendant is not required…to justify every word of the alleged defamatory matter; it is sufficient if the substance, the gist, the sting of the libelous charge be justified, and if the gist of the charge be established by the evidence the defendant has made his case."[22]

Truth, however, is only the best defense in all the states. As noted earlier, the Fifth Circuit U.S. Court of Appeals interpreted Massachusetts's law as providing plaintiffs with the right to argue that even though a defamatory statement about matters of private concern is true, the defendant communicated it with ill will.[23] This ruling in 2009 caught many lawyers by surprise. Perhaps that is because they, like the Texas Supreme Court in *Casso v. Brand*, 776 SW 2d 551, 558 (Tex: Supreme Court 1989), believed "actual malice, as used in defamation cases, is a term of art which is separate and distinct from traditional common law malice. It does not include ill will, spite or evil motive.…"

In contrast, the authors of *The First Amendment and the Fourth Estate: The Law of Mass Media* noted the following in 2008: "A minority of states have required the truth to have been spoken with 'good motives' or for 'justifiable ends' or both, but in the wake of *Sullivan* and its progeny, such requirements are not constitutional—at least where issues of public concern are involved."[24] As noted in Chapter 5, where courts' definitions of reckless disregard are discussed, most jurisdictions do not permit juries to determine recklessness based solely on ill will, but will allow them to consider evidence of it. As for the plaintiff in *Noonan v. Staples, Inc.*, D.C. Mass, No. 06–10716, he was an employee of Staples, the office supply chain. He claimed that he had been defamed by an email broadcast that contained truthful accusations against him. He lost at trial.

Fair Comment and Criticism

Many states afford individuals qualified immunity from libel actions when they voice their opinions about matters of public concern including conduct of political candidates, policies and activities of prominent social institutions, corporations that affect the public welfare, and any communications submitted to the public for its approval such as plays, books, and advertisements. But such comments are generally accorded the qualified privilege only when they are (i) a comment, (ii) based on true facts, and (iii) the commenter makes them without implying or saying that the plaintiff is corrupt or dishonorable.

Constitutional

A statement that is truly an opinion is not actionable. That is because "there is no such thing as a false idea. However pernicious an opinion may seem, we depend for its correction not on the conscience of judges and juries but on the competition of other ideas," Justice Lewis F. Powell said in *Gertz v. Welch*, 418 U.S. 323, 339–340 (1974). If there is a reasonable possibility that challenged statements are not assertions of facts, a defendant will try to persuade a judge or a jury that such statements are protected under the opinion defense. Accordingly, the courts have created two doctrinal tests to distinguish protected statements deemed opinion or hyperbole—not to be taken literally—from actionable statements asserting facts.

First, the U.S. Court of Appeals for the District of Columbia's fashioned the four-factor *Ollman* test in *Ollman v. Evans*, 750 F.2d 970 (D.C. Cir. 1984; cert denied 471 US 1127, May 28, 1985), to assess whether the average juror should view a defamatory statement as opinion or a statement of fact: (1) Whether the statement has a precise common usage or meaning; (2) Can the statement be proved true or false; (3) The context of the statement; (4) The genre, setting, or format in which the statement was conveyed.

The U.S. Supreme Court, however, devised a different test in *Milkovich v. Lorraine Journal*, 497 U.S. 1 (1990). In contrast, *Milkovich* held that where a statement of opinion about public matters reasonably implies false and defamatory facts regarding public figures or officials, such plaintiffs must show that statements were made with knowledge of their false implications or with reckless disregard of their truth. Under *Milkovich*, there is no clear line separating defamatory factual statements from defamatory opinion, no "artificial dichotomy between 'opinion' and 'fact.'"[25]

Consequently, just because a defamatory statement is labeled "opinion," or found in a newspaper opinion column, does not protect the speaker from a libel action. Thus, the fourth leg of the *Ollman* test—"the broader context or setting in which the statement appears"—is irrelevant under *Milkovich*, or should be. The determinative question under *Milkovich* is similar to the second factor in *Ollman:* Is the statement capable of being objectively characterized as true or false? In other words, does a statement imply knowledge of facts that can be proved false even though it appears to be a subjective opinion?

Consequently, to state a defamation claim that survives a First Amendment challenge, a plaintiff must present evidence of a statement of fact that is provably false. And under *Milkovich*, when statements do not imply a verifiably false factual assertion, they also can fall under the category of loose figurative language or rhetorical hyperbole because the average person does not take their meaning to be literal descriptions. Earlier, in *Greenbelt Cooperative Publishing Assn., Inc. v. Bresler*, 398 U.S. 6 (1970), the Court ruled that rhetorical hyperbole was protected under the First Amendment.

On its face, it would seem as though the *Milkovich* test supersedes the *Ollman* test. The *Milkovich* court even expressly rejected the *Lorain Journal* newspaper's argument that it endorse "another First-Amendment-based protection for defamatory statements which are categorized as 'opinion' as opposed to 'fact,'" explaining that it did not think the *Gertz* dictum "was intended to create a wholesale defamation exemption for anything that might be labeled 'opinion.'"[26] But some federal and state courts still rely on *Ollman*'s "totality of the circumstances" analysis. Those courts apply that test as part of the Milkovich analysis, and still others apply *Ollman*-like factors based on their own state constitutions. Accordingly, defendants in libel cases, depending on the jurisdiction, may rely on the indicia of the *Ollman*'s four-factor test to evaluate the totality of the circumstances "in assessing whether the average reader would view the statement as fact or, conversely, opinion": [27]

> (i)…the common usage or meaning of the specific language of the challenged statement itself. Our analysis of the specific language under scrutiny will be aimed at determining whether the statement has a precise core of meaning for which a consensus of understanding exists or, conversely, whether the statement is indefinite and ambiguous…the statement's verifiability (ii)…the entire article or column, for example—inasmuch as other, unchallenged language surrounding the allegedly defamatory statement will influence the average reader's readiness to infer that a particular statement has factual content…(iii) the broader context or setting in which the statement appears…(iv) widely varying social conventions which signal to the reader the likelihood of a statement's being either fact or opinion.[28]

In the abstract, the *Ollman* test is more protective of a defendant's free speech interest than the *Milkovich* test. That difference is largely attributable to the broader context factor that allows judges or jurors to consider whether the statement appeared in an editorial, opinion column, or a sports broadcast, to name a few contexts in which the expression of opinion is assumed. Yet, weighing the broader context doesn't always tip the scale in the defendant's favor. *In the Matter of Liskula Cohen* v. *Google*, a judge applied a New York three-part test similar to *Ollman*'s, including "whether either the full context of the communication in which the statement appears or the broader social context and surrounding circumstances are such as to signal readers or listeners that what is being read or heard is likely to be opinion, not fact." As discussed earlier, the judge found that "skank" was not protected under the opinion defense based on a dictionary definition and the sexually provocative photographs that also appeared on the blog. It should be noted that New York law provides an exception to the opinion defense. An accusation of criminal activity, even in the form of opinion, is not constitutionally protected.[30]

In contrast, a California appeals court in *Seelig v. Infinity Broadcasting Corp.*, 119 Cal. Rptr. 2d 108 (2002), applied the *Milkovich* test and found the word "skank" hyperbolic and protected under the opinion defense. The judge ruled that the word was too vague, "a derogatory slang term of recent vintage that has no generally recognized meaning."[31] The judge also noted that the plaintiff failed to provide an accepted dictionary definition for the term "skank."

Could that have been all that distinguished the *Cohen* analysis from *Seelig*? No. Though the court grounded its analysis in *Milkovich* and never mentioned *Ollman*, it explicitly applied an *Ollman* "totality of the circumstances" test based on California state precedent,[32] taking into account the context of the irreverent and hyperbolic language of the morning radio talk program where the statement was voiced.[33]

Retraction

Some jurisdictions allow media outlets to limit the amount and types of damages that can be awarded against them by issuing a retraction or correction of the allegedly false and defamatory statement. Some jurisdictions require plaintiffs to request a retraction or correction. A retraction should not repeat the offending statement. It should be given the same play as the original statement, and be issued in a timely manner.

Statute of Limitations

Courts will not entertain a libel, or any other civil or criminal action for that matter, except murder in the first degree, after the statute of limitations runs, or expires. Each state has its own statute of limitations, and for libel the time that a plaintiff has to bring a libel action ranges from one to three years. The clock starts running on the plaintiff when the defamatory statement is published, i.e, when a third party hears or reads the statement.

The Single Publication Rule

In most states, the publication of a single issue of a newspaper, a book, or magazine marks the start of the statute of limitations for the communication, even though that publication consists of thousands of copies. It is sometimes referred to as the "one publication which gives rise to one cause of action" rule. Therefore, republication of that issue does not give rise to a new cause of action under libel. If such a limitation did not exist, a plaintiff may sue multiple times for a book that continues to circulate. If another entity republishes the defamatory communication, or if the communication is published in what constitutes a new edition, the single publication rule does not apply.

But what about republication on the Internet? Most states have applied the rule to Internet postings. As an example, in *Firth v. State of New York*, 775 NE 463 (NY: Court of Appeals 2d 2002), an appeals court ruled that a modification of a web posting does not constitute republication of defamatory communication.

Wire Service Defense

In states that have recognized this defense, a news outlet is not required to verify the facts of a story provided to it by a "reputable news-gathering agency." The rationale behind the defense, the Michigan

Court of Appeals explained in *Howe v. Detroit Free Press, Inc.*, 555 NW 2d 738, 741 (1996), "is that no local news organization could assume the burden of verifying every news item reported to it by established news-gathering agencies and continue to satisfy the demands of modern society for up-to-the-minute global information." The news outlet, however, is obligated to know that the service is reputable, check the wire service story for inconsistencies, and must not publish if it knows the story to be false or is aware of inconsistencies.

Breaking News Defense

In evaluating whether news media defendants behaved recklessly, jurors may take into account whether the news report was "breaking news." In other words, jurors will be asked to consider the nature of the story in question and the time constraints imposed on the news outlet to report the story.[34]

Defenses: Anti-Slapp Laws

In 1989, law professor George W. Pring identified an explosion of litigation that he called, "strategic lawsuits against public participation" or SLAPP, which started after 1970. Plaintiffs who filed SLAPPs, he discovered, did not really intend to win their lawsuits. Rather their goal was to silence critics with the threat of the costly burden of defending themselves in a civil action: "The apparent goal of SLAPPs is to stop citizens from exercising their political rights or to punish them for having done so. SLAPPs send a clear message: that there is a 'price' for speaking out politically. The price is a multimillion-dollar lawsuit and the expenses, lost resources, and emotional stress such litigation brings."[35]

In response, states passed anti-SLAPP protection laws. According to The Legal Project, as of January 2009, 29 states had anti-SLAPP statutes.[36] Those statutes may allow, among other things, a defendant to request the dismissal of a libel lawsuit because under certain circumstances a libel lawsuit may be nothing more than a SLAPP. But few states are like California and Indiana, where the anti-SLAPP statute is applicable to news reporting and editorial content. In those two states, the anti-SLAPP statutes provide protection against lawsuits that chill the valid exercise of free speech on public issues. In contrast, most other states provide protection for a limited range of political speech and activities, such as comments on applications of zoning permits and a homeowner's right to petition government.

SUMMARY: A defendant may prevail in a libel action by negating one or more of the essential elements of a plaintiff's case, and by employing the truth, fair comment and criticism, opinion and hyperbole, the expiration of the Statute of Limitations, single publication, wire service, or breaking news defenses. Truth is not an absolute defense; it is, however, the best defense. And under the Court's ruling in *Milkovich v. Lorain Journal Co.*, 497 U.S. 1 (1990), a defendant arguing that an allegedly defamatory statement is a protected opinion must show that it does not imply knowledge of facts that can be proved false, even though it appears to be an opinion. *Milkovich* also provides a defense for hyperbole, language that is exaggerated and figurative which no reasonable person would understand as stating facts.

Privileges to Defamation

It has been long recognized under common law that an open society is served well by allowing individuals to make defamatory statements in certain venues and under conditions without fear of legal liability. The defense or privilege rests upon the idea that conduct which otherwise would be actionable is immunized from legal liability because society in general benefits. As an example, *Sullivan* created a constitutional privilege. The privilege allows those who criticize government and elected officials to make minor or inconsequential factual errors in stories they believed to be true. Society benefits because news outlets and citizens are more likely to publicize alleged corruption by elected and government officials and openly discuss government policies and practices with little fear that a misstatement will subject them to an expensive libel suit. Before *Sullivan*, the Constitution, as well as federal and state common law, allowed similar immunities.

Absolute Immunity

Under the U. S. Const., Art. I, § 6., statements by members of both Houses of Congress communicated in "any speech, debate, vote, report, or action done in session" is shielded from liability.[37] Federal judges, officers of judicial branch and branches related to the judicial process, and the Postmaster General also enjoy absolute immunity from libel liability.[38]

Absolute Immunity: Consent

A defendant may successfully argue that a plaintiff in a libel action gave the defendant permission to share defamatory statements with third parties. In other words, the plaintiff implicitly or explicitly consented that defamatory statements about him or her would be or were likely to be shared. Such situations often develop from an employer-employee relationship as occurred in *Baker v. Lafayette College*, 350 Pa. Superior Ct. 68 (1986), in which an assistant professor sued claiming that statements in his performance evaluations were defamatory. Baker asked the court to look at the alleged inaccuracy and biasness of the evaluations. The Pennsylvania appeals court, however, said Baker's argument failed "because it is inconsistent with the nature of an absolute privilege…The courts of our sister states…have consistently held that consensual publications are absolutely privileged and that the absolute character of the privilege forbids inquiry into ill will, negligence or actual malice (knowledge of or recklessness as to falsity)."[39]

Absolute Immunity: Political Broadcasts

Section 315 of the Federal Communications Act requires radio broadcasters to provide reasonable access to political candidates and the broadcasters cannot censor candidates' comments. If such candidates libel someone, broadcasters enjoy absolute immunity from libel, the U.S. Supreme Court ruled in *Farmers Educational and Co-op. Union of America, North Dakota Div. v. WDAY, Inc.*, 360 U.S. 525 (1959).

Qualified Privilege: Fair Report

As early as the 1890s, state courts recognized a qualified privilege for news reporters and citizens to inform about what went on in judicial, legislative, and other public proceedings. In states that recognized the fair report privilege, a defendant will be protected from a libel suit when he or she (i) accurately quotes and describes with neutrality and balance, and (ii) properly attributes statements from (iii) an official public document, or statements made by a public official on a public matter. Such reports do not have to be comprehensive; they may be a summary, as are most news reports. The defendant carries the burden of showing that the privilege applies to the defamatory communication.

Qualified Privilege: Neutral Reportage

In *Edwards v. Audubon Society*, 556 F.2d 113 (2d Cir. 1977), the U.S. Court of Appeals for the Second Circuit established a First Amendment privilege for reporting that differs from the fair report privilege in the following way: The neutral reportage privilege is not tied to public proceedings or documents. Rather, it requires that when responsible individuals or groups make accusations against public officials, figures, or organizations involved in newsworthy public controversies, a reporter who quotes, paraphrases and summarizes those statements will be protected so long as the news account is accurate, balanced, and neutral. The reporter is not required to verify the accuracy of the accusation. As of 2006, 17 jurisdictions adopted the privilege and 13 rejected it.[40] The U.S. Supreme Court has declined to address the constitutionality of the neutral report privilege, most recently in *Norton v. Glenn*, 860 A. 2d 48 (PA: Supreme Ct. 2004) (cert. denied March 28, 2005). In that ruling, the Pennsylvania court held that neither federal nor state constitutions mandated that the court adopt the neutral reportage privilege.

Qualified Privilege: § 230 the Communications Decency Act of 1996.

Because Congress believed that online service providers would be reluctant to allow individuals to use the blogs, chat rooms, and bulletin boards that online companies provide, it chose to grant such entities immunity from libel suits stemming from the comments made by individuals. Some argue that social media networks such as Facebook and Twitter would not have been developed out of fear that the cost of policing the defamatory comments of millions of daily users would have been prohibitive. Section 230(c) provides: "No provider or user of an interactive computer service shall be treated as the publisher or speaker of any information provided by another information content provider." Online service providers are immune even when they exercise editorial control, unless they alter the meaning of the content because § 230 (2)(a) provides: "No provider or user of an interactive computer service shall be held liable on account of—(A) any action voluntarily taken in good faith to restrict access to or availability of material that the provider or user considers to be obscene, lewd, lascivious, filthy, excessively violent, harassing, or otherwise objectionable, whether or not such material is constitutionally protected."

SUMMARY: Statutes and common law accord speakers communicating during or about certain types of public forums—typically legislative, judicial, and other official proceedings—an absolute privilege to speak without fear that their comments will subject them to libel actions. The law grants the privilege to foster free-flowing discussion about important public matters. For example, members of Congress, federal judges, and the Post Master enjoy absolute immunity when speaking in their official capacities. Also, plaintiffs who have implicitly or explicitly given permission to use their statements cannot sue that individual or institution for libel.

News reporters and others benefit from the qualified fair and neutral report privileges. The fair report privilege provides that a defendant will be protected from a libel suit when he or she (i) accurately quotes and describes with neutrality and balance, and (ii) properly attributes statements from (iii) an official public document, or statements made by a public official on a public matter. The neutral report privilege provides that when responsible individuals or groups make accusations against public officials, figures, or organizations involved in newsworthy public controversies, a reporter who quotes, paraphrases, and summarizes those statements will be protected so long as the news account is accurate, balanced, and neutral. Section 230 of the Communications Decency Act of 1996 creates a qualified priviledge for online publishers. They are not responsible for libelous postings of others unless the publisher excercises editorial control over the content.

ONLINE RESOURES

1. "Defamation," Citizen Media Law Project, http://www.citmedialaw.org/legal-guide/defamation
2. "The First Amendment Handbook," Reporter's Committee for Freedom of the Press, http://www.rcfp.org/first-amendment-handbook/1-libel
3. "Frequently Asked Media Law Questions," Media Law Resource Center, http://www.medialaw.org/Content/NavigationMenu/Public_Resources/Libel_FAQs/Libel_FAQs.htm

QUESTIONS

1. Which of the following statements should be considered libelous per se or libelous per quod and why:
   a. Rush Limbaugh is a big fat idiot.
   b. Dr. Sanjay Gupta, CNN's medical reporter and practicing neurosurgeon, is not qualified to be a "certified medical examiner" as CNN claims.
   c. CNN's charismatic Anderson Cooper and his boyfriend, club owner Ben Maisani, turned up at the gayest party in town on Wednesday night.
   d. Unfortunately, former NBA player Joe Dunk's successes on the court couldn't stop him from losing career earnings worth $120 million, including over $4 million for a corporate jet that was grounded just months after he bought it.
2. Which of the following statements would be protected under the *Milkovich* opinion defense:

a. In my opinion, the football coach is a tyrant.

b. It's reasonable to assume that Fred Smith is nuts.

c. Everyone knows that Kristen Smith cannot be trusted.

d. Rush Limbaugh is a big fat idiot.

3. Would the following statement be protected under fair comment and criticism immunity: "The author's account of several events are so erroneous that it reminds this critic why the author is widely considered an untrustworthy scoundrel."

ENDNOTES

1. See *Estate of Richard Jewell v. Cox Enterprises*, A11A0510 (2011).
2. Jewell died in 2007. Though one cannot libel the dead, Jewell was alive when the defamatory statement was published. Thus, his family was allowed to continue the lawsuit.
3. "Criminalizing Speech about Reputation:The Legacy of Criminal Libel in the U.S. after Sullivan & Garrison," Media Law Resource Center (January 2003), http://www.medialaw.org/Template.cfm?Section=News& Template=/ContentManagement/ContentDisplay.cfm&ContentID=699
4. See *Lieberman v. Fieger*, 338 F.3d 1076 (9th Cir. 2003).
5. "Civil Jury Instructions, Damages for Libel/Slander Per Se, 3.11–8," State of Connecticut Judicial Branch (January 2008), http://www.jud.ct.gov/ji/Civil/part3/3.11–8.htm
6. *Yonaty v. Mincolla*, 97 A.D.3d 141, 945 N.Y.S.2d 774, 779 (2012).
7. *In the Matter of Liskula Cohen v. Google, Inc., and Blogger.com*, 887 N.Y.S.2d 424, 428–429 (NY: Supreme Court, Aug. 17, 2009).
8. *Bryson v. News America Publications, Inc.* 672 NE 2d 1207, 1217 (1996).
9. *Tolley v. Fry & Sons, Ltd.* 1 K.B. 467, 479 (1930).
10. See *McKinney v. County of Santa Clara*, 110 Cal.App.3d 787 (1980) for discussion of the two exceptions to this rule.
11. W. Page Keeton (Ed.). *Prosser and Keeton on the Law of Torts*. St. Paul, MN: West Publishing (1984), 799.
12. *Schoenfeld v. Journal Co.*, 235 N.W. 442 (1931).
13. *Cardillo v. Doubleday & Co.*, Inc., 518 F.2d 638 (2d Cir. 1975).
14. *Ryckman v. Delavan*, 25 Wend. 186, 202 (N.Y. 1840).
15. *Restatement of Torts (Second)* § 626, Disparagement of Property in Quality of Land, Chattels, and Intangible Things.
16. *Chapadeau v. Utica Observer*, 38 NY 2d 196, 199 (1975).
17. *Letter Carriers v. Austin*, 418 U.S. 264 (1974).
18. See *Gertz v. Robert Welch, Inc.*, 323, 348–350 (1974).
19. "American Libel Trials: A Short Primer for Canadian Practitioners," Media Law Resource Center (May 12–13, 2005), 1, http://www.medialaw.org/Content/.../About.../AmericanLibelTrialsAPrimer.pdf
20. Ibid.
21. *Anderson v. Liberty Lobby, Inc.*, 477 U.S. 242, 248 (1986).
22. *Kurata v. Los Angeles News Publishing Co.*, 4 Cal. App. 2d 224, 227–228 (1935).
23. *Noonan v. Staples*, 556 F. 20, 26 (1 Cir. 2009).
24. T. Baron Carter, Marc A. Franklin, and Jay B. Wright. *The First Amendment and the Fourth Estate: The Law of Mass Media*. New York: Thomson Reuters/Foundation Press (2008), 99.
25. Milkovich, 497 U.S. at 19.
26. *Milkovich v. Lorraine Journal*, 497 U.S. 1, 18 (1990).
27. *Ollman v. Evans*, 750 F.2d 970, 979 (D.C. Cir. 1984) (cert denied 471 U.S. 1127, May 28, 1985).
28. Ibid. 979.
29. Milkovich, 497 U.S. at 19.
30. *Hoffman v. Landers*, 146 A.D.2d 744, 746 (NY. 2d Dept. 1989).
31. *Seelig v. Infinity Broadcasting Corp.*, 119 Cal. Rptr. 2d 108, 118 (2002).

32. Ibid. 117.

33. Ibid. 118.

34. *Curtis Publishing v. Butts*, 388 U.S. 130 (1967); *Tavoulareas v. Piro*, 817 F.2d 762 (D.C. Cir. 1985), cert. denied 484 U.S. 870) (1987).

35. George W. Pring. "SLAPPs: Strategic Lawsuits against Public Participation," 7 Pace Environmental Law Review 5–6 (1989).

36. Jacqueline Kline. "Anti-SLAPP Statutes in the US by State," (January 14, 2009), http://www.legal-project.org/149/anti-slapp-statutes-in-the-us-by-state

37. *Kilbourn v. Thompson*, 103 U.S. 168 (1881).

38. *Barr v. Matteo*, 360 U.S. 564, 570 (1959).

39. *Baker v. Lafayette College*, 350 Pa. Superior Ct. 68, 74 (1986).

40. Jennifer J. Ho. Annotation, Construction and Application of the Neutral Reportage Privilege, 13 A.L.R.6th 111 (2006).

CHAPTER FIVE

Defamation

Constitutional and Cyber Law

CONTROVERSY: In late August 2008, two individuals who worked in the modeling profession in New York told Liskula Cohen about what they had read on a blog, "Skanks in NYC." They told Cohen, a former *Vogue* model, that an anonymous blogger had described her as a "psychotic, lying, whoring skank I would have to say that the first place award for 'Skankiest in NYC' would have to go to Liskula Gentile Cohen." The anonymous blogger also called her a "ho," an "old hag," and a "fortysomething" who "may have been hot 10 years ago," among other disparaging remarks.

Cohen, 36 at that time, petitioned a New York state court for pre-action discovery from Google, Inc., in January 2009 so that she could sue the anonymous blogger for libel. (Blogger.com, where the comments were posted, is a subsidiary of Google.) Google grumbled a bit; it said it would not comply unless a judge ordered it to do so. Eventually, a judge ordered the search engine company to out the blogger. Before that occurred, the still-anonymous blogger removed the postings, and, through an attorney, argued that she had not defamed Cohen. That August, however, the judge, persuaded that an average person would find the words in question defamatory and that Cohen had established a strong enough case to go to trial, ordered Google to comply.[1]

Later that month, Cohen dropped her $3 million libel suit against the blogger Rosemary Port. Meanwhile, Port's vow to sue Google for allegedly breaching its fiduciary duty to protect her anonymity has yet to materialize.

Chapter's Scope

In the previous chapter, you learned that the landmark First Amendment and libel ruling *New York Times Co. v. Sullivan*, 376 U.S. 254 (1964), reconfigured the libel landscape in the U.S. This chapter explains why the Court chose to change libel law by expanding protections for news outlets against libel actions in *New York Times Co. v. Sullivan* and its progeny, most notably in *Gertz v. Robert Welch, Inc.*, 418 U.S. 323, 345 (1972), and in *Philadelphia Newspapers, Inc. v. Hepps*, 475 U.S. 767 (1986). The chapter also addresses two areas of law arising from libel in cyberspace. Cyberspace law in the U.S. requires plaintiffs like Cohen to lift additional heavy burdens: they must first persuade a judge to order intermediaries like Google, which enjoy immunity from libel suits under Section 230 of the Communications Decency Act of 1996, to identify anonymous defamers who enjoy qualified First Amendment protection. Cyberspace also has created new personal jurisdiction concerns. Traditionally, courts impose personal jurisdiction—their authority to rule on a lawsuit—based on whether a substantial number of copies of an allegedly defamatory statement are regularly sold and distributed in their state or nation, or whether the defendant conducts substantial business in their jurisdiction. On what basis does a New York court, for example, have the authority to impose its judgment on a website operating out of California? Can courts in foreign nations impose their jurisdiction on libel defendants who upload content only in the U.S.? So far, federal appeals courts and Congress have offered only some solutions for these new personal jurisdictional concerns.

New York Times v. Sullivan, 376 U.S. 254 (1964). The Civil Rights public protest movement was in its fifth year when four black students from North Carolina A&T College reinvigorated it on February 1, 1960. The students tried to obtain service at a segregated Woolworth's lunch counter in Greensboro, N.C., and triggered a wave of student sit-ins and protests throughout the South. On March 19, 1960, the *New York Times* ran a paid advertisement, "Heed Their Rising Voices," that applauded the student protests.

"As the whole world knows by now, thousands of Southern Negro students are engaged in widespread nonviolent demonstrations in positive affirmation of the right to live in human dignity as guaranteed by the U.S. Constitution and the Bill of Rights," read the first paragraph of the advertisement endorsed by former First Lady Eleanor Roosevelt, baseball star Jackie Robinson, Martin Luther King Jr. and Hollywood stars Marlon Brando and Harry Belafonte, among others. But the drafters of the advertisement made erroneous statements, accusing "southern violators" and police in Montgomery, Alabama, of misdeeds and crimes in the third and fifth paragraphs of the 723-word statement.

Approximately 394 copies of the March 19, 1960, edition circulated in Alabama, and only about 35 were distributed in Montgomery County. As discussed in the section "Identification: 'Of and Concerning'" in the previous chapter, the ad did not identify L.B. Sullivan by name or by his governmental title. Yet, Sullivan sued in Alabama court, winning a $500,000 damage award, quite a large sum for that period.

Like most states, Alabama made a defendant strictly liable for false defamatory statements; it did not matter that the false statements were minor and that the gist of the ad taken as a whole was true. All Sullivan had to prove was that the *New York Times* published the ad, that it was about him, and it contain factual errors, even insignificant ones. The Alabama Supreme Court affirmed the verdict as consistent with its state law and rejected the *New York Times'* argument that the First Amendment protected the ad.

The U.S. Supreme Court unanimously overturned the verdict, and created a constitutional privilege for defamatory statements, requiring elected and government officials to prove reckless disregard for the truth or knowing falsity with clear and convincing evidence to warrant an award of damages. In reaching its decision, the Court also established that punitive damages cannot be based on negligence or presumed when public officials sue for defamatory statements concerning their public conduct. The plaintiff must prove reckless disregard for the truth or knowing falsity to win punitive damages. The First Amendment protects paid political advertisements, the Court said, setting a foundation for expanding First Amendment protection for advertising (see Chapter 15). The Court shifted the the the burden of proof to elected and government officials in libel suits in which public officials sue for defamatory statements concerning their public conduct. Lastly, the Court repudiated the Sedition Act of 1798.

Sullivan is landmark because it established a precedent that substantially changed libel law—it overturned 175 years of libel law—and crystallized our understanding of the First Amendment's role in protecting and promoting the press as a forum for discussion and debate of public affairs and as a watchdog of official public conduct. As Justice Brennan put it: "Thus, we consider this case against the background of a profound national commitment to the principle that debate on public issues should be uninhibited, robust, and wide-open, and that it may well include vehement, caustic, and sometimes unpleasantly sharp attacks on government and public officials."[2] Why allow news outlets to get away with factual errors? Because, as Brennan explained, "erroneous statement is inevitable in free debate, and that it must be protected if the freedoms of expression are to have the 'breathing space' that they 'need…to survive' . . ."[3]

Beyond the text of the opinion, *Sullivan* and its progeny helped to spur the boom in investigative reporting in the 1970s and 1980s because journalists had less concern that getting minor facts wrong in a story would lead to massive monetary damages against them and their employers. On the other hand, many have argued that *Sullivan* and its progeny have encouraged dubious and sloppy practices among journalists covering elected officials and public figures.

Defining "Actual Malice": Reckless Disregard for the Truth Standard

In *St. Amant v. Thompson*, 390 U.S. 727, 730–731 (1968), the Court said that reckless disregard "cannot be fully encompassed in one infallible definition. Inevitably its outer limits will be marked out through case-by-case adjudication, as is true with so many legal standards for judging concrete cases, whether the standard is provided by the Constitution, statutes, or case law." Truer words, as they say, were never spoken. What follows are definitions of the fault standard offered by the Court, federal appeals courts, and one state court. Notice that federal courts have not eliminated consideration of the pre-*Sullivan* meaning of **actual malice** when determining whether a defendant's defamatory statement was made with reckless disregard for the truth.

In *Garrison v. Louisiana*, 379 U.S. 64, 74, 79 (1964), the Court said a plaintiff must show that a false statement was made with a "high degree of awareness of…probable falsity." *Curtis Publishing Co. v. Butts*, 388 U.S. 130, 153 (1967), states that evidence of either deliberate falsification or reckless publication "despite the publisher's awareness of probable falsity" is essential to recovery by public officials in defamation actions. In *St. Amant v. Thompson*, 390 U.S. 727, 731–732 (1968), the Court said a defendant must be shown to have "entertained serious doubts as to the truth of his publication." A federal court ruled in *Tavoulareas v. Piro*, 817 F.2d 762, 795 (D.C. Cir.1987) (en banc), that evidence of ill will, combined with other circumstantial evidence indicating that the defendant acted with either reckless disregard of the truth, may support a finding of actual malice. In *Harte-Hanks Communications, Inc. v. Connaughton*, 491 U.S. 657, 667 (1989), the Court said, "It also is worth emphasizing that the actual malice standard is not satisfied merely through a showing of ill will or 'malice' in the ordinary sense of the term." The *Harte-Hanks Communications* Court also said that profit motive and ethical lapses are insufficient evidence for a finding of knowing or reckless falsity. The Court, however, noted, "Although courts must be careful not to place too much reliance on such factors, a plaintiff is entitled to prove the defendant's state of mind through circumstantial evidence...*and it cannot be said that evidence concerning motive or care never bears any relation to the actual malice inquiry* [emphasis added]."[4]

In *Masson v. The New Yorker, Inc.*, 501 U.S. 496, 517 (1991), the Court held that "...a deliberate alteration of the words uttered by a plaintiff does not equate with knowledge of falsity for purposes of *New York Times Co. v. Sullivan*...unless the alteration results in a material change in the meaning conveyed by the statement." In *Dunn v. Air Line Pilots Association*, 193 F.3d 1185, 1198 n. 17 (11th Cir.1999), a court noted that "Ill-will, improper motive or personal animosity plays no role in determining whether a defendant acted with 'actual malice.'" In *Huckabee v. Time Warner Entertainment Co.*, 19 SW 3d 413 (Tex: Supreme Court 2000), a state court ruled that, "Actual malice in a defamation case is a term of art. Unlike common-law malice, it does not include ill-will, spite, or evil motive...Rather, to establish actual malice, a plaintiff must prove that the defendant made the statement 'with knowledge that it was false or with reckless disregard of whether it was true or not.'"

SUMMARY: *New York Times v. Sullivan*, 376 U.S. 254 (1964), reshaped the libel landscape in the U.S. Before *Sullivan*, defendants in libel cases did not enjoy First Amendment protection, though they may have been able to invoke state-provided free press and free speech guarantees. Typically, under state laws, defendant news outlets could be found liable for criticism of public officials based on trivial errors or misstatements, even though the gist of the news account was accurate. Now, government officials and public figures have to show with convincing clarity that the news outlet knew its report was false or produced it with reckless disregard for the truth. The *Sullivan* Court also included "actual malice" as part of the fault standard. But actual malice, a term of art taken from common law that connotes ill will or spite, is problematic because, for one thing, a news story can be accurate and truthful, but an advocacy or investigative reporter is often motivated by contempt or vendetta. Accordingly, in *Harte-Hanks Communications, Inc. v. Connaughton*, 491 U.S. 657, 667 (1989), the Court said, "Juries may consider evidence concerning motive or care but '[a]ctual malice may not be inferred alone from evidence of personal spite, ill will or intention to injure on the part of the writer.'"

Gertz v. Robert Welch, Inc., *418 U.S. 323, 345 (1972), Plaintiff Status and Fault.*

In *Gertz*, the Court, 5–4, held that a private person does not have to show recklessness or knowing falsity to recover damages in libel even when the defamatory content concerns matters of public controversy. As discussed earlier, private figures are required to show negligence, in some jurisdictions gross negligence. The private individual is limited to recovery of compensation for actual injury, loss of revenues or a job, or mental anguish or suffering. Regardless of whether a plaintiff is a public or private figure, punitive or presumed damages can be recovered only if recklessness or knowing falsehood is proved.

Some background and context: *Sullivan*, of course, required that public officials suing for defamatory statements about their public conduct had to show reckless disregard or knowing falsity. The Court in *Rosenblatt v. Baer*, 383 U.S. 75 (1966), limited the scope of public officials for libel purposes to government employees who have control over government affairs and policy. In other words, a police commissioner is a public official in the libel context. Typically, a police officer on the beat would not be deemed a public figure because he or she does not ordinarily have control over government affairs and policy. In *Rosenblatt*, the Court also said plaintiffs must meet the reckless or knowing falsehood standard when the defamatory statements pertain to matters of public concern; even private persons must meet that standard. The Court in *Curtis Publishing Co. v. Butts*, 388 U.S. 130 (1967), said public figures—celebrities—also must show recklessness and knowing falsity.

Gertz, however, rejected the plurality opinion of *Rosenblatt* that relied on the "public concern concept," which states that all plaintiffs must prove recklessness-or-knowing-falsity when the defamatory statements are about public matters. There was no majority ruling in *Rosenbloom*. Eight justices voiced their views in five opinions. No opinion received more than three votes. Thus, *Rosenblatt* provided poor guidance for lower courts. In contrast, *Gerz* said private individuals should not have to meet the *Sullivan* test because, unlike public officials and public figures, they have little or no access to counter false statements through the news media and they have not voluntarily sought public office or involvement in public affairs and controversies. Thus, *Gertz* established four classifications of libel plaintiffs: (i) public officials, (ii) all-purpose public figures, (iii) limited-purpose public figures, and (iv) private persons. As noted earlier, it is to a plaintiff's advantage to have a judge declare him or her a private figure because the standard of fault—typically negligence—is easier to meet than recklessness or knowing falsity. Trial judges designate whether a plaintiff is a public or private figure and appeals court may scrutinize such classifications.

Public Official

Of course, no elected official can be deemed private, though some appointed officials and employees might fall into the class of private figure for libel purposes. According to *Rosenblatt v. Baer*, 383 U.S. 75, 85 (1966), "It is clear…the 'public official' designation applies at the very least to those among the hierarchy of government employees who have, or appear to the public to have, substantial responsibility for or control over the conduct of governmental affairs."

All-Purpose Public Figure

Gertz defined the all-purpose public figure as one who has achieved pervasive fame or notoriety in a particular community, or in a larger geographical scope. The widely cited D.C. Circuit Court of Appeals' ruling in *Waldbaum v. Fairchild Publications*, Inc., 627 F.2d 1287, (D.C. Cir.1980), is perhaps most useful in illustrating the full scope of the all-purpose public figure. The plaintiff, Eric Waldbaum, had been president and CEO of Greenbelt Consumer Services, Inc., the second-largest consumer cooperative in the U.S., until his dismissal in 1976. Waldbaum sued Fairchild Publications, the publisher of *Supermarket News*, which had published a five-sentence article that said Greenbelt had "been losing money the last year and retrenching." Waldbaum appealed a summary judgment that said he was a limited-purpose public figure, and the D.C. Circuit affirmed. The Circuit explained that an all-purpose public figure is a celebrity, a person the public follows with great interrerst, and one who has access to the news media if defamed. Courts and jurors, the D.C. Circuit said, may look to several factors to weigh whether a plaintiff is an all-purpose public figure: statistical surveys that concern the plaintiff's name recognition, previous press coverage, or whether the plaintiff shapes public opinion.

Limited-Purpose Public Figure

There is no firm line drawn for determining when an otherwise private individual steps over into the category of plaintiff who will have to meet the *Sullivan* fault standard. But there is a guideline: the plaintiff who has thrust himself or herself into the vortex of a public controversy. In determining that Waldbaum was a limited-purpose public figure, the D.C. Circuit in *Waldbaum v. Fairchild Publications, Inc.*, 627 F.2d 1287, 1292 (D.C.Cir.1980), elaborated on the *Gertz* definition by adding that such a limited-purpose figure "is attempting to have, or realistically can be expected to have, a major impact on the resolution of a specific public dispute that has foreseeable and substantial ramifications for persons beyond its immediate participants." The court said that Waldbaum's status as a corporate CEO did not alone make him a limited-purpose public figure. Waldbaum, however, had become a public activist promoting his image and had held press conferences, attempting to influence the supermarket industry.

Federal Circuit Courts of Appeal have developed various tests to aid judges in applying *Gertz*'s limited purpose public figure standard. The Second Circuit applies a four-part test, requiring a defendant to show that the plaintiff has (i) successfully invited public attention to his views in an effort to influence others prior to the incident that is the subject of litigation; (ii) voluntarily injected himself into a public controversy related to the subject of the litigation; (iii) assumed a position of prominence in the public controversy; and (iv) maintained regular and continuing access to the media.[5] In *Silvester v. American Broadcasting Co.*, 839 F.2d 1491, 1494 (11th Cir.1988), the U.S. Court of Appeals for the Eleventh Circuit adopted a three-prong test to determine whether a person is a limited-purpose public figure. Under this test, the court must (i) isolate the public controversy; (ii) examine the plaintiff's involvement in the controversy; and (iii) determine whether the alleged defamation was germane to the plaintiff's participation in the controversy. The U.S. Court of Appeals for the Fifth Circuit's three-part test requires that (i) the controversy at issue must be public both in the sense that people are discussing it and people other than the immediate participants in the controversy are likely to feel the impact of its resolution, (ii) the plaintiff must have more than a trivial or tangential role in the controversy, and (iii) the alleged defamation must be germane to the plaintiff's participation in the controversy. Courts, however, will not allow the news media to **bootstrap** a private figure into a public one by relying on the coverage that triggered the libel lawsuit. As the Court in *Hutchinson v. Proxmire*, 443 U.S. 111, 135 (1979), stressed, "Clearly, those charged with defamation cannot, by their own conduct, create their own defense by making the claimant a public figure."

Involuntary Limited-Purpose Public Figure

The Court in *Gertz* also recognized the possibility that an individual can be "drawn into a particular public controversy," as well as taking affirmative steps to be part of one.[6] For example, in *Dameron v. Washington Magazine, Inc.*, 779 F.2d 736 (D.C. Cir. 1985) (cert denied 476 U.S.1141) (1986), the D.C. Circuit ruled that an air traffic controller on duty when a plane crashed was a public figure for the limited purpose of discussing the plane crash, though he had not thrust himself into the vortex of the controversy.

Private Figure

Typically, a private figure is defined by what the plaintiff is not—not an elected official or either of the two types of public figures. Still, reaching the determination is rarely simple. In the seminal case of *Gertz v. Welch*, Elmer Gertz, a defense attorney involved in three cases that gained national attention, published books and was a well-known figure among the Chicago legal community, all before the publication of the offending article in 1969. Yet, the U.S. Supreme Court said he was not a public figure mostly because none of the prospective jurors at the libel trial had heard of him.[7]

In *Time, Inc. v. Firestone*, 424 U.S. 448 (1976), the first significant application of *Gertz*, the Court ruled that the plaintiff, recently divorced from a member of one of the richest families in the U.S., was a private figure despite the prominence of the Firestone family and the fact that the Florida Supreme Court dubbed their divorce a "cause celebre." The Court said that a divorce proceeding is not the sort of public controversy contemplated in *Gertz* because resorting to the judicial process is not voluntary when a defendant must appear in court to defend her interests.

Businesses: Private or Public Figures?

The two justifications for the *Gertz* private/public dichotomy do not provide a general rule for corporations. Some corporations have routine and easy access to the mass media, and some do not. Some corporations advertise widely and routinely—their brands are household words. Most corporations, however, are barely known by name. Consequently, courts have developed criteria on a case-by-case basis. For instance, the Fifth Circuit in *Snead v. Redland Aggregates Ltd.*, 998 F.2d 1325, 1329 (5th Cir. 1993), weighed (i) the notoriety of the corporation to the average individual in the relevant geographical location and the size and nationality of the corporation; (ii) the nature of the corporation's business, because the makers of prominent consumer goods and services are more likely to attain public-figure status; and (iii) whether the corporation has been the target of frequent and intense media scrutiny.

SUMMARY: *Gertz v. Welch, Inc.*, 418 U.S. 323 (1972), established four classifications of libel plaintiffs: (i) public officials, (ii) all-purpose public figures, (iii) limited-purpose public figures, and (iv) private persons. Only public officials who have substantial responsibility for or control over the conduct of governmental affairs, command attention from news organizations, or have made themselves well-known in their communities qualify as public officials for libel. All-purpose public figures are most easily understood as celebrities. Limited-purpose public figures are those otherwise private individuals who have made themselves publicly known by their voluntary involvement in a public controversy. Under a limited set of circumstances, an otherwise private person can be pulled into a public controversy and become a public figure. Public officials, all-purpose, and limited-purpose public figures must prove knowing falsity or reckless disregard for the truth. Private persons, anyone who does not fit into the public figure categories, need to prove only that a reporter was negligent, that the reporter made a mistake that a reasonable reporter would not commit, or, in some states, that the reporter was grossly negligent.

The Matters of "Public Concern" Standard

Gertz repudiated reliance on whether matters of public concern can be used as the touchstone to judge whether to apply the recklessness-or-knowing-falsity test. According to *Gertz*, the plaintiff's private or public status is the measure. Nevertheless, a minority of jurisdictions applies the concept of "public concern." That is largely a result of the U.S Supreme Court's plurality ruling in *Dun & Bradstreet Inc. v. Greenmoss Builders, Inc.*, 472 U.S. 749 (1985), and in *Philadelphia Newspapers, Inc. v. Hepps*, 475 U.S. 767 (1986).

In *Dun & Bradstreet*, the Court held that when the false and defamatory statements involve matters of private concern, a private-figure plaintiff does not have to show recklessness or knowing falsity to win presumed or punitive damages. Dun & Bradstreet, the defendant, had informed some of its clients that Greenmoss Builders had filed for bankruptcy, a statement that was false. The mistake was not one of recklessness or knowing falsity. A 17-year-old high school student, paid to review Vermont bankruptcy pleadings, made the mistake of attributing a bankruptcy filing by one of Greenmoss's ex-employees to the company. Greenmoss won a $350,000 judgment without a finding that Dun & Bradstreet's error was the result of recklessness or knowing falsity. Dun & Bradstreet appealed, arguing that under *Gertz*, plaintiffs had to show recklessness or knowledge of falsity to recover presumed or punitive damages.

Writing for a plurality, Justice Powell said the Court in *Gertz* had not addressed the issue raised in *Dun & Bradstreet*: "We have never considered whether the *Gertz* balance obtains when the defamatory statements involve no issue of public concern. To make this determination, we must employ the approach approved in *Gertz* and balance the state's interest in compensating private individuals for injury to their reputation against the First Amendment interest in protecting this type of expression."[8]

Powell reasoned that speech on matters of private concern warrants less First Amendment protection than speech on matters of public concern. In contrast, the state's interest in awarding presumed and punitive damages was substantial when the defamatory statement concerned private matters. Consequently, "in light of the reduced constitutional value of speech involving no matters of public concern, we hold that the state interest adequately supports awards of presumed and punitive damages—even absent a showing of 'actual malice.'"[9] The four dissenting justices, however, argued that the plurality opinion departed "completely from the analytic framework and result of that case: '*Gertz* was intended to reach cases that involve any false statements...whether or not [they] implicat[e] a matter of public importance.'"[10]

In *Philadelphia Newspapers, Inc. v. Hepps*, 475 U.S. 767 (1986), the Court held that at least where a media outlet publishes speech of public concern, a private-figure plaintiff bears the burden of proving falsity and recklessness before recovering damages. The Court ruled that the plaintiff's status was not determinative, an approach that departs from the rationale underlining *Gertz*. The *Hepps* approach is anchored in the public speech concept, speech concerning "the legitimacy of the political process," as the *Hepps* court described it.[11] Placing the burden of proving truth upon media defendants who publish speech of public concern is unconstitutional because such a " 'chilling' effect would be antithetical to the First Amendment's protection of true speech on matters of public concern," the Court said.[12]

What constitutes speech that involves matters of public concern? *Sullivan* and its progeny tell us that statements about the public conduct of elected officials or statements about all- purpose public figures meet the standard. In the government-employee context, the Court in *Connick v. Myers*, 461 U.S. 138, 146 (1983), said it is speech "relating to any matter of political, social, or other concern to the community." The U.S. Court of Appeals for the Fourth Circuit applies a test: "whether the public or the community is likely to be truly concerned with or interested in the particular expression, or whether it is more properly viewed as essentially a private matter between employer and employee."[13]:

> SUMMARY: Defamatory statements concerning public matters are accorded greater First Amendment protection than ones about private matters. Thus, where a media outlet publishes speech concerning a public matter or controversy, even a private-figure plaintiff bears the burden of proving falsity and recklessness before covering damages. In contrast, a private-figure plaintiff suing a private defendant or a media outlet over statements that do not concern a public controversy or matter, only needs to prove negligence in most states.

Libel on the Internet

This chapter opened with a brief account of fashion model Liskula Cohen's successful legal effort to obtain the identity of an anonymous blogger who defamed her. As a libel plaintiff, Cohen is hardly alone, in one respect. Increasingly, targets of online defamation are going to court to unmask anonymous and pseudonymous defamers. Unlike Cohen, most fail. But that trend may be ending.

Virtual defamation differs from traditional defamation in at least two legally significant ways: § 230 of the Communications Decency Act shields ISPs from (i) civil actions, such as libel, negligence, and fraud, and (ii) state false-advertising laws stemming from the content posted by users. This protection makes it extremely difficult for plaintiffs to unmask the identities of anonymous Internet users. So when anonymous individuals post defamatory comments in cyberspace provided by online intermediaries, plaintiffs cannot sue the intermediaries who provide websites, social networks, or online forums for libel. To uncover an anonymous source's identity, the plaintiff can sue the user who created the content and submit a request to the intermediary during discovery, or subpoena the intermediary to get the anonymous user's identity. Online service providers should be able to identify an anonymous user by obtaining the Internet Protocol number assigned to every computer using the Internet. But plaintiffs also have to persuade a judge that their case is jury-worthy to get the identity of the defendant. In most jurisdictions, their task is made more difficult by the fact that anonymous speech enjoys First Amendment protection.

It wasn't always that way. Under traditional libel law, "one who repeats or otherwise republishes defamatory matter is subject to liability as if he had originally published it."[14] In some jurisdictions, distributors, such as newsstands and bookstores, were exempt from liability so long as they had no knowledge that a publication they were selling contained defamatory statements. Such was the case in New York, when plaintiffs Cubby Inc. and Robert Blanchard sued CompuServe Inc. for defamatory statements posted on one of the online forums the company provided. In *Cubby, Inc. v. CompuServe Inc.*, 776 F. Supp. 135, 140 (Dist. Court, SD New York 1991), a federal district court granted summary judgment for CompuServe, finding that, "CompuServe has no more editorial control over such a publication than does a public library, book store, or newsstand, and it would be no more feasible for CompuServe to examine every publication it carries for potentially defamatory statements than it would be for any other distributor to do so."

So under *Cubby, Inc. v. CompuServe Inc.*, an online service provider was shielded from libel lawsuits as long as it assumed no role in editing the content of the online sites it provides. At first, Prodigy's practice was to edit; it monitored and removed objectionable content. Thus, a New York judge ruled on summary judgment in *Stratton Oakmont, Inc. v. Prodigy Services Co.*, 23 Media L. Rep. 1794 (N.Y. Sup. Ct. May 24, 1995), that Prodigy was a publisher, not a distributor, and could be held liable for defamatory statements posted on one of its electronic bulletin boards.

After Prodigy ceased engaging in editorial activities, a New York appeals court granted it summary judgment in an action alleging infliction of emotional harm stemming from a posting that made it seem as though the plaintiff was sending threatening messages. In *Lunney v. Prodigy Services*, Inc., 250 A.D.2d 230, 238 (1998), the court interpreted the terms of Prodigy's service member agreement to negate "any possible extension of tort liability to third parties based on any alleged failure, on the part of Prodigy, to monitor its bulletin boards."

Congress stepped in and granted ISPs immunity under § 230 the Communications Decency Act of 1996. Section 230(c) provides: "No provider or user of an interactive computer service shall be treated as the publisher or speaker of any information provided by another information content provider." Online service providers are immune even when they exercise editorial control, unless they alter the meaning of the content, because § 230 (2)(a) provides: "No provider or user of an interactive computer service shall be held liable on account of—(A) any action voluntarily taken in good faith to restrict access to or availability of material that the provider or user considers to be obscene, lewd, lascivious, filthy, excessively violent, harassing, or otherwise objectionable, whether or not such material is constitutionally protected."

Under § 230 immunity, an online service provider is not required to remove offending messages even when it is informed of their content, the U.S. Court of Appeals for the Fourth Circuit ruled in *Zeran v. America Online, Inc.*, 129 F.3d 327 (4th Cir. 1997). So § 230 immunity is broader than the traditional distributor immunity, which was lost once a vendor was informed of the defamatory content in one of its books or periodicals.

Anonymous Speech and Online Libel

It is well-settled law that the First Amendment protects those who engage in anonymous speech.[15] This principle is often underscored by referencing the anonymous pamphlets of American revolutionaries and the pseudonym "Publius," the author of the Federalist Papers, now believed to be Alexander Hamilton, James Madison, and John Jay. Accordingly, courts have devised balancing tests weighing the First Amendment rights of anonymous Internet speakers with libel plaintiffs' common law right to protect reputation, a right that predates the First Amendment, in response to plaintiff's subpoena seeking disclosure.

In one of the earliest rulings involving a libel action, *In re Subpoena Duces Tecum to America Online, Inc.*, 2000 WL 1210372 (Cir. Ct. Va., January 31, 2000), reversed on other grds., sub. nom., *America Online Inc. v. Anonymous Publicly Traded Co.*, 542 S.E.2d 377 (Va. 2001), a Virginia court reviewed a subpoena seeking the identity of John Doe defendants who had allegedly made defamatory statements and disclosed confidential information online. The Virginia court recognized the First Amendment right to Internet anonymity, and held that an Internet service provider could assert that right on behalf of its users.[16] The court applied a two-part test determining whether the subpoena would be enforced: (i) the court must be convinced by the pleadings and evidence submitted that the party requesting the subpoena has a good faith basis to contend that it may be the target of defamatory conduct, and (ii) the information sought must be central to pursuing the cause of action. In *America Online Inc.*, discovery was allowed because the court concluded that the plaintiff had met those requirements.

In *Dendrite Int'l, Inc. v. Doe No. 3*, 775 A.2d 756, 760–761 (N.J. Super. A.D. 2001), a New Jersey appeals court required the plaintiff to: (i) use the Internet to notify the anonymous posters that they are subject of a subpoena, (ii) withhold action to allow the defendants a reasonable opportunity to file and serve opposition to the application, (iii) quote verbatim the allegedly actionable content on the ISPs related site, (iv) allege all the elements of the cause of action, (v) present evidence supporting the claim, and (vi) show the court that the right to identify the speaker outweighs the First Amendment right of anonymous speech. The plaintiff, however, failed to persuade the judge to disclose the poster's identity. The criteria, the court acknowledged, was more demanding than "a traditional motion to dismiss for failure to state a cause of action."[17]

Doe v. 2TheMart.com, Inc., 140 F. Supp. 2d 1088 (Dist. Court, WD Washington 2001), marked the first time a federal court addressed a case in which a libel plaintiff sought to unmask anonymous posters. 2TheMart.com presented a subpoena to InfoSpace in an attempt to learn the identities of at least three people who had used pseudonyms to hide behind criticism of 2TheMart.com. A federal court in Seattle, Washington, considered four factors in determining whether the subpoena should be issued: "…whether: (i) the subpoena seeking the information was issued in good faith and not for any improper purpose, (ii) the information sought relates to a core claim or defense, (iii) the identifying information is directly and materially relevant to that claim or defense, and (iv) information sufficient to establish or to disprove that claim or defense is unavailable from any other source."[18] The court ruled that 2TheMart.com "failed to demonstrate that the identifies of these Internet users is directly and materially relevant to a core defense in the underlying securities litigation."[19]

The extra burden § 230 immunity imposes on libel plaintiffs is hardly an arcane legal matter, as evidenced by the press coverage devoted to the AutoAdmit case, or *Doe I and Doe II v. Individuals, whose true names are unknown using the following pseudonyms*, later amended to *Doe I v. Ciolli*, No. 307-cv0090-CFD (D.Conn June 8, 2007).[20] In the AutoAdmit case, two female Yale Law School graduates, Brittan Heller and Heide Iravani, filed a federal lawsuit against Anthony Ciolli, the former chief education director of a popular law school admissions forum, AutoAdmit, and users employing 39 pseudonyms, who had posted sexually explicit, male-locker-room vulgarity and threatening comments about the women on the forum between 2005 and 2007. The plaintiffs alleged defamation, among other actions. The site drew between 800,000 to one million visitors each month.

In February 2008, the women issued a subpoena to AT&T Internet Services, seeking identities of anyone who had used the name Anthony Ciolli and other user names and logins. A&T complied within 19 days. And, in a June 13, 2008, ruling, a federal trial judge in Connecticut denied one defendant's motion to proceed anonymously. In reaching his decision, the judge analyzed five factors, much as in *Dendrite Int'l, Inc. v. Doe No. 3*: (i) whether the plaintiff attempted to notify the anonymous posters, (ii) whether the plaintiff identified all the defamatory statements, (iii) whether there was an alternative means of obtaining the information, (iv) whether the defendant's identity was central to pressing the plaintiff's claims, and (v) the extent of the defendant's expectation of privacy when the content was posted.[21] But most important to the judge's ruling was determination that the plaintiff had made "a concrete showing as to each element of a prima facie case"[22] of defamation, similar to the judge's analysis in *In the Matter of Liskula Cohen v. Google, Inc., and Blogger.com*. By October 2009, the plaintiffs had reached settlements with one of the unmasked posters and dropped their legal actions against the remaining still anonymous posters.

Meanwhile, the plight of the two women, who at the time were not able to land law firm positions despite their impressive credentials earned at one of the highest ranking law schools in the U.S., had become the poster case, so to speak, for those who argued that § 230 immunity for online service providers comes at the expense of innocent victims of false and reputation-damaging gossip from anonymous sources. Section 230's detractors say the statute tips the balance between free expression and reputation protection too heavily in favor of the free expression rights of gossipers, hate-mongers, and bullies. They point out that online service providers can and have successfully defied subpoenas. For example, JuicyCampus.com, a website devoted to anonymously posted, reputation-damaging gossip, successfully defied a subpoena from a New Jersey prosecutor for about a year. According to the website owner, Matt Ivester, JuicyCampus.com closed in February 2009 only because of inadequate revenue.

SUMMARY: Virtual defamation differs from traditional defamation in at least two legally significant ways: §230 of the Communications Decency Act shields ISPs from (i) civil actions such as libel, negligence, and fraud and (ii) state false-advertising laws stemming from the content posted by users, making it extremely difficult for plaintiffs to unmask the identities of anonymous Internet users. Generally, the First Amendment protects the anonymity of Internet users. Therefore, plaintiffs who wish to sue anonymous authors of allegedly defamatory comments posted on blogs, social networking sites, and electronic bulletin boards, for example, must first subpoena the owner of the website to seek the identity of the author. Courts are now devising balancing tests weighing the First Amendment rights of anonymous Internet speakers with libel plaintiffs' common law right to protect reputation in response to plaintiff's subpoena seeking disclosure.

Libel Tourism

The universality of the Web has made media outlets far more vulnerable to plaintiffs seeking the best jurisdiction for their libel actions. Aggrieved parties shop for nations with plaintiff-friendly libel laws rather than media-defendant-friendly jurisdictions, such as the U.S., to sue media outlets and book publishers. Great Britain is a favorite libel tourism spot.

Great Britain appeals to libel plaintiffs mostly because defamatory statements on matters of public concern are presumed to be false and injurious. Thus, a defendant has the burden of proving truth. A defendant who attempts to prove truth and fails may face aggravated damages for failing to publish a correction in a timely manner. In contrast, under U.S. law—*Philadelphia Newspapers v. Hepp*—defamatory statements concerning public officials, figures, and public matters are presumed true and the plaintiff carries the burden of proof. Also, there is a uniformed fault standard in Great Britain; whether the plaintiff is famous or not does not matter. Media defendants, however, may invoke a "responsible journalism" privilege, basically arguing that, though the statements are false, the journalist acted responsibly, or without negligence. In the U.S., however, a plaintiff suing a media defendant that published a defamatory statements about a matter of public concern must show that the defendant's statement was false and it acted with reckless disregard for the truth, clearly a more difficult standard of fault than negligence.

Libel tourists also find Great Britain attractive because its courts have been willing to exert jurisdiction control—in personam jurisdiction—over defendants, even when they have never set foot in the nation and do no business there except for the sales of a small number of books or periodicals. A court that has in personam, or personal jurisdiction, has the authority to compel a nonresident defendant to appear in court and comply with the court's judgment. Typically, a court will legitimately hold personal jurisdiction in a civil matter where the tort, a wrongful act, occurred. Under the landmark ruling *International Shoe Co. v. Washington*, 326 U.S. 310 (1945), a civil defendant cannot be subjected to in personam jurisdiction by out-of-state courts unless the defendant had certain "minimum contacts" within that state. So if a publisher's place of business was in Illinois, but the plaintiff wanted to try her civil action in New York where she lived, she would have to persuade a judge that the defendant had a place of business or residence in New York, or distributed to a certain number of subscribers in New York, the forum state, in order for the judge to establish personal jurisdiction over the Illinois-based publisher. But how does one determine the proper jurisdiction in cyberspace where a publisher has no control over where his content will be viewed?

As the U.S. Court of Appeals for the Second Circuit noted in *Best Van Lines, Inc. v. Walker*, 490 F.3d 239, 251 (2d Cir. 2007), many courts rely on *Zippo Manufacturing Company v. Zippo Dot Com, Inc.*, 952 F. Supp. 1119 (W.D.Pa.1997), the "seminal authority regarding personal jurisdiction based upon the operation of an Internet web site." The Zippo sliding scale analysis applies traditional due process "minimum contacts" personal jurisdictional principles to Internet operations to determine whether jurisdiction over an out-of-state website is constitutionally valid. The scale focuses on the nature and quality of the website's commercial activities in a particular jurisdiction:

> At one end of the spectrum are situations where a defendant clearly does business over the Internet. If the defendant enters into contracts with residents of a foreign jurisdiction that involve the knowing and repeated transmission of computer files over the Internet, personal jurisdiction is proper. At the opposite end are situations where a defendant has simply posted information on an Internet Web site which is accessible to users in foreign jurisdictions. A passive Web site that does little more than make information available to those who are interested in it is not grounds for the exercise [of] personal jurisdiction. The middle ground is occupied by interactive Web sites where a user can exchange information with the host computer. In these cases, the exercise of jurisdiction is determined by examining the level of interactivity and commercial nature of the exchange of information that occurs on the Web site.[23]

But many legal systems in other nations do not follow the same analysis to determine personal jurisdiction. The British defamation case, *Berzovsky v. Michaels and Others (Forbes)*, illustrates the vulnerability of Internet publishing media outlets when judges in other nations rule on jurisdiction. In December 1996, *Forbes* magazine published an investigative story about a Russian oligarch Boris Berezovsky that portrayed him as something akin to a powerful gangland boss. A total of 13 copies were mailed to subscribers in Russia where Berezovsky lived. *Forbes*, however, is headquartered in New York City, and 785,710 copies of the December 1996 issued were read in the U.S. and Canada. *Forbes* argued before the House of Lords in London that either Russia or the U.S. was the proper jurisdiction for a libel suit brought by Berezovsky.

But 1,915 copies of the issue were distributed in England and Wales. Berzovsky and another plaintiff filed a defamation action in London and persuaded The House of Lords that 6,000 readers in the United Kingdom had read the story when website viewers were counted. Consequently, their ability to raise funds from London investors, where they frequently did business, was seriously damaged, the plaintiffs argued. The House of Lords ruled that London was the proper jurisdiction because the wrongful act had been committed there.[24]

Having to defend itself in a British court would not have been overly burdensome for *Forbes* if British libel laws were similar to those in the U.S. But, as discussed above, the libel laws in the U.S. and Great Britain are dissimilar in significant ways to the advantage of plaintiffs. According to Charles J. Glasser, Bloomberg News' Global Media Counsel, "The law holds that UK media defendants are faced with considerable legal presumptions to overcome at trial: both falsity and damage are presumed by law"[25] and in the U.S. the *Forbes* story "would have been protected by a plethora of privileges."[26] *Forbes* settled the case in 2003 with a reading of a statement in the High Court, and published a retraction and a correction.

In recent years, several states and the U.S. have passed anti-libel tourism laws, spurred by Dr. Rachel Ehrenfeld's legal campaign. In 2003, Ehrenfeld, director of the American Center for Democracy and the Economic Warfare Institute, authored the book, *Funding Evil: How Terrorism Is Financed and How to Stop It*. She identified Saudi businessman Khalid bin Mahfouz and his sons as terrorist financiers. Mahfouz sued Ehrenfeld in London, even though the book was not distributed there. Twenty-three copies, however, were obtained in England, purchased from online booksellers. Tried in absentia, Ehrenfeld lost and the British court ordered her to pay the equivalent of $225,000 in damages, publish a correction and apology, and imposed an injunction preventing the book from being distributed in Great Britain.

Ehrenfeld countersued in New York, seeking a judgment declaring that Mahfouz could not prevail on a libel claim against her under federal or New York law. Such a finding would make the British judgment unenforceable in the United States, and New York in particular, on constitutional and public policy grounds. The New York Court of Appeals, however, dismissed the action, finding that it did not have personal jurisdiction over Mahfouz.[27] The U.S. Court of Appeals for the Second Circuit upheld the ruling in *Ehrenfeld v. Bin Mahfouz*, 489 F.3d 542 (2d Cir. 2007).

The New York State Legislature's response was quick. The legislative body passed the Libel Terrorism Reform Act, or "Rachel's Law," in April 2008. The act allows New York courts to assert jurisdiction over a plaintiff who wins a foreign libel judgment against a New York writer or publisher and limit enforcement to satisfy First Amendment standards. Several states, including Illinois, California, Florida, New Jersey, and Hawaii have passed similar protections.

In 2010, Congress passed the Securing the Protection of our Enduring and Established Constitutional Heritage (SPEECH) Act. The SPEECH Act prohibits courts here from enforcing, among other things, a foreign defamation judgment unless U.S. judges determine that the foreign law is consistent with the First Amendment and prohibits recognition in the U.S. of a foreign judgment when a party establishes that foreign law is inconsistent with U.S. jurisdiction due process guarantees.

SUMMARY: Any communication posted on the Worldwide Web is instanteously global. That unique nature of the Web makes a speaker vulnerable to libel plaintiffs in states and nations where the defendants do little or no business, and allows plaintiffs to shop for plaintiff-friendly jurisdictions in other nations, Great Britain in particular. Domestically, many courts rely on *Zippo Manufacturing Company v. Zippo Dot Com, Inc.*, 952 F. Supp. 1119 (W.D.Pa.1997), the "seminal authority regarding personal jurisdiction based upon the operation of an Internet web site." The *Zippo* sliding scale analysis applies traditional due process "minimum contacts" personal jurisdictional principles to

Internet operations to determine whether jurisdiction over an out-of-state website is constitutionally valid. The scale focuses on the nature and quality of the websites' commercial activities in a particular jurisdiction. The Securing the Protection of our Enduring and Established Constitutional Heritage (SPEECH) Act, enacted in 2010, provides protection against foreign libel judgments enforceability in the U.S. when such judgments do not conform to U.S. libel laws.

ONLINE RESOURCES

1. "The Advertisement: Heed Their Rising Voices," http://faculty-web.at.northwestern. edu/commstud/freespeech/cont/cases/nytsullivan1.html
2. Ronald K. L. Collins, "*New York Times Co. v. Sullivan:* The Case that Changed First Amendment History," http://catalog.freedomforum.org/SpecialTopics/NYTSullivan/ summary.html
3. "Legal Guide for Bloggers," https://www.eff.org/issues/bloggers/legal/liability/230
4. "Libel," http://www.rcfp.org/digital-journalists-legal-guide/libel
5. Section 230 of the Communications Decency Act, http://www.citmedialaw.org/section-230

QUESTIONS

HillaryHaters.com is a website owned and operated by Arthur Stein, a shadowy Republican operative. Stein's site aims to "rescue" America from "the radical ideas of Hillary Clinton," providing space for anyone to comment on Hillary Clinton. One day, an anonymous user posted the following words: "In my opinion, and from what I have learned from other sources who should know, Hillary Rodman Clinton is a practicing illuminist witch, a member of the Illuminati Order, I'm not making this up. She's also a bitch, a traitor to her country, and a pants-suit wearing, lesbian feminist skank who was complicit in the murder of Vince Foster in 1993. Yeah, she sucks."

1. Identify all the words or statements that are arguably defamatory in the above statement and explain why.
2. Are any of the words or statements libelous per se? Which ones?
3. Is it likely that the opinion defense will provide protection for the defendant or defendants?
4. What role would U.S.C. 47, § 230 play in Clinton's libel case.
5. Clearly, Clinton is an all-purpose public figure. Is she likely to prevail in her libel suit under the appropriate fault standard?

ENDNOTES

1. *In the Matter of Liskula Cohen v. Google, Inc., and Blogger.com*, 887 N.Y.S.2d 424 (NY: Supreme Court, Aug. 17, 2009).
2. *New York Times v. Sullivan*, 376 U.S. 254, 270 (1964).
3. Ibid. 271–272.
4. *Harte-Hanks Communications, Inc. v. Connaughton*, 491 U.S. 657, 668 (1989).
5. *Lerman v. Flynt Distribrution. Co., Inc.*, 745 F.2d 123, 136–137 (2d Cir.1984) cert. denied, 471 U.S. 1054 (1985).

6. *Gertz v. Robert Welch, Inc.* at 351.

7. Ibid. 351–352.

8. *Dun & Bradstreet* at 757.

9. Ibid. 761.

10. Ibid. 775.

11. *Philadelphia Newspapers, Inc. v. Hepps,* 475 U.S. 767, 778 (1986).

12. Ibid. 777.

13. *Berger v. Battaglia,* 779 F.2d 992, 999 (4th Cir. 1985).

14. *Cianci v. New Times Publishing Co.,* 639 F.2d 54, 61 (2d Cir. 1980).

15. *Buckley v. American Constitutional Law Foundation,* 525 U.S. 182, 197–99 (1999); *McIntyre v. Ohio Elections Comm.,* 514 U.S. 334 (1995); *Talley v. California,* 362 U.S. 60 (1960).

16. See *In re Subpoena Duces Tecum To America Online, Inc.,* http://pub.bna.com/eclr/40570.htm

17. *Dendrite Int'l, Inc. v. Doe No. 3,* 775 A.2d 756, 771 (N.J. Super. A.D. 2001).

18. *Doe v. 2TheMart.com, Inc.,* 140 F. Supp. 2d 1088, 1095 (Dist. Ct., WD Washington 2001).

19. Ibid. 1097–1098.

20. See David Margolick. "Slimed Online," *Portfolio.com,* (February 11, 2009), http://upstart.bizjournals.com/news-markets/national-news/portfolio/2009/02/11/Two-Lawyers-Fight-Cyber-Bullying.html

21. *Doe I and Doe II, v. Individuals, whose names are unknown, defendant,* No. 4:07 CV 909 (CF) (June 13, 2008) at ¶¶8–9.

22. Ibid. ¶10.

23. *Zippo Manufacturing Company v. Zippo Dot Com, Inc.,* 952 F. Supp. 1119, 1124 (W.D.Pa. 1997).

24. See *Berezovsky v. Michaels* [2000] W.L.R. 1004 (H.L.), http://www.publications.parliament.uk/pa/ld199900/ldjudgmt/jd000511/bere-1.htm

25. Charles J. Glasser, (Ed.) *International Libel & Privacy Handbook.* New York: Bloomberg Press (2006), 274.

26. Ibid. xvii.

27. *Ehrenfeld v Bin Mahfouz,* 9 N.Y.3d 501 (2007).

CHAPTER SIX

Privacy

CONTROVERSY: As the first decade of the 21st century ended, more Americans voiced concerns about privacy. They questioned whether they were paying too high a price to hook up with "friends," see views of strangers' front doors around the world, buy books via the Internet, or surf the Web. The high price was a loss of privacy. Companies, such as Facebook and Google, were selling personal data to advertisers without obtaining explicit consent from users.

Online users targeted Facebook in 2009 and 2010. Each time, the biggest social networking site changed users' privacy settings in response to complaints, it seemed as though users lost more control of their privacy instead. There were calls for boycotts against Facebook, and four Facebook users led a class action lawsuit against the network in 2010. Google managed to draw government scrutiny and the ire of individuals. Probes by several countries, including the U.S., showed that its Street View project had inadvertently intercepted emails, passwords, and URLs from unencrypted Wi-Fi networks. Earlier, a Franklin Park, Pennsylvania, couple sued Google, arguing that Street View online mapping invaded their privacy. Google settled the novel federal lawsuit for $1, acknowledging that its Street View vehicle had trespassed when it photographed the couple's private road.[1] In December 2010, the Federal Trade Commission (FTC) issued a report endorsing a "do not track" list that would allow users to opt out of having their online activity tracked and sold. The Commerce Department also recommended privacy codes of conduct for online companies. The Obama administration called for new rules regulating the protection of consumer privacy online, including the creation of a federal privacy office and a nationwide "Privacy Bill of Rights."

Chapter's Scope

This chapter examines legal doctrines, cases, statutes, and regulations protecting privacy. Though there is no single definition of the term, for our purposes "privacy" is the right to be left alone and to control information about ourselves. This chapter looks at two categories of privacy protection theories: (i) invasion of privacy torts, which are statutory protections, allowing individuals to bring claims against defendants; and, to a lesser extent, (ii) the Fourth Amendment, which prohibits unreasonable search and seizure by government officials. In the 1890s and early 20th century, courts and state legislatures started fashioning invasion of privacy torts to allow individuals to sue newspapers for publishing photographic images of them. Today, all states recognize some or all of the traditional invasion of privacy torts, which are discussed at length below: **appropriation** or misappropriation and the related right of publicity, public disclosure of private facts, false light, and intrusion and the related trespass tort. Now, email, search engines, and social media are some of the online innovations forcing legislators, regulators, and the courts to confront digital privacy concerns, as the introductory controversy illustrates. Thus, this chapter also discusses invasion of privacy controversies stemming from, and statutes affecting, online activity, some of which raise Fourth Amendment concerns; identifies the most significant federal statutes protecting digital privacy; takes note of the FTC's recent campaign to regulate online privacy; and examines how the courts are handling traditional privacy claims of trespass, misappropriation, and right to publicity stemming from online activities.

Invasion of Privacy and Media Technologies

For almost a decade, privacy rights advocates and civil libertarians have urged the government to do something about behavioral marketing—corporations' unauthorized use of the personal information individuals post on social networking sites or reveal inadvertently through their online searches and transactions. Online companies sell computer browser histories and information from users' social networking pages, often without explicit user permission, to advertisers whose targeted ads appear on browsers or users' social media pages. But, for the most part, Congress has refrained from passing laws to protect individuals' online data privacy. Consequently, individuals have appealed to companies to self-regulate or have sued in court. Perhaps the actions of the FTC, Commerce, and the Obama administration in 2010 marked a turning point? Some evidence to support that belief might be found in the settlements the FTC reached with Facebook, Twitter, and Google over their privacy policies and practices discussed later in this chapter.

The actions of the European Union (EU), however, leave little doubt that this economic and political partnership between 27 European nations is cracking down on social media companies' unauthorized use of personal information. In January 2012, the EU took an emphatic step toward reining in Internet companies that make billions of dollars from private user information. The EU proposed laws that, if approved by the European Parliament, would go into effect in 2014, allowing users to demand, among other things, that their data vanish from the Internet ("right to be forgotten").

Once again, the introduction of a new mass media technology has triggered a flurry of legislative and judicial responses to protect privacy concerns. The first time was in the late Victorian Age with the advent of photography. New photo camera technology allowed amateurs to "snap" photos of the unsuspecting rich and famous at public, semi-public, and private settings. New print technology allowed gossip-mongering newspapers to print those photos. Many Victorians were not amused.

Musical stage actress Marion Manola was one such camera-shy Victorian. For an actress, wearing tights on stage was acceptable in 1890. Off-stage and in public? Apparently not. After a flashlight photographer surprised her by photographing her performing in tights on a Broadway stage, Manola covered her face and ran off stage. She sued to prevent the photograph from going public. She prevailed when the defendants—a photographer, and the theater manager—failed to appear in a New York court to oppose the injunction.

Samuel Dennis Warren and Louis D. Brandeis cited *Manola v. Myers & Stevens* in their highly influential 1890 *Harvard Law Review* article, "The Right to Privacy."[2] Harvard Law School graduates Warren and Brandeis were founding partners of the Boston law firm Nutter McClennen & Fish LLP. In 1916, Brandeis would become the first Jewish U.S. Supreme Court justice. With "The Right to Privacy," the young lawyers proved influential in reshaping the law's treatment of privacy. They argued that under court-made law, the Declaration of Independence's "right to life" guarantee had broadened into a right to sue to protect the intangible property of privacy.

A New York Supreme Court Judge cited Warren and Brandeis' "The Right to Privacy" in *Schuyler v. Curtis*, 15 N.Y.S. 787 (1892), the first reported case in which the right of privacy was unambiguously recognized.[3] But the New York Court of Appeals reversed the ruling in 1895. In 1893, in *Marks v. Jaffa*, 26 N.Y.S. 908, 6 Misc. 290, a New York court imposed an injunction to stop the publication of a picture of a plaintiff in a newspaper, part of a contest in which readers would choose between the plaintiff's photograph and another to decide which one was most popular.[4]

The New York Court of Appeals' reversal in *Roberson v. Rochester Folding Box Company*, 171 N.Y. 538 (1902) had a ripple effect locally and nationwide. In *Roberson*, Franklin Mills, a flour manufacturer and sales businessman, used the likeness of Roberson, a young girl, on its bags of flour without her consent. Roberson, who claimed that she suffered emotionally from the ridicule heaped on her by people who recognized her from the flour bag images, won on the trial court level. But the Court of Appeals reversed, ruling that there was no precedent for a cause of action for invasion of privacy. In response, the New York legislature passed a law making it a misdemeanor and tort to use the name or image of a person for advertising or trade without consent in 1903.[5] Meanwhile, courts elsewhere declined to recognize the Warren-Brandeis proposed right to sue until the Supreme Court of Georgia's ruling in *Pavesich v. New England Life Insurance Co.*, 50 S.E. 68 (1905).

When legal scholar William Lloyd Prosser codified the right to privacy laws in a 1960 law review article, "Privacy," only four states had failed to recognize such rights.[6] Five decades later, the four branches of invasion of privacy Prosser identified remain unchanged: (i) appropriation or misappropriation, (ii) public disclosure of private facts, (iii) false light, and (iv) intrusion. But that does not mean all states recognize all four invasion of privacy torts, or wrongful acts. For example, the Ohio Supreme Court did not recognize the false light tort until 2007.[7] Also, some states recognize a right of publicity, which is closely related to appropriation. Another tort related to the four privacy torts is intentional infliction of emotional distress.

Elements of Invasion of Privacy Torts

The four traditional privacy torts and two of more recent vintage, the right of publicity and intentional infliction of emotional harm, provide a plaintiff with legal remedies for humiliation, mental distress and, sometimes, economic harm caused by a defendant's unauthorized use of a plaintiff's persona, private intangible interests, or tangible property.

Appropriation

One who appropriates to his own use or benefit the name or likeness of another is subject to liability to the other for invasion of his privacy.[8] As noted above, the New York legislature and the Georgia Supreme Court recognized appropriation as the first invasion of privacy cause of action. Appropriation gives a plaintiff a property right—the exclusive control of his or her name, likeness, image, voice, or performance. Generally, to state a valid cause of action in appropriation, the plaintiff must establish each of the following elements: The defendant (i) wrongfully—intentionally or accidently—appropriated (ii) the plaintiff's name, likeness, image, voice, performance, or some other personal aspect and (iii) published it for commercial gain or advantage.

Generally, the commercial element is an essential part of the plaintiff's case. But in some states, plaintiffs are not required to show that a defendant sought to benefit financially from the unauthorized use of the plaintiff's name or likeness. It is sufficient to show that the defendant's action caused embarrassment, shame, or other emotional harm. Unlike the tort of false light, appropriation does not involve falsity; truth is not a defense. Unlike the public disclosure of private facts tort, appropriation does not require the invasion of someone's secrecy or privacy.

Right of Publicity

Courts and legislatures have extended appropriation to cover the right of publicity. Jurisdictions have recognized a right of publicity, either by expressly acknowledging it as a separate tort for the right of publicity or by finding it within appropriation. In *Zacchini v. Scripps Howard Broadcasting*, 433 U.S. 562, 576 (1977), the U.S. Supreme Court said appropriation included a "'right of publicity'—involving, not the appropriation of an entertainer's reputation to enhance the attractiveness of a commercial product, but the appropriation of the very activity by which the entertainer acquired his reputation in the first place." The U.S. Court of Appeals for the Second Circuit was first to recognized the right of publicity in *Haelan Laboratories Inc. v. Topps Chewing Gum, Inc.*, 202 F.2d 866, 868 (2d Cir. 1953), cert. denied, 346 U.S. 816 (1953). The activity at issue in *Zacchini* was a 15-second shot-out-of-a-cannon-into-a-net performance. The Court ruled that the broadcast of the entire performance posed a substantial threat to the economic value of Zacchini's performance and that the First Amendment does not immunize the news media when they broadcast a performer's entire act without consent.

In the traditional appropriation cases such as *Roberson v. Rochester* and *Pavesich*, "the personal injury is measured in terms of the mental anguish that results from the appropriation of an ordinary individual's identity."[9] The right of publicity, however, "seeks to protect the *property* interest that a celebrity has in his or her name; the injury is not to personal privacy, it is the economic loss a celebrity suffers when someone else interferes with the property interest that he or she has in his or her name."[10] There is another major distinction. Plaintiffs suing for traditional appropriation cannot be decedents suing on behalf of a deceased relative. The right of publicity, however, survives the death of its owner and is inheritable.

Consent

A plaintiff cannot prevail in appropriation if she has given a defendant permission to use her persona or likeness. Consequently, disputes often arise over the specific intent of consent agreement language, oral agreements, or the plaintiff's conduct that might imply consent. *Lane v. MRA Holdings*, LLC, 242 F.Supp. 1205 (M.D. Fla. 2002), is instructive. A videographer working for MRA Holdings,

LLC, the company that produced *Girls Gone Wild– College Girls Exposed*, approached Lane on a public street and persuaded her to expose her breasts. Lane had signed a waiver and proof of age statement, and received a T-shirt and a hat for posing. She, however, argued that she did not agree to allow her image to be publicly sold as part of a *Girls Gone Wild* tape and promotional advertisement. A Florida court, however, ruled that no reasonable jury could conclude that her consent was limited to viewing by only the film crew.[11]

Newsworthiness and Public Interest Defenses

Warren and Brandeis drew the bright line between privacy and the public interest when they asserted that, "The right to privacy does not prohibit any publication of matter which is of public or general interest."[12] Consequently, courts or state legislatures have recognized that communication of matters in the public interest, "which rests on the right of the public to know and the freedom of the press to tell it," is an affirmative defense against appropriation.[13]

Non-news media defendants may evoke the public interest defense. The U.S. Court of Appeals for the Ninth Circuit, however, rejected Hallmark Cards' argument that its line of birthday cards, depicting a cartoon waitress with an oversized photograph of Paris Hilton's head, concerned matters of public interest. Hilton, the celebrity famous for being famous, argued that the card appropriated the role she played on *The Simple Life* television show and implicated "no *issue* of public interest because it involves no issue at all, only a celebrity who interests many people."[14] The appeals court agreed, finding that the defense protects a communication about a previous publication of information and matters of recent events. Hallmark's cards did not publish or report such information, the Ninth Circuit ruled.[15]

Non-news media may invoke the incidental benefits defense, which protects references to real individuals in documentaries and other nonfictional and fictional works as long as references are not primarily for commercial purposes.[16]

News media defendants may invoke the newsworthy defense, which is related to the public interest defense in that it seeks to balance an individual's privacy interest against the public's right to know, stemming from the First Amendment. Typically, courts consider "a variety of factors, including the social value of the facts published, the depth of the article's intrusion into ostensibly private affairs, and the extent to which the party voluntarily acceded to a position of public notoriety" to determine whether a publication is of legitimate public concern."[17]

Additionally, courts adhering to the Booth Rule have carved out a First Amendment newsworthiness exception for news media that use individuals—typically celebrities—in commercials promoting news media outlets' news coverage to gain increased ratings, subscriptions, or sales. The commercials, however, must be truthful and not imply or claim that the celebrity has endorsed them.[18] But, as the U.S. Supreme Court ruled in *Zacchini v. Scripps Howard Broadcasting*, the newsworthiness defense will not protect "the media when they broadcast a performer's entire act without his consent."[19]

Transformative-Use Defense

In California, which has seen a good number of appropriations and right of publicity challenges brought by celebrities, defendants may avail themselves of the transformative defense. Related to copyright law's transformative fair use defense, California courts ask: Does the appropriated work, a video game, for example, change a celebrity's likeness or persona into something new, such as a parody or a fictional characterization?[20]

SUMMARY: The original invasion of privacy tort, as envisioned by Warren and Brandeis in "The Right to Privacy," is appropriation, which measures personal injury in terms of mental anguish. The closely related right of publicity, typically brought by celebrities, protects a property interest, measuring the economic loss a celebrity has suffered as a result of the unauthorized use of his or her name, likeness, or identity. Under both claims, defendants may prevail by showing consent, that the communication was of public interest or newsworthy, or a transformative use.

Public Disclosure of Private Facts

"One who gives publicity to a matter concerning the private life of another is subject to liability to the other for invasion of his privacy, if the matter publicized is of a kind that (i) would be highly offensive to a reasonable person, and (ii) is not of legitimate concern to the public."[21] In this branch of invasion of privacy, a plaintiff claims a publication has publicized allegedly private aspects of his or her life. As the Appeals Court of Massachusetts put it, "The notion of right of privacy is founded on the idea that individuals may hold close certain manuscripts, private letters, family photographs, or private conduct which is no business of the public and the publicizing of which is, therefore, offensive."[22]

A plaintiff must show that the facts were publicized. The emphasis is on the word publicity, meaning that disclosure of a private fact to one or several individuals is generally not enough to meet the disclosure standard. Rather, as the word "publicity" connotes, the fact must have widespread disclosure. Massachusetts is an exception; there, the courts have concluded that "the disclosure of private facts about an employee among other employees in the same corporation can constitute sufficient publication" under the state privacy statute.[23]

Private Facts

Generally, private facts are defined by what is reasonably and traditionally determined to be of a private nature—personal information that we seek to keep from public view. The disclosed private facts must truthfully reflect the plaintiff's private life; they cannot be false or fictionalized facts.[24] Typically, information about an individual's sexual behavior, medical condition, or financial status is considered private. The key inquiry, then, is: Were the private facts unknown publicly or inaccessible to the public before the allegedly infringing communication was published? If such facts were already a matter of general interest and circulated in a local or regional community via publication, no right of privacy may apply.

Highly Offensive to a Reasonable Person

The question here is whether the disclosure of the private facts offends the ordinary reasonable person. Because jurors typically make this determination, "highly offensive" is frequently a matter of community standards. California courts, for example, require plaintiffs to show that defendants published private facts "with reckless disregard for the fact that reasonable men would find the invasion highly offensive."[25]

Legitimate Concern to the Public or Newsworthiness

Plaintiffs cannot bring a successful disclosure of private facts action unless they can show that the communication was not public in nature. But the flip side of that element of a plaintiff's case also provides an often effective defense; when the private fact is a matter of public concern, it is newsworthy. Consequently, it is difficult for plaintiffs suing over a news outlet's widespread dissemination of an already publicly available, but previously undisclosed, fact to prevail. For the same reason, it is difficult for elected figures and celebrities to defeat a newsworthy defense, as virtually all aspects of their lives may be rendered public due to their widespread fame.

In *Cox Broadcasting Co. v. Cohn,* 420 U.S. 469, 496 (1975), the U.S. Supreme Court held that under the First Amendment there can be no recovery for a disclosure of private facts action when the facts are a matter of public record: "Such a rule would make it very difficult for the media to inform citizens about the public business and yet stay within the law. The rule would invite timidity and self-censorship and very likely lead to the suppression of many items that would otherwise be published and that should be made available to the public."[26] In *Smith v. Daily Mail Publishing Co.*, 443 U.S. 97 (1979), the Court said *Cox Broadcasting* and related rulings "all suggest strongly that if a newspaper lawfully obtains truthful information about a matter of public significance then state officials may not constitutionally punish publication of the information, absent a need to further a state interest of the highest order."[27]

In *Ostergren v. Cuccinelli*, 09–1723, 09–1796 (2010), the U.S. Court of Appeals for the Fourth Circuit applied the aforementioned *Smith* test to rule that a blogger's publication of lawfully obtained Social Security Numbers (SSNs) of Virginia government officials was protected under the First Amendment newsworthy standard. The federal appeals court said Virginia may not prosecute the blogger as long as the state continued to post public land records online without removing the SSNs.

Also, once an individual becomes newsworthy, he or she is always newsworthy, but only for the public retelling of the original newsworthy events and controversies and when there exists a current news justification for republication.[28]

Consent

Defendants carry the burden of proving consent, and, typically, such disputes involve the specific scope of the plaintiff's agreement. In *McCabe v. Village Voice*, a model argued that she had agreed that her nude photograph would appear in a book, and not the *Village Voice* newspaper. McCabe, the model, said that's what the photographer told her. Some three years later, when the photographer sold McCabe's and other photos to the newspaper, her release forms did not have her true signature and the *Voice* was unable to locate her to clarify her intentions. The judge ruled that a jury could find that the newspaper unreasonably assumed that the plaintiff had consented to have a photograph appear in a newspaper.[29]

> SUMMARY: If a defendant publicizes facts about a plaintiff that are highly offensive to a reasonable person and not of public concern, a plaintiff may win a public disclosure of embarrassing facts lawsuit. A defendant, however, may win by showing that the elements of the tort—private facts, offensiveness to a reasonable person, and not of public

concern—do not exist. Additionally, media defendants often prevail by showing that the facts are newsworthy. Under *Cox Broadcasting v. Cohen*, the U.S. Supreme Court established broad protection under the First Amendment for media to accurately report otherwise private information that is part of in an official public document. But once an individual becomes newsworthy, he or she is always newsworthy for the public retelling of the original newsworthy events and controversies and when there exists a current news justification for republication.

Publicity Placing a Person in a False Light

"One who gives publicity to a matter concerning another that places the other before the public in a false light is subject to liability to the other for invasion of privacy, if (i) the false light in which the other was placed would be highly offensive to a reasonable person, and (ii) the actor had knowledge of or acted in reckless disregard as to the falsity of the publicized matter and the false light in which the other would be placed."[30]

A majority of jurisdictions has adopted the false light tort.[31] Yet, there is strong opposition to it; a minority of jurisdictions has declined to adopt it and "scholarly critique of the tort has at times been sharp."[32] Critics of the false light tort say it borders on redundancy because it "duplicates or overlaps the interests already protected by the defamation torts of libel and slander."[33]

There is no disputing that the two torts are analogous. Both provide plaintiffs with remedies for harm caused by false or misleading communication. When a public figure brings a false light invasion of privacy claim or a private figure sues a media outlet over a story of public interest for false light, the reckless disregard for the truth or knowing falsity libel standard applies.[34] But courts recognizing false light draw at least two key distinctions: "Defamation reaches injury to reputation; privacy actions involve injuries to emotions and mental suffering."[35] For a plaintiff to succeed in defamation, he or she must show that the statement was shared with a third party. In contrast, the false light plaintiff must show that the statement was publicized, that it became public knowledge. In some jurisdictions, it is enough that the false information was circulated within a particular community, such as among evangelical protestant Christians.[36]

Falsehood

To prove a false light claim, a plaintiff must show that the communication was factually inaccurate. False light claims are based on the implication of falsehoods. The Indiana Court of Appeals in *Branham v. Celadon Trucking Services, Inc.*, 744 NE 2d 514 (2001), illustrates this standard. In *Branham*, the plaintiff sued for false light after his co-workers photographed him sleeping during a break while a partially clad fellow worker made a lewd gesture. Branham became a subject of derision at the workplace. But the Indiana court dismissed his suit because the photo was an accurate depiction of the plaintiff sleeping, the unfortunate target of a prank. In some jurisdictions, the factually inaccurate communication does not have to be private. Even though false light is a privacy tort, not all jurisdictions require that "the publicized facts concern the private life of plaintiffs."[37]

Offensiveness

The factually inaccurate communication must also be highly offensive to a reasonable person. In considering whether publicity is highly offensive, one must ask whether "the plaintiff, as a reasonable man, would be justified in the eyes of the community in feeling seriously offended and aggrieved by the publicity."[38] A District of Columbia court found that a false statement sexually linking a plaintiff to a known porn king would be offensive to a reasonable person.[39] An Illinois appeals court ruled that the false "implication that a plaintiff had an extramarital affair, filed for divorce from his spouse, abused alcohol, and misused personal funds would be offensive to a reasonable person."[40]

Fault

Since the U.S. Supreme Court's ruling in *Time v. Hill*, 385 U.S. 374 (1967), plaintiffs bringing false light actions must meet libel fault standards. That means plaintiffs who are public figures must establish that the defendant's communication was false, or publicized the false light statement with reckless disregard of the truth. The Court established that fault standard for defamation in *New York Times v. Sullivan*, 376 U.S. 254 (1964). The Court ruled later in *Philadelphia Newspapers Inc. v. Hepps*, 475 U.S. 767 (1986), that public and private figures must show falsity and reckless disregard for the truth when suing the media for defamation. Consequently, all plaintiffs bringing false light actions against the media must meet the *Hepps* standard as well.

Actors and models have found false light claims useful. In a number of such actions against media outlets, actors and models claimed that an outlet's use of their photographic image implied that they endorsed the outlet or assertions made in articles or broadcasts. For example, Jose Solano Jr., an actor from the *Baywatch* television show, sued *Playgirl* for publishing a cover photograph of the bare-chested actor. The cover headline read, "TV Guys. Primetime's Sexy Young Stars Exposed." But Solano had not given permission for the magazine to use the photograph, and there was no nude photo of him inside the magazine. Solano sued for false light and other claims. Applying the First Amendment reckless disregard for the truth or knowing falsity standard, the U.S. Court of Appeals ruled in *Solano v. Playgirl, Inc.*, 292 F.3d 1078, 1089 (9th Cir. 2002), that "where a defendant uses a plaintiff's name and likeness in a knowingly false manner to increase sales of the publication" the First Amendment does not apply.

SUMMARY: False light is the only invasion of privacy tort in which truth is a defense. It is a close cousin to libel and plaintiffs bringing false light actions must meet libel fault standards. That means plaintiffs who are public figures must establish that the defendant knew that the communication was false, or publicized the false light statement with reckless disregard of the truth. False light plaintiffs must also establish that the false light in which they were placed is highly offensive to a reasonable person. But there is no requirement to show that a false statement, embellished report, or a misleading or doctored photograph harmed the plaintiff's reputation, as is essential to libel. False light involves injuries to the plaintiff's emotional and mental well-being, not reputation.

Intrusion

One who intentionally intrudes, physically or otherwise, upon the solitude or seclusion of another or his private affairs or concerns is subject to liability to the other for invasion of his privacy, if the intrusion would be highly offensive to a reasonable person.[41] Intrusion is the only invasion of privacy tort in which publicity plays no role. The harm does not arise because a defendant publishes a photograph of the plaintiff as she frolicked nude in her backyard hot tub, or reads quotes from her personal diary during a radio broadcast. The public disclosure of private facts claim covers the harms caused by the public disclosure of such information. In contrast, intrusion stems from the harm caused by the defendant's physical presence or the mechanical or electronic extension of that presence onto the plaintiff's private property or into his private affairs. Plaintiffs bringing intrusion claims must show (i) intent on the part of the defendant to intrude; (ii) that the intrusion was highly offensive to a reasonable person; and (iii) that the plaintiff had a reasonable expectation of privacy regarding his person, place, or information. The third element—reasonable expectation of privacy—is central to the plaintiff's case.

Intentional Conduct

Accidental intrusion into a plaintiff's private activities does not provide sufficient cause to bring an intrusion action. The defendant must have intended to intrude. Accordingly, courts examine defendants' motives for intruding. If the plaintiff cannot establish that the defendant had the intent to interfere with his privacy, there is no intentional conduct. The facts presented in *Hamrick v. Wellman Products Group*, 2004 Ohio 5170 (2004), provide some idea of the type of conduct that, though intrusive, shows no intent upon the intruders to invade the privacy of the plaintiff. Plaintiff Hamrick argued that two cleaning women, who pushed open a closed door to a stall located in workplace restroom to find him sitting there partially clothed, invaded his privacy. The Ohio court rejected his claim, noting that the cleaning women were not trying to catch him in an embarrassing position; they were merely trying to do their jobs.

Highly Offensive to Reasonable Person

Triers of fact—jurors or judges—decide whether a person of reasonable sensitivity would find a defendant's intrusion highly offensive. But there is no clear definition of "highly offensive" intrusion. Pennsylvania courts, for example, require the plaintiff to allege facts "sufficient to establish that the intrusion could be expected to cause mental suffering, shame, or humiliation to a person of ordinary sensibilities."[42] Consequently, the Borings—the Franklin Park, Pennsylvania, couple that sued Google's Street View online mapping for intrusion and other privacy torts—failed to persuade a federal judge in Pennsylvania that it had a valid intrusion claim: "While it is easy to imagine that many whose property appears on Google's virtual maps resent the privacy implications, it is hard to believe that any—other than the most exquisitely sensitive—would suffer shame or humiliation," the judge ruled.[43] California courts consider factors such as "the degree and setting of the intrusion, and the intruder's motives and objectives."[44] In *Randolph v. ING Life Insurance and Annuity Co.*, 973 A. 2d 702, 710 (D.C. 2009), a case resulting from the theft of a life insurance agent's laptop in which were stored customers' social security numbers, a court said, "In this age of identity theft and other wrongful conduct through the unauthorized use of electronically-stored data, we have little difficulty agreeing that conduct giving rise to unauthorized viewing of personal information such as a plaintiff's Social Security number and other identifying information can constitute an intrusion that is highly offensive to any reasonable person."

Reasonable Expectation of Privacy

The intrusion tort provides a common law source for use of the reasonable expectation of privacy standard, a standard similar to one derived from the search and seizure clause of the U.S. Constitution's Fourth Amendment.[45] Once intent and offensiveness are established, a plaintiff's case hinges on a showing that it was reasonable for the plaintiff to believe that the information, property, or space that the plaintiff or her property occupied at the time of the intrusion was private. Perhaps it may be helpful to see this concept as a spectrum, with the home and its various compartments, particularly a locked bathroom, on the reasonable-expectation-of-privacy end. Typically, it is reasonable to expect that a locked home or locked rooms inside a private residence signal privacy. In contrast, public sidewalks or commons, such as a public park, are zones situated on the opposite end of the spectrum, where it is unreasonable to expect protection from intrusion. When you walk on a public street, it is unreasonable to expect that others cannot observe your conduct and appearance.

The reasonable-expectation-of-privacy analysis, however, is not limited to identifying where the intrusion took place. A plaintiff's conduct may diminish or eliminate his or her reasonable expectation of privacy even in otherwise private settings. For example, a plaintiff who sunbathes topless in her backyard has no reasonable expectation of privacy if her neighbors can see her from their second-story windows, despite the eight-foot fence that surrounds the plaintiff's backyard. If, however, the neighbors need a telescopic lens to see her, she is more likely to have a reasonable expectation of privacy.

Likewise, even on a New York City public street, individuals—even world-famous, public figures—still have a degree of a reasonable expectation of privacy. In *Galella v. Onassis*, 487 F.2d 986 (1973), the U.S. Circuit Court of Appeals, for example, upheld a modified restraining order against a paparazzi photographer, limiting him from blocking the movement of the former First Lady Jackie Kennedy Onassis in public places. It should not, however, be surprising that it is reasonable to expect that parts of our bodies and undergarments, which are typically covered from view when we are in public places, are still deemed private, as the Supreme Court of Alabama declared in the intrusion case *Daily Times Democrat v. Graham*, 162 S0.2d 474 (1964).

Trespass

As noted at the chapter's outset, Google paid the nominal fee of $1 to the Borings for trespassing upon their land to take video for their street mapping project. Under trespass—technically trespass to chattels—the defendant intentionally uses or interferes with the personal property owned by the plaintiff.[46] It is a tort closely related to intrusion, and, typically, plaintiffs claim both for the same wrongdoing. (For further discussion of newsgathering torts of trespass and intrusion, see Chapter 7.)

Defenses

Obviously, a defendant may negate any of the elements of the intrusion claim as a defense, and a defendant may argue consent. Though newsworthiness is not a complete defense, the newsworthy status of the plaintiff may mitigate against the severity of the plaintiff's remedies, as in *Galella v. Onassis*,

487 F.2d 986 (1973), in which the federal appeals panel reduced the yardage of the distance the paparazzi had to maintain between Onassis and himself. Of course, the reasonable expectation of privacy test can be used as a defense.

SUMMARY: Plaintiffs pursuing intrusion claims do not have to establish that the invasion of privacy led to publication. It is the only privacy tort in which the harm occurs from the act of violating seclusion—taking a photograph, electronically eavesdropping on a telephone conversation, or making copies of someone's private notes—and not the subsequent publicizing of the information. Once intent and offensiveness are established, most intrusion cases are won and lost on the reasonable expectation of privacy standard. That standard requires plaintiffs to show that they believed that their person, information, or the space they occupied was private and that it was reasonable to hold such a belief. A plaintiff's conduct can diminish his or her reasonable expectation of privacy in private places or increase it in public places.

Privacy & Cyberspace

As noted at the outset of this chapter, Congress has done little to regulate digital privacy interests, leaving the markets and the courts to establish most of the standards. As a result, the law has been slow to mark the boundaries of privacy in cyberspace. Take email, for example. Ray Tomlinson wrote the first email programs in 1972, and with the advent of the World Wide Web in the early 1990s, online-mail use became as common as telephoning by the 21st century's start. Meanwhile, whether users could invoke the Fourth Amendment's reasonable expectation of privacy standard to prevent the government from obtaining their emails from Internet Service Providers (ISPs) without first obtaining a court-ordered warrant remained an unsettled question for nearly 40 years. In contrast, warrantless searches of persons, homes, telephones, and mail are presumptively unconstitutional. In determining whether a right to privacy exists under the Fourth Amendment, courts apply the *Katz v. U.S.*, 389 U.S. 347, 361 (1967), reasonableness standard, asking first whether an individual has "exhibited an actual (subjective) expectation of privacy and, second, that the expectation be one that society is prepared to recognize as 'reasonable.'" However, email joined the list of Fourth Amendment-protected zones of privacy only in the jurisdiction of the U.S. Court of Appeals for the Sixth Circuit in December 2010. In a landmark ruling, the Sixth Circuit held in *U.S. v. Warshak*, 2010 FED App. 0377P Slip Op at 22 (6th Cir. 2010), that under the Fourth Amendment a subscriber to an Internet service "enjoys a reasonable expectation of privacy in the contents of emails 'that are stored with, or sent or received through, a commercial ISP.'" The Sixth Circuit in *Warshak* also found 18 U.S.C. 2703(b) of the Stored Communications Act (SCA), which is part of the Electronic Communications Privacy Act (ECPA), unconstitutional because it allows government to get private emails without a warrant.[47]

Thus, in the wake of *Warshak*, privacy activists renewed their efforts to persuade Congress to revise the ECPA to require the government to produce a warrant based on probable cause to get users' emails. Congress enacted the ECPA in 1986 as an amendment to Title II of the Omnibus Crime Control and Safe Streets Act (Wiretap Statute) to extend Fourth Amendment due process protection to transmission of electronic data via computer. Title II of the ECPA, the Stored Communications Act (SCA), protects communications held in electronic storage, most notably messages stored on computers. The act, however, only covers emails that are stored by ISPs for up to six months. But that is not how most ISPs operate; they tend to keep users' transmitted emails for more than six months. Privacy activists argue that Congress needs to rewrite the ECPA to reflect the industry's practice. Otherwise, as the *Warshak* ruling recognized, users' reasonable expectations that their emails are private go unprotected.

Privacy activists argue that Congress also must update the ECPA to extend Fourth Amendment due process protection to data stored in the Internet, the tracking of GPS data in cell phones and mobile Internet devices, shared information and photographs on social networking sites, and other digital activities.

Meanwhile, Congress responded to privacy concerns raised by the misuse of cell phone video cameras when it passed the Video Voyeurism Prevention Act of 2004. Though it creates criminal penalties, the statute borrows from the reasonable-expectation-of-privacy standard articulated in intrusion tort law. The statute amends the federal criminal code to make it a misdemeanor to videotape, photograph, film, record, or broadcast an image of an individual's private area without consent under "circumstances in which *a reasonable person* would believe that he or she could disrobe in privacy...or circumstances in which *a reasonable person* would believe that a private area of the individual would not be visible to the public, regardless of whether that person is in a public or private place."[48]

Likewise, Congress passed the Driver's Privacy Protection Act of 1994 (DPPA), spurred in part by the murder of young actress Rebecca Shaeffer. Her murderer, an obsessed fan, obtained her address from a California online database. The information was part of the public record which is why Shaeffer's attacker was able to obtain her address legally. But now the DPPA forbids states from releasing such information, unless a request meets one of fourteen exceptions. In effect, the act expands the privacy zone while shrinking the public and press's right to access records that were previously public. The act creates a conflict between reasonable expectation of privacy and right to access government public records interests. But in *Reno v. Condon*, 528 U.S. 141 (2000), the Court upheld the act under the 10th Amendment, ruling that it is a proper exercise of Congress's authority to regulate interstate commerce under the Commerce Clause.

In another effort to protect privacy, Congress invoked §5 of the Federal Trade Commission Act to police Internet marketers who target children by collecting their personal information from websites without parental knowledge. Specifically, the Children's Online Privacy Protection Act (COPPA) protects the privacy of children under the age of 13 by requesting parental consent for the collection or use of personal information of the users. COPPA targets commercial websites and online services that are directed at children and the FTC can fine violators as much as $11,000 for each violation.

The FTC Reins in Social Media Companies

Under Section 5(a) of the FTC Act, the commission has authority to sue companies for deceptive and unfair acts affecting commerce. In 2010 and 2011, the FTC charged Twitter, Google, and Facebook with such practices stemming from the companies' handling of users' personal data. All three companies reached settlements with the agency in which they admitted to misleading customers about the effectiveness of their efforts to safeguard personal information. In March 2011, the FTC reached a settlement with Twitter resolving charges that the company deceived consumers and put their privacy at risk by failing to safeguard personal information after hackers had obtained private tweets and other information, and were able to send out fake tweets from user accounts between January and May of 2009. Under the settlement terms, an independent auditor will assess Twitter's newly established security program every other year for 10 years.[49] Google Inc. reached a settlement with the FTC stemming from charges that it used deceptive tactics and violated its own privacy promises to consumers when it launched its social network, Google Buzz, in 2010. Settlement terms include a requirement that Google put a comprehensive privacy program in place and subject itself to independent privacy audits for 20 years.[50] Facebook reached an agreement on charges that it misled its users about the effectiveness of privacy settings and what information they were sharing and with whom. The terms of the settlement require, among other things, that Facebook prevent anyone from accessing a user's material within 30 days of a user's deletion of an account, to undergo periodic privacy audits, and to obtain users' express consent before the company shares their information beyond the privacy settings users have established.[51]

SUMMARY: Federal laws protecting digital privacy vary; they address specific concerns. Still, they fall into two groups; they protect against government access to private records, or the unauthorized use of digitally captured, collected, or stored information. The Electronic Communications Privacy Act falls into the former group and the Driver's Privacy Protection Act, Video Voyeurism Prevention Act, and the Children's Online Privacy Protection Act fall into the latter category. Privacy advocates, however, contend that Congress must rewrite federal privacy laws to keep pace with new threats to privacy posed by digital technologies such as GPS-enabled phones, digital book purchase records, search engines, and social networking sites. Meanwhile, the FTC has established itself as the leading regulator of online companies' privacy policies and practices by bringing successful actions against Twitter, Google, and Facebook in 2011.

Trespass in Cyberspace

Early in this chapter, you learned that Google admitted its street mapping project trespassed on private property. But that settlement arose from the company's actions in real space. Does the law of trespass to chattel, as discussed above, apply to actions in the virtual reality? While Google has not been sued for trespass in cyberspace, it may be vulnerable to such a legal action, depending on the jurisdiction, because its search engines, like other search engines, use robots, bots, spiders, or web crawlers; Google calls its program "Googlebot." Generally, plaintiffs argue that the unauthorized use of such software allows defendants unauthorized use of their property. Plaintiffs argue that a trespass action is appropriate because, in effect, defendants have intentionally sneaked into their stores and warehouses and walked away with personal or business possessions.

Generally, defendants argue that websites are publicly accessible. Therefore, consent has been given to the public. They also contend that the electronic search devices are insufficiently tangible to apply to the brick-and-mortar trespass law because trespass must result in physical damage or functional interference with property. There are fewer than a dozen rulings on the application of trespass to the unauthorized use of computers and the Internet, so the issue is far from settled law.

At least five federal trial judges have ruled that Internet service providers whose computers are overburdened with spam email may sue under trespass without having to show a substantial interference with the right to possess their own computers. For example, the judge in *CompuServe Inc. v. Cyber Promotions, Inc.*, 962 F.Supp. 1015, 1017 (S.D.Ohio1997), held "that where defendants engaged in a course of conduct of transmitting a substantial volume of electronic data in the form of unsolicited e-mail to plaintiff's proprietary computer equipment…continued such practice after repeated demands to cease and desist, and…deliberately evaded plaintiff's affirmative efforts to protect its computer equipment from such use, plaintiff has a viable claim for trespass to personal property and is entitled to injunctive relief to protect its property."[52]

In *eBay, Inc. v. Bidder's Edge, Inc.,* 100 F. Supp. 2d 1058 (N.D. Cal. 2000), a federal court preliminarily enjoined Bidder's Edge from accessing eBay's computer systems by use of an automated querying program without eBay's written consent. Though eBay suffered no damage or functional interference with its website's operation, the federal court ruled that "conduct which consists of intermeddling with or use of another's personal property, is sufficient to establish a cause of action for trespass to chattel."[53]

The California Supreme Court and at least two other courts reached an opposing conclusion.[54] In *Intel Corporation v. Hamidi,* 1 P. 3d 296 (2003), Intel claimed that an ex-employee committed trespass when he used the email system to share his dissatisfaction with his ex-employer with several thousand employees. The court, however, reversed an injunction against the employee because there was no evidence that his use of the email system harmed or interfered with the operation of the company's computers. The court said that, while other torts may be applicable to the Internet, trespass is not one of them because the alleged injury must stem from a loss of or interference with tangible property.

Misappropriation, Right of Publicity Claims, and Social Networking Sites

It seems reasonable to assume that the conduct of social networking sites might make them vulnerable to misappropriation claims, alleging that they have used others' names or likenesses without consent, or right of publicity claims, because they used others' names and likenesses to enhance their commercial endeavors. That is because Facebook and MySpace profit from the sale of user information and photographs directly by selling user content to advertisers and marketers, or indirectly by using the content to attract new users.

On the other hand, it is no secret that Facebook, for example, sells user information to advertisers and marketers and the core reason for its existence is to make it easy for users to share personal information with a large circle of individuals. Social media networks' user policies appear to warn users about the public nature of their systems.

Ostensibly, user policies spell out terms of service, rules that users must abide by to use the site, and terms that give the site permission to collect and sell user information to data brokers, credit rating agencies, advertisers, employers, and health insurers, or to hand over to the government. But privacy advocates say that most policies are vague to the site's advantage: "In many cases, the privacy policies of social networking services lack a definition of critical terms or broadly state purposes of data collection (e.g., 'to provide you with a better experience') to allow limitless use of data."[55]

If a user wishes to object to a specified use of private information—to withhold consent—sites typically provide either an opt-in or opt-out of the agreement choice. Privacy advocates prefer the opt-in process, which typically requires a user to click approval or send an email request to the site owners. If the user fails to opt-in, then the site cannot exploit the personal information.

Generally, companies prefer the opt-out process. If the user fails to opt-out, he or she has given consent; the site may use the information.[56] Because privacy policies of many social networking sites employ vague terms and require users to opt-in, the issue of consent, or lack of, is often pivotal in misappropriation claims brought against social networking sites.

In *Doe v. Friendfinder Network, Inc.*, 2008 WL 803947 (D.N.H. Mar. 27, 2008), "Jane Doe" sued the social networking site "Adult Friendfinder," alleging, among other claims, a violation of her right of publicity. A registered user posted a profile of a "recently separated 40-year old woman in the Upper Valley region of New Hampshire who was seeking 'Men or Women for Erotic Chat/E-mail/Phone Fantasies and Discreet Relationships'" and listed other biographical data. The plaintiff said she and others in her community recognize the profile as a description of her, though she had not posted it. The site also used the description to promote its services on other sexual-oriented websites. A federal judge ruled that the plaintiff had a legitimate case for infringement of the plaintiff's right to publicity. The judge also ruled that the plaintiff's claim against the website owner was not barred by CDA §230. The federal statute that immunizes Internet service providers from many state law legal claims based on user-generated content does not apply to right of publicity claims.

In *Cohen v. Facebook*, C 10–5282 RS (N.D. Cal. June 28, 2011), a federal trial judge dismissed a plaintiffs' class action misappropriation claim because the plaintiffs were unable to show that their names and likenesses had any general commercial value, and, in the alternative, failed to show that Facebook's promotion of its Friend Finder service caused them to suffer mental anguish. The plaintiffs claimed that Facebook used their names and photographs for commercial purposes to promote the service without their consent or knowledge. Plaintiffs argued that they were entitled to statutory damages even absent a showing of harm. The court, however, did allow the plaintiffs to amend their complaint by showing that they had indeed suffered mental anguish.

Toward the end of 2011, a federal trial judge sitting in California ruled that another class action alleging misappropriation against Facebook could proceed to trial. Facebook earns money primarily through the sale of targeted advertising that appears on member pages. One such advertising effort is sponsored stories, which appear on a member's Facebook page and consist of a friend's (another member's) name, photograph, the friend's endorsement of an advertiser, and the advertiser's logo. The plaintiffs in *Fraley v. Facebook*, 11-CV-01726-LHK (N.D. Cal. Dec. 16, 2012), however, argued that Facebook used their names and photographs in sponsored stories without their consent. The judge ruled that the issue of consent was one that could be sorted out at trial because the plaintiffs were Facebook members before the company started its sponsored stories advertising campaign. Thus, whether Facebook's Statement of Rights and Responsibilities, Privacy Policy, or Help Center pages were proof of user consent, as Facebook asserted, remained a disputed question of fact for a jury to sort out. The judge also ruled that the plaintiffs had evidence showing that Facebook directly benefited from the sponsored story ads in the form of quotes from the CEO and COO, claiming that "friend endorsements are two to three times more valuable than generic advertisements sold to Facebook advertisers…Thus, Plaintiffs have alleged facts showing that their personal endorsement has concrete, measurable, and provable value in the economy at large."[57]

Public Disclosure of Private Facts & Social Networking Sites

Given that this tort requires a plaintiff to show that a publication has publicized private aspects of a plaintiff's life, blogs and other postings can generate such lawsuits. But when the plaintiff's conduct is partly responsible for publication of private information, then the plaintiff doesn't have a triable case. *Moreno v. Hanford Sentinel, Inc.*, 172 Cal. App. 4th 1125 (Cal. Ct. App. 2009), is illustrative. The plaintiff, Cynthia Moreno, ridiculed her hometown of Coalinga, California, on her MySpace page. The article was downloaded, passed on to the local newspaper, which then published it as a letter to the editor. It was not well received by the townsfolk. Her family was threatened with death, gun shots were fired at the Moreno home, her family moved out of town, and patronage to the family business fell off so much that the 20-year-old business closed. The family sued the newspaper for public disclosure of private facts, lost at trial, and a California appeals court affirmed the verdict. Under California law, to adequately state a claim for violation of the constitutional right of privacy, a party must establish (1) a legally protected privacy interest, (2) a reasonable expectation of privacy under the circumstances, and (3) a serious invasion of the privacy interest. The court noted that the doctrine of reasonable expectation does not require that information be held in total secrecy; information disclosed to a close circle of friends still may be deemed private. But Moreno's expectation that only a limited audience would view it was unreasonable and her deletion of the item soon after it was posted was irrelevant, the court said; her unsecured MySpace page was accessible to the public, making her potential audience vast.

The Stored Communications Act (SCA) & Facebook

So far, Facebook has fended off a class action lawsuit, *In re Facebook Privacy Litigation*, 791 F. Supp 705 (N D Cal 2011). The lawsuit claims that,among other wrongs, the company's system that allows advertisers to obtain user IDs, or "usernames," when Facebook users click on advertisements, violates the SCA because it discloses the plaintiffs' communications to advertisers who were not the intended recipients of the private communications. Under the SCA,an entity that provides electronic communication services shall not knowingly divulge the contents of information stored in its computers or other forms of electronic storage to unintended recipients. A federal trial judge sitting in California said that the plaintiffs failed to have a claim under the SCA because, whether the software sent communications to Facebook or to the advertisers, either entity appeared to have a lawful right to receive the communication.

Privacy, Social Networking Sites, and Criminal and Civil Discovery Proceedings

Cyberspace creates no special zone of privacy for parties in criminal and civil trials subpoenaed by courts to obtain information. Instead, courts weigh a party's reasonable expectation of privacy under the Fourth Amendment against fair trial interests and traditional discovery principles when deciding whether to order a party to disclose information stored in cyberspace. Generally, courts allow discovery of photographs, postings, emails, and other information from social networking websites when the information is relevant to the litigation and the discovery request is narrowly tailored. In *U.S. v. Lifshitz*, 369 F.3d 173, 190 (2004), the Second Circuit held that individuals whose emails have reached their recipients, or who post communications on the Internet, do not enjoy a reasonable expectation of privacy under the Fourth Amendment. In *Beye v. Horizon Blue Cross Blue Shield of N.J.*, 568 F. Supp. 2d 556, 579 (D.N.J. 2008), a federal trial judge ordered plaintiffs to produce information posted on their daughters' Facebook and MySpace pages, which the girls had shared with others, but not information that had been kept private.

So far, courts have rejected the argument that information posted on social networking sites is categorically private. One New York judge, however, reached the opposite conclusion: social media sites are inherently public. The judge granted a defendant access to a plaintiff's current and older Facebook and MySpace pages and accounts, including all deleted pages and related information in *Romano v. Steelcase Inc.*, 30 Misc.3d 426 (2010). The judge, quoting a law review article, said there was no reasonable expectation of privacy on social networking sites, even when privacy settings are put into play, because "given the millions of users, '[i]n this environment, privacy is no longer grounded in reasonable expectations, but rather in some theoretical protocol better known as wishful thinking.'"[58] In contrast, in *Tompkins v. Detroit Metro. Airport*, 10–10413 (E.D. Mich. 2012), a Michigan judge rejected the *Romano* position when it declined to grant a defendant access to a plaintiff's entire Facebook account. Even though information posted on Facebook set for private access is not generally privileged, the judge said, a defendant does not have a right "to rummage at will through information that Plaintiff has limited from public view." The defendant must show that the sought-after information is reasonably calculated to lead to admissible evidence.

SUMMARY: "You have zero privacy anyway," Sun Microsystems Chief Executive Scott McNealy said in 1999, "get over it." "People have really gotten comfortable not only sharing more information and different kinds, but more openly and with more people," Facebook CEO Mark Zuckerberg said in January 2010, "that social norm is just something that has evolved over time." Some CEOs of online companies and others would have us believe that the Internet has changed our traditional conceptions of privacy, or gives us little choice but to abandon such notions. Yet, early in the third decade of the cyber age, the overwhelming majority of the small number of courts that has addressed cyberspace privacy issues has applied traditional, if not ancient, privacy law doctrines to online activities. Several courts have ruled that a lawsuit alleging trespass is a legitimate claim for cyberspace activities even though the ancient doctrine requires interference with an individual or an individual's tangible property. The California Supreme Court and at least two other courts, however, have said trespass is not applicable to cyberspace activities. Courts have not walled off cyberspace from misappropriation and right of publicity claims, either. Still, plaintiffs' toughest tasks are persuading judges that, by allowing access to only a small group of individuals, a user did not make his or her pages public, and that their acquiescence to a social media site's terms and use policies did not include consent to use of their personal images and data. That is pretty much the same task that plaintiffs bringing public disclosure of private facts actions face. And in *Moreno v. Hanford Sentinel, Inc.*, a court said there is a reasonable expectation of privacy from full-public disclosure of information posted on social networking pages when information is limited to a close circle of friends.

Some say that since social media exists to facilitate the sharing of personal information, traditional notions of privacy have little meaning there. Many users, however, advance the opposite view. When they designate certain information on their pages for private access, a court has no right to make them disclose that information. But in rulings on whether a party in a criminal or civil action must comply with an order to disclose, most courts reject the argument that information posted on social media sites marked private is immune to such orders. Instead, they balance the Fourth Amendment's reasonable expectation of privacy interest against fair trial concerns to determine whether disclosure is required. One ruling stands out, however. In *Romano v. Steelcase*, a New York judge said there is no reasonable expectation of privacy on social networking sites.

ONLINE RESOURCES

1. Electronic Privacy Information Center, http://www.informationshield.com/usprivacy laws.html
2. *Europe v. Facebook*, http://www.europe-v-facebook.org/
3. Privacy and the Press, http://www.freedomforum.org/packages/first/privacyandthe press/resources.htm
4. Privacy in Cyberspace, http://cyber.law.harvard.edu/privacy/module1.html
5. United States Privacy Laws, http://www.informationshield.com/usprivacylaws.html

QUESTIONS

1. The reasonable expectation of privacy standard requires plaintiffs to show that they believed that their person, information, or property, or the zone they occupied, was private and that it was reasonable to hold such a belief. Apply the standard to the following facts to determine whether Ms. Godiva Chocolate, a fictional character, has a reasonable expectation of privacy. Ms. Chocolate, a wealthy, but eccentric, retired actress lives in Coventry, Connecticut, where she vacuums her living room in the nude every Saturday at 9 a.m. Often the curtains covering the large windows are left open. Her living room's large window faces the street, which is 60 yards from the house. The sidewalk spans 10 yards from the street to her front yard. Her front yard stretches 50 feet before it reaches the window. Therefore, if you stand on the sidewalk in front of her house, you will have to look about 50 yards—half the size of a football field—to see inside her living room. Celebrity TV learns about Ms. Chocolate's vacuuming habits and videotapes her from an unmarked van parked in front of her house. Has Celebrity TV illegitimately intruded on Ms. Chocolate's privacy?

2. Your cell phone leaves a record of your location every time you make a call, and your mobile phone service supplier keeps such records. Do you believe you have a reasonable expectation of privacy regarding information revealing when and where you have made a phone call, or should police be able to obtain your phone logs from your mobile phone service supplier without obtaining a warrant? The legal ground rules remain unclear, but that was the question before the U.S. Court of Appeals for the Third Circuit in the case, *In the Matter of the Application of the U.S. for an Order Directing a Provider of Electronic Communication Service to Disclose Records to the Government*, 08–4227 (2010), scheduled for arguments in 2011.

3. Do you think there should be a law that gives people the right to know everything that a website knows about them, or do you feel such a law is unnecessary? Do you believe there should be a law that requires websites and advertising companies to delete all stored information about an individual, or do you believe such a law is unnecessary? Berkeley Center for Law and Technology at the University of California, Berkeley School of Law, sponsored a nationally representative telephone survey of Americans to understand the public's views of both online and offline privacy issues. The findings, reported in "How Different are Young Adults from Older Adults When it Comes to Information Privacy Attitudes and Policies?" can be downloaded at, http://papers.ssrn.com/sol3/papers.cfm? abstract_id=1589864&rec=1&srcabs=1588163. See if your views correspond with other young adults, ages 18–24.

ENDNOTES

1. *Boring v. Google, Inc.*, 598 F.Supp.2d 695 (W.D. Pa. 2009), *affirmed in part, reversed in part, and remanded,* 362 Fed. Appx. 273 (3d Cir. 2010), cert. denied,131 S.Ct. 150(2010).
2. Samuel Warren and Louis Brandeis. "The Right to Privacy, " 4 *Harvard Law Review* 193, fn 13 (1890), http://www.jjllplaw.com/The-Right-to-Privacy-Warren-Brandeis-Harvard-Law-Review-1890.html
3. *Schuyler v. Curtis et al.* Supreme Court of New York, Special Term, New York County, 15 N.Y.S. 787; 1891 N.Y.; *Pavesich v. New England Life Insurance Co,* 50 S.E. 68, 75 (1905).
4. *Pavesich v. New England Life Insurance* at 75.
5. N.Y. Session Laws 1903, ch. 132,§§ 1–2. Amended in 1921, N.Y. Civ. Rights Law.
6. William L. Prosser. "Privacy," 48 *California Law Review* 383, 388(1960).
7. *Welling v. Weinfeld,* 866 N.E. 2d 1051 (Ohio 2007).
8. *Restatement of the Law, Second, Torts,* §652, American Law Institute, http://cyber.law.harvard.edu/privacy/Privacy_R2d_Torts_Sections.htm
9. *PETA v. Bobby Berosini, Ltd.,* 895 P. 2d 1269, 1283 (Nevada 1995).
10. Ibid.
11. Ann Margaret Eames. "Caught on Tape: Exposing the Unsettled and Unpredictable State of the Right of Publicity," 3 *Journal of High Technology Law* 41(2004).
12. Samuel Warren and Louis Brandeis. "The Right to Privacy," 4 *Harvard Law Review* 193 (1890), http://www.jjllplaw.com/The-Right-to-Privacy-Warren-Brandeis-Harvard-Law-Review-1890.html
13. *Montana v. San Jose Mercury News, Inc.,* 40Cal.Rptr. 2d 639, 640 (1995).
14. *Hilton v. Hallmark Cards,* 599 F.3d 894, 905 (9th Cir. 2010).
15. Ibid. 912.
16. *Benavidez v. Anheuser-Busch, Inc.,* 873 F.2d 102, 104 (5th Cir. 1989).
17. *Kapellas v. Kofman,* 1 Cal.3d 20, 36 (1969).
18. *Booth v. Curtis Publishing,* 182 N.E. 2d 812 (1962).
19. *Zacchini v. Scripps Howard Broadcasting,* 433 U.S. 562, 575–576 (1977).
20. See *Comedy III Productions v. Gary Saderup,* Inc., 106 Cal.Rptr.2d 126 (2001); *Winter v. DC Comics,* 30 Cal.4th 881, 134 Cal.Rptr.2d 634, 69 P.3d 473, 475 (2003); *Kirby v. Sega of Am., Inc.,* 144 Cal. App.4th 47, 50 Cal.Rptr. 607 (2006).
21. *Restatement of Law, Second, Torts,* §652, http://cyber.law.harvard.edu/privacy/Privacy_R2d_Torts_Sections.htm
22. *Cefalu v. Globe Newspaper Co.,* 391 NE 2d 935 (Mass. Appeals Court 1979).
23. *Bratt v. International Business Machines Corp.,* 467 NE 2d 126 (Mass. Supreme Judicial Court 1984).
24. See *Restatement of the Law, Second, Torts* §652D.
25. *Briscoe v. Reader's Digest Association,* 4 Cal. 3d 529 (1971).
26. See also *The Florida Star v. B.J.F.,* 491 U.S. 524 (1989).
27. *Smith v. Daily Mail Publishing Co.,* 443 U.S. 97, 103 (1979).
28. *Briscoe v. Reader's Digest Association,* 483 at 41.
29. *McCabe v. Village Voice, Inc.,* 550 F. Supp. 525, 530 (Dist. Court, ED Pennsylvania 1982).
30. *Restatement of the Law, Second, Torts,* §652e.
31. *West v. Media General Convergence, Inc.,* 53 SW 3d 640, 644 (Tenn. 2001).
32. *Howard v. Antilla,* 294 F.3d 244, 248 (1st Cir. 2002).
33. *West v. Media General,* 53 SW 3d at 645.
34. *New York Times v. Sullivan,* 376 U.S. 254 (1964); *Philadelphia Newspapers, Inc. v. Hepps,* 475 U.S. 767(1986).
35. *Branham v. Celadon Trucking Services, Inc.,* 744 NE 2d 514, 524 (2001).
36. See *Duncan v. Peterson,* 835 N.E.2d 411 (2005).
37. *In re Lansaw,* 424 BR 193, 200 (Bank.Court, WD Pennsylvania 2010).
38. See *Restatement (Second) of Torts,* § 652E, cmt. c.
39. *Benz v. Washington Newspaper Publishing Co.,* No. 05–1760 (EGS), 2006 WL 2844896, at *6 (D.D.C. Sept. 29, 2006).

40. *Duncan v. Peterson*, No. 2–09–1078 (ILL: Appellate Court, 2d Dist. 2010).

41. *Restatement of the Law, Second, Torts*, § 652B.

42. *Boring v. Google, Inc.*, 598 at 700.

43. Ibid.

44. *Hernandez v. Hillsides, Inc.*, 47 Cal. 4th 272, 287 (California Supreme Court 2009).

45. See *Stengart v. Loving Care Agency*, 990 A. 2d 650. 660 (New Jersey Supreme Ct. 2010).

46. *Restatement (Second) of Torts* §218.

47. *U.S. v. Warshak*, 2010 FED App. 0377P Slip Op at 22 (6th Cir. 2010).

48. U.S.C.A. § 1801.

49. *In the Matter of Twitter, Inc.*, 092 3093 (2011), http://www.ftc.gov/os/caselist/0923093/index.shtm

50. *In the Matter of Google, Inc.*, 102 3136 (2011), http://www.ftc.gov/os/caselist/1023136/index.shtm

51. *In the Matter of Facebook, Inc.*, 092 3184 (2011), http://www.ftc.gov/os/caselist/0923184/index.shtm

52. See also *America Online, Inc. v. IMS,* 24 F.Supp.2d 548 (E.D.Va.1998); *Hotmail Corp. v. Van$ Money Pie Inc.,* 1998 WL 388389 (N.D.Cal. Apr. 16, 1998); *America Online, Inc. v. LCGM, Inc.,* 46 F.Supp.2d 444 (E.D.Va.1998); *America Online, Inc. v. Prime Data Systems, Inc.,* 1998 WL 34016692 (E.D.Va. Nov.20,1998).

53. *eBay, Inc. v. Bidder's Edge, Inc.,*100 F. Supp. 2d 1058, 1070 (N.D. Cal. 2000).

54. See also *Pearl Investments, LLC v. Standard I/O, Inc.*, 257 F.Supp.2d 326 (2003); *Sotelo v. Directrevenue*, 384 F.Supp.2d 1219 (2005).

55. Katitza Rodriguez Pereda. "Comments of the Electronic Frontier Foundation to the Council of Europe Committee of Experts on New Media," MC-NM(2010)003_en, 6, https://www.eff.org/sites/default/files/filenode/documents/EFF-CoE-Social-Networks-FINAL_1.pdf,

56. See Michael Birnhack and Niva Elkin-Koren. "Does Law Matter Online? Empirical Evidence on Privacy Law Compliance," 17 *Michigan Telecommunications and Technology Law Review* 337 (2011), http://www.mttlr.org/vol-seventeen/birnhack&elkin-koren.pdf

57. *Fraley v. Facebook*, 11-CV-01726-LHK * 16 (N.D. Cal. Dec. 16, 2012).

58. *Romano v. Steelcase Inc.*, 30 Misc.3d 426, 434 (2010); see also *McMillen v. Hummingbird Speedway, Inc.*, 2010 WL 4403285 (Pa.Com.Pl. 2010).

CHAPTER SEVEN

Prior Restraints & Subsequent Punishment

CONTROVERSY: Perhaps Julian Assange should call his anti-secrecy operation "WikiFloods." Assange named it WikiLeaks, of course, but "leaks" undersells its impact. WikiLeaks unleashed a torrent of secret information in 2010—nearly 800,000 U.S. government classified records. In doing so, the group earned the wrath and scrutiny of the U.S. Justice Department, which, in turn, drove the debate about the First Amendment, media, and lawbreaking from the pages of legal journals and onto the front pages of newspapers, to the top of the line-up for news broadcasters, and into the minds and mouths of bloggers. Not since the initial publication of the top-secret Pentagon Papers excerpts by the *New York Times* in June 1971 have so many Americans debated the legitimacy of the state prosecuting a media outlet for alleged criminal wrongdoing.

Vice President Biden called Assange a "high-tech terrorist." U.S. Senator Joseph Lieberman and other lawmakers introduced legislation that would make it a federal crime to publish the name of a U.S. intelligence source. Lieberman also said the Justice Department should determine whether WikiLeaks and the mainstream newspapers that published the classified documents could be tried under the 1917 Espionage Act. In response, part of the Columbia Journalism School faculty declared their support for WikiLeaks, arguing that "any prosecution of WikiLeaks' staff for receiving, possessing or publishing classified materials will set a dangerous precedent for reporters in any publication or medium, potentially chilling investigative journalism and other First Amendment-protected activity."[1]

Chapter's Scope

The uproar over WikiLeaks opened a new front on the decades-old struggle to define the limits imposed by the First Amendment on government authority to censor or punish media newsgathering and publication that might break the law or encourage others to do so. The struggle to prevent government from banning speech that might threaten national security and public safety predates the First Amendment and the founding of this nation. But this chapter focuses on the First Amendment doctrines the U.S. Supreme Court developed in the 20th century to address federal and state statutes that sought to impose criminal and civil penalties on media activities and individual expression that, the government argued, threatened national security, encouraged violence and other forms of lawbreaking, and harmed individuals' well-being or property. Those First Amendment free press and free speech doctrines are prior restraint and the subsequent punishment doctrines, specifically incitement, threats, and **newsgathering torts**. This chapter also looks at the intentional infliction of emotional distress tort, which may function as a newsgathering tort, or a subsequent punishment claim. Under the claim, plaintiffs argue that they suffered severe emotional distress as the result of a defendant's extreme and outrageous conduct. When the defendant is the news media, that extreme and outrageous conduct can arise during the course of newsgathering in which a private zone or a reasonable expectation of privacy is breached. Thus, the tort may function like a newsgathering tort. Plaintiffs, however, can also allege that published content alone was extreme and outrageous. Thus, it may function as an additional punishment action.

Prior Restraint

A prior restraint is a statute, regulation, judicial order, sometimes a tax, or other form of government action that either prevents publication or imposes government review as a prerequisite for publication—in a word, censorship. In the Anglo-American tradition, prior restraints were the British monarchy's response to the printing press, specifically in the form of licensing. In an effort to suppress the publication of political and religious dissent, the British Crown required book publishers and printers to obtain permission from the state in the form of a license, starting in 1534. John Milton wrote his famous and influential *Areopagitica* (1644) in opposition to the 1643 licensing law. After the Glorious Revolution of 1688 and the new monarchy's acceptance of *An Act Declaring the Rights and Liberties of the Subject and Settling the Succession of the Crown*—most often referred to as the English Bill of Rights (1689)—the licensing law expired.

There is near universal agreement among scholars that the Founding Fathers understood the First Amendment guarantees of free speech and press to protect against prior restraints, but allowed government and individuals to bring legal actions after the offending speech was made public. Such legal actions are called subsequent punishment laws. Incitement, threats, and newsgathering torts are among the many types of legal actions that fall under the category of subsequent punishment. As 18th-century British legal scholar, attorney, and judge William Blackstone, whose writings greatly influenced the legal thinkers among the Constitution's framers and ratifiers, famously put it, "Every freeman has an undoubted right to lay what sentiments he pleases before the public; to forbid this is to destroy the freedom of the press; but if he publishes what is improper, mischievous or illegal he must take the consequences of his own temerity."[2]

But protections against prior restraints are not absolute, as the U.S. Supreme Court established in its landmark ruling *Near v. Minnesota ex rel Nelson*, 283 U.S. 697 (1931). In *Near*, a county prosecutor won a court injunction—an order restraining a party from undertaking a specific action—to prevent a Minneapolis newspaper from continuing to print articles alleging that gangsters controlled gambling, bootlegging, and racketeering in Minneapolis, and that law enforcement officials were doing little to stop him. But on review, the Court reversed the injunction. The Court ruled that the state statute on which the injunction was based was an impermissible prior restraint because it sought to control communications about public officials and their public conduct.

There is heavy presumption that any prior restraint on publication of information or ideas is constitutionally invalid. But there are exceptions. The *Near* Court, invoking precedent, identified three exceptions to the rule that prior restraints are presumptively unconstitutional:

> 'When a nation is at war many things that might be said in time of peace are such a hindrance to its effort that their utterance will not be endured so long as men fight and that no Court could regard them as protected by any constitutional right'…No one would question but that a government might prevent actual obstruction to its recruiting service or the publication of the sailing dates of transports or the number and location of troops. On similar grounds, the primary requirements of decency may be enforced against obscene publications. The security of the community life may be protected against incitements to acts of violence and the overthrow by force of orderly government. The constitutional guaranty of free speech does not 'protect a man from an injunction against uttering words that may have all the effect of force.' [3]

That passage alludes to (i) speech that harms national security interests, meaning state secrets, combat, and espionage efforts; (ii) sexually explicit content found by a court or jury to be obscene; (iii) speech that incites others to break the law or to use force to rebel against the state. The Court also permits trial judges who meet strict standards to impose prior restraints on lawyers, jurors, and the press, as discussed in Chapter 10. Though the Founding Fathers were strongly opposed to the governmental censorship of printing press licensing, it is still constitutional to require broadcasters to obtain licenses from the Federal Communications Commission, another form of prior restraint discussed further in Chapter 11. The Court also ruled that public school officials have the authority to impose prior restraints on student newspapers in *Hazelwood School District v. Kuhlmeier*, 484 U.S. 260 (1988). Government authority to limit public protest by time, place, and manner restrictions, and also court injunctions to prevent violation of copyright laws, are other forms of permissible prior restraints.

Prior Restraints and National Security

Courts seek to balance the government's need to prevent disclosure of classified information that others might use to harm U.S. officials, diplomats, spies, secret contacts, and armed forces personnel against the citizens' right keep government accountable. Yet, because opposition to prior restraint is almost synonymous with free expression in our legal tradition, the Court has made it difficult for government to censor speech, even when the government claims national security is at risk. In such cases, the government must persuade a judge to issue an injunction to prevent a media outlet or individual from disseminating the allegedly harmful message, or to keep the speaker from continuing to publish. A judge must apply the serious-and-imminent danger test to determine whether the speech deserves First Amendment protection. The test—first articulated in the incitement case, *Brandenburg v. Ohio*, 395 U.S. 444 (1969)—is a departure from, and more protective of free expression than, the clear-and-present-danger test established in *Schenck v. U.S.*, 249 U.S. 47 (1919).

In a ruling handed down per curiam—by the whole court without a particular judge writing for the majority—the court applied the serious-and-imminent test in *New York Times Co. v. U.S.* (Pentagon Papers), 403 U.S. 713 (1971), and said that the publication of top-secret documents by the *Times* and other newspapers did not harm national security. The Court acknowledged that the disclosure may have had a serious impact, but in his concurrence, Justice William J. Brennan explained why the impact was not imminent. Brennan said that President Nixon's administration argued only that the publication "'could,' or 'might,' or 'may' prejudice the national interest in various ways. But the First Amendment tolerates absolutely no prior judicial restraints of the press predicated upon surmise or conjecture that untoward consequences may result."[4] Therefore, to show imminent harm, Brennan said, government must prove that the type of publication that "inevitably, directly, and immediately" causes harm is analogous to "imperiling the safety of a transport already at sea."[5]

In *U.S. v. Progressive, Inc., Erwin Knoll, Samuel Day, Jr., and Howard Morland*, 467 F. Supp. 990 (1979), a federal judge, applying the serious-and-imminent test, issued a prior restraint in the form of a temporary injunction preventing publication, the first such injunction in the country's history. *Progressive* magazine had planned to publish technical, highly classified instructions on how to build a hydrogen bomb. The federal judge ruled that such disclosure was "analogous to publication of troop movements or locations in time of war and falls within the extremely narrow exception to the rule against prior restraint."[6] But the case never reached the U.S. Supreme Court because reality intruded, demonstrating that the disclosure of the H-bomb instructions did not pose a serious-and-imminent threat. Several publications, including a college newspaper, published the same secrets, and the government dropped the case.

The Court, however, has upheld the Central Intelligence Agency's licensing system, "contracts of silence," which require its employees to get approval before publishing information related to the agency and its intelligence activities. In *U.S. v. Marchetti*, 466 F.2d 1309 (4th Cir. 1972), the Fourth Circuit held that enforcement of a secrecy agreement and a secrecy oath did not violate the First Amendment despite the prior restraint on Marchetti's speech. In *Snepp v. U.S.*, 444 U.S. 507 (1980), the Court did not apply the serious-and-imminent test. Instead, it ruled that "undisputed evidence in this case shows that a CIA agent's violation of his obligation to submit writings about the Agency for prepublication review impairs the CIA's ability to perform its statutory duties."[7] Together, *Marchetti* and *Snepp* stand for the proposition that government and ex-government employees' speech can be subjected to prior restraints when the government is seeking to protect its legitimate national security interests.

SUMMARY: *Near v. Minnesota* carved out three exceptions from the presumption that prior restraints are unconstitutional: (i) speech that harms national security interests, (ii) sexually explicit content found by a court or jury to be obscene, and (iii) speech that incites others to break the law or to use force to rebel against the state. Judges who grant a government request to impose a prior restraint in the form of a temporary injunction apply the serious-and-imminent test to determine whether the speech may be censored. To meet the test, government must prove that the speech will "inevitably, directly, and immediately cause" a specific harm.

Chilling Free Speech

Most laws, particularly criminal ones, have a chilling effect on human behavior. They create a deterrent against illegal activity and are constitutionally valid. But when laws chill constitutionally protected conduct, courts should strike them down as unconstitutional. For example, when a law "chills" the legitimate exercise of First Amendment-protected expression, courts may declare such a law unconstitutional.

A prior restraint hinders speech before it occurs. That is what makes it distinct from a subsequent punishment law. Yet, a law that has an impermissible deterring effect on free speech can come in the form of subsequent punishment and have the same effect as a prior restraint. Such laws might impose a vague or overbroad content restriction, prescribe draconian punishment on free expression, have the practical effect of discouraging the exercise of constitutionally protected political rights, or one that targets non-speech conduct but has an indirect censorial effect on free expression. In other words, simply because a legal regulation does not have the explicit purpose of an impermissible prior restraint, it may still have an unconstitutionally censorial impact.

The Court first used the term "chilling" in the free expression context to strike down McCarthy-era, government-imposed loyalty oaths. Such oaths indirectly infringed upon government employees' right of association protected under the First Amendment guarantees of speech, assembly, and petition. In a concurrence in *Wieman v. Updegraff,* 344 U.S. 183, 195 (1952), Justice Felix Frankfurter noted that an Oklahoma loyalty requirement had "an unmistakable tendency to *chill* [emphasis added] that free play of the spirit which all teachers ought especially to cultivate and practice; it makes for caution and timidity in their associations by potential teachers." After *Wieman*, the Court found in a number of cases that constitutional violations may arise from the chilling effect of governmental regulations that indirectly affect the exercise of First Amendment rights.[8]

The potential chilling effect of the Stolen Valor Act of 2005 proved constitutionally fatal to the law, which imposed criminal penalties on individuals who falsely claimed that they had received military decorations and medals. Applying strict scrutiny, the Court struck the content-based restriction down as unconstitutional in *U.S. v. Alvarez,* 132 S. Ct. 2537, 2548 (2012).

> Were the Court to hold that the interest in truthful discourse alone is sufficient to sustain a ban on speech, absent any evidence that the speech was used to gain a material advantage, it would give government a broad censorial power unprecedented in this Court's cases or in our constitutional tradition. The mere potential for the exercise of that power casts a *chill*, a *chill* [emphasis added] the First Amendment cannot permit if free speech, thought, and discourse are to remain a foundation of our freedom.

SUMMARY: Laws that are not prior restraints—they do not explicitly prevent speech from occurring—may nevertheless have the practical impact of a prior restraint when they "chill" speech. Thus, a law that chills or discourages individuals from exercising their free expression rights of speech, publication, or assembly may be struck down as unconstitutional. A law that impermissibly chills speech can come in the form of a vague or overbroad content restriction; one that imposes draconian punishment on free expression; one that has the practical effect of discouraging the exercise of constitutionally protected political rights; or one that targets non-speech conduct, but has an indirect censorial effect on free expression.

Subsequent Punishment

Even when government fails to obtain an injunction to prevent disclosure of information it claims harms national security, the federal government can still seek to punish the media outlet or leaker. In the *Pentagon Papers* ruling, several of the justices acknowledged that the federal government had two possible alternatives: criminal prosecution under statutes requiring anyone who obtains stolen property to return it to public officers, or the federal statute 18 U.S.C. § 798 of the Espionage Act of 1917. Does the First Amendment protect journalists or operations like Assange's WikiLeaks from prosecution for possession of stolen documents? Yes, under certain conditions, the Court ruled in *Bartnicki v. Vopper*, 532 U.S. 514 (2001) discussed later in this chapter.

Does the First Amendment protect journalists from prosecution under the Espionage Act § 798? A majority of the *Pentagon Papers* Court suggested that journalists and others were not immune from prosecution for possessing stolen government secrets. To date, there has been only one ruling on the application of the Espionage Act to nongovernment individuals, *U.S. v. Rosen*, 445 F. Supp. 2d 602 (E.D. Va. 2006). *Rosen* involved two pro-Israel lobbyists indicted in 2005 for conspiracy to disclose national security secrets to Israel officials and others. They were accused of conspiracy to possess the information without authorization. A federal judge ruled that the government could prosecute them under the Espionage Act, but had to show that the classified information, if disclosed, was potentially harmful to the U.S. and that the defendants *knew* that the disclosure was potentially harmful. Apparently, the Obama administration, which inherited the case from the Bush administration, would have had an extremely difficult task proving that disclosure was potentially harmful. The Obama administration killed the *Rosen* prosecution by filing a motion to dismiss in May 2009 because it was faced with having to confront testimony from a former Information Security Office director, who was expected to testify that the information was generally known to Israeli national security officials before the *Rosen*-related disclosure. Consequently, disclosure by the defendants could not have harmed national defense interests.

As this publication went to press, the federal government had declined to seek an injunction against WikiLeaks or any of the traditional news outlets, such as the *New York Times*, that published classified documents provided by Assange's organization. Had federal prosecutors done so, it seems unlikely that they could have met the serious-and-imminent test. There has been no concrete evidence that the leaks harmed U.S. national security. The federal government, however, left open the possibility of prosecuting Assange under the Espionage Act. But Assange, though he has been critical of U.S. foreign policy, has portrayed himself as a crusading journalist dedicated to increasing government's accountability to citizens. Such statements, many observers say, would make it difficult for federal prosecutors to prove intent under the *Rosen* test.

SUMMARY: *U.S. v. Rosen*, 445 F. Supp. 2d 602 (E.D. Va. 2006), raises the possibility that journalists and operations such as WikilLeaks may be tried for conspiracy to communicate national defense information to unauthorized persons in violation of the Espionage Act of 1917. Under the *Rosen* test, the government must prove that disclosure of the classified information is potentially harmful to the U.S. and that the defendant knew that the disclosure was potentially harmful.

Incitement to Imminent Lawlessness

Federal and local prosecutors can bring criminal charges against the media and individuals for advocating unlawfulness, including violent overthrow of government and other kinds of criminal or dangerous behavior. Individuals also can bring civil actions alleging that a media outlet or an individual's communication spurred others to act wrongfully. The First Amendment does not protect advocacy that incites or produces unlawful action or is likely to produce such action.[9] The government must show that the defendant had intended to incite others to unlawfulness, and that the speech was the direct and immediate cause of the unlawful acts, or was likely to cause such acts. In *Hess v. Indiana*, 414 U.S. 105 (1973), the Court said there had to be "evidence, or rational inference from the import of the language" that a defendant's "words were intended to produce imminent disorder" and that it was not enough that "speech had a tendency to lead to violence."[10]

The mid-1970s saw the emergence of lawsuits testing the reach of the *Brandenburg-Hess* incitement test. Individuals who brought wrongful death actions against entertainment media outlets argued that the First Amendment protection of the incitement test applied only to political speech cases. These plaintiffs argued that their loved ones—typically children—engaged in fatal activities urged on by the messages and images in rock and rap music, television and movie content, and books. The plaintiffs were inspired by a successful wrongful death suit against a radio deejay in *Weirum v. RKO General, Inc.*, 539 P. 2d 36 (Cal: Supreme Court 1975). In *Weirum*, a radio station with a large teenage audience ran a contest in which it rewarded the first contestant to locate a deejay personality, who was driving throughout the Los Angeles area with money to give away. In an effort to pursue the deejay, a minor forced a car off a highway, killing its driver. The dead driver's wife and children brought a wrongful death suit against RKO, a radio and television company. The California court ruled that RKO was liable because the broadcast had stimulated the young drivers to engage in reckless conduct that resulted in another driver's death, an event that was foreseeable. The California court rejected RKO's First Amendment defense.

Soon after, in *Zamora v. CBS*, 480 F. Supp. 199 (S.D. Florida 1979), a Florida judge, citing *Hess* and other incitement cases involving political speech, rejected a plaintiff's lawsuit claiming that the then three national television networks were to blame for a teenager's deadly misconduct. First Amendment protection provided under the incitement test also defeated the efforts of plaintiffs in *Olivia N. v. NBC*, 126 Cal. App. 3d 488 (1981), and in *McCollum v. CBS, Inc.*, 202 Cal. App. 3d 989 (1988), whose plaintiffs claimed that rock star Ozzy Osbourne's lyrics were the proximate cause of a relative's suicide. Since *Weirum*, no plaintiff alleging that media content led to bodily harm or death has prevailed under the incitement theory. The suits failed mostly because courts require plaintiffs to show specific intent to promote criminal activity and a direct causal link between exposure to words and resulting deaths consistent with the *Brandenburg* incitement standard.

Aiding & Abetting

Undaunted, plaintiffs attempting to hold media liable for the unlawful acts and reckless conduct of members of their audiences pursued other legal theories. The U.S. Circuit Court of Appeals for the Eleventh Circuit allowed a jury award to stand against a magazine publisher in *Braun v. Soldier of Fortune Magazine*, 968 F. 2d 1110 (1992). The appeals court ruled that "the First Amendment permits a state to impose upon a publisher liability for compensatory damages for negligently publishing a commercial advertisement where the ad on its face, and without the need for investigation, makes it apparent that there is a substantial danger of harm to the public."[11] The parties reached an out-of-court settlement. Note, however, *Braun* can be distinguished from the vast majority of incitement cases because commercial speech was at issue. Commercial speech, or advertising, enjoys less First Amendment protection than other forms of speech (see Chapter 15).

Conversely, the speech in *Hit Man: A Technical Manual for Independent Contractors* was not commercial speech. It was speech concerning instructions and ideas; it purported to teach what must be done to murder for pay. Police found the manual in the possession of a contract killer who killed a mother, her son, and a nurse. The contract killer followed the *Hit Man*'s detailed instructions of how to solicit, prepare, and commit murder. The victims' guardian and relatives brought a wrongful death action against Paladin Press, the publisher of the book, arguing that the publisher had aided and abetted murder. In *Rice v. Paladin Press*, 128 F. 3d 233 (4th Circuit 1997), cert. denied, 523 U.S. 1074 (1998), the U.S. Circuit Court of Appeals for the Fourth Circuit reversed a grant of summary judgment favoring Paladin Press, sending the suit to trial. The Fourth Circuit adopted a new theory of liability for publishers, still not recognized in any other federal jurisdiction. The First Amendment, it said, did not protect a publisher who intentionally provides methodical and comprehensive instructions to aid individuals in committing a specific crime from civil or criminal prosecution. The case was settled out of court.

The *Rice v. Paladin* aiding-and-abetting liability standard is far less protective of free speech than the *Brandenburg-Hess* test. That is largely because, under the aiding-and-abetting theory, a plaintiff or prosecutor does not have to establish immediacy. In other words, days, months, or years may pass between the would-be contract killer's possession of the book and the commission of the crime, yet the publisher is still liable.

True Threats

Courts may also rule that *Brandenburg-Hess* does not control when speech directly threatens an individual or group with violence. Instead, the doctrine of true threats controls and the First Amendment does not protect true threats. In *Planned Parenthood of the Columbia/Willamette Inc. v. American Coalition for Life Activists* (2002), the U.S. Court of Appeals for the Ninth Circuit, applying the true threat doctrine, held that an anti-abortion website was liable for the murder of doctors identified on their site. These doctors, who performed abortions, were represented on the website in illustrated wanted posters. A true threat, the appeals court said, is "a statement which, in the entire context and under all the circumstances, a reasonable person would foresee would be interpreted by those to whom the statement is communicated as a serious expression of intent to inflict bodily harm upon that person."[12] In *Virginia v. Black*, 538 U.S. 343 (2003), the U.S. Supreme Court said that under the true threat doctrine the Ku Klux Klan's symbolic act of burning a cross was not protected speech. The Court said cross burning directed at specific individuals is a clear example of a ban not on the politics that incites the threat, but on the threatening or intimidating aspect of the expression: "Intimidation in the constitutionally proscribable sense of the word is a type of true threat, where a speaker directs a threat to a person or group of persons with the intent of placing the victim in fear of bodily harm or death."[13]

There is no consensus among courts, however, whether *Virginia v. Black* requires that the government show intent on the speaker's part to intimidate, intent to merely communicate to another individual what a reasonable person would regard as a serious expression of harm, or whether criminality should be determined from the perspective of a reasonable speaker or the reasonable target of the speech.

SUMMARY: Criminal and civil actions may be brought against media outlets and individuals whose speech incites, aids, and abets lawlessness, or threatens specific individuals with harm. Under the *Brandenburg* incitement test, prosecutors and plaintiffs must prove that the speech posed a serious and imminent threat and that the speaker intended the specific harm to occur. The *Rice v. Paladin* aiding-and-abetting test provides that the First Amendment will not protect a publisher who intentionally provides methodical and comprehensive instructions to aid individuals to commit a specific crime from civil or criminal prosecution. According to the ruling in *Planned Parenthood of the Columbia/Willamete Inc. v. American Coalition for Life Activists*, the First Amendment will not protect a true threat—speech, words, and images that, when viewed in their entire context, would be interpreted by a reasonable person as a serious expression of intent to inflict bodily harm. Nor will the First Amendment protect speech, under the true threat doctrine, where the speaker intended to communicate a serious expression of harm to a specific target, though the speaker may not actually have intended to carry out the threat, the Court said in *Virginia v. Black*.

Newsgathering Torts

In its landmark 5–4 decision, *Cohen v. Cowles Media Co.*, 501 U.S. 663 (1991), the Court held that the First Amendment did not prevent a plaintiff from recovering damages stemming from a newsperson's failure to keep a promise not to reveal a source's identity. Under promissory estoppel, a plaintiff argues that he suffered economic harm because he relied, to his detriment, on a defendant keeping his promise. In *Cohen v. Cowles*, the source lost his job when his identity was disclosed. The Court said the enforcement of general laws against the news media is not subject to First Amendment analysis greater than would be applied to enforcement against nonnewspersons. It explained that a "well-established line of decisions" held "that generally applicable laws do not offend the First Amendment simply because their enforcement against the press has incidental effects on its ability to gather and report the news."[14]

Cohen v. Cowles Media triggered a spurt of lawsuits in which plaintiffs targeted journalists for alleged wrongs committed during newsgathering, such as invasion of privacy claims, trespass, misrepresentation, inducing sources to breach contracts, fraud, aiding and abetting, intentional infliction of emotional distress, and possession of illegally obtained information. Such newsgathering torts invoke common law and statutes that are generally applicable, meaning that everyone is expected to abide by such laws. Thus, plaintiffs argued that, under *Cohen v. Cowles Media*, journalists who intentionally deceive targets or benefit from a source's lawbreaking do not enjoy First Amendment immunity for such actions. Typically, newsgathering suits stem from newspersons' use of undercover techniques of deception and disingenuousness to gain access to places and information they otherwise would not be privy to.

But the proposition that journalists enjoy *no* First Amendment immunity for newsgathering is not easily squared with the Court's acknowledgement in *Branzburg v. Hayes*, 408 U.S. 665, 681 (1972), that "without some protection for seeking out the news, freedom of the press could be eviscerated," or in *Globe Newspaper Co. v. Superior Court*, 457 U.S. 596, 604 (1982), where it said that the right to gather news is among the freedoms, that "while not unambiguously enumerated in the very terms of the Amendment, are nonetheless necessary to the enjoyment of other First Amendment rights." The Court also has recognized a limited First Amendment protection for newsgathering in *Pell v. Procunier*, 417 U.S. 817 (1974), as has the U.S. Ninth Circuit in *Fordyce v. City of Seattle*, 55 F.3d 436, 439 (9th Cir. 1995), and the U.S. Eleventh Circuit in *Smith v. City of Cumming*, 212 F.3d 1332, 1333 (11th Cir. 2000).

Consequently, many courts seek to balance a newsperson's limited First Amendment newsgathering right against a plaintiff's right to invoke her common and statutory legal rights. Such balancing often allows a newsperson to minimize liability by arguing that the newsgathering led to the dissemination of information of serious concern, the imposition of the statute would have a significant effect on newsgathering and reporting, or the statute is a direct restriction on speech. Even so, in most newsgathering cases, where typically defendants allege a host of claims, news media defendants have persuaded judges to eliminate many of the plaintiff's claims and reduce monetary damages by proving that their actions caused little or no harm.

In the mid-1990s, a newsgathering lawsuit, invoking *Cohen v. Cowles* and brought by the Food Lion Inc. supermarket company against Capital Cities/ABC Inc., threatened to make investigative reporting too costly to pursue. Food Lion sued ABC TV's *Prime Time Live* under the generally applicable laws of fraud, trespass, intrusion, misrepresentation, and breach of loyalty stemming from the television show's undercover probe of food preparation at a Food Lion store. The allegations of unsanitary food preparation were apparently true; they were caught on camera. Nevertheless, a jury awarded the company an astounding $5,545,750 in punitive damages and $1,400 in actual damages in 1997. The size of the punitive damage award, many in the media argued, posed a grave threat to freedom of the press. Two years later, however, the U.S. Court of Appeals for the Fourth Circuit reduced the award to a mere two dollars. The court ruled that undercover journalists did not defraud the company or disadvantage it to any significant degree.[15] In *Desnick v. American Broadcasting Companies, Inc.*, 44 F. 3d 1345 (7th Cir. 1995), an eye clinic sued ABC for its undercover investigation of the clinic's practices, claiming, among other torts, infringement of the right of privacy, illegal wiretapping, fraud, trespass, invasion of privacy, and defamation. Only the defamation claim survived judicial review. In *Veilleux v. National Broadcasting Co.*, 206 F.3d 92 (1st Cir. 2000), a truck driver, his employer, and his employer's wife sued NBC over a *Dateline* story on long-distance trucking, alleging defamation, misrepresentation, negligent infliction of emotional distress, invasion of privacy, and loss of consortium. A Maine jury awarded them $525,000. The U.S. Court of Appeals for the First Circuit, however, reversed or vacated the judgments except for part of the misrepresentation claim that it remanded for further proceedings.

Under certain conditions, the First Amendment protects news media defendants who benefit from a source's illegal behavior. In *Bartnicki v. Vopper*, 532 U.S. 514 (2001), the defendant Vopper, a radio commentator, knew or had reason to know that the recording of a conversation he played on the air, in which members of a local teachers union made self-incriminating threats of violence, had been illegally intercepted from a cell phone. An opposition member, who claimed he found the tape in his mailbox, gave it to Vopper. The U.S. Supreme Court held that "a stranger's illegal conduct does not suffice to remove the First Amendment shield from speech about a matter of public concern" as long as the news media plays no role in the illegal act.[16]

A small minority of state courts also allow journalists to mount a substantive First Amendment defense during a criminal trial; that is, a judge allows journalists to argue to a jury that he or she broke the law solely to publicize a publicly significant matter, did not benefit from the illegal act in the manner which the law sought to proscribe, or did not cause the harm the statute was designed to prevent.[17] In *U.S. v. Matthews*, 209 F.3d 338 (4th Cir. 2000), a federal appeals court rejected a journalist's bid to use the First Amendment defense in a case in which he was charged with trafficking child pornography on the Internet. Lawrence Charles Matthews, an experienced newsperson, claimed that only by trading in child pornography could he infiltrate the online child pornography world. The appeals court, however, did not preclude the possibility that a First Amendment defense could be used even in a child pornography case: "Because we conclude that Matthews cannot avail himself of whatever protection the First Amendment offers to those who disseminate child pornography, we, too, need not define the exact parameters of a possible First Amendment defense. We do note, however…that one could invoke a First Amendment defense only if the depictions did not threaten the enormous harms to children the Court identified."[18]

> SUMMARY: Newspersons, the U.S. Supreme Court said in *Cohen v. Cowles Media Co.*, must obey generally applicable laws. Consequently, the First Amendment, as a rule, does not shield them from criminal and civil claims stemming from their newsgathering activities. The Court, however, carved out an exception in *Bartnicki v. Vopper* for newspersons when a stranger's illegal actions lead to disseminating information of public concern and the news organization plays no role in aiding or encouraging the illegal conduct. Courts also recognize, under certain conditions, that newspersons may invoke the First Amendment as an affirmative defense.

Intentional Infliction of Emotional Distress

To succeed on a claim for intentional infliction of emotional distress, a plaintiff typically must demonstrate that (i) the defendant intended to inflict emotional distress; (ii) the conduct of the defendant was extreme and outrageous; (iii) the actions of the defendant were the cause of the plaintiff's distress; and (iv) the resulting emotional distress to the plaintiff was severe. Historically, courts have been skeptical about the merits of the intentional infliction of emotional distress tort. The legal action, they fear, attracts overly sensitive plaintiffs bringing trivial claims or dishonest plaintiffs bringing fictitious claims. The principal problem is identifying the nature and measuring the extent of an alleged mental injury. Over the years, those concerns arose, for example, from plaintiffs claiming emotional distress because of an employer's conduct, the receipt of false information about the death of a loved one, viewing the death of a family member in an accident, from racial insults, sex discrimination, and false imprisonment.

When the conduct in question is speech about public figures or matters of public concern, the courts have an additional apprehension. Courts are concerned about what jurors determine is "outrageous" speech. "'Outrageousness' is a highly malleable standard with 'an inherent subjectiveness about it which would allow a jury to impose liability on the basis of the jurors' tastes or views, or perhaps on the basis of their dislike of a particular expression,'" Chief Justice John Roberts said in *Snyder v. Phelps*, 131 S. Ct. 1207, 1219 (2011), quoting *Hustler Magazine, Inc. v. Falwell*, 485 U.S. 46, 53 (1988).

In *Hustler*, the Court held that public figure plaintiffs bringing intentional infliction of emotional distress claims must meet the *New York Times v. Sullivan*'s reckless disregard for the truth or knowing falsity standard to prevail. *Hustler* magazine ran a parody of a then-popular liquor ad that featured televangelist fundamentalist minister and political commentator Jerry Falwell talking about his "first time," a drunken, incestuous encounter. The ad displayed a disclaimer: "ad parody–not to be taken seriously." Falwell's claim failed, the Court said, because it was a parody and no reasonable person would believe that it was expressing facts.

In *Snyder v. Phelps*, the Court overturned a verdict of $5 million awarded to Albert Snyder for the emotional distress he suffered when members of the Westboro Baptist Church picketed the funeral of his son, a Marine killed in Iraq. The church members, who had picketed other solders' funerals, carried signs that said, among other statements, "America is doomed," "You're going to hell," "God hates you," "Fag troops," "Semper fi fags," and "Thank God for dead soldiers." The Court said the Westboro protesters were entitled to special protection under the First Amendment because their speech took place in a public location, a public street, and was about matters of public concern, the nation's moral conduct and homosexuality in the military, among other topics.

> SUMMARY: Plaintiffs suing media outlets for intentional infliction of emotional harm stemming from speech have a difficult task. The public-figure plaintiff must show reckless disregard for the truth or knowing falsity. The private-figure plaintiff must meet the same standard when the speech is deemed to be about matters of public concern.

ONLINE RESOURCES

1. "Advocacy of Unlawful Action and the 'Incitement Test,'" *Exploring Constitutional Conflicts*, http://law2.umkc.edu/faculty/projects/ftrials/conlaw/incitement.htm
2. David L. Hudson Jr., "True Threats," *First Amendment Center,* http://www.firstamend mentcenter.org/true-threats
3. "Prior Restraints and the Presumption of Unconstitutionality," *Exploring Constitutional Conflicts*, http://law2.umkc.edu/faculty/projects/ftrials/conlaw/priorrestraints.htm
4. Anthony L. Fargo and Laurence B. Alexander, "Testing the Boundaries of the First Amendment Press Clause: A Proposal for Protecting the Media from Newsgathering Torts," 32 *Harvard Journal of Law & Public Policy* 1093 (2009), http://www.harvard-jlpp.com/wp-content/uploads/2009/05/FargoFinal.pdf

QUESTIONS

1. Serious, but not imminent. A quick Internet search of "how to build an H-bomb" reveals illustrations and instructions. If you can access these instructions, so can terrorists. So why do you think the public disclosure of the instructions does not pose a serious-and-imminent threat to the U.S. or global safety?
2. "O, what a tangled web we weave when we try to deceive." You are an editor assigned to an investigative news team. The team's editors and reporters meet to discuss a proposed investigation of suspected secret Pentagon-sponsored DNA experiments conducted within the walls of BioLab Inc., an otherwise private company. The Pentagon not only pays for the experiments, but half of the scientists working on the project are Pentagon officials.

    Brenda Starr, a prize-winning reporter, says the following: "We've been told by one current and four former BioLab employees that the government and the company are breaking international law in their joint effort to develop a gene-changing weapon that has the potential to mutate humans. Here's what I propose we do: We should conduct a two-prong probe. My sources have introduced me to several scientists who are opposed to the experiments. They say the weapon has the potential to change humans into other species.

"Since these scientists are experts in DNA research, we shouldn't have any problems getting them jobs at BioLab. We can equip them with hidden microphones and cameras. They should be able to get video footage of the experiments that would later be scrutinized by other scientists, so there will be little doubt as to the true nature of the experiments.

"Now, the scientists we plan to send in say they have friends who are already employed by BioLab and the friends are willing to tap into BioLab's computers to obtain virtually irrefutable evidence of the true nature of the experiments. But the computer search might take some time, so my plan is to have those scientists give me codes that will allow me to search the database from office computers. That way, we will reduce the likelihood that any employee will get caught."

But one editor objects to the plan. He argues that the news outlet should inform the U.S. Justice Department of its suspicions about the threat of the DNA experiments. "Let the proper authorities investigate," Perry Prudent argues.

The team's chief editor adds that she's concerned about the legal problems that might arise. She says that she's a bit queasy about going undercover: "What if we have to go to court and defend ourselves? Do we have any legal defenses? Where are we legally vulnerable?"

a) She tells you to write a memo that identifies and applies the relevant case law.
b) She also asks you to weigh the legal advantages and disadvantages in pursuing each undercover tactic and Prudent's argument.
c) Finally, she asks: what is the most legally sound course of action the investigative team can pursue?

ENDNOTES

1. "Faculty Speaks Out Against WikiLeaks prosecution," [Press release] *Columbia Journalism School* (January 4, 2011), http://www.journalism.columbia.edu/news/295
2. William Blackstone. *Commentaries on the Laws of England* (Vol. 4). Chicago: University of Chicago Press (2002), 152.
3. *Near v. Minnesota ex rel Nelson*, 283 U.S. 697, 716 (1931).
4. *New York Times Co. v. U.S.*, 403 U.S. 713, 725–726 (1971).
5. Ibid. 727.
6. *U.S. v. Progressive, Inc., Erwin Knoll, Samuel Day, Jr., and Howard Morland*, 467 F. Supp. 990, 996 (1979).
7. *Snepp v. U.S.*, 444 U.S. 507, 512 (1980).
8. See *Baggett v. Bullitt*, 377 U. S. 360 (1964), *Lamont v. Postmaster General*, 381 U. S. 301 (1965); *Keyishian v. Board of Regents*, 385 U. S. 589 (1967); and *Baird v. State Bar of Arizona*, 401 U.S. 1 (1971).
9. *Brandenburg v. Ohio*, 395 U.S. 444 (1969).
10. *Hess v. Indiana*, 414 U.S. 105, 109 (1973).
11. *Braun v. Soldier of Fortune Magazine*, 968 F.2d 1110, 1119 (1992).
12. *Planned Parenthood of the Columbia/Willamette Inc. v. American Coalition for Life Activists*, 290 F. 3d 1058, 1077 (2002).

13. *Virginia v. Black*, 538 U.S. 343, 360 (2003).

14. *Cohen v. Cowles Media Co.*, 501 U.S. 663, 669 (1991).

15. *Food Lion, Inc. v. Capital Cities/ABC, Inc.*, 194 F.3d 505 (4th Cir. 1999).

16. *Bartnicki v. Vopper*, 532 U.S. 514, 535 (2001).

17. See Brief for The Reporters Committee for Freedom of the Press, National Public Radio, Inc., The Radio-Television News Directors Association, and the Society of Professional Journalists as Amici Curiae Supporting Petitioner, *Matthews v. U.S.*, 209 F.3d 338 (4th Cir. 2000) (No. 00–5605), cert. denied 531 U.S. 910 (2000).

18. *U.S. v. Matthews*, 209 F.3d 338, 347 (4th Cir. 2000).

CHAPTER EIGHT

Reporter's Privilege

CONTROVERSY: Without exaggeration, the Medill Innocence Project is unique. Its news reporters are Northwestern University journalism students. Their investigations led to the release of 11 wrongly convicted men from prison, five of them from death row, the suspension of the Illinois death penalty in 2000 and its abolishment in 2011. Of all the news reporters in all the world, few have had such a life- and social-policy-changing impact. But were the students really journalists? They interviewed, investigated, wrote, and published like journalists. But were they conducting journalism as defined by the Illinois Reporter's Privilege Act, a shield law, which grants news reporters the privilege of keeping unpublished information secret?

The Cook County State's Attorney's Office said the students did not qualify as news reporters under the state shield law and subpoenaed their professor, David Protess, in 2009. The prosecutors wanted Protess to hand over, among other evidence, his grading criteria, student grades and notes related to the project's probe into the conviction of Anthony McKinney, who was seeking to overturn a life sentence for murder. Protess refused to comply. Newspapers, news agencies, and journalism groups filed amici briefs in support of the project. In September 2011, a Cook County Judge rejected the Project's arguments. Generally, student journalists may invoke the protections of the state shield law, but the Innocent Project students did not qualify as journalists because they acted as criminal investigators under the direction of McKinney's lawyers, the judge said. The university did not appeal the ruling. In 2011, Protess and the university parted ways after a dispute over his response to the subpoena, and Protess announced plans to start his own investigative effort, the Chicago Innocence Project.

Chapter's Focus

Protess's unsuccessful effort to resist the subpoena arising from *People of Illinois v. Anthony McKinney*, No. 78 CR 5267 (Ill. Cir. Ct. Cook Cty. 2009), is a classic example of the clash of interests that results when journalists seek to withhold confidential information sought in criminal and civil judicial proceedings. A prosecutor or a defendant claims the subpoenaed witness's evidence is essential for the fair administration of justice and the witness, therefore, should not be allowed to invoke the news reporter's privilege to keep the information secret. The witness, an individual affiliated or unaffiliated with a news outlet, invokes the news reporter's privilege, arguing that, under the First Amendment or a state shield law, a journalist has a qualified privilege not to testify about information given to him in confidence, and even an absolute privilege depending on the terms of the shield law. A journalist who fails to comply with a judge's order to testify may face fines and jail time. Yet, from the view of a prosecutor, criminal defendant, or libel plaintiff, the absence of the testimony and evidence can mean the difference between winning and losing a case. In criminal cases, the absence of the evidence could mean that an innocent individual is found guilty. What follows is a brief account of the news reporter's privilege as it developed in the U.S. and the public policy undergirding it. This chapter also discusses the mixed impact of the Supreme Court's landmark ruling in *Branzburg v. Hayes*, 408 U.S. 665 (1972), the recognition and expansion of the privilege by lower federal courts and state legislature's in the aftermath of *Branzburg* to cover nonfiction-content producers working in media other than newspapers, and Congress's effort to create a federal shield law currently in the form of the proposed Free Flow of Information Act of 2007, revised in 2009.

How Society Benefits from Secret Sources

In just about every edition of the *New York Times, Washington Post,* or nightly television news broadcast, you will hear or see words similar to, "According to White House sources" or "Pentagon sources say . . ." Such attribution signals to the reader that a government employee or elected official leaked highly newsworthy information or documents about closed-door government activities to a news reporter and received a promise from the reporter not to reveal the source's name. Such leaks can reveal corruption, hypocrisy, or disclose information beneficial to the public's health and safety. It is a symbiotic relationship that government employees and the press have practiced in the U.S. at least since 1848, when then-U.S. Secretary of State and future president James Buchanan is widely believed to have given a copy of a secret draft of a proposed treaty to end the Mexican-American War to *New York Herald News* reporter John Nugent. Nugent holds the distinction of being the first news reporter arrested for refusing to identify his source.[1]

Confidential agreements among news reporters and their sources serve an important societal interest in a democracy. Buchanan and thousands of subsequent government officials have used confidential agreements with news reporters to give voters civically valuable information that they would not otherwise receive. Government and nongovernment sources would not likely disclose information in exchange for anonymity, if reporters had no recourse but to reveal their anonymous sources' names when subpoenaed.

There are other concerns. Unchecked compelled disclosure allows the government to intrude into newsgathering and editing, burdens journalists' time and resources, and makes news outlets appear as an investigative arm of the judicial system. Thus, forcing a news reporter to reveal a confidential source, the argument goes, is a form of censorship. It infringes press freedom by imposing a limitation on the public's right to know.[2] That is largely why many U.S. senators heartily support the proposed federal Free Flow of Information Act. Many senators, but not enough, as the Senate has yet to vote on the bill.

How Society Is Harmed When a Source Is Kept Secret

Sources have hidden behind anonymity and a reporter's promise of confidentiality to falsely accuse Richard A. Jewell, a security guard, of planting a bomb at the Atlanta, Georgia, 1996 Summer Olympics, and Wen Ho Lee, a Taiwanese-American scientist, of spying for the People's Republic of China in 1999, and also for outing CIA agent Valerie Plame to embarrass her husband, former Ambassador Joseph C. Wilson, in 2003. In addition to potentially protecting false accusers, a journalist's refusal to testify about a crime can jeopardize a defendant's Sixth Amendment fair trial rights. What if the news reporter's secret source seems to have information that may prove a defendant's innocence? What if the source has evidence that may show that a defendant is not entitled to retrial, as the Cook County State attorney contends in *People of Illinois v. Anthony McKinney*? And what if a news reporter is subpoenaed to testify before a grand jury investigating alleged criminal activities that the news reporter seems to have knowledge about based on published news stories? That was generally the question the Supreme Court addressed in *Branzburg v. Hayes*: "whether requiring newsmen to appear and testify before state or federal grand juries abridges the freedom of speech and press guaranteed by the First Amendment."[3]

The Mixed Message of Branzburg v. Hayes

In *Branzburg v. Hayes*, 408 U.S. 665 (1972), the Court ruled on appeals stemming from four related cases. *Branzburg v. Hayes* and *Branzburg v. Meigs* involved Louisville, Kentucky, *Courier-Journal* Paul M. Branzburg. In one story, the *Courier-Journal* published a detailed description of hashish makers and sellers. The other story involved the same news reporter's detailed account of local marijuana use, including interviews with drug users.

The third case, *In re Pappas*, did not involve publication. It arose from the presence of a news photographer inside the New Bedford, Massachusetts, headquarters of the militant Black Panther Party. The fourth case, *U.S. v. Caldwell*, also did not involve publication. *New York Times* news reporter Earl Caldwell refused to testify before a grand jury about the information he had gathered on the Black Panther Party as a staff writer assigned to cover the political group. All the defendants had argued that a "reporter should not be forced either to appear or to testify before a grand jury or at trial until and unless sufficient grounds are shown for believing that the reporter possesses information relevant to a crime the grand jury is investigating, that the information the reporter has is unavailable from other sources, and that the need for the information is sufficiently compelling to override the claimed invasion of First Amendment interests occasioned by the disclosure."[4]

On review, the Court, 5–4, reaffirmed lower court rulings in *Branzburg* and *Pappas* rejecting the reporters' First Amendment defense, and reversed Caldwell's favorable ruling. The Court said the reporters were asking it to endorse concealment of evidence of criminality

> on the theory that it is better to write about crime than to do something about it. Insofar as any reporter
> in these cases undertook not to reveal or testify about the crime he witnessed, his claim of privilege under

the First Amendment presents no substantial question. The crimes of news sources are no less reprehensible and threatening to the public interest when witnessed by a reporter than when they are not.[5]

The majority also rejected the argument that its ruling would have a chilling effect on the free flow of information between sources, the news media, and citizens. Only a small percentage of such agreements are targeted by grand juries, it said. Moreover, the Court said, "The Constitution does not, as it never has, exempt the newsman from performing the citizen's normal duty of appearing and furnishing information relevant to the grand jury's task."[6]

Had *Branzburg* stopped there, its holding would be easy to discern: the First Amendment does not give news reporters a privilege to keep their sources secret from grand jury investigations. But Justice Lewis F. Powell Jr. wrote a concurrence that has allowed lower courts to interpret *Branzburg* as providing a test to balance press freedom and the obligation of citizens to testify about criminal conduct:

> The Court states that no harassment of newsmen will be tolerated. If a newsman believes that the grand jury investigation is not being conducted in good faith he is not without remedy. Indeed, if the newsman is called upon to give information bearing only a remote and tenuous relationship to the subject of the investigation, or if he has some other reason to believe that his testimony implicates confidential source relationships without a legitimate need of law enforcement, he will have access to the court on a motion to quash and an appropriate protective order may be entered. The asserted claim to privilege should be judged on its facts by the striking of a proper balance between freedom of the press and the obligation of all citizens to give relevant testimony with respect to criminal conduct. The balance of these vital constitutional and societal interests on a case-by-case basis accords with the tried and traditional way of adjudicating such questions.[7]

In his dissent, Justice Potter Stewart provided such a balancing test: "I would hold that the government must (1) show that there is probable cause to believe that the newsman has information that is clearly relevant to a specific probable violation of law; (2) demonstrate that the information sought cannot be obtained by alternative means less destructive of First Amendment rights; and (3) demonstrate a compelling and overriding interest in the information."[8]

SUMMARY: Five justices in *Branzburg v. Hayes* held that unless a journalist can prove that a grand jury was convened in bad faith, a journalist must comply with a grand jury subpoena. Compelled testimony before a grand jury does not abridge reporters' First Amendment rights, these justices said. But five justices—one concurring opinion and four dissents—recognized a qualified privilege allowing reporters to refuse to testify in criminal and civil proceedings about secret sources and information.

Beyond Branzburg

A fair reading of Powell's concurrence combined with the dissenting opinions of four justices, including Stewart's proposed balancing test, has led many federal appeals courts, and state courts and legislatures, to find a reporter's privilege for confidential and nonconfidential information in the First Amendment, state constitutions, or evidentiary and procedural rules. Broadly speaking, there are two types of privileges, absolute and qualified, and they are applied to either criminal grand jury investigations or trials, or both. Ostensibly, under an absolute privilege, which appears only in state shield laws, judges cannot compel reporters to disclose confidential or nonconfidential information. But absolute privileges are interpreted by courts and written narrowly. They are limited to either sources or documents and written materials, and in some states, only pertain to specific kinds of sources, documents, and materials. The qualified privilege, which is Justice Stewart's balancing test or a variant, can be applied to criminal or civil cases.

Additionally, many states and federal circuits, following Powell's declaration that "no harassment of newsmen will be tolerated," allow reporters to challenge grand jury subpoenas by arguing that the probe is being conducted in bad faith, the relationship between the information sought and the target of the investigation is remote, or the investigation does not implicate a legitimate law enforcement need, which is typically referred to as a fishing expedition.[9]

According to the Reporter's Committee for Freedom of the Press (RCFP), twelve federal circuits recognize a qualified privilege, applying Stewart's test or a variation of it.[10] Note, however, that U.S. Court of Appeals for the Seventh Circuit Judge Richard Posner questioned the validity of *Branzburg* as a precedent supporting protection for nonconfidential information in *McKevitt v. Pallasch*, 339 F.3d 530 (2003). Also, the Federal Circuit, which hears patent and customs cases, has not recognize the privilege. As a matter of policy, the U.S. Justice Department applies a test "to provide protection for the news media from forms of compulsory process, whether civil or criminal, which might impair the news gathering function" by striking "the proper balance between the public's interest in the free dissemination of ideas and information and the public's interest in effective law enforcement and the fair administration of justice."[11]

By late 2010, 39 states and the District of Columbia offered some form of statutory protection for the reporter's privilege.[12] Alaska, Arizona, California, Indiana, Kentucky, Maryland, Minnesota, Montana, Nebraska, Nevada, New Jersey, New York, Oregon, and Pennsylvania have shield laws that have been interpreted to provide an absolute privilege against testimony in criminal and civil cases. In some of those states, however, the absolute privilege applies only to certain types of sources. Ohio's absolute privilege—Ohio Rev. Code § 2739.04 (broadcast) and Ohio Rev. Code § 2739.12 (newspapers)—for example, protects only the identities of sources, not notes or documents. The Ohio shield law states, in part, that no individual qualifying as a news reporter "shall be required to disclose the source of any information…in any legal proceeding, trial, or investigation before any court, grand jury, petit jury, or any officer thereof, before the presiding officer of any tribunal, or his agent, or before any commission, department, division, or bureau of this state, or before any county or municipal body, officer, or committee thereof."[13]

Need, Exhaustion, & The Public Interest

At least 16 states provide qualified immunity. The Illinois Reporter's Privilege Act, key to Protess and his students' unsuccessful defense, is such a shield law. Typically, under qualified immunity shield laws, prosecutors, defendants, and litigators, such as libel plaintiffs, must satisfy three criteria: need, exhaustion, and public interest. The need prong, which also is part of common law qualified immunity, has been described as requiring that the information sought is essential or goes to the heart of the prosecutor's, defendant's or litigant's case.[14] Exhaustion does not require that every other possible source testify, but certainly a "very substantial" number, the D.C. Circuit Court of Appeals explained in *Zerilli v. Smith*, 656 F.2d 705, 714 (D.C. Cir. 1981).

Like many shield laws providing qualified immunity, the Illinois Reporter's Privilege Act has a public interest requirement. It requires that courts weigh whether the information is "essential to the protection of the public interest involved or, in libel or slander cases, the plaintiff's need for disclosure of the information sought outweighs the public interest in protecting the confidentiality of sources of information used by a reporter as part of the news gathering process under the particular facts and circumstances of each particular case."[15]

What types of public interests outweigh a reporter's interests in protecting sources? In *People v. Pawlaczyk*, 724 N.E. 2d 901, 914 (2000), for example, the Illinois Supreme Court held that "the compelling public interest that *Branzburg* found inherent in the functioning of a grand jury" outweighed the interest in protecting confidential sources. Parties seeking disclosure are also likely to prevail when leaked information causes great harm to national security interest, such as the exposure of a covert agent, the disclosure of a top secret nuclear weapon, or information about an imminent strike.[16]

Note, however, federal appeals courts have not adopted the public interest prong, despite U.S. Court of Appeals Judge David S. Tatel's contention that the "public interest" balancing prong is necessary because "need and exhaustion will almost always be satisfied" in a leak case, "leaving the reporter's source unprotected regardless of the information's importance to the public."[17]

SUMMARY: Though federal courts do not recognize a First Amendment privilege allowing reporters to refuse to comply with a grand jury subpoena, 12 of the 13 federal appeals court jurisdictions allow certain individuals to invoke a qualified reporter's privilege stemming from federal evidentiary and First Amendment law in criminal trials and civil proceedings. Thirty-nine states have shield laws, with a minority providing absolute immunity for confidential information. Generally, the test for the qualified privilege under federal common law and state shield laws mimics or modifies Justice Stewart's proposed test requiring parties seeking disclosure to show need, exhaustion, and public interest: (i) that there is probable cause to believe that the news person has information that is clearly relevant to a specific, probable violation of law; (ii) demonstrate that the information sought cannot be obtained by alternative means less destructive of First Amendment rights; and (iii) demonstrate a compelling and overriding interest in the information to compel disclosure.

Function Tests: Who Qualifies for Protection?

There are four ways to qualify as a journalist to invoke the confidentiality privilege: (i) the privilege is granted to a specific class in the language of the governing state shield law or under a state common law precedent; (ii) qualifying under the shield law's function test, which identifies specific activities such as newsgathering and publishing; (iii) in federal jurisdictions, qualifying under a common law, First Amendment-based "intent" test; and (iv) as an alternative argument under state law, persuading a judge to go beyond the language of a shield law by adopting an intent test under the First Amendment or state law. Whether the argument is tethered to a shield law or common law, petitioners typically raise policy concerns. In other words, the petitioner argues that granting the privilege will promote the free flow of important information to citizens.

The arguments in the friend-of-the-court brief filed by the *Press Amici* in The Circuit Court of Cook County, Ill., Criminal Division, *People of Illinois v. Anthony McKinney*, No. 78 CR 5267 (Ill. Cir. Ct. Cook Cty. 2009), are illustrative of the application of the function test. As discussed earlier in this chapter, the Illinois Cook County State's Attorney's Office effort to compel Protess to testify about Northwestern University journalism students' notes and other materials implicates the state's shield law, the Illinois Reporter's Privilege Act.

The Act's § 8–902 provides a functional test to determine the eligible class: "any person regularly engaged in the business of collecting, writing or editing news for publication through a news medium on a full-time or part-time basis; and includes any person who was a reporter at the time the information sought was procured or obtained." Section 8–902 (b), defines a news medium as "any newspaper or other periodical issued at regular intervals whether in print or electronic format and having a general circulation; a news service whether in print or electronic format; a radio station; a television station; a television network; a community antenna television service; and any person or corporation engaged in the making of news reels or other motion picture news for public showing."

The *Press Amici* in The Circuit Court of Cook County, Ill., Criminal Division, *People of Illinois v. Anthony McKinney*, No. 78 CR 5267 (2009), argued that the journalism students met the shield law's functional test, and they cited, among other precedents, *People v. Degorski*, 34 Media L. Rep. 1954, 1959 (Ill. Cir. Ct. Cook Cty. 2005), in which the Better Government Association watchdog group was entitled to invoke the privilege. Regarding § 8–902 (b), the amici brief noted that the students published on hard copy and via their website, in addition to collaborative efforts with local and national news media.

Prosecutors, however, argued that the students were really engaged in an investigation, compiling evidence to aid defendants who claimed they were wrongly convicted, and they did not publish until two years after they completed their investigation. Thus, prosecutors argued that under the shield law, the students were not "regularly engaged in the business of collecting, writing, or editing news for publication." Additionally, the prosecutors argued that the students were not writing for a news medium as they were not on the school paper's staff.

The Function Test and Bloggers

Three state courts have addressed whether a blogger can invoke the privilege under a function test. In *O'Grady v. Superior Court*, 139 Cal. App. 4th 1423 (2006), the court applied California's shield law and a qualified constitutional privilege to bloggers who leaked information about Apple computer products. The California appeals court boiled down the function test to a succinct definition: "The shield law is intended to protect the gathering and dissemination of *news*, and that is what petitioners did here. We can think of no workable test or principle that would distinguish 'legitimate' from 'illegitimate' news."[18] In *Mortgage-Specialists, Inc. v. Implode-Explode Heavy Industries, Inc.*, 999 A.2d 184, 190 (N.H. 2010), the New Hampshire Supreme Court concluded that under the state constitution a website served an "informative function" and contributed "to the flow of information to the public."

The New Jersey Supreme Court, however, ruled that an online message board acting as a pornography watchdog was not the functional equivalent of traditional news outlets in *Too Much Media, LLC v. Hale*, 20 A.3d 364 (N.J. Supreme Ct. 2011). The court declined to adopt an intent test as the defendant and amici had urged, relying instead on the state shield law which required petitioners to show "a connection to news media…a purpose to gather, procure, transmit, compile, edit, or disseminate news; and…that the materials sought were obtained in the course of pursuing professional newsgathering activities."[19] According to the court, "In essence, message boards are little more than forums for conversation. In the context of news media, posts, and comments on message boards can be compared to letters to the editor. But message-board posts are actually one step removed from letters that are printed in a newspaper because letters are first reviewed and approved for publication by an editor or employee whose thought processes would be covered by the privilege."[20] The court added that an individual did not have to acquire certain credentials or adhere to professional journalism standards to invoke the shield law.

> SUMMARY: Many state shield laws allow nonfiction information gatherers unaffiliated with traditional media outlets to invoke the reporter's privilege based on a function test. Typically, the test requires that the individual be regularly engaged in information gathering and publishing. Some require that those seeking to invoke the privilege receive payment to qualify as a journalist. Recently enacted or revised shield laws are broadly written to include journalists working in all forms of print, broadcast, and electronic media. Courts, however, have been slow to recognize bloggers as journalists eligible to invoke shield laws.

The Federal Intent Test

In the absence of a federal shield law, federal courts have crafted an intent test to judge a petitioner's eligibility to invoke the reporter's privilege. Five federal circuits apply intent tests by looking at objective criteria to determine whether an individual seeking to invoke the reporter's privilege had the intent to publish information for the public. The five circuits also have said that the medium a petitioner uses does not make a dispositive difference in the degree of protection accorded to his or her work.

In *Silkwood v. Kerr-McGee Corp.*, 563 F.2d 433 (10th Cir. 1977), the court found that a documentary filmmaker was eligible to invoke the privilege. The court said, "His mission in this case was to carry out investigative reporting for use in the preparation of a documentary film. He is shown to have spent considerable time and effort in obtaining facts and information of the subject matter in this lawsuit, but it cannot be disputed that his intention, at least, was to make use of this in preparation of the film."[21] In *von Bulow v. von Bulow*, 811 F.2d 136 (2d Cir. 1987), the court crafted an intent test in which the critical question is "whether the person, at the inception of the investigatory process, had the intent to disseminate to the public the information obtained through the investigation."[22] The Second Circuit reasoned that the medium did not matter because "[t]he press in its historic connotation comprehends every sort of publication which affords a vehicle of information and opinion."[23] The Ninth Circuit adopted the *von Bulow* test in *Shoen v. Shoen*, 5 F.3d 1289 (9th Cir. 1993). In *In re: Mark Madden*, 151 F.3d 125, 131 (3d Cir. 1988), the Third Circuit held that petitioners seeking to invoke the reporter's privilege "must demonstrate the concurrence of three elements: that they: (i) are engaged in investigative reporting; (ii) are gathering news; and (iii) possess the intent at the inception of the newsgathering process to disseminate this news to the public." The court reasoned that, "As we see it, the privilege is only available to persons whose purposes are those traditionally inherent to the press; persons gathering news for publication."[24] Citing *Shoen*, *von Bulow*, and *Madden*, the First Circuit in *Cusumano v. Microsoft Corp.*, 162 F.3d 708 (1st Cir. 1998) said an MIT professor and author could invoke the privilege.

Would WikiLeaks's Julian Assange qualify to invoke the privilege under an intent test? WikiLeaks released nearly 800,000 U.S. government classified records in 2010, as discussed in Chapter 7. One article, "WikiLeaks Would Not Qualify to Claim Federal Reporter's Privilege in Any Form," was widely circulated on the Web, contending that based on the "intent" rulings, investigative reporting involves "more than the mere dumping of documents—that the person asserting the privilege 'adopts words and metaphors, solves a narrative puzzle and assesses and interprets,' all by his or her own effort…In contrast, the backbone of WikiLeaks is a high-security drop box that allows people anonymously to submit documents for the site's staff to review."[25] But *Shoen, von Bulow, Madden*, and *Cusmano* do not define "investigative journalism," leaving the matter up to further interpretation. Additionally, Harvard University Law Professor Yochai Benkler concluded that the federal intent tests would allow WikiLeaks to invoke the privilege: "We come, then, to the conclusion that as a matter of First Amendment doctrine, *Wikileaks* is entitled to the protection available to a wide range of members of the fourth estate, from fringe pamphleteers to the major press organizations of the industrial information economy."[26]

But by 2012, it did not appear that the federal government was interested in subpoenaing Assange to learn who leaked the documents. Rather, it appeared that the government was preparing to indict Assange under the 1917 Espionage Act for unauthorized possession of classified government documents, as discussed in Chapter 7.[27] Meanwhile, the federal government accused U.S. Army Private Bradley E. Manning, whose pretrial hearing ended in December 2012, of leaking the documents to WikiLeaks.

> SUMMARY: Five federal circuits apply an intent test that looks at objective criteria to determine whether an individual seeking to invoke the reporter's privilege (i) was engaged in investigative reporting, (ii) engaged in news gathering, and (iii) possessed the intent at the inception of the newsgathering process to disseminate news to the public.

Contempt of Court, Promises, and Waivers

In October 2004, Chief Judge Thomas F. Hogan, of the U.S. District Court for the D.C. Circuit, found *New York Times'* Judith Miller, *Time* magazine's Matthew Cooper, and *Time* Inc. in civil contempt for refusing to give evidence in response to grand jury subpoenas served by Special Counsel Patrick J. Fitzgerald. In separate rulings, Hogan sentenced Miller to 18 months in jail. Cooper also received an 18-month jail sentence, and Hogan fined *Time* Inc. $1,000 a day for the 18-month-period.

Fitzgerald subpoenaed Miller, Cooper, and *Time* in an effort to ferret out the identity of the individual or individuals who told the news media in 2003 that Valerie Plame was a secret CIA agent involved in monitoring weapons of mass destruction. Miller spent three months in jail before she disclosed to a grand jury that her source was Lewis "Scooter" Libby, Vice President Dick Cheney's chief of staff. Cooper and *Time* complied with the court order. Cooper's source was Karl Rove, President George W. Bush's senior advisor. In 2007, President Bush commuted Libby's 30-month prison sentence for perjury, obstruction of justice, and lying during the Plame investigation.

Miller, Cooper, and *Time* cooperated with the grand jury investigation largely because the confidential sources signed waivers releasing them from their confidentiality promises. As the *American Journalism Review* noted, "The Valerie Plame case marks the first widespread use of waivers that release journalists to disclose confidential conversations with their sources to prosecutors."[28] The Plame case, which also spurred the current effort to create a federal shield law as discussed below, illustrates the bind a pledge of confidentiality imposes on journalists.

Though journalists may feel the need to get a waiver from sources, the majority of courts say the law does not require that the journalist get consent from the source to testify. The privilege belongs to the journalists, according to many courts and shield laws.[29] Even so, many journalists argue that professional ethics demands that once they make a promise to keep a source's identity secret, they will not divulge it under any condition. To do so undermines the long-term ability to persuade other potential sources to talk.

Journalists also should consider that if they disclose a source's identity without permission from that source, the source may sue them under the doctrine of promissory estoppel, which allows the individual who relies on a false promise to his detriment to sue for damages. Promissory estoppel is a claim in equity, not contracts. In its landmark 5–4 decision, *Cohen v. Cowles Media Co.*, 501 U.S. 663 (1991), the U.S. Supreme Court held that the First Amendment did not prevent a plaintiff from recovering damages stemming from a newsperson's failure to keep a promise not to reveal a source's identity under the promissory estoppel doctrine. (See Chapter 7 for additional discussion of *Cohen v. Cowles Media*.) Only one court has addressed whether a reporter has a legal obligation to a source with unclean hands. A federal district court in Washington, D.C., ruled in *Steele v. Isikoff*, 130 F. Supp. 2d 23 (D.C.C. 2000), that a confidential source who intentionally lies cannot sue a reporter for breach of contract, fraud, unjust enrichment, intentional infliction of emotional harm, or breach of duty of confidentiality.

SUMMARY: A reporter who breaks a promise of confidentiality may be sued by the source based on the doctrine of promissory estoppel, which allows the individual who relies on a false promise to his detriment to sue for damages. But if a reporter refuses to testify, he or she may be held in contempt of court and face fines and confinement in jail. Consequently, some recommend that a reporter seek a waiver from the secret source to avoid incarceration. Some argue that, ethically, a reporter has no obligation to a source that lies and one court has recognized that deceptive sources may not sue reporters for breach of a promise of confidentiality.

A Federal Shield Law?

Congress has talked about passing a federal shield law for nearly 40 years. Ninety-nine proposals were introduced between 1972 and 1978.[30] The current effort has been largely attributed to Congress's concern over the jailing of reporters, including Miller, and an uptick in subpoenas issued to reporters. But the proposal has stalled four times since 2005. The House passed its current version, S. 448/H.R. 985, in March 2009. The identical Senate version of the Free Flow of Information Act of 2009 has yet to become law.

The 2010 Senate version provides greater protection for journalists than federal common law. It provides qualified immunity in federal criminal and civil proceedings, and employs an expansive function test to determine who may invoke the privilege. It provides protection for a host of nonfiction news gatherers, including student journalists. It also specifically includes Internet service providers. It offers qualified immunity from testifying in criminal and civil proceedings for confidential information. It also has language that provides a public interest balancing test similar to Judge Tatel's proposal that federal courts have rejected. Disclosure is required unless "the covered person has not established by clear and convincing evidence that disclosure of the protected information would be contrary to the public interest, taking into account both the public interest in gathering and disseminating the information or news at issue and maintaining the free flow of information and the public interest in compelling disclosure (including the extent of any harm to national security)."[31]

In the absence of a federal shield law, journalists challenging federal subpoenas may invoke common law-imposed privileges in federal courts. As noted earlier, 12 federal circuits recognize a qualified privilege, applying Justice Stewart's test or variations of it. For example, in *U.S. v. Sterling*, 818 F. Supp. 2d 945, 951 (E. D. Va. July 29, 2011), a federal district court ruled that "the Fourth Circuit recognizes a qualified First Amendment reporter's privilege that may be invoked when a subpoena either seeks information about confidential sources or is issued to harass or intimidate the journalist" in a grand jury probe. *U.S. v. Sterling* stems from one of nine investigations undertaken by the Obama administration to find the source of leaks.[32]

In *U.S. v. Sterling*, the federal government subpoenaed journalist and book author James Risen to testify at the criminal trial of Jeffrey Sterling, a former Central Intelligence Agency officer charged with disclosing classified information to Risen. In January 2006, Risen published *State of War: The Secret History of the CIA and the Bush Administration*. Chapter 9 of the book describes "Operation Merlin," an allegedly failed CIA attempt, as told from the view of a CIA case officer assigned to persuade a scientist to go along with the operation.[33] The government's subpoena sought "(1) testimony about where the disclosures occurred; (2) testimony about what information each source disclosed and when the disclosure occurred; (3) testimony about how Risen received classified information; and 4) testimony to authenticate Chapter 9."[34]

The Fourth Circuit district judge applied the circuit's two-part test. First, the court must determine whether the subpoena seeks confidential reporting information, or was issued to harass the reporter. If either condition is found, the circuit applies the LaRouche test, asking (i) whether the information is relevant, (ii) whether the information can be obtained by alternative means, and (iii) whether there is a compelling interest in the information.

The subpoena was not harassment. Rather, the judge found that the confidentiality agreement covered information as well as the source's identity: "Courts have long held that the reporter's privilege is not narrowly limited to protecting the reporter from disclosing the names of confidential sources, but also extends to information that could lead to the discovery of a source's identity."[35]

Applying the Fourth Circuit LaRouche test, the federal district court judge found that the source of the classified information was relevant. The judge also ruled that government had failed to show that it had exhausted alternative sources of information such as email messages or recordings of telephone calls in which Sterling disclosed classified information to Risen. Additionally, the judge noted, the government had the grand jury testimony of an ex-intelligence official who said that Risen had told him that Sterling was his source for information about the classified operation. Thus, there was no need to have Risen testify about such information.

The government failed to meet the compelling interest standard because it merely argued that Risen's testimony would "simplify the trial and clarify matters for the jury" and "allow for an efficient presentation of the Government's case."[36] The information must be necessary or, at the very least, critical to the litigation at issue, to meet the compelling interest test, the judge said.

National Shield Laws in Foreign Counties

When famed First Amendment lawyer Floyd Abrams testified before the U.S. Senate Judiciary Committee about a proposed federal shield law he asked, "How can the United States provide no protection when countries such as France, Germany, and Austria provide full protection and nations ranging from Japan to Argentina and Mozambique to New Zealand provide a great deal of protection?"[37] Abrams's question implied that the U.S. prides itself on having press freedoms stronger that the nations he listed, arguably the most protective in the world. Yet, its national government has not produced a shield law to clarify a journalist's right to keep sources confidential, even when many other nations in Europe, Asia, Africa, and South America already do because those governments understand that protection of journalistic sources is a basic condition of press freedom.

The European Court of Human Rights (ECtHR), for example, recognized the importance of the reporter's privilege in *Goodwin v. United Kingdom* (1996) 22 EHRR 123. The court's ruling is binding in the 47 nations that make up the Council of Europe, including France, Germany, the United Kingdom, and the Russian Federation.

In *Goodwin*, a journalist, William Goodwin, working for the British publication *The Engineer* magazine, refused to divulge the identity of the source of a confidential corporate plan and was found in contempt by the British Court of Appeal, which was upheld by the House of Lords. Goodwin appealed to the (ECtHR), alleging that the British court's action violated Article 10 of the Convention for the Protection of Human Rights and Fundamental Freedoms, which the (ECtHR) follows. Article 10 states that the right to freedom of expression includes the right "to hold opinions and to receive and impart information and ideas without interference by public authority and regardless of frontiers."[38] Section 2 of Article 10, however, says that free expression guarantees are subject to interference "in the interests of national security, territorial integrity or public safety, for the prevention of disorder or crime, for the protection of health or morals, for the protection of the reputation or rights of others, for preventing the disclosure of information received in confidence, or for maintaining the authority and impartiality of the judiciary."[39]

The Court ruled that the disclosure sought by the corporation was "not necessary in a Democratic society" and that the human rights Convention required "that any compulsion imposed on a journalist to reveal his source had to be limited to exceptional circumstances where vital public or individual interests were at stake."[40]

Consequently, all of the 47 Council of Europe nations must, at the very least, recognize that journalists enjoy a qualified privilege to keep sources confidential and information secret. *Goodwin's* influence extends beyond Europe's borders, notes Jane Kirtley, Silha Professor of Media Ethics and Law at the University of Minnesota: "Other international and regional bodies, including the Inter-American Commission on Human Rights and the African Commission on Human and People's Rights, have issued declarations recognizing the right of journalists to maintain the confidentiality of their sources and unpublished information."[41]

SUMMARY: The proposed federal Free Flow of Information Act of 2009 would create a federal shield law providing qualified immunity to a wide class of news and information gatherers, including bloggers. Yet, as of 2012, the U.S. government still had no shield law. Meanwhile, journalists challenging grand jury subpoenas in federal courts relied on each circuit's interpretation of a First Amendment- or common law-based privilege, and many foreign nations, including 47 in Europe, recognized that journalists have a qualified privilege to keep information confidential and sources secret.

The Privacy Protection Act of 1980, 42 § 2000aa

The PPA does not provide reporters and publishers with a shield, but with a counterpunch, the right to sue for damages after an illegal search or seizure of work products such as notes, drafts, and outtakes. It provides, in part, that it is "unlawful for a government officer or employee, in connection with the investigation or prosecution of a criminal offense, to search for or seize any work product materials possessed by a person reasonably believed to have a purpose to disseminate to the public a newspaper, book, broadcast, or other similar form of public communication, in or affecting interstate or foreign commerce."

For example, in 2004, the Associated Press and the *Hattiesburg American* filed a lawsuit accusing U.S. Marshals of violating their rights under the PPA and the Constitution. A U.S. Marshall erased and seized reporters' tape recordings of U.S. Justice Antonin Scalia's speech at a high school in Hattiesburg, Pennsylvania. In a settlement reached that year, the U.S. Justice Department conceded that the marshals had violated the PPA by seizing the journalists' work product, and that the journalists were entitled to $1,000 in damages and reasonable attorneys' fees.[42]

The PPA ban on search and seizure has exceptions. Most notably § 2000aa(b)(1) allows authorities to search and seize when they have probable cause to believe that a reporter or publisher has evidence linking him or her to a crime, and under § 2000aa(b)(2) when authorities seek to prevent death or serious injury. PPA restrains federal and state authorities. Some states—California, Connecticut, Illinois, Nebraska, New Jersey, Oregon, Texas, Washington, and Wisconsin—have passed similar press protections.

SUMMARY: The Privacy Protection Act of 1980 creates a civil action for reporters and publishers to sue for illegal search and seizure of their work product, typically notes, drafts, film outtakes, and digital records.

ONLINE RESOURCES

1. Stephen Bass, "Getting to the Source: The Curious Evolution of Reporter's Privilege," http://www.slate.com/articles/news_and_politics/jurisprudence/2003/12/getting_to_the_source.html
2. "Free Flow of Information Act of 2009," http://www.c-spanvideo.org/appearance/595210164
3. "The Reporter's Privilege: An Historical Overview," http://www.gsspa.org/conferences/fall/10051964_1%20-%20Historical%200veriview%200f%20the%20Reporter_s%20Privilege.PDF
4. Kathleen Ann Ruane, "Journalists' Privilege: Overview of the Law and the Legislation in Recent Congresses," http://www.fas.org/sgp/crs/secrecy/RL34193.pdf
5. State Shield Laws, http://www.citmedialaw.org/state-shield-laws

QUESTIONS

In Gotham, they have a Cape Law instead of a Shield Law.

Gotham City Ordinance 2831.Confidential Sources: The bill provides a qualified privilege from disclosing sources and other information. The privilege applies to a compelled disclosure request by a municipal prosecutor, a request by a criminal defendant, and in civil litigation. The privilege is overcome if (1) the party seeking the disclosure has exhausted alternate sources; (2) there are reasonable grounds, based on an alternate source, to believe the information sought is relevant; (3) the information sought is essential; and (4) the public interest in compelling disclosure outweighs the public interest in newsgathering.

Who is covered: The act applies to a "journalist," which it defines as "a person who, for financial gain or livelihood, is engaged in gathering, preparing, collecting, photographing, recording, writing, editing, reporting, or publishing news or information as a salaried employee of or independent contractor for a newspaper, news journal, news agency, book publisher, press association, wire service, radio or television station, magazine, Internet news service, or other professional medium or agency which has, as one of its regular functions, the processing and researching of news or information intended for dissemination to the public."

Vicki Vale, a freelance photojournalist for Ipod News, reports that Batman is multi-billionaire Bruce Wayne. She says a top-level municipal official told her so. Vale hasn't worked as a photojournalist for long. She got the scoop on Wayne-Batman one week before she started freelancing with Ipod News. Soon after Vale's story is published, it is widely believed that the Joker and his henchmen torched Wayne Mansion in an attempt to kill Batman.

Vale's source is Police Commissioner Gordon. It seems that he was furious with Batman because his alter ego, Wayne, had made public statements critical of police corruption that Batman/Wayne believes has not been adequately investigated. Gordon had been drinking when he was speaking with Vale and said that Batman is "just some spoiled rich kid with a butler named Alfred." Vale put two and two together and correctly concluded that Bruce Wayne is Batman. She called Gordon to confirm her conclusion, and he said first you have to promise me that you will never reveal that I am your source. "I promise to keep your identity secret," Vale replied.

Gotham D.A. Harvey Dent opens a grand jury investigation into the Wayne Mansion fire, the attempted murder of Wayne/Batman, and related matters. Dent subpoenas Vale, demanding she identify the anonymous top-level Gotham official who revealed Batman's secret identity to her. Note that Batman's secret identity is classified top secret under Gotham City law.

1. How should Vale respond to the subpoena based on legal precedent and identify the societal interest supporting her position?
2. Make D.A. Dent's argument. What legal precedents support his position? Identify the societal interest supporting his position.
3. Under the terms of Gotham City Ordinance 2831, is Dent likely to persuade a judge that Vale should identify her source? Explain.

ENDNOTES

1. "The Senate Arrests a News reporter." United States Senate, http://www.senate.gov/artandhistory/history/minute/The_Senate_Arrests_A_Reporter.htm
2. See *Garland v. Torre*, 259 F.2d 545, 548 (2d Cir.1958).
3. *Branzburg v. Hayes*, 408 U.S. 665, 667 (1972).
4. Ibid. 680.

5. Ibid. 692.
6. Ibid. 691.
7. Ibid. 710.
8. Ibid. 743.
9. See *In re Contempt of Stone*, 397 N.W. 2d 244 (Mich. Ct. App. 1986).
10. See "Reporter's Privilege: B. Absolute of Qualified Privilege," Reporters Committee for Freedom of the Press (2007), http://www.rcfp.org/privilege/index.php
11. *Department of Justice Guidelines for Issuance of Subpoenas to News Media*, 28 C.F.R Sec. 5010, 2005) § 50.10, 28 Code of Federal Regulations, Ch. I (7–1–03 Edition), http://edocket.access.gpo.gov/cfr_2003/julqtr/pdf/28cfr50.10.pdf
12. Anthony McClure. "Reporter's Privilege Receives Increasing Attention from States," *Litigation News*, American Bar Association, (December 15, 2010), http://apps.americanbar.org/litigation/litigationnews/top_stories/121510-reporter-privilege-shield-law.html
13. Ohio Rev. Code § 2739.04.
14. *Garland v. Torre*, 259 F.2d 545, 550 (2d Cir. 1958).
15. Chapter 735 Illinois Compiled Statutes Act 5/8—907.
16. *In re Grand Jury (Judith Miller)*, 397 F.3d 964, 996 (D.C. Cir. 2005).
17. *Hatfill v. Gonzales*, 505 F. Supp. 33, 46 (D.D.C. (2007) citing *In re Grand Jury (Judith Miller)*, 397 F.3d 964, 997 (D.C. Cir. 2005).
18. *O'Grady v. Superior Court*, 139 Cal. App.4th 1423, 1457 (2006).
19. *N.J.S.A.* 2A:84A-21.3.
20. *Too Much Media, LLC v. Hale*, 20 A.3d 364, 379 (2011).
21. *Silkwood v. Kerr-McGee Corp.*, 563 F.2d 433, 436–37 (10 Cir.1977).
22. *von Bulow v. von Bulow*, 811 F.2d 136, 143 (2d Cir. 1987) *cert denied* 481 U.S. 1015, 107 S.Ct. 1891, 95 L.Ed.2d 498 (1987).
23. Ibid. 144, citing *Lovell v. Griffin,* 303 U.S. 444, 452 (1938).
24. *In re: Mark Madden*, 151 F.3d 125, 129–130 (3d. Cir. 1988).
25. Jonathan Peters. "WikiLeaks Would Not Qualify to Claim Federal Reporter's Privilege in Any Form," 63 *Federal Communications Law Journal* 668, 678 (2011), http://www.law.indiana.edu/fclj/pubs/v63/n03/Vol.63–3_2011-May_Art.-04_Peters.pdf
26. Yochai Benkler. "A Free Irresponsible Press: WikiLeaks and the Battle over the Soul of the Networked Fourth Estate," 46 *Harvard Civil Rights-Civil Liberties Review* 331, 362 (2011).
27. "Stratfor Emails: US has Issued Sealed Indictment Against Julian Assange," [Press release], WikiLeaks.org (February 8, 2012), http://wikileaks.org/Stratfor-Emails-US-Has-Issued.html
28. Rachel Smolkin. "Waivering," *American Journalism Review* (February/March 2006), http://www.ajr.org/article_printable.asp?id=4038
29. See Kurt Wimmer and Stephen Kiehl. "Who Owns the Journalist's Privilege—the Journalist or the Source?" 28 *Communications Lawyer* 9 (August 2011), http://www.americanbar.org/content/dam/aba/publications/communications_lawyer/august2011/who_owns_journalists_privilege_journalist_source_comm_law_28_2.authchec kdam.pdf
30. See Robert D. Lystad. "Anatomy of a Federal Shield Law: The Legislative and Lobbying Process," 23 *Communications Lawyer* 1 (2005).
31. Text of S. 448 [111th]: Free Flow of Information Act of 2009, http://www.govtrack.us/congress/billtext.xpd?bill=s111–448
32. Charlie Savage. "Nine Leak-Related Cases," *New York Times* (June 20, 2012), http://www.nytimes.com/2012/06/20/us/nine-leak-related-cases.html?ref=wikileaks
33. *U.S. v. Sterling*, 818 F. Supp. 2d 945, 947 (E. D. Va. July 29, 2011).
34. Ibid.
35. Ibid. 954.
36. Ibid. 959.

37. "Testimony of Floyd Abrams," *Reporters' Shield Legislation: Issues and Implications: Hearing Before the S. Comm. on the Judiciary,* 108th Cong. (July 20, 2005), http://www.judiciary.senate.gov/hearings/testimony.cfm?id=e655f9e2809e5476862f735da108e42e&wit_id=e655f9e2809e5476862f735da108e42e-1-4

38. See *Goodwin v. United Kingdom* (1996) 22 EHRR 123 *11, http://www.5rb.com/docs/Goodwin-v-%20United%20Kingdom%20ECHR%2027%20Mar%201996.pdf

39. Ibid.

40. Ibid. 13.

41. Jane Kirtley. *Media Law Handbook.* New York: Avalon Publishers (2012), 18–19. http://www.america.gov/media/pdf/books/media-law-handbook.pdf#popup

42. Phil Currie. "U.S. Marshals Service Admits Wrongdoing, Sets New Policy After Hattiesburg Presses Case on Seizure of Recordings," News Watch, *Gannett,* (October 1, 2004), http://159.54.227.112/go/newswatch/2004/october/nw1001–1.htm

CHAPTER NINE

Access to Government Records, Property & Services

CONTROVERSY: What is the Department of Homeland Security (DHS) hiding? It has 2,000 naked images of airline passengers, and it refuses to let the Electronic Privacy Information Center (EPIC) see them. Airport security full-body scanners captured the images. The center, a privacy advocacy group, says it needs them to determine if the screening violates the Fourth Amendment and federal statutory laws protecting privacy. EPIC filed requests in 2009 to obtain information about the screening under the Freedom of Information Act (FOIA). FOIA, enacted in 1966, requires federal agencies to make government records available to the public. DHS produced 1,766 pages of documents, but withheld the images, invoking one of the FOIA's nine exemptions to disclosure, Exemption 2-High. EPIC challenged DHS's reliance on Exemption 2-High, but lost on summary judgment in January 2011.[1] For some time, courts used the term "Low 2" for human resources and employee relations records and "High 2" for records whose disclosure would risk circumvention of the law.

That classification disappeared, however, less than two months after *EPIC v. DHS*. In March 2011, the U.S. Supreme Court eliminated Exemption 2-High in *Milner v. U.S. Department of the Navy*, No. 09–1163 (2011), thereby changing the law that the judge had relied on in *EPIC v. DHS*, and giving EPIC another chance. But EPIC's bid to get the judge to reconsider and vacate his ruling failed on a technicality. The group filed its motion for reconsideration ten days after the appeal period ended. DNS still has the pictures.

Chapter's Scope

Here, we examine your right to access government-held information, places, and services. That right is chiefly defined by the FOIA, the Federal Sunshine Act of 1976, state open meeting and record statutes, and the First Amendment public forum doctrine that defines the scope of protection accorded speech-related activities conducted at government-owned and -controlled facilities and spaces. Federal and state open records and meetings laws and the public forum doctrine seek to strike a balance between the public's right to access property that the government holds on its behalf and the government's right to withhold its property to protect a variety of important societal interests. Open records laws, typically referred to as Freedom of Information laws, affect the public's right to access the records government departments and agencies compile. Open meetings laws, or Sunshine Laws, accord citizens the right to obtain certain public documents and attend meetings convened by departments, agencies, and at the state level, commissions, some legislative bodies, and private bodies involved in government decision making. The chapter ends with a discussion of the First Amendment public forum doctrine.

Openness vs. Secrecy

Often, getting a government agency to hand over what appear to be public documents can be a futile red-tape struggle. That is mostly because there is no First Amendment right to access government-held records and documents. In *Zemel v. Rusk*, 381 U.S. 1, 17 (1965), the U.S. Supreme Court said, "The right to speak and publish does not carry with it the unrestrained right to gather information."

Your right to access government-held records and documents is protected only by federal and state statutes, such as the federal FOIA. That shortcoming weakens the public's right to access government information because statute-guaranteed rights are easily trumped by countervailing constitutional rights, checked by opposing important societal interest, and vulnerable to the changing currents of politics and ideology.

National security, law enforcement, and medical and financial privacy are some of those important countervailing societal interests. Federal agencies, such as DHS, the FBI, Office of Personnel Management, the U.S. Army, Security Exchange Commission, Department of Agriculture, and the Federal Communications Commission, to name only a handful, need to keep a great deal of information they collect secret from the public's view to protect those interests. The federal government has an old precedent for tightly controlling access to documents and records. The housekeeping statute of 1789 (now 5 U.S.C. section 22) allowed each government department to maintain control of its own information dissemination policies, and ever since, secrecy and claims of privilege have become the norm.[2]

Yet, democracy requires openness to thrive and the principle of public access to government information stretches back to English common law.[3] For the last 50 years, Congress and state legislators have tried to reconcile these antithetical imperatives by enacting open records and information statutes.

Federal and state legislatures, agencies, and institutions also have justifications for denying the public access to government-controlled public property. Municipalities need to exclude the press and public during labor negotiations meetings, for example. For national security reasons, the military must limit the times when the public and press may enter bases and facilities. Public school educators, of course, must screen who enters school buildings out of concern for the safety of children.

At the same time, legislative meetings, public schools, and military bases are public institutions accountable to the public to some degree. Thus, the public and news media have a right to attend legislative meetings where public matters are discussed and deliberated, and enter schools and military bases under certain circumstances. As the California Supreme Court noted in a courtroom access case, "'Access theory' asserts that the public's right to receive and disseminate communications about public affairs implies at least some right to acquire relevant information at the source. It draws on the right to assemble in places and at proceedings traditionally public. It presumes the deterrent effect of public scrutiny on official misconduct. And it emphasizes the unique role of the media in vindicating the right to know."[4]

But note that the U.S. Supreme Court established in *Pell v. Procunier*, 417 U.S. 848 (1974) and *Houchins v. KQED, Inc.*, 438 U.S. 1 (1978), that the news media has no greater constitutional right of access to government-controlled places than accorded to the general public. And the public's First Amendment right to access government-controlled places and services is qualified under the public forum doctrine.

> SUMMARY: In our system, constitutional law trumps statutory law, and the federal Freedom of Information Act is merely statutory law. There is no federal constitutional right to access government-held records. As a result, the public's right to access records held by federal and state departments, commissions, and agencies is often trumped when in conflict with constitutionally guaranteed rights and often checked by important, competing government interests.

The Freedom of Information Act, 5 U.S.C. § 552

Conflicts between the press and the government over secrecy during the early years of the Cold War led to the formation of a Special Subcommittee on Government Information, more popularly known as the Moss subcommittee after its 1955 chair, California Democratic Representative John E. Moss. Meanwhile, prominent journalists and the American Society of Newspaper Editors (ASNE) spearheaded efforts to fight government secrecy. The ASNE formed the Freedom of Information Committee. Their efforts led to the passage of the Federal Public Records Law, known as the federal Freedom of Information Act or FOIA, in 1966. FOIA provides the public with a presumptive right of access to government records. The 1972 Federal Advisory Committee Act (5 U.S.C. App.) requires executive branch federal advisory committees to be open. The 1976 Government in the Sunshine Act (5 U.S.C. 552b) requires that federal boards, commissions, and councils be open to the public. The 1996 Electronic Freedom of Information Act requires access to electronically stored databases. All, however, are subject to exemptions.

A Hobbled Act

The vulnerability of the statute-protected right to access government-held information has been demonstrated by the federal government's post-9/11 efforts to combat terrorism. According to the

Reporters Committee on Freedom of the Press, "Federal FOI Act officers now act under directions to give strong consideration to exemptions before handing out information, and to protect 'sensitive but unclassified' information. Federal Web sites have come down, a measure to protect 'homeland security' records became law in 2002, and federal courts have ruled that the government is owed deference in its FOI Act denials when it claims national security might be affected—even if the records are not classified."[5] If the right to access government-held information were protected under the First Amendment, it is less likely that judges, imposing strict scrutiny, would have ruled that deference was due to denials of FOIA requests when the government claimed national security concerns.

Similarly, if access was constitutionally protected, it is unlikely that courts would allow government agencies to flout the act's mandate to respond to requests within 20 working days and an additional 10 days for unusual circumstances. According to the National Security Archives 2003 report, median processing times for FOIA requests range from a low of "two business days at the Small Business Administration to ranges with a high of 905 business days at the Department of Agriculture and a high of 1113 business days at the Environmental Protection Agency…some cases leaves FOIA requesters waiting for over a decade for substantive responses to FOIA requests."[6] The oldest unfulfilled request dates back to 1987.[7]

Bureaucrats vs. The Public

Despite such shortcomings, the FOIA process has yielded significant, beneficial information to the public including secret government documents on Martin Luther King Jr., John Lennon, FBI surveillance documents on protestors, brake problems in the F/A-18 Hornet jet, and broken locks in Richmond, Virginia, jails which led to at least 15 breakouts in 2004, just to name a few. The FOIA 5 U.S.C. § 552(a)(3)(A) accords "any person" a right to obtain any records held by a federal agency and sue when disclosure appears incomplete. An FOIA request must be a brief written, faxed, or emailed and sent to the agency most likely to hold the records. Specific agencies covered by the FOIA include "any executive department, military department, Government corporation, Government controlled corporation, or other establishment in the executive branch of the Government (including the Executive Office of the President), or any independent regulatory agency."[8]

Accessible records include all that an agency created or obtained and possessed when a request is filed. They include print documents, photographs, videos, maps, email, and electronic records. If an agency refuses to furnish records, a requester may file suit in federal court and obtain an injunction ordering "the production of any agency records improperly withheld."[9] The FOIA, however, does not cover public records held by the President, Congress, or federal court system. The Presidential Records Act covers presidential records. Congress has its own set of rules covering access. Most federal court records are publicly available.

"Exemptions Are To Be Narrowly Construed"

Federal agencies do not have to honor requests that fall under nine exemption categories. Congress created the exemptions out of concern that "legitimate governmental and private interests could be harmed by release of certain types of information."[10] The U.S. Supreme Court, however, has "consistently stated that FOIA exemptions are to be narrowly construed."[11] It is beyond this chapter's scope to provide court rulings on each exemption, but included here are the nine exemptions and case law interpreting the scope of exemptions 1, 2, 4, 6, and 7.

Exemption 1(A) covers records that are "specifically authorized under criteria established by an Executive order to be kept secret in the interest of national defense or foreign policy and (B) are in fact properly classified pursuant to such Executive order."[12]

Exemption 2 covers records "related solely to the internal personnel rules and practices of an agency."[13]

Exemption 3 provides for the exemption of records that are specifically exempted from disclosure by other federal statutes. Some of those statutes are the Internal Revenue Code, the Homeland Security Act, National Security Agency Acts of 1947 and 1959, Privacy Act of 1974, the Consumer Product Safety Act, and the CIA Information Act.

Exemption 4 provides for the exemption of trade secrets and commercial or financial information obtained from a person that is privileged or confidential.

Exemption 5 Inter-agency or intra-agency memorandums or letters which would not be available by law to a party other than an agency in litigation with the agency.

Exemption 6 Personnel, medical files, and similar files the disclosure of which would constitute a clearly unwarranted invasion of personal privacy.

Exemption 7 Records or information compiled for law enforcement purposes, but only to the extent that the production of such law enforcement records or information (A) could reasonably be expected to interfere with enforcement proceedings; (B) would deprive a person of a right to a fair trial or an impartial adjudication; (C) could reasonably be expected to constitute an unwarranted invasion of personal privacy; (D) could reasonably be expected to disclose the identity of a confidential source, including a state, local, or foreign agency or authority, any private institution which furnished information on a confidential basis; (E) would disclose techniques and procedures for law enforcement investigations or prosecutions, or would disclose guidelines for law enforcement investigations or prosecutions if such disclosure could reasonably be expected to risk circumvention of the law; or (F) could reasonably be expected to endanger the life or physical safety of any individual.

Exemption 8 Information that concerns the supervision of financial institutions.

Exemption 9 Geological and geophysical information and data, including maps, concerning wells.

Requesters seeking release of national security classified records start at a disadvantage because it is well settled that courts are obligated to give "substantial deference" to agency documents that implicate national security under Exemption 1.[14] Still, the agency carries the burden of justifying nondisclosure.[15] For instance, the D.C. Circuit upheld the Defense Department and CIA's redaction of documents about 14 "high-value" detainees held at the U.S. Naval Base in Guantanamo Bay, Cuba, based on exemptions 1 and 3 in *ACLU v. U.S. Dept. of Defense*, 628 F.3d 612 (D.C. Cir. (2011). Citing precedent, the court said the standard for upholding the agencies' decision and awarding summary judgment was to determine whether the justifications for withholding were specific and detailed, that they logically fell within the claimed exemption, and that they were not contradicted by evidence in the record or by evidence of the agencies' bad faith. Additionally, a court must take into account that claims of threatened harm to national security will always be speculative. Ultimately, the justification must be logical and plausible.[16]

In *ACLU v. U.S. Dept. of Defense*, the CIA identified five potential threats to national security stemming from disclosure: propaganda value to al Qaeda, undermining "the CIA's ability to interrogate detainees, improving al Qaeda's insight into the United States' intelligence activities, and hinder[ing] the CIA's ability to obtain assistance from foreign nations."[17] The court said the information could be withheld under Exemption 1 because disclosure "reasonably could be expected to result in damage to the national security.'"[18]

As noted at the opening of this chapter, *Milner v. U.S. Department of the Navy* limited the scope of Exemption 2. Prior to *Milner*, three federal appeals courts had adopted the D.C. Circuit's definition of Exemption 2's scope in *Crooker v. Bureau of Alcohol, Tobacco & Firearms*, 670 F.2d 1051 (1981). The *Crooker* approach made a distinction between "Low 2" for materials concerning human resources and employee relations and "High 2" for records whose disclosure would risk circumvention of the law. But Justice Elena Kagan ruled that the exemptions should be construed narrowly. The Court must adhere to the specific language of the exemption—"related solely to the internal personnel rules and practices of an agency"—and Congress's intent. Under such a standard, Exemption 2 could not be construed to provide for the "High 2" category. Accordingly, the Court ruled that the Navy could not use Exemption 2 to withhold maps and data used to help store explosives at a naval base in Washington State because they did not pertain to human resources and employee relations.

Courts will apply Exemption 4, covering confidential trade secrets and commercial or financial information, when the following three-prong test is met: (i) The information for which exemption is sought must be a trade secret or commercial or financial in character; (ii) it must be obtained from a person; and (iii) it must be privileged or confidential.[19] Additionally, the Second and D.C. Circuits apply a two-part test to determine whether information is privileged or confidential under Exemption 4: (i) Disclosure would impair the government's ability to obtain necessary information in the future, or (ii) cause "substantial harm to the competitive position of the person from whom the information was obtained."[20] The First and D.C. Circuits allow agencies to withhold information under Exemption 4, if withholding serves a valuable purpose and is useful for the effective execution of its statutory responsibilities, "the program effectiveness test."[21]

The Second Circuit considered all three tests in *Bloomberg, LP. v. Board of Governors of the Federal Reserve*, 601 F.3d 143 (2d Cir. 2010), but settled on the three-prong test. The case involved the Bloomberg news organization's FOIA request to obtain information regarding loans that the twelve Federal Reserve Banks made to private banks in April and May 2008, specifically: the identity of the borrowing banks, the dollar amounts of the loans, the loan origination and maturity dates, and the collateral securing the loans. The court rejected the program effectiveness test, reasoning "a test that permits an agency to deny disclosure because the agency thinks it best to do so (or convinces a court to think so, by logic or deference) would undermine 'the basic policy that disclosure, not secrecy, is the dominant objective of [FOIA].'"[22] The court relied on the three-part test to determine that the information the Federal Reserve wanted to withhold was "generated within a Federal Reserve Bank upon its decision to grant a loan. Like the loan itself, it did not come into existence until a Federal Reserve Bank made the decision to approve the loan request," and, therefore was not "obtained from a person" as required under part two of the three-part test.[23]

Exemptions 6 and 7 protect the privacy interests of individuals whose medical, personnel, and law enforcement records are collected and filed by federal agencies. Exemption 6 permits withholding only when disclosure "would constitute a clearly unwarranted invasion of personal privacy." Exemption 7(C) permits withholding when disclosure "could reasonably be expected to constitute an unwarranted invasion of personal privacy."

In *U.S. Dept. of Justice v. Reporters Committee for Freedom of the Press*, 489 U.S. 749, 776 (1989), the Court said the proper application of both exemptions requires balancing the individual's privacy interest against the public interest. In *Nava v. Favish*, 541, U.S. 157, 172 (2003), the court said the requester must establish "the public interest sought to be advanced is a significant one, an interest more specific than having the information for its own sake. Second, the citizen must show the information is likely to advance that interest."

In *ACLU v. Department of Justice*, No. 08–1157 (D.D.C. March 26, 2010), appeal docketed, No. 10–5159, an ACLU requests for documents related to the government's use of cell phone tracking in criminal investigations and prosecutions without judicial approval implicated Exemptions 6 and 7. The ACLU argued that the public interest in disclosure of the government's warrantless and once-secret surveillance was substantial, that the public stood to gain an understanding of the scope, purpose, and outcomes of the cell phone tracking. But the ACLU received mixed results from a federal district court judge. Applying the balancing test, the judge found that the public interest outweighed the privacy interest for those who have been convicted or entered guilty pleas. Those documents were not protected under Exemptions 6 and 7. But the exemptions protected the information about individuals who were acquitted, dismissed or whose cases had been sealed.

Redaction

In *ACLU v. U.S. Dept. of Defense* discussed above, redaction—the censoring of portions of released documents by agencies—was at issue. Redaction is a point of contention in many FOIA requests that go to court. Plaintiffs argue that agencies abuse their discretion by deleting information from records that are not entitled to exemption, or by deleting so much information as to make the released documents meaningless. For instance, after six years and under legal threat, the U.S. Justice Department released heavily redacted documents of the government's secret history of post-World War II Nazi-hunting operations and collaboration to the National Security Archive in 2010. A month later, the *New York Times* obtained a complete version.[24]

Agencies draw their authority to redact from Section 552(b) of FOIA, which provides that an agency must disclose any "reasonably segregable portion" of an otherwise exempt record. Courts, however, have ruled that if the nonexempt material is so "inextricably intertwined" that disclosure of it would "leave only essentially meaningless words and phrases," then the entire record may be withheld.[25] An agency, however, must justify redaction by "identifying the reasons why a particular exemption is relevant and correlating those claims with the particular part of a withheld document to which they apply."[26]

SUMMARY: The FOIA accords an individual a right to obtain records—including print documents, photographs, videos, maps, email, and electronic records—that an agency, department, commission, or government-controlled corporation subject to the law has created or obtains when a request is made. A requester who believes the government entity has failed to comply with disclosure may sue and obtain an injunction ordering "the production of any agency records improperly withheld." The Act, however, provides nine exemptions that allow the government to withhold records or redact portions of them to protect legitimate government and private interests. The courts have said that the exemptions should be narrowly construed. Nevertheless, some agencies have disclosure request backlogs ranging from more than two years to nearly four years.

"Sunlight Is Said To Be the Best of Disinfectants"

So said U.S. Supreme Court Justice Louis Brandeis in a December 20, 1913, *Harper's Weekly* magazine article, "What Publicity Can Do." Brandeis spoke of the need to compel bankers to disclose information about their commissions and profits. But his words are now associated with principles of openness and transparency in government, in general, and the Government in Sunshine Act, 5 U.S.C. § 552b, in particular. While the FOIA makes records of government agencies accessible to the public, the Government in Sunshine Act, enacted in 1977, focuses on promoting public access to government agency decision making. It requires multi-member federal agencies to hold their meetings in public and to announce the time, place, and subject matter of public meetings at least one week before the meeting date. The act provides ten exemptions, most of them similar or identical to the FOIA's nine exemptions. Indeed, plaintiffs seeking disclosure often bring actions under both acts.

The act covers agencies "headed by a collegial body composed of two or more individual members, a majority of whom are appointed to such position by the President with the advice and consent of the Senate." Thus, the Federal Communications Commission, Federal Election Commission, Federal Trade Commission, Federal Energy Regulatory Commission, and Securities and Exchange Commission must comply with the act and are periodically audited. The Florida Bar Association lists 53 agencies covered by the act.[27] Some well-known and large agencies, such as the Environmental Protection Agency, do not fall under the scope of the act that regulates collegial bodies "composed of two or more individual members." A single individual heads the EPA.

Under the act, a meeting is any agency deliberation that focuses on agency business involving a quorum of the agency heads. Take the FCC, for example. It has five commissioners. If only two commissioners meet, the meeting does not have to be open. Exploratory discussions or briefings that do not predetermine official agency action are not meetings under the act. The act also requires that the deliberations "determine or result in the joint conduct or disposition of official agency business," regardless of whether a formal vote is required or taken.[28]

SUMMARY: The federal Government in Sunshine Act requires multi-member federal agencies to hold their meetings in public and to announce the time, place, and subject matter of public meetings at least one week before the meeting date. The act provides ten exemptions, most of them similar or identical to the FOIA's nine exemptions.

State Open Meetings and Records Laws

Like all state public records laws, Washington's Public Records Act requires disclosure of all nonexempt public records upon request by any person. Additionally, Washington routinely discloses the identities of signers of referendum petitions in response to public records requests. In 2009, however, Project Marriage Washington, an anti-gay group, which spearheaded a campaign in Washington to have voters determine whether to extend domestic partnership rights to gays in 2009, challenged the state's authority to disclose such records. The Project argued that disclosure would open those who had signed its petition opposing gay domestic partnership rights to harassment. Thus, the Project made the novel argument that compelled disclosure burdens petition signers' ability to speak, and infringes on privacy of association and belief guaranteed by the First Amendment.

When the case made its way to the U.S. Supreme Court, news and journalists organizations weighed in against the Project. An amicus curiae brief opposing the Project's position warned that,

> Allowing petitioners to prevail on the claim that referendum petition signatures are private would have far-reaching and devastating effects on this country's system of open government and governmental accountability…If governmental acts are allowed to occur anonymously under the guise of protecting speech, this Court will pave the way for any government acts involving personal expression to trump accountability and openness laws, risking the elimination of open meetings, governmental disclosure requirements, and almost any government accountability law.[29]

In *John Doe v. Reed*, 130 S. Ct. 2811 (2010), the Court handed down a ruling with mixed results. The Court ruled that disclosure of referendum petition signers' identities generally does not violate the First Amendment rights of the signers. At the same time, a majority of the court acknowledged that compelled disclosure of names and other personal information included in referendum petitions may, under certain circumstances, violate a First Amendment right to anonymity. Such compelled disclosure laws are subject to "exacting scrutiny," the Court said. Exact scrutiny requires a substantial relation between the disclosure requirement and a sufficiently important government interest. The high court sent the matter back to lower courts to consider whether the particular claim had merit.

Consequently, state open records laws requiring disclosure of the identities of signers to referendum petitions are still vulnerable to a First Amendment privacy challenges. Additionally, state legislatures have the authority to exempt the identities of those who sign referendum petitions from disclosure mostly because access is not a constitutionally protected right.

In his concurrence, which read more like a dissent, Justice Scalia argued that the Court was wrong to acknowledge the existence of a First Amendment privacy right that subjects laws requiring disclosure of referendum petitioners' identities to exacting scrutiny:

> Requiring people to stand up in public for their political acts fosters civic courage, without which democracy is doomed. For my part, I do not look forward to a society which, thanks to the Supreme Court, campaigns anonymously…and even exercises the direct democracy of initiative and referendum hidden from public scrutiny and protected from the accountability of criticism. This does not resemble the Home of the Brave.[30]

An Overview of State Open Meetings and Records Laws

It is far too early to tell if we are headed down the slippery slope that Justice Scalia described. But all 50 states and the District of Columbia have open record statutes similar to Washington's and open meetings laws. The open meetings laws generally provide the public with access to state, county, and municipal meetings of governing and policy-making bodies such as town councils, commissions, agencies, school board and advisory boards, and state-held documents. Generally, open meetings laws require government bodies to give advance notice to the public about public meetings, and to allow the public to attend, and obtain transcripts or recordings of public meetings. Many state sunshine laws predate the federal access laws.

With the advent of the Internet, a good number of municipal government bodies post meeting notices, agendas, and minutes of official action taken at meetings online in compliance with open meetings laws. Space limitations do not allow for a review of all 51 open meeting and records statutes. What follows, then, is a look at Florida's open meeting and open records statutes, considered by many to be some of the strongest in the U.S.

The Florida open public record laws date to 1909. Voters made the right of access to government information an amendment to the state constitution and included the state government's legislative, executive, and judicial branches in 1992. Florida §286.011 Public Meetings and Records law defines public meetings as, "meetings of any board or commission of any state agency or authority or of any agency or authority of any county, municipal corporation, or political subdivision…at which official acts are to be taken." Government entities covered by the statute must provide "reasonable notice" of public meetings and minutes must be promptly recorded and open to public inspection.

The law covers gatherings where "two or more members of a public board or commission discuss some matter on which foreseeable action will be taken by that board or commission."[31] Public boards, commissions, and regional agencies under the "dominion and control" of the state legislature, members-elect of boards or commissions, and private bodies that government has delegated decision making authority to fall under the act.[32] But typically, the statute does not apply to administrative proceedings or government staff meetings.[33] Failure to comply may result in a fine not exceeding $500.

As with all federal and state public access laws, the Florida statute provides exemptions—more than 200! Some of the exempted gatherings are meetings between city councils and city attorneys when discussing pending litigation involving the city; advisory committees involved solely in fact-finding activities; proceedings of peer review panels, committees, and governing bodies of public hospitals or surgical centers relating to discipline; certain meetings of Judicial Nominating Commissions and Judicial Qualifications Commissions; and strategy discussions between a governmental body and its chief executive officer prior to collective bargaining negotiations actions.

According to Florida's Public Records Law, 119.01, "It is the policy of this state that all state, county, and municipal records are open for personal inspection and copying by any person." Under the law, public records are "all documents, papers, letters, maps, books, tapes, photographs, films, sound recordings, data processing software, or other material, regardless of the physical form, characteristics, or means of transmission, made or received pursuant to law or ordinance or in connection with the transaction of official business by any agency." The state legislature has exempted "more than 850 separate records," including "medical, birth and adoption records; autopsy photographs, and video and audio recordings of an autopsy, Social Security numbers contained in official public records; personal identifying and financial information contained in the Department of Health's records; investigative and criminal intelligence records of law enforcement agencies that are related to active investigations; and driver license and motor vehicle records unless driver consents to disclosure."[34]

SUMMARY: The 50 states, the District of Columbia, and the federal government have adopted open meetings and records laws, typically referred to as "sunshine laws." Open meetings laws require public bodies to deliberate and act in public view. There are exceptions. Typically, public bodies such as town councils and school boards may close all or portions of meetings to discuss, for example, government personnel matters and labor talks. State open records laws allow requesters to obtain documents from state and local governing bodies. Many of the state open records exemptions are similar to the FOIA, but as the Florida statute shows, exemptions may number into the hundreds.

The First Amendment and Access to Government-Controlled Spaces, Services, and Facilities

As noted earlier in this chapter, the Court ruled in *Zemel v. Rusk* that the First Amendment does not bestow upon the public or the press an unrestrained right to gather information. *Zemel v. Rusk*, however, does not preclude the right under the First Amendment for the public and the press to enter "places which by long tradition or by government fiat have been devoted to assembly and debate."

The quoted phrase is language from *Perry Education Association v. Perry Local Educators' Association*, 460 U.S. 37 (1983), where the Court revised its public forum doctrine by creating three forum types, which it currently categorizes as "traditional, designated or limited, and nonpublic."[35] The Court has applied public forum analysis to determine when a government entity seeking to regulate its own property may place limitations on expressive activities, including information gathering, assembly, and discussion. In *Cornelius v. NAACP*, 473 U.S. 788, 802 (1985), the Court explained that government transforms its property that has been traditionally closed to assembly and debate into a public forum "only by intentionally opening a nontraditional forum for public discourse." To determine the government's intent, the Court examines the government's policy and practice, "the nature of the property, and its compatibility with expressive activity to discern the government's intent."

Traditional public forum. The Court established the traditional public forum doctrine in *Hague v. Committee for Industrial Organization*, 307 U.S. 496 (1939), where it ruled that, under the First Amendment, government may not ban speech-related activities such as demonstrations, leafleting, and speaking in public areas traditionally provided for speech such as public streets and parks. In a democracy, government controls public property as a trustee for the public, the Court said: "Such use of the streets and public places has, from ancient times, been a part of the privileges, immunities, rights, and liberties of citizens."[36]

The Court further explained in *Perry Education Association* that a government-imposed content-based restriction on expressive activity conducted in a traditional public forum must survive strict scrutiny analysis; it must promote a compelling state interest and be narrowly drawn to achieve that end. A content-neutral regulation of expressive activity conducted in a traditional public forum, however, is subject to time, place, and manner limits and must be narrowly tailored to serve a significant government interest, and leave open ample alternative channels of communication, the *Perry* Court said.

A designated or limited public forum "consists of public property which the State has opened for use by the public as a place for expressive activity. The Constitution forbids a State to enforce certain exclusions from a forum generally open to the public even if it was not required to create the forum in the first place."[37] Moreover, "Government restrictions on speech in a designated public forum are subject to the same strict scrutiny as restrictions in a traditional public forum."[38] An example of a designated public forum is a municipality leasing a private theater, thus, making it a government facility. When it denied the use of the theater to a New York production company based on the nudity, foul language, and drug-use references in the play *Hair*, the Court struck down the ban as an impermissible prior restraint of the use of a public forum in *Southeastern Promotions, Ltd. v. Conrad*, 420 U.S. 546 (1975). In *Widmar v. Vincent*, 454 U.S. 263 (1981), the Court ruled that a state university created a designated public forum when it dedicated facilities for meetings of registered student organizations. Consequently, the university would have to show that its denial of the use of the facilities to student religious organizations was necessary to serve a compelling state interest and a restriction that was narrowly drawn to achieve that end. The university argued that as a public institution it had a compelling state interest in maintaining separation of church and state under the U.S. First Amendment and the Missouri State Constitution. But the Court said it could not exclude the religious groups based on the content of their speech because use of the "open forum in a public university does not confer any imprimatur of state approval on religious sects or practices" and the use by more than 100 secular student groups was evidence that the religious groups would not dominate the forum.[39] The university also could have regulated the religious groups use with reasonable time, place and manner restriction, the Court noted.

The use of public school rooms for school board meetings or municipal council meetings held at town halls are examples of limited public forums.[40] Any member of the public or press may attend such meetings and engage in discussions about relevant issues.[41] It stands to reason, however, that government has an interest in conducting orderly public meetings and federal courts have recognized that interest as significant.[42] Government may impose time, place, and manner restrictions on speech as long as the restrictions are content neutral and narrowly tailored to serve a significant governmental interest and leave open ample alternatives for communication.[43] When the school board or council is not in session, government may limit access to teachers, administrators, and students in the case of public schools and to credentialed individuals at municipal buildings.

A public forum does not have to be spatial or geographic. In *Rosenberger v. University of Virginia*, 515 U.S. 819 (1995), the Court said that once the University of Virginia established a fund to support extracurricular on-campus student activities, it had created a public forum. Therefore, the University could not deny funds to a student-run religious publication, the Court ruled.

In contrast, a state educational institution, like Hastings College of Law, that has designated a forum by funding student organizations may deny funding to a student organization that discriminates unlawfully on the basis of race, color, religion, national origin, ancestry, disability, age, sex or sexual orientation, the Court ruled in *Christian Legal Society v. Martinez*, 130 S.Ct. 2971 (2010). How did Hastings College of Law's actions differ from the University of Virginia's? The university's funding program singled out an organization for disfavored treatment. In contrast, Hasting's funding program made no such distinction; it required that all funding recipients treat all students equally.

The nonpublic forum category includes: military bases (*Greer v. Spock*, 424 U.S. 828 (1976); post office mail boxes (*U.S. Postal Service v. Council of Greenburgh Civic Association*, 453 U.S.114 (1981); public utility poles (*Members of the City Council of Los Angeles v. Taxpayers for Vincent*, 466 U.S. 789 (1984); military bases even when open to the non-military personnel (*U.S. v. Albertini*, 472 U.S. 675 (1985); solicitation of votes and the display or distribution of campaign materials near polling places (*Burson v. Freeman*, 504 U.S. 191 (1992); and airport and transportation terminals (*International*

Society for Krishna Consciousness v. Lee, 505 U.S. 672 (1992). Government may impose time, place, and manner restrictions on the use of nonpublic forums. Intermediate scrutiny is imposed to test the constitutionality of a viewpoint-neutral regulation of nonpublic forums. But when government targets political expression, courts apply exacting scrutiny: the State must show that the regulation is necessary to serve a compelling state interest and that it is narrowly drawn to achieve that end.

SUMMARY: The Court has applied public forum analysis to determine when a government entity seeking to regulate its own property may place limitations on expressive activities, including information gathering, assembly, discussion and speech making.

- First, in "traditional" public forums, such as public streets and parks, restrictions based on content must satisfy strict scrutiny. Government also can limit individuals' use of such forums by enforcing reasonable content-neutral time, place, and manner restrictions.
- Second, strict scrutiny also applies to content-based regulations restricting "designated or limited" public forums, which are government-controlled properties that do not fall within the "traditional" category, but which the government has opened for public expressive purposes. Government may also impose reasonable viewpoint-neutral time, place, and manner restrictions to regulate expression in "limited" or "designated" public forums. Municipal-owned theaters, town meetings, and university student organization funds are examples of "designated" or "limited" public forums.
- Lastly, government can regulate speech in "nonpublic forums," such as military bases, mail boxes, utility poles, polling areas, airport and transportation terminals by imposing content-neutral time, place, and manner restrictions. Additionally, when a statute targets political speech in a nonpublic forum, courts subject the restriction to exacting scrutiny.

ONLINE RESOURCES

1. "The Government in the Sunshine Act," http://www.rcfp.org/federal-open-government-guide/federal-open-meetings-laws/government-sunshine-act
2. "Eight Federal Agencies Have FOIA Requests a Decade Old, According to Knight Open Government Survey," National Security Archive, http://www.gwu.edu/~nsarchiv/NSAEBB/NSAEBB349/index.htm
3. "The Sunshine in Government Initiative," http://www.sunshineingovernment.org/index.php?cat=213
4. U.S. Department of State Freedom of Information Act (FOIA), http://www.state.gov/m/a/ips/
5. "What is the Public Forum Doctrine?" http://www.freedomforum.org/packages/first/publicforumdoctrine/

QUESTIONS

1   In May 2011, the Associated Press (AP) filed an FOIA request to obtain the release of photographs and video taken during the raid on Osama Bin Laden's compound in Abbottabad, Pakistan. Identify the exemption or exemptions that might justify the government's refusal to release the photographs and videos?

2.   In a presentation, "City Meetings and the First Amendment," delivered at Texas City Attorneys Association's 2006 Summer Conference, attorneys Steven L. Weathered and Leonard V. Schneider asked the following: "…if the municipality has created a…forum on its agenda for 'public comment' with a limitation that comments are limited to subjects that address city and citizen concerns, is the city allowed to prohibit a citizen from making a statement that the 'mayor and council are liars and thieves' on the premise this is a personal attack?…what if the speaker stated 'council members that support property tax rate hikes are liars and thieves because they promised, if elected, there would be no tax rate hikes?'" What do you think? See: *White v. City of Norwalk*, 900 F.2d 1421, 1425 (9th Cir. 1990); *Gault v. City of Battle Creek*, 73 F.Supp.2d 811, 814 (W.D. Michigan 1999); and "Free Speech Restrictions at Auburn City Council Meetings," http://www.nyclu.org/regions/central-new-york/auburn_meetings_speech

3.   What kind of forum is a government-owned website? Traditional? Designated or Limited? Nonpublic? Apply the precedents above and analogize. Also, see *Putnam Pit v. City of Cookeville*, 221 F.3d 834 (6th Cir. 2000).

ENDNOTES

1. *EPIC v. U.S. Department of Homeland Security (DHS)*, 09–2084 (RMU) (D.D.C. January 12, 2011).
2. See John J. Mitchell. "Government Secrecy in Theory and Practice: 'Rules and Regulations' As an Autonomous Screen," 58 Columbia Law Review 199 (1958).
3. See Robert L. Hughes. "The Common Law of Access to Government Records," 16 Newspaper Research Journal 39 (1995).
4. *San Jose Mercury-News v. Municipal Court*, 30 Cal.3d 498, 502 (1982).
5. Reporters Committee for Freedom of the Press. "Freedom of Information." In Homefront Confidential: How the War on Terrorism Affects Access to Information and the Public's Right to Know (September 2005),, http://www.rcfp.org/homefrontconfidential/foi.html
6. National Security Archive. Justice Delayed Is Justice Denied: The Ten Oldest Pending FOIA Requests. Washington, D.C.: George Washington University (2003), 2, http://www.gwu.edu/~nsarchiv/NSAEBB/NSAEBB102/tenoldest.pdf
7. Ibid, 3.
8. The Freedom of Information Act, 5 U.S.C. § 552(B)(f)(1),http://www.justice.gov/oip/foia_updates/Vol_XVII_4/page2.htm
9. Ibid. 5 U.S.C. § 552 (4)(B).
10. *FBI v. Abramson*, 456 U.S. 615, 621 (1982).
11. *Department of Justice v. Julian*, 486 U.S. 1 (1988).
12. Ibid. The Freedom of Information Act, 5 U.S.C. § 552(F)(b)(1)(A).
13. Ibid. F(b)(2).
14. *Doherty v. Department of Justice*, 775 F.2d 49, 52 (2d Cir.1985); *Diamond v. FBI*, 707 F.2d 75, 79 (2d Cir.1983),cert. denied, 465 U.S. 1004, 104 S.Ct. 995, 79 L.Ed.2d 228 (1984).
15. *Donovan v. FBI*, 806 F.2d 55, 58 (2d. Cir. 1986).
16. *ACLU v. U.S. Dept. of Defense*, 628 F.3d 612, 619 (D.C. Cir. 2011).

17. Ibid. 625.

18. Ibid.

19. See *GC Micro Corp. v. Defense Logistics Agency*, 33 F.3d 1109, 1112 (9th Cir.1994); *Nadler v. FDIC*, 92 F.3d 93, 95 (2d Cir. 1996)

20. *Nadler v. FDIC*, 92 at 96.

21. *Org. for Women Office Workers v. Bd. of Governors of Federal. Reserve System*, 721 F.2d 1, 11 (1st Cir.1983); see also *Critical Mass Energy Project v. Nuclear Regulatory Commission*, 830 F.2d 278, 287 (D. C. Cir. 1987) (adopting program effectiveness test), overruled on other grounds by *Critical Mass Energy Project v. Nuclear Regulatory Commission*, 975 F.2d 871, 879 (D. C. Cir. 1992) (en banc).

22. In *Bloomberg, L.P. v. Board of Governors of the Federal Reserve*, 601 F.3d 143, 151 (2d Cir. 2010), citing *Department of Air Force v. Rose*, 425 U.S. 352 (1976).

23. In *Bloomberg, L.P. v. Board of Governors of the Federal Reserve*, 601 F.3d 143, 148 (2d Cir. 2010).

24. See Judy Feigin. "The Office of Special Investigations: Striving for Accountability in the Aftermath of the Holocaust," U.S. Department of Justice (December 2006), http://documents.nytimes.com/confidential-report-provides-new-evidence-of-notorious-nazi-cases?ref=us#p=1

25. *Neufeld v. IRS,* 646 F.2d 661, 663 (D.C. Cir. 1981).

26. *King v. U.S. Department of Justice*, 830 F.2d 210, 224 (D.C. Cir. 1987).

27. Joseph Z. Fleming and Jose I. Leon. "The Federal Government in the Sunshine Act: A Federal Mandate for Open Meetings," The Florida Bar (August, 2008), http://www.floridabar.org/DIVCOM/PI/RHandbook01.nsf/1119bd38ae090a748525676f0053b606/33db31567bc6b028852569cb004c8736?OpenDocument#I.%20Introduction._0

28. *Pacific Legal Foundation v. Council on Environmental Quality*, 636 F.2d 1259, 1266 (D.C. Cir. 1980).

29. Brief for the Reporters Committee for Freedom of the Press et al. as Amici Curiae Supporting Respondents, *John Doe No. 1 v. Reed*, 130 S. Ct. 2811 (2010) (No. No. 09–559), 4.

30. *John Doe No. 1 v. Reed*, 130 S. Ct. at 2837.

31. Brechner Center for Freedom of Information. Florida Government in the Sunshine: A Citizen's Guide, , 4, http://brechner.org/citizen%20guide%202006.pdf

32. Ibid. 6.

33. Ibid.

34. Ibid. 14–15.

35. See *Christian Legal Society v. Martinez*, 130 S. Ct. 2971, n. 11 (2010) for the Court's most current nomenclature for the three categories.

36. *Hague v. Committee for Industrial Organization*, 307 U.S. 496, 515–516 (1939).

37. *Perry Education Association v. Perry Local Educators' Association*, 460 U.S. 37, 45 (1983).

38. *Pleasant Grove City, Utah v. Summum*, 129 S. Ct. 1125, 1132 (2009).

39. *Widmar v. Vincent*, 454 U.S. 263, 274 (1981).

40. See *White v. City of Norwalk*, 900 F.2d 1421, 1425 (9th Cir. 1990).

41. See *City of Madison, Joint School District. v. Wisconsin Employment Relations Commission*, 429 U.S. 167 (1976).

42. *Jones v. Heyman*, 888 F.2d. 1328, 1332 (11th Cir. 1989) citing City of Madison at n.8.

43. *Burson v. Freeman*, 504 U.S. 191, 197 (1992); *Ward v. Rock Against Racism*, 491 U.S. 781, 791 (1989).

CHAPTER TEN

Fair Trial/Free Press

CONTROVERSY: As you read this, certain federal trial courts are engaged in an experiment that could dramatically change their relationship with the media and the public. Starting in July 2011, 14 federal trial court districts allowed their civil proceedings to be video recorded as part of a three-year project to evaluate the effects of cameras in courtrooms. The U.S. Judicial Conference—composed of federal trial and appellate judges—pursued a similar pilot program in the 1990s. It pulled the plug in 1994. Many judges were horrified by the media coverage of the O.J. Simpson trial. As Ninth Circuit U.S. Court of Appeals Judge Alex Kozinski and his law clerk Robert Johnson wrote, "You can't talk about cameras in the courtroom without talking about The Juice."[1] In 1996, the conference allowed electronic coverage of federal appeals proceedings as part of an experiment and the Ninth and Second participated. Now, under the current pilot program, you can watch the video recordings at www.uscourts.gov and on local participating court websites at the court's discretion. In contrast, most states allow each judge to determine whether commercial news outlets may cover specific criminal and civil proceedings.

Meanwhile, as far as the majority of the U.S. Supreme Court is concerned, it does not matter one bit how the experiment turns out. Though retired U.S. Supreme Court Justice David H. Souter now lives blissfully somewhere in New Hampshire, most of his ex-colleagues, apparently, are determined to live up to the spirit of Souter's vow, "I can tell you the day you see a camera come into our courtroom, it's going to roll over my dead body." Live or recorded video broadcasts of U.S. Supreme Court oral arguments are forbidden.[2]

Chapter's Scope

The more than 50-year-long debate over the impact of television cameras in courtrooms, alluded to above, is just one manifestation of the U.S. Supreme Court's effort to strike the proper balance between fair trial and free press rights. Many believe the Court's ban on televising its own proceedings misses the mark. Criminal defendant's fair trial rights are protected under the Sixth Amendment[3] and the Fourteenth Amendment's due process clause.[4] The fair trial rights of parties in civil actions are protected under the Seventh and Fourteenth Amendments.[5] The First, Sixth, and Seventh Amendments, however, provide the public and news media with rights to attend trials and other judicial proceedings and to discuss them publicly. Additionally, state common law and judicial policy also confer fair trial and free press rights to the public, press, and parties involved in criminal and civil trials. Starting with the Warren Court (1953–1969), the U.S. Supreme Court has sought to achieve a fair balance between the constitutional rights of press, the public, parties in criminal and civil proceedings, and the legal system by creating legal doctrines from cases involving (i) pretrial news coverage, (ii) news coverage during and after trial, (iii) citizens and journalists' efforts to attend courtroom proceedings, (iv) and the news media's and the public's efforts to photograph, film, videotape or use digital technology to record, photograph, and tweet courtroom proceedings. A discussion of those cases and doctrines follows.

First Amendment & Pretrial Speech Prejudicial to Fair Trials

As soon as the defendant is indicted by a grand jury or arraigned at a hearing, sometimes earlier, intensive and widespread bad press can undermine a criminal defendant's ability to get a fair trial. The Court first addressed the impact such media coverage can have on a defendant's right to have his case heard by an impartial jury in *Irvin v. Dowd*, 366 U.S. 717 (1961). Leslie Irvin, convicted for multiple murders in Indiana, brought a habeas corpus appeal to the Court, alleging that media coverage including newspapers carrying stories about his alleged confession and criminal background had reached about 95% of the dwellings in the two counties, and similar radio and TV coverage in one of the counties made it impossible to pick jurors who had not concluded that he was guilty before hearing evidence at trial. Irvin noted that newspapers running stories about his alleged confession and criminal background reached about 95% of the dwellings in the two counties and similar radio and TV coverage occurred in one of the counties. He sought two changes of venue, but received only one because of limits imposed by Indiana law. The Court noted, "Almost 90% [of the jury pool]…entertained some opinion as to guilt—ranging in intensity from mere suspicion to absolute certainty. A number admitted that, if they were in the accused's place in the dock and he in theirs on the jury with their opinions, they would not want him on a jury."[6] The jury pool was tainted, the Court said. The Court, finding clear and convincing prejudice against Irvin based on the totality of the circumstances, vacated his conviction and remanded his case for a new trial because, as Justice Tom C. Clark reasoned, "With his life at stake, it is not requiring too much that petitioner be tried in an atmosphere undisturbed by so huge a wave of public passion and by a jury other than one in which two-thirds of the members admit, before hearing any testimony, to possessing a belief in his guilt."[7] On retrial, Irvin was convicted and sentenced to life imprisonment.

In *Rideau v. Louisiana*, 373 U.S. 723 (1963), the Court overturned a murder conviction because a filmed jailhouse confession of the defendant was broadcast three times over a local television station, reaching about 65% of the community. The trial court denied Rideau's requests to remove jurors and for a change of venue, which could have mitigated the adverse effect of the prejudicial broadcasts. Writing for a 7–2 majority, Justice Potter Stewart noted, "For anyone who has ever watched television the conclusion cannot be avoided that this spectacle, to the tens of thousands of people who saw and heard it, in a very real sense *was* Rideau's trial—at which he pleaded guilty to murder. Any subsequent court proceedings in a community so pervasively exposed to such a spectacle could be but a hollow formality."[8]

In its 8–1 ruling in *Sheppard v. Maxwell*, 384 U.S. 333 (1966), the Court overturned the murder conviction of Dr. Sam Sheppard on Fourteenth Amendment due process grounds because a carnival atmosphere caused by news reporters pervaded the trial. The *Sheppard* Court also took note of the massive and intensive defendant-averse publicity before and during trial. The trial judge failed to minimize the influence of pretrial publicity by changing the trial's venue or sequestering the jury, the Court said.

Sheppard v. Maxwell is also notable for the Court's identification of the interest at stake in its balancing analysis. It acknowledged the role a "responsible press" has played as "the handmaiden of effective judicial administration, especially in the criminal field...The press does not simply publish information about trials but guards against the miscarriage of justice by subjecting the police, prosecutors, and judicial processes to extensive public scrutiny and criticism." Accordingly, the Court said, it has been "unwilling to place any direct limitations on the freedom of the news media" to cover what transpires in courtrooms.[9]

On the other hand, the *Sheppard* Court said trials are not elections "to be won through the use of the meeting-hall, the radio, and the newspaper" and freedom of discussion must not undermine the need to have jurors reach verdicts based only on the evidence and argument produced in the courtroom.[10] Dr. Sheppard was retried and acquitted in 1966, and his fight for exoneration inspired the 1960s television series *The Fugitive* and the 1993 movie of the same title.

Juror exposure to extensive pretrial publicity alone does not deprive a defendant of his fair trial rights. Though the constitutional standard of fairness requires that a defendant be judged by an impartial jury, "qualified jurors need not, however, be totally ignorant of the facts and issues involved," the Court ruled in *Murphy v. Florida*, 421 U.S. 794, 800 (1975). In *Patton v. Yount*, 467 U.S. 1025 (1984), the Court, citing language in *Irvin v. Dowd*, held that appeals courts may overturn a trial court's ruling regarding a jury panel's impartiality only when it has made a "manifest," or indisputably obvious, error in reaching its decision.

SUMMARY: Though news outlets play a role supported by the First and Sixth Amendment, serving as watchdogs of the criminal justice system for the public and the defendant's benefit, criminal defendants are entitled to be tried by a jury weighing only the evidence presented at trial. When it is found that a majority of a jury panel has reached a criminal conviction based solely on widespread and intense pretrial evidence, the Sixth and Fourteenth Amendments demand that an appeals court overturn such a verdict. In *Irvin v. Dowd*, for example, the Court noted that "the pattern of deep and bitter prejudice" in the community "was clearly reflected in the sum total of the voir dire...370 prospective jurors or almost 90% of those examined on the point...entertained some opinion as to guilt," and "[8] out of the 12 [jurors] thought [the defendant] was guilty."[11]

Judicial Remedies to Publicity before, during, and after Trial

In the previous section, you learned that courts must overturn criminal convictions to remedy the effects of pretrial publicity that made it impossible for a defendant to receive a fair trial because a majority of a jury had predetermined the defendant's guilt, regardless of the evidence presented at trial. The terms voir dire, change of venue, and sequester were also introduced. They, along with continuance, are trial procedures a judge may impose to mitigate the adverse effects of publicity before and during trial. Such procedures do not infringe upon journalists' free press rights. Thus, journalists do not have standing to challenge a judge's decision to employ them. All of them, however, create risks or disadvantages for defendants and can undermine the fair administration of justice.

- **Voir Dire.** In criminal trials, the pretrial procedure voir dire—"to speak the truth"—starts with the creation of the jury pool made up of citizens residing in a district where the offense was committed, or venue. Next, the judge or attorneys subject members of the pool to oral questioning with the aim of selecting jurors they believe are capable of rendering an impartial verdict. But is voir dire effective in screening out biased jurors? Social science studies have shown that voir dire is not effective in eliminating juror bias because most jurors do not recognize their pretrial-publicity-induced bias or admit to it.[12] Defense attorneys are further hampered by the Court ruling in *Mu'Min v. Virginia*, 500 U.S. 415 (1991), which held that a trial judge's refusal to question prospective jurors about the specific contents of pretrial news reports to which they had been exposed did not violate the defendant's Sixth Amendment fair trial or Fourteenth Amendment due process rights. Thus, potential jurors do not have to erase from their memories everything they have read, seen, and heard about a case to qualify as impartial.
- **Change of Venue.** The Sixth Amendment states that "in all criminal prosecutions, the accused shall enjoy the right to a speedy and public trial, by an impartial jury of the State and district wherein the crime shall have been committed." Venue is defined as the proper place to hold a civil or criminal trial and, in a criminal case, venue is the county or district where the crime occurred. Generally, in a civil action, a plaintiff may sue in the district or county where the defendant does business or lives. To minimize the effects of pretrial publicity, a judge may move a trial to a jurisdiction that has been exposed to little or no publicity about the case. In *Patton v. Yount*, the Court said a change of venue determination requires an examination of the nature of the publicity surrounding the trial, the voir dire of the jury panel as a whole, and individual jurors. Some states require a judge to make such a determination based on a reasonable likelihood pretrial prejudicial news will prevent a fair trial; others require a judge to find that the pretrial publicity made it impossible for a defendant to get a fair trial. Though a case can be moved only to a location within the same state, a change can mean that a trial occurs hundreds of miles from where the victims and their community live, or where the defendant's peers reside. And can changing the venue make a difference when a high-profile criminal case receives nationwide media coverage?
- **Continuance.** The Sixth Amendment guarantees defendants a "speedy trial." Consequently, when suspending or postponing a trial because of pretrial and continuing news coverage, a judge must balance the defendant's and the legal system's interests in reaching a verdict in a timely manner against the adverse effects of news coverage on the jury. The purpose in postponing a trial, or granting a continuance, is to allow the

memories of pretrial news coverage to fade and improve the likelihood of seating an impartial jury.

- **Sequestration.** Obviously, isolating jurors in hotels to avoid exposure to news coverage and contact with individuals who might convey knowledge of trial news coverage helps only during a trial, not to mitigate pretrial prejudice. Commentators also question the quality of justice provided by jurors who might be more concerned about freeing themselves from isolation than in reaching a well-considered verdict.

Gag Orders

The *Sheppard's* Court call to judges to get tough on pretrial prejudicial publicity—"[T]he cure lies in those remedial measures that will prevent the prejudice at its inception"[13]—spurring a rise in the use of gag orders, a form of prior restraint, to prevent journalists, lawyers, parties to the case, and jurors from talking publicly about a pending or ongoing trial, and even during the aftermath of a trial. A judge may hold journalists who fail to comply with a gag order in contempt and fine or jail them.

In *Nebraska Press Association v. Stuart*, 427 U.S. 539 (1976), a plurality of the Court crafted a three-part test for gag orders imposed on the press that is extremely free-press protective, mostly because, under First Amendment law, prior restraints are presumed unconstitutional, with a few exceptions as discussed in earlier chapters. To impose a gag order, a judge must show that (i) intense widespread publicity will occur, (ii) other less speech-restrictive measures will be ineffective, and (iii) the gag order will be effective in shielding potential jurors from prejudicial information. There are less speech-restrictive alternatives at the judge's disposal in the forms of voir dire, continuance, change of venue, and sequestration. So, a judge will have to explain why those alternatives are not likely to blunt the effects of pretrial publicity.

News outlets have defied gag orders because they believed that the orders were unconstitutional, or, perhaps, after conducting a cost-benefit analysis, decided paying fines or serving a brief jail sentence was worth the risk of publishing. In *U.S. v. Noriega*, 752 F. Supp. 1032 (1992), U.S. District Judge William Hoeveler imposed a gag order to prevent the Cable News Network (CNN) from airing the deposed Panama General Manuel Noriega's privately tape-recorded messages between him and his lawyers. The order was upheld in *U.S. v. Noriega*, 917 F. 2d 1543 (11th Cir. 1990) and the U.S. Supreme Court denied certiorari *In re Cable News Network (CNN) v. Noriega*, 498 U.S. 976 (1990). CNN, however, violated the gag order and in *U.S. v. Cable News Network, Inc.*, 865 F. Supp. 1549 (D. Fla. 1994), Judge Hoeveler held CNN in criminal contempt. As part of the sentence, CNN aired an apology to the judge and paid the government's legal fees of $85,000.[14]

Gagging Trial Participants

Some jurisdictions have recognized that media outlets have standing to challenge gag orders imposed on lawyers,[15] jurors, parties, and witnesses. To gain standing in a case, a media outlet must show that it has a personal stake in the outcome of the litigation and that a law protects that interest. Accordingly, media outlets argue that gags on trial participants deny them the ability to gather news, an interest protected under the First Amendment. Gaining standing, however, hardly guarantees an outlet a favorable outcome. For example, the Radio & Television News Association, an umbrella group for news broadcasters, won standing in *Radio & Television News Association v. U.S. Dist. Ct.*, 781 F. 2d 1443 (9th Cir. 1986), but failed to get a gag order lifted from a trial attorney because, as the court reasoned, the "media never has any guarantee of or 'right' to interview counsel in a criminal trial."[16]

The Public and Journalists' Access to Courtroom Proceedings

Under the common law we have inherited from the British system, it is presumed that criminal trials are open to the public because, as future-U.S. Supreme Court Justice Oliver Wendell Holmes observed as a Massachusetts Supreme Court judge, "It is of the highest moment that those who administer justice should always act under the sense of public responsibility, and that every citizen should be able to satisfy himself with his own eyes as to the mode in which a public duty is performed."[17] The Sixth and Seventh Amendments also provide the public and the news media with a right of access. Courts have interpreted fair trial rights to include public scrutiny of courtroom proceedings: "The knowledge that every criminal trial is subject to contemporaneous review in the forum of public opinion is an effective restraint on possible abuse of judicial power."[18]

The First Amendment also provides the public and news media with a qualified right to attend criminal courtroom proceedings. Citing the Anglo-American tradition of open criminal trials, seven U.S. Supreme Court justices recognized for the first time in *Richmond Newspapers, Inc. v. Virginia*, 44 U.S. 555 (1980), that under the First Amendment certain criminal courtroom proceedings are open to the public: (i) "where the people generally—and representatives of the media—have a right to be present, and (ii) where their presence historically has been thought to enhance the integrity and quality of what takes place."[19] This has been referred to as the experience-and-logic test.

Accordingly, the U.S. Supreme Court and lower courts have established a First Amendment right of access to many stages of the criminal and civil court proceedings and documents. In *Globe Newspaper Co. v. Superior Court*, 457 U.S. 596 (1982), the Court struck down a Massachusetts mandatory rule barring press and public access to criminal sex-offense trials during the testimony of minor victims. It applied a hybrid scrutiny to the mandatory ban, considering the compelling government interest and how narrowly tailored the language was written, concluding that a trial court can determine on a case-by-case basis whether closure is necessary to protect the welfare of a minor victim.

The criminal voir dire and trial is presumed to be open to the public, the Court held in *Press Enterprise v. Superior Court ("Press Enterprise I")*, 464 U.S. 501 (1984). A judge, however, may close the voir dire and trial by identifying an "overriding interest based on findings that closure is essential to preserve higher values and is narrowly tailored to serve that interest. The interest is to be articulated along with findings specific enough that a reviewing court can determine whether the closure order was properly entered."[20]

In *Press Enterprise II*, 478 U.S. 1 (1986), the Court held that the press has a First Amendment right to a transcript of a criminal prosecution preliminary hearing. The Court reaffirmed the right of the public to attend the voir dire in *Presley v. Georgia*, 130 S. Ct. 721 (2010), a 7–2 per curiam opinion. The Court ruled that a trial judge must consider alternatives to excluding the public from the voir dire, even when the party opposing closure fails to ask for specific alternatives.

Lower Federal Courts and Access

By applying the *Richmond Newspapers* experience-and-logic analysis, federal and state appellate and trial courts have recognized a qualified right of access to various proceedings during the criminal prosecution process and to related documents. What immediately follows is a sample of rulings by federal appeals courts opening up access to various stages of the criminal prosecution process and documents. *U.S. v. Danovaro*, 877 F. 2d 583, 589 (7th Cir. 1989), ruled that, "As members of the public, [co-defendant] and his attorneys may attend proceedings at which pleas are taken and inspect the transcripts, unless there is strong justification for closing them." The Second Circuit included pretrial hearings on motions to suppress evidence in *U.S. v. Klepfer* (*In re Herald Co.*), 734 F. 2d 93, 99 (2d Cir. 1984). The same court ruled in *U.S. v. Haller*, 837 F. 2d 86–87 (2d Cir. 1988), that a right of access to plea hearings and agreements existed. In *Huminski v. Corsones*, 396 F. 3d 53 (2d Cir. 2004), the Second Circuit ruled that an individual has a First Amendment right to enter the courthouse merely out of curiosity or because he wants to monitor the activities of a judge he believes is unjust. In *U.S. v. Chagra*, 701 F. 2d 354, 363–364 (5th Cir. 1983), the Fifth Circuit said pretrial bond reduction hearings are open. In *Hearst Newspapers, Inc. v. Cardenas-Guillen*, No. 10–40221 (5th Cir. 2011), the Fifth Circuit ruled that the press and public have "a First Amendment right of access to sentencing hearings, and that the district court should have given the press and public notice and an opportunity to be heard before closing the sentencing proceeding in this case."

The U.S. Supreme Court declined to resolve a split between the Sixth and Third federal circuits on whether Immigration and Naturalization Service deportation hearings are open to the public when it denied certiorari in *North Jersey Media Group, Inc. v. Ashcroft*, No. 02–1289 (2003). Applying the experience-and-logic analysis, the Third Circuit in *North Jersey Media Group, Inc. v. Ashcroft*, 308 F. 3d 198, 201 (3d Cir. 2002), said, "In our view the tradition of openness of deportation proceedings does not meet the standard required by *Richmond Newspapers*, or even its Third Circuit progeny." A little more than a month earlier, the Sixth Circuit reached the opposite conclusion in *Detroit Free Press v. Ashcroft*, 303 F. 3d 681 (6th Cir. 2002). The Sixth Circuit applied the experience-and-logic analysis and concluded that deportation hearings had been traditionally open and the public and news media's presence there had enhanced the integrity and quality of the proceedings.

Juvenile Court Proceedings

Consistent with the *Richmond Newspapers*' experience-and-logic test, most judges have been reluctant to open juvenile court proceedings to the public and the press because such proceedings have traditionally been closed to the public.[21] Just as important, the U.S. Supreme Court has never ruled that the press and the public have a right of access to such proceedings. But, partly as a response to a rise in violent and deadly crimes committed by teenagers in the 1990s, all states and the District of Columbia now allow juveniles to be criminally prosecuted as adults under certain circumstances.[22] Accordingly, many states have opened juvenile proceedings and documents to the public when a minor is charged with a crime that would be a felony if committed by an adult.

Civil Proceedings

The U.S. Supreme Court has not handed down a ruling on the public's and press's First Amendment right of access to civil proceedings. Nevertheless, the Seventh Circuit noted in *Bond v. Utreras*, 585 F. 3d 1061, 1074 (7th Cir. 2009), it follows from common law-based open court principles "that most documents filed in court are presumptively open to the public; members of the media and the public may bring third-party challenges to protective orders that shield court records and court proceedings from public view." In *Bond v. Utreras*, the Seventh Circuit also ruled that the common law right of access does not extend to unfiled discovery materials because they are not a part of the public record. *Nixon v. Warner Communications, Inc.*, 435 U.S. 589, 599 (1978), instructs that under the common law, "decision as to access is one best left to the sound discretion of the trial court, a discretion to be exercised in light of the relevant facts and circumstances of the particular case." Courts must weigh the competing public and private interests, such as privacy in attorney-client privileged documents and contractual nondisclosure terms, to determine whether a significant interest outweighs the presumption of openness.[23]

Still, it is important to note that the First Amendment's guarantee of public access to civil court proceedings and records is much stronger than the guarantee provided by the common law because *Press Enterprise I* requires that the "presumption of openness may be overcome only by an overriding interest based on findings that closure is essential to preserve higher values."[24]

Courts also have applied the *Richmond Newspapers* two-part test to determine whether quasi-judicial forums such as government administrative hearings and public university student disciplinary board proceedings are presumptively open to the public.

Post-Verdict Access Bans

The *Press Enterprise I* test also applies to restrictions on news media contact with jurors after a trial has ended, the Third Circuit ruled in *U.S. v. Antar*, 38 F. 3d 1348 (1994). Strict scrutiny also may be applied to test the constitutionality of such restrictions. In a pre-*Press Enterprise I* ruling, the Fifth Circuit applied strict scrutiny to strike down a similar ban on post-verdict interviews in *In re The Express-News Corp.*, 695 F. 2d 807 (5th Cir.1982), because the statutory-imposed ban might have prevented jurors from talking with relatives, friends, and associates. In *U.S. v. Cleveland*, 128 F. 3d 267 (5th Cir.1997), applying strict scrutiny, the Fifth Circuit upheld a post-verdict restriction on jurors discussing their deliberations that said, in part, "absent a special order by me, no juror may be interviewed by anyone concerning the deliberations of the jury."[25] The court said the restriction was more narrowly tailored than the one in *In re The Express-News Corp.* because it did not restrict interviews with relatives and friends and did not prevent discussion about the verdict, just the deliberations. In an issue of first impression, the New Jersey Supreme Court in *State v. Neulander*, 801 A. 2d 255 (2002), upheld an order banning interviews of members of a hung jury that could not reach a verdict in the guilt phase of a capital murder trial, even though jurors' identities were publicly disclosed throughout the voir dire proceeding. The court said the risk was sufficiently substantial that such interviews would reveal information about the strengths and weaknesses in the prosecution's case that could provide the prosecution with an undue advantage in the retrial.

> SUMMARY: *Richmond Newspapers, Inc. v. Virginia*, 44 U.S. 555 (1980), provides that under the First Amendment certain criminal courtroom proceedings are open to the public (i) "where the people generally—and representatives of the media—have a right to be present, and (ii) where their presence historically has been thought to enhance the integrity and quality of what takes place." This has been referred to as the experience-and-logic test. Accordingly, grand jury and juvenile court proceedings are presumed to be closed to the press and public. In *Press Enterprise I*, the Court said the presumption of openness could be overcome only by an "overriding interest based on findings that closure is essential to preserve higher values and is narrowly tailored to serve that interest." Federal appeals and trial courts and state courts have recognized a First Amendment right of access to pretrial suppression, plea hearings, sentencing, Immigration and Naturalization Service deportation hearings, civil hearings and trials, and related documents. Judges' restrictions on what jurors say after the verdict are subject to the *Press Enterprise I* test or strict scrutiny. The Sixth and Seventh Amendments and state common laws also provide the public and the news media with a qualified right of access to courtroom proceedings.

Access to Courtroom Proceedings Via Electronic Media

Judicial skepticism of electronic coverage of trials and other courtroom proceedings stems mostly from the press's unrestrained conduct during the trial of Bruno Hauptmann. Hauptmann was convicted of kidnapping and murdering the son of world-famous aviator Charles Lindbergh in 1937. His Flemington, New Jersey, trial was crammed with more than 700 reporters, as many as 129 photographers and lights to assist the photography, and large motion-picture newsreel cameras.[26] In 1937, the American Bar Association (ABA) Committee, formed to study the news media's impact on the fair administration of justice, concluded that Hauptman's trial was "the most spectacular and depressing example of improper publicity and professional misconduct ever presented to the people of the United States…That the use of cameras in the courtroom should be only with the knowledge and approval of the trial judge and the consent of counsel for the accused in criminal cases and of counsel for both parties in civil cases."[27] In its wake, an ABA committee adopted Judicial Canon 35, which ultimately recommended banning photographic and broadcast coverage of courtroom proceedings to prevent the disruptive presence of photographic, motion picture, and video cameras. Ever since, it has been argued that banning cameras from courtrooms infringes on citizens' and the news media's free press and fair trial interests. Indeed, a presumption that criminal trials are open to the public and the press predates the U.S. Constitution. So what is wrong with allowing journalists to bring in extra tools to give the public instantaneous access to courtroom proceedings?

The Constitution's framers offer no answers. They did not contemplate image-capturing technologies. Image-capturing technologies, however, did not seem to bother judges during the first four decades of the 20th century. Many judges allowed reporters to bring microphones for radio transmission, and photography and movie cameras with their necessary lights and cables into courtrooms, and all that clutter of equipment and their attendant journalists did not always end up in the media circus witnessed at Hauptmann's trial. But the so-called trials of the century—such as Hauptmann and Simpson—have had a disproportionate impact on the public and judiciary's perceptions. After the ABA's Judicial Canon 35 recommended in 1937 that courts closed their doors to electronic broadcasting, the federal government and all states banned cameras and broadcasting equipment from courtroom proceedings.

Even now, no court has held that the news media have a First Amendment right to televise or film courtroom proceedings. The Court, however, ruled in *Chandler v. Florida*, 449 U.S. 560 (1981), that states may televise trials as long as a defendant's right to a fair trial is protected. Under Federal Rules of Criminal Procedure 53, only the Court and Congress have the authority to permit cameras at federal criminal trials. The Court exercised that authority when it declined to allow the oral arguments of *Bush v. Gore*, 531 U.S. 98 (2000), to be televised and in *Hollingsworth v. Perry*, 130 S. Ct. 705 (2010) when it stopped the live audio-video streaming of the federal trial over a lawsuit challenging the constitutionality of California's Proposition 8 same-sex marriage ban.

The shift away from the television, film, and photography ban started in Texas, one of two states— Colorado was the other—that never followed the ABA recommendation. In *Estes v. Texas*, 381 U.S. 532 (1965), the Court, 5–4, reversed defendant Billy Sol Estes's conviction for swindling because the televised broadcast of his trial deprived him of his due process rights under the Fourteenth Amendment. The defendant was not required to show evidence of the broadcast's harmful effects. The majority contended that the presence of cameras distracted the defendant and "while it is practically impossible to assess the effect of television on jury attentiveness, those of us who know juries realize the problem of jury 'distraction'…Human nature being what it is, not only will a juror's eyes be fixed on the camera, but also his mind will be preoccupied with the telecasting rather than with the testimony."[28] The majority, however, said that, though the news media have no First Amendment right to broadcast from a courtroom, the Constitution does not require that judges ban them.

By 1979, six states had adopted rules allowing electronic coverage of trials, and another ten conducted pilot programs to test the impact of cameras on the conduct of trial participants.[29] Florida was one such state and its Supreme Court concluded "that on balance there [was] more to be gained than lost by permitting electronic media coverage of judicial proceedings subject to standards for such coverage."[30] But two Florida men, convicted of conspiracy to commit burglary, grand larceny, and possession of burglary tools, sought to overturn their conviction, arguing that the presence of television and photography cameras in the courtroom deprived them of a right to a fair trial.

In *Chandler v. Florida*, the Court held that Florida and other states were permitted to experiment with cameras in courtrooms as long as a presiding judge exercised authority to guarantee fairness: "An absolute constitutional ban on broadcast coverage of trials cannot be justified simply because there is a danger that, in some cases, prejudicial broadcast accounts of pretrial and trial events may impair the ability of jurors to decide the issue of guilt or innocence uninfluenced by extraneous matter."[31]

Cameras and the Federal Court System

The Judicial Conference excludes all electronic media coverage of all federal civil and criminal proceedings. Since 1946, the Federal Rules of Criminal Procedure 53 has banned photography and broadcasting cameras in federal courtrooms. Each court of appeals, however, may permit electronic media coverage of its proceedings. In 2004, the now defunct Court TV network argued that the federal and New York State constitutions gave it the right to televise the federal criminal trial of Zacarias Moussaoui, who was later convicted of conspiracy to murder for his involvement in the September 11 attacks. A New York appeals court panel made fast work of Court TV's contention. It said Rule 53 was a content-neutral restriction that "is sufficiently tailored to further an important state interest, namely, the preservation of the value and integrity of live witness testimony in state tribunals."[32] New York constitutional law, the court added, has "never been interpreted…as granting any greater access rights than those provided under *Richmond Newspapers, Inc. v Virginia* and its progeny."[33]

Electronic & Digital Coverage of Courtrooms in the 21st Century

State courts do not have to comply with Rule 53. By 2011, according to the Radio Television Digital News Association (RTNDA), California, Colorado, Florida, Georgia, Idaho, Kentucky, Michigan, Montana, Nevada, New Mexico, New Hampshire, North Dakota, South Carolina, Tennessee, Vermont, Washington, West Virginia, Wisconsin, and Wyoming allowed extended camera coverage at the trial and appellate levels of criminal and civil trials. Alaska, Arizona, Connecticut, Hawaii, Iowa, Kansas, Massachusetts, Mississippi, Missouri, Nebraska, New Jersey, North Carolina, Ohio, Oregon, Rhode Island, Texas, and Virginia allowed cameras at certain phases of civil and criminal proceedings. Alabama, Arkansas, Delaware, Illinois, Indiana, Louisiana, Maine, Maryland, Minnesota, New York, Oklahoma, Pennsylvania, South Dakota, and Utah allow only appellate court coverage. Thus, all the states allow cameras into some phase of the trial or appeals process. Many states also webcast their proceedings. The District of Columbia allows only photography under some circumstances in criminal and juvenile court proceedings.[34]

Why do so many judges still oppose televised trial proceedings? Typically, like the majority in *Estes*, opponents say lawyers, judges, witnesses, and jurors tend to play to the cameras, creating a circus-like atmosphere. As a result, judges have greater difficulty controlling the decorum in such an atmosphere, making it more likely that jurors are exposed to impermissible evidence. Judges subject to reelection are particularly apt to play to the cameras, the argument goes. Opponents also argue that jurors are more likely to be intimidated by public opinion when they are aware that millions of viewers see their image. Opponents also contend that commercial televised trials that focus on the sensational and sound bites tend to distort what courts do, thereby reducing the public's understanding of judges, the judicial system, and the complexity of legal controversies.

Typically, proponents of cameras in courtrooms proceedings argue that broadcasting trials is merely an extension of the principles of openness that predated the Constitution. Proponents also cite empirical studies on the effect of televised coverage on judges and attorneys that show minimal adverse consequences.

U.S. Court of Appeals Judge for the Ninth Circuit Kozinski is an advocate for cameras in courtrooms. He says the decisions by the overwhelming majority of states to allow televised broadcast of trials or hearings "tell us more than any survey data ever could. And, if that's not enough for you, empirical evidence from the states is also positive. After reviewing multiple studies of state judiciaries, the Federal Judicial Center concluded that, 'for each of several potential negative effects of electronic media on jurors and witnesses, the majority of respondents indicated the effect does not occur or occurs only to a slight extent.'"[35]

Digital Technologies

Even as the Judicial Conference's current cameras-in-the-courtroom project unfolded in 2011, media technological innovations—the World Wide Web, webcasting, cell phones, smartphones, BlackBerrys, iPhones, Palm Pilots, laptop computers, iPads, earpiece devices such as Bluetooth, and digital or other types of video cameras and audio recorders—continued to create new threats to fair trial interests.

In *In re Sony BMG Music Entertainment*, 564 F. 3d 1 (1st Cir. 2009), a case of first impression, the First Circuit overturned a federal district court's order permitting webcasting of non-evidentiary motions in a civil case: "While the new technology characteristic of the Information Age may call for the replotting of some boundaries, the venerable right of members of the public to attend federal court proceedings is far removed from an imagined entitlement to view court proceedings remotely on a computer screen."[36] In *United States v. Shelnutt*, No. 09-cv-14 (M.D. GA. Nov. 2, 2009), a federal judge prohibited a journalist from tweeting from his courtroom because "contemporaneous transmission of electronic messages from the courtroom describing the trial proceedings, and the dissemination of those messages in a manner such that they are widely and instantaneously accessible to the general public, falls within the definition of 'broadcasting' as used in Rule 53."

In response to reports of a rash of incidents of jurors' misusing social media, cell phones, and search engines that have resulted in mistrials, exclusion of jurors, and imposition of fines, the Judicial Conference Committee on Court Administration and Case Management issued model jury instructions in 2010 that it recommends federal district judges use. The instructions include the following admonishment to jurors: "You may not communicate with anyone about the case on your cell phone, through e-mail, Blackberry, iPhone, text messaging, or on Twitter, through any blog or website, through any internet chat room, or by way of any other social networking websites, including Facebook, MySpace, LinkedIn, and YouTube."[37]

Because state courts are not subject to Rule 53, their rulings on the use of cell phones, laptops, and iPads by journalists, the public, and jurors vary. Connecticut law, for example, prohibits broadcasting of trials. But did that statute include tweeting? *In State v. Komisarjevsky*, 2011 WL 1032111 (Conn. Super. Ct. Feb. 22, 2011), a defendant facing a trial for sexual assault asked the court to ban tweeting during trial, arguing that tweeting was tantamount to broadcasting under the statute. The court denied his bid, finding that tweeting did not constitute broadcasting under the statute because the statute's primary purpose is to spare a victim of sexual assault from having her voice and image conveyed to the public. The court also said that although it had discretionary authority to restrict disruptive electronic devices, tweeting was not disruptive.

New York has a revised recommended jury instruction that some say may serve as a model for other states.[38] It says in part, "In this age of instant electronic communication and research, I want to emphasize that in addition to not conversing face to face with anyone about the case, you must not communicate with anyone about the case by any other means, including by telephone, text messages, email, internet chat or chat rooms, blogs, or social websites, such as Facebook, MySpace or Twitter."[39]

SUMMARY: In *Chandler v. Florida*, 449 U.S. 560 (1981), the U.S. Supreme Court held that the Constitution did not prohibit states from experimenting with cameras in courtrooms as long as a presiding judge exercises authority to guarantee fairness. Now, all states allow cameras into some phase of the trial or appeals process. On the federal level, where Federal Rules of Criminal Procedure 53 bans them, the Judicial Conference has permitted limited experiments with cameras in courtrooms such as the one begun in July 2011. No court, however, has held that the news media have a First Amendment right to televise or film courtroom proceedings. Meanwhile, federal and state courts face a new electronic communications threat to fair-trial interests—digital devices such as cell phones, iPads, BlackBerrys, and laptops.

ONLINE RESOURCES

1. "Access to Courts," Reporters Committee for Freedom of the Press, http://www.rcfp.org/first-amendment-handbook/7-access-courts
2. "Cameras in the Court: A State-By-State Guide," Radio Television Digital News Association, http://www.rtnda.org/pages/media_items/cameras-in-the-court-a-state-by-state-guide55.php
3. "Fair Trials and a Free Press," C-SPAN Video Library, http://www.c-spanvideo.org/program/298109–5
4. "Gag Orders," Reporters Committee for Freesom of the Press, http://www.rcfp.org/first-amendment-handbook/6-gag-orders
5. *The Reporter's Key: Rights of Fair Trial and Free Press. ABA National Conference of Lawyers and Representatives of the Media* http://www.abanow.org/2006/01/the-reporters-key-rights-of-fair-trial-and-free-press-third-edition/

QUESTIONS

1. Three Bronx, New York, police officers are scheduled to go on trial three days from now for the fatal beating of an African immigrant. You are the editorial chief of Channel 22 NYNews and today an amateur videographer walks into your office. The videographer shows you a grainy tape of three Bronx police officers clubbing someone. The tape runs for about five minutes and, after viewing it, you're certain it's a tape of the immigrant being beaten by the three officers. He is on the ground and appears to be unable to fight back, but the beating continues until his body goes limp. You make a decision to air the tape for the next day's news cycle. Within 24 hours, the tape is viewed by 80% of the adult population in the Bronx. The next day, you are in court standing before the judge who will preside over the police officers' trial. Their attorney is asking the judge to issue an injunction ordering you to stop broadcasting the tape.

    (a) Identify the argument the attorney would make to persuade the judge to issue the gag order.

    (b) Identify your counter argument.

    (c) Citing precedent, who is likely to win the argument and why?

2. What if Osama bin Laden had been captured alive and brought here to stand trial? Should the trial have been opened to broadcast cameras, cell phones, and devices that tweet and text? Identify the arguments for allowing such access. Identify the arguments for denying such access.

3. What's the worst that could happen? Is there any legal disincentive for a news outlet not to publish a defendant's alleged confession before a trial is about to start? The *Nebraska Press Association v. Stuart* three-part test makes it difficult for a judge to impose an injunction against the news media. With the news media's ability to publish instantaneously via the Internet, a gag order is not likely to provide a timely remedy, anyway. What about the judge's contempt of court powers? Read the following cases and decide: *U.S. v. Cable News Network, Inc.*, 865 F. Supp. 1549 (D. Fla. 1994); *U.S. v. McVeigh*, 955 F. Supp. 1281, 1282 (D. Colo. 1997). Lastly, is it ethical for journalists to rush to print "confessions," or to defy gag orders not to print such materials, immediately before a trial is scheduled to begin? The Society of Professional Journalists Code of Ethics "Minimize Harm" principle says, "Journalists should…Balance a criminal suspect's fair trial rights with the public's right to be informed."

ENDNOTES

1. Alex Kozinski and Robert Johnson. "Of Cameras and Courtrooms," 20 *Fordham Intellectual Property, Media & Entertainment Law Journal* 1107 (2010).

2. "On Cameras in Supreme Court, Souter Says, 'Over My Dead Body,'" *New York Times* (March 30, 1996), http://www.nytimes.com/1996/03/30/us/on-cameras-in-supreme-court-souter-says-over-my-dead-body.html

3. U.S. Const. amend. XI, §. "In all criminal prosecutions, the accused shall enjoy the right to a speedy and public trial, by an impartial jury of the State and district wherein the crime shall have been committed, which district shall have been previously ascertained by law, and to be informed of the nature and cause of the accusation…"

4. U.S. Const. amend. XIV, §. "No State shall make or enforce any law which shall abridge the privileges or immunities of citizens of the United States; nor shall any State deprive any person of life, liberty, or property, without due process of law . . ."

5. U.S. Const. amend. VII. "In Suits at common law, where the value in controversy shall exceed twenty dollars, the right of trial by jury shall be preserved, and no fact tried by a jury, shall be otherwise re-examined in any Court of the United States, than according to the rules of the common law."

6. *Irwin v. Dowd*, 366 U.S. 717, 727 (1961).

7. Ibid. 728 (1961).

8. *Rideau v. Louisiana*, 373 U.S. 723, 726 (1963).

9. *Sheppard v. Maxwell*, 384 U.S. 333, 350 (1966).

10. Ibid.

11. *Irwin v. Dowd* at 727.

12. See Jeffrey T. Frederick. *Mastering Voir Dire and Jury Selection: Gain an Edge in Questioning and Selecting Your Jury*. Chicago: American Bar Association (2005), 244–245.

13. *Sheppard v. Maxwell* at 363.

14. See also Philip Taylor. "Colliding with Contempt," *News Media & the Law* (Summer 2002), http://www.rcfp.org/browse-media-law-resources/news-media-law/news-media-and-law-summer-2002/colliding-contempt

15. The American Bar Association's Model Rules of Professional Conduct Rule 3.6 requires that, "A lawyer who is participating or has participated in the investigation or litigation of a matter shall not make an extrajudicial statement that the lawyer knows or reasonably should know will be disseminated by means of public communication and will have a substantial likelihood of materially prejudicing an adjudicative proceeding in the matter."

16. *Radio & Television News Association v. U.S. Dist. Ct.*, 781 F. 2d 1443, 1447 (9th Cir. 1986).

17. *Cowley v. Pulsifer*, 137 Mass. 392, 394 (1884).

18. *In re Oliver*, 333 U.S. 257, 270 (1948).

19. *Richmond Newspapers, Inc. v. Virginia*, 44 U.S. 555, 578 (1980).

20. *Press Enterprise v. Superior Court ("Press Enterprise I")*, 464 U.S. 501, 510 (1984).

21. "Hearings in juvenile court originally were intended to be informal, nonadversarial, and private in the belief that this was more consistent with the rehabilitative goals of the juvenile court than were the traditional adversarial proceedings employed in the adult criminal court." *San Bernardino County Department of Social Services v. Superior Court*, 232 Cal. App. 3d 188, 198 (1991) (citing *In re Gault*, 387 U.S. 1, 25–27 (1967)).

22. Patrick Griffin, Patricia Torbet, and Linda Szymanski. *Trying Juveniles as Adults in Criminal Court: An Analysis of State Transfer Provisions*. U.S. Department of Justice, Office of Justice Programs, Office of Juvenile Justice and Delinquency Prevention, 1998.

23. See *Virginia Department of State Police v. Washington Post*, 386 F. 3d 567 (4th Cir. 2004).

24. *Press Enterprise v. Superior Court ("Press Enterprise I")*, 464 U.S. at 510.

25. *U.S. v. Cleveland*, 128 F. 3d 267, 269 (5th Cir. 1997).

26. See Jacob Marvelley. "Note: Lights, camera, mistrial: Conflicting federal court local rules and conflicting theories on the aggregate effect of cameras on courtroom proceedings," 16 *Suffolk Journal of Trial & Appellate Advocacy* 30, 35 (2011), http://www.law.suffolk.edu/highlights/stuorgs/moot/upload/2-Note-Marvelley-Jake.pdf

27. "The Press: After Flemington," *Time Magazine* (October 04, 1937), http://www.time.com/time/magazine/article/0,9171,931651,00.html

28. *Estes v. Texas*, 381 U.S. 532, 546 (1965).

29. *Chandler v. Florida*, 449 U.S. 560, 565 (1981).

30. Ibid.

31. Ibid. 575.

32. *Courtroom Television Network LLC v. State*, 8 AD 3d 164, 166 (NY: Appellate Div., 1st Dept. 2004).

33. Ibid.

34. "Cameras in the Court: A State-by-State Guide," Radio Television Digital News Association (2012),

http://www.rtnda.org/pages/media_items/cameras-in-the-court-a-state-by-state-guide55.php

35. Alex Kozinski and Robert Johnson. "Of Cameras and Courtrooms," 20 *Fordham Intellectual Property, Media & Entertainment Law Journal* 1115 (2010).

36. *In re Sony BMG Music Entertainment*, 564 F. 3d 1, 9 (1st Cir. 2009).

37. Judge Julie A. Robinson, Chair of the Judicial Committee on Court Administration and Case Management, to Judges, United States District Courts, January 28, 2010, "Juror Use of Electronic Communication Technologies," Attachment, http://federalevidence.com/downloads/blog/2010/Memorandum.On.Juror.Use.Of. Electronic.Communication.Technologies.pdf

38. Harry A. Valetk. "Facebooking in Court: Coping with Socially Networked Jurors," (October 11, 2010), http://www.law.com/jsp/article.jsp?id=1202473157232

39. "Jury Admonitions in Preliminary Instructions," New York State Unified Court System (May 5, 2009), 2, http://www.nycourts.gov/cji/1-General/CJI2d.Jury_Admonitions.pdf

CHAPTER ELEVEN

Broadcast & Cable Television Regulation

CONTROVERSY: "Indecent Exposure: *FCC v. Fox* and the End of an Era." "Why Regulate Broadcasting?" "Red Lion and Pacifica: Are They Relics?"[1] As the titles of these three law review articles indicate, many commentators had anticipated big things from *Federal Communication Commission (FCC) v. Fox Television Stations, Inc.*, perhaps the end of the decades-old First Amendment broadcast regulatory model.[2] Under the model, the Court allows Congress and the FCC to regulate over-the-airways broadcasting based on standards that are fundamentally different than print, cable, the Internet, and any other medium. That approach is unconstitutional, critics say, because it relegates broadcasters to the lowest level of free expression protection among media speakers. It's indefensible, they argue, because the Court's justifications for such unequal treatment—the spectrum scarcity, pervasiveness, and unique accessibility to children doctrines—are unsupportable in our era of spectrum abundance, media diversity, and filtering technologies that allow parents to block out unwanted programming. Moreover, it makes little sense to apply a unique First Amendment standard to broadcast programming when TV content is syndicated on Cable TV and streamed on the Internet, they say. The Court, however, saw things differently. *FCC v. Fox Television Stations*, 132 S.Ct. 2307 (2012), was only about the legitimacy of the FCC's new fleeting expletive indecency policy, which did not require consideration of the First Amendment spectrum scarcity, pervasiveness, or accessibility doctrines, the Court said.[3] The unanimous[4] Court, however, ruled that sanctions imposed on Fox and ABC were invalid because the FCC had not given them fair notice of what was prohibited under the revised indecency policy.

Chapter's Scope

Despite the continued drumbeat to abolish it, the First Amendment broadcast model and the related FCC administered regulatory regime remain intact, certainly at least for the near future. This chapter, then, identifies why and how the free expression rights of radio and television outlets are treated uniquely under the First Amendment. It discusses the key and landmark judicial rulings upholding federal authority to regulate the broadcast spectrum—a portion of the electromagnetic spectrum used for telecommunication—and limits broadcasters' free expression rights starting with *Great Lakes Broadcasting v. FRC*, 37 F.2d 993 (1930). The Court applies the less rigorous intermediate-level scrutiny to test the constitutionality of content-based restrictions on broadcast, and allows the FCC to: require broadcasters to obtain licenses to operate; to impose content requirements such as the Fairness Doctrine , time limits on advertising during children's programming, and, of course, indecency standards; and to limit the number and type of media outlets a broadcaster may own. This chapter discusses those limitations and requirements.

The chapter also covers cable TV laws and regulations by providing a brief examination of how the industry went from an unregulated mass medium with undefined First Amendment rights to one regulated by the FCC within a 50-year span. Under the cable TV regulatory model, government restrictions on programming must meet the highest level of judicial scrutiny. That is the same standard imposed upon newspapers, for example. At the same time, applying intermediate-level scrutiny, the Court has ruled that cable TV operators are subject to must-carry obligations, requiring them to transmit public access channels for use by local individuals or groups. In contrast, the Court has ruled that government cannot impose such requirements on newspapers.[5]

"As Public Convenience, Interest, or Necessity Requires"

Congress and the FCC's authority to treat broadcasters uniquely under the First Amendment, upheld by the Court for more than 70 years, derives from the public interest standard, a key clause of the Communications Act of 1934, 47 U.S.C.A. 3003(a)(g): "the Commission from time to time, as public convenience, interest, or necessity requires, shall . . ." The Communications Act established the FCC as a successor to the Federal Radio Commission (FRC), giving it authority to police the airways and license broadcasters.

The public interest standard evolved from the need, as Congress and the radio industry perceived it in the 1920s, for the federal government to play the role of sheriff, bringing law and order to the free-for-all of the unregulated AM radio spectrum. In contrast to business's traditional position, corporate radio interests asked for government intervention.[6] The standard is inextricably tied to the spectrum scarcity doctrine—the belief that because all who wish to cannot use the airways at the same time, government must act as a public trustee by placing the broadcast spectrum in the public domain, and allocating its limited resources so that all may benefit. The standard justifies, for example, the FCC's authority to grant and revoke licenses, to impose fines on broadcasters for indecent content, to set limits on the kind and number of media properties licensees may own, or affiliate with, and apparently, even to allow Congress to tell broadcasters to lower the volume of the commercials they air.[7]

Regulating in the Public Interest

Then-U.S. Commerce Secretary Herbert Hoover was the first to apply a "public interest" concept to radio when he told the Fourth National Radio Conference in 1926 that "the ether is a public medium, and its use must be for a public benefit."[8] The following year, Congress enacted the Radio Act of 1927 [47 U.S.C. Chapter 4][9] creating the FRC to license use of the airways, as the Radio Act of 1912 failed to create any real federal regulatory authority. The 1927 statute empowered the FRC to, "from time to time, as public convenience, interest, or necessity requires," regulate radio. The FRC's authority derived from the Interstate Commerce Clause. The Congressional Record, however, sheds little light on precisely which public interest was meant in the context of radio regulation.

In 1928, however, the FRC issued its first interpretation of the standard in *Great Lakes Broadcasting Co.*, 3 FRC Ann. Rep. 32 (1929). In short, the FRC explained that, since the number of individuals seeking to broadcast far exceeded the number of channels, the FRC intended to favor licensees who would place the listening public above the interest, convenience, or necessity of themselves or their advertisers because the "public interest requires ample play for the free and fair competition of opposing views, and the Commission believes that the principle applies...to all discussion of issues of importance to the public."[10]

In 1930, the U.S. Court of Appeals for the District of Columbia affirmed the FRC's authority under the public interest standard to allocate and deny use of the radio spectrum in *Great Lakes Broadcasting v. FRC*, 37 F.2d 993 (1930). The D.C. Circuit continued to uphold the FRC's authority to regulate radio in the public interest, for convenience, and for necessity under the Radio Act of 1927 in at least five other cases from 1929–31: *Technical Radio Laboratory v. FRC*, 36 F.2d 111 (D.C. Cir. 1929); *City of New York v. FRC*, 36 F.2d 115 (D.C. Cir. 1929); *Chicago Federation of Labor v. FRC*, 41 F.2d 422 (D.C. Cir. 1930); *KFKB Broadcasting Association v. FRC*, 47 F.2d 670 (D.C. Cir. 1931); and *Reading Broadcasting v. FRC*, 48 F.2d 458 (D.C. Cir. 1931).

Free Speech vs. the Public Interest

None of the complaining parties in the above series of cases challenged the FRC's rulings on free speech grounds. Perhaps the issue was not raised because the FRC rulings in those cases did not directly affect licensees' programming choices. In the 1930s and 1940s, however, licensees did challenge the FRC's—and after 1934, its successor, the FCC's—authority on statutory and First Amendment free speech grounds in *KFKB v. FRC*, 47 F.2d 670 (1931), *Trinity Methodist Church, South v. FRC*, 62 F.2d 850 (1932); *FCC v. Pottsville Broadcasting*, 309 U.S. 134 (1940); *FCC v. Saunders Bros. Radio Station*, 309 U.S. 470 (1940); *NBC v. U.S.*, 319 U.S. 190 (1943); and *WOKO, Inc. v. FCC*, 153 F.2d 623 (1946). Of those rulings, the *NBC v. U.S.*, 319 U.S. 190 (1943); is seminal in establishing the federal government's authority to regulate broadcasters' contractual arrangements affecting programming consistent with First Amendment rights of licensees and networks.

The National Broadcasting Company (NBC), formed in 1926, was the first radio network, meaning it created content and delivered it to affiliated radio stations. At the time of the ruling, the two networks—Columbia Broadcasting System (CBS) was established in 1928—provided the much-needed content at a high price. They restricted affiliate stations from associations with other local stations, for example. In an effort to prevent such restrictive agreements, the FCC promulgated its Chain Broadcasting Regulation in 1941, limiting networks control and ownership of affiliates in the public interest. (The FCC licenses stations, not networks.) In a 5–2 ruling, the Court upheld the

FCC's authority to issue the Chain Broadcasting Regulations and its intervention into programming matters. It justified the FCC's authority to choose between two financially and technically qualified license applicants based on what would become the scarcity rationale—"There is a fixed natural limitation upon the number of stations that can operate without interfering with one another" [11]—and the need to consider more than an applicant's financial and technical qualifications to meet its public interest, convenience, or necessity mandate.[12] When a broadcaster enters into a contract with a network that limits the broadcaster's ability to make the best use of the station, the broadcaster is not serving the public interest, the Court said. It also affirmed the FCC's exercise of its authority to affect networks, entities the agency has no explicit statutory authority to regulate, as a way to prevent private entities from monopolizing broadcasting. Lastly, the Court held that license denial or revocation based on public interests grounds does not deprive broadcasters of their First Amendment free speech rights: "Freedom of utterance is abridged to many who wish to use the limited facilities of radio. Unlike other modes of expression, radio inherently is not available to all. That is its unique characteristic, and that is why, unlike other modes of expression, it is subject to governmental regulation. Because it cannot be used by all, some who wish to use it must be denied."[13]

> SUMMARY: The public interest standard evolved from the need—as Congress and the radio industry perceived it in the 1920s—for the federal government to play the role of sheriff, bringing law and order to the free-for-all of the unregulated AM radio spectrum. In 1934, Congress created the Federal Communications Commission to regulate the electromagnetic spectrum "as the public convenience, interest, or necessity requires." In *NBC v. U.S.*, 319 U.S. 190 (1943), the Court said the FCC's licensing authority did not deprive broadcasters of their First Amendment rights because government must impose technical and content demands on broadcasters seeking to use the limited airwaves in order to best serve the public's interest.

The Public Interest, Content Regulation, & the First Amendment

Empowered by the Court's affirmation of its mandate to regulate broadcast licensees in the public interest, the FCC has promulgated several rules and policies affecting licensees' programming, ownership and management, and technological and operational obligations. It has also modified or repealed public interest standard-supported rules, as it is empowered under Section 202(h) of the Communications Act, to "repeal or modify any regulation it determines to be no longer in the public interest." This section focuses on the major FCC rules, policies, and court rulings affecting programming: the fairness doctrine, editorial advertisements, Equal Opportunities for Political Candidates rules, Broadcast News Distortion and Hoaxes, Sponsorship Identification rules, Equal Opportunities rule, The Children's Television Act (1990), rules regulating political speech on non-commercial public broadcasting stations, and the FCC's rules banning indecent speech.

The Fairness Doctrine

In May 2010, news website *Politico.com* obtained FBI documents about death threats issued against elected officials in 2009. In one such threat, a Texas man left the following message on U.S. Senator

Debbie Stabenow's (D-MI) voicemail: "We're gonna (expletive) get you…we're gonna get you with a lot of (expletive) bolt action. Like we did RFK, like we did MLK. We know who you are. We'll get you." Later, the man told the FBI that he left the message because he was "really, really drunk" and was "venting" after hearing a discussion of the "Fairness Doctrine" and was concerned that the government would reinstate the doctrine and abolish the radio shows of Sean Hannity and Rush Limbaugh.

A highly irrational response, of course, but some people—primarily those on the right of the political spectrum—get awfully riled up over the possibility that the FCC might breathe new life into the Fairness Doctrine. They say that it's more than 20-year absence allowed right-wing talk radio to flourish because, without it, the FCC had no authority to force such stations to give airtime to those they attacked. Revive it, and right-wing talk radio will grow silent, they say.[14]

The doctrine, really a policy, stems from the FCC's rulings in *In the Matter of Mayflower Broadcasting Corp. and the Yankee Network, Inc.*, 8 F.C.C. 333 (1940), and findings in the FCC's *Report on Editorializing by Broadcast Licensees*, 13 F.C.C. 1246 (1949). According to Applicability of the Fairness Doctrine in the Handling of Controversial Issues of Public Importance, 29 Fed. Reg.10426 (1964), the Fairness Doctrine consists of two basic requirements: that licensees devote a reasonable portion of their broadcast time to the discussion and consideration of controversial issues of public importance and that they endeavor to make their facilities available for the expression of contrasting viewpoints. As the U.S. Supreme Court would later explain in *Columbia Broadcasting System, Inc. v. Democratic National Committee*, 412 U.S. 94, 112–113 (1973), "broadcasters are responsible for providing the listening and viewing public with access to a balanced presentation of information on issues of public importance" because it is "the right of the public to be informed, rather than any right on the part of the Government, any broadcast licensee or any individual member of the public to broadcast his own particular views on any matter."

In 1967, the FCC beefed up its fairness policy by adopting the personal attack and political editorial rules. Under the personal attack rule [47 C.F.R. § 73.123], broadcasters had to give notice and free response time to individuals or groups whose honesty, character, or integrity were impugned "during the presentation of views on a controversial issue of public importance," whether the accusation was truthful or not. The rule affected mostly radio and television talk shows. The rule, however, exempted accusations targeting public figures, foreign groups, or attacks made by political candidates or their authorized spokesperson during a political campaign. The rule also exempted commentary, interviews, interpretation, and analysis spoken in a newscast or news reporting.

The political editorial rule [47 C.F.R. § 73.123(c)] required broadcast stations that endorsed a political candidate in an editorial to notify and give free rebuttal time to that candidate's political rival. As a result, many broadcasters complained that they were discouraged from airing editorials concerning political races. Many also argued that the doctrine impermissibly infringed on their First Amendment right of editorial autonomy, a right enjoyed by the print and film media, and later the Internet.

Those arguments failed before the U.S. Supreme Court, as it ruled in its landmark opinion *Red Lion Broadcasting v. FCC*, 395 U.S. 367, 391 (1969), that a license to broadcast does not give a broadcaster exclusive control of the airwaves: "As we have said, the First Amendment confers no right on licensees to prevent others from broadcasting on 'their' frequencies and no right to an unconditional monopoly of a scarce resource which the Government has denied others the right to use." In other words, the scarcity doctrine was still a legitimate rationale for government regulation of over-the-air broadcasting.

In *Red Lion*, Reverend Billy James Hargis, a fundamentalist Christian evangelist and Anti-Communist whose *Christian Crusade* ministry aired on radio and television, delivered a 15-minute broadcast that was highly critical of author Fred J. Cook on WGCB, which was licensed by Red Lion Broadcasting Company. In 1964, Hargis, a staunch supporter of Republican presidential candidate U.S. Senator Barry Goldwater, attacked Cook for his book, *Goldwater: Extremist on the Right*. Hargis said Cook had been fired by a newspaper for making false charges, that he had attacked FBI Director J. Edgar Hoover and the CIA, and that the book was written to smear and destroy the senator, among other accusations.

Cook said Hargis had personally attacked him, and demanded free reply time. WGCB refused. Cook contacted Red Lion Broadcasting and the FCC. The FCC concluded the broadcast was a personal attack in violation of the personal attack rules and that Red Lion and the station must provide reply time. These actions led to the question of whether the FCC had the authority to create and to enforce the Fairness Doctrine.

In upholding Congress's authority to confer power to the FCC to enforce the doctrine and its component personal attack and political editorializing rules, the Court said, "In light of the fact that the 'public interest' in broadcasting clearly encompasses the presentation of vigorous debate of controversial issues of importance and concern to the public; the fact that the FCC has rested upon that language from its very inception a doctrine that these issues must be discussed, and fairly...the fairness doctrine and its component personal attack and political editorializing regulations are a legitimate exercise of congressionally delegated authority."[15] But the Court also suggested that a future Court might reconsider the matter when presented with evidence that the Fairness Doctrine and related rules stifle, rather than encourage, discussion and coverage of controversial issues.[16]

Not surprisingly, the attacks against government-imposed fairness continued. The doctrine became a key target of broadcast journalists and business deregulation proponents, mostly Republicans. The election of economic supply-sider President Ronald Reagan ushered in an era of business deregulation in the 1980s that engulfed the FCC. Reagan appointee, FCC Chairman Mark Fowler, who famously declared in 1981 that "the television is just another appliance—it's a toaster with pictures," led the deregulation revolution of the broadcast and telecommunication industries. Under Fowler's leadership, the FCC issued its *Report Concerning General Fairness Doctrine Obligations of Broadcast Licensees*, 102 FCC 2d 143, 146 (1985), declaring that the doctrine was "chilling speech" because broadcasters avoided discussions of certain controversial issues to avoid compliance, it interfered with journalistic liberty, and the emerging media technologies provided citizens with diverse views, all evidence that the doctrine was counterproductive and unnecessary.

Though Fowler was no longer FCC chairman in 1987, the FCC voted to stop enforcing the doctrine, relying on the findings of its 1985 Fairness Report. The U.S. Court of Appeals for the D.C. Circuit affirmed the FCC's argument that the Fairness Doctrine did not serve the public interest in *Syracuse Peace Council v. FCC*, 867 F.2d 654 (D.C. Cir. 1989). The same appeals court ordered the FCC to repeal the related personal attack and political editorializing rules in *Radio-Television News Directors Association v. FCC*, 229 F. 3d 269 (2000), which the FCC did.

Today, the Fairness Doctrine and the related personal attack and political editorializing rules dwell in a legal limbo. A Republican-dominated FCC repealed the doctrine. Congressional legislators have proposed bills to reinstate it, and to prevent its reinstatement. Courts have questioned its validity. But no court has ever declared the doctrine and related rules unconstitutional, and that is partly why some Republicans and conservatives such as Hannity and Limbaugh fear that the Democrats will move to revive the doctrine during the Obama administration. President Obama, however, said he would not pursue such a course.

Personal Attack and Political Editorial Rules

Starting in 1967, the FCC enforced the personal attack and political editorializing rules as corollaries to the Fairness Doctrine. Once the FCC stopped enforcing the doctrine, it was no surprise that it would abolish the related rules, particularly since broadcast journalists had targeted them for several years. The personal attack rule required, with several exceptions, that broadcasters gave individuals or groups an offer of a reasonable opportunity to respond to attacks on honesty, character, and integrity made during a broadcast. The political editorial rule did the same for political candidates. It required that broadcasters give candidates a reasonable opportunity to respond to editorials opposing them or endorsing their rivals. In *Radio-Television News Directors Association v. FCC*, 229 F. 3d 269 (D.C. Cir. 2000), the court ordered the FCC to justify the rules in light of its decision to repeal the Fairness Doctrine. The FCC ordered their repeal in October 2000.

Equal Opportunities for Political Candidates

Section 315 of the Communications Act [47 U.S.C. § 315] is distinct from the Fairness Doctrine-related personal attack and political editorializing rules, also known as equal time rules . The FCC still enforces its equal time rules. Under Section 315, when a broadcast station permits a legally qualified candidate for any public office to use its station, the broadcaster must provide all other legally qualified candidates with an equal opportunity to use its facilities. Generally, its purpose is to prohibit broadcasters from siding with or taking action against any legally bona fide candidate for public office. But the rules exempt a legally qualified candidate's appearance on a bona fide newscast, bona fide news interview, bona fide news documentary, or on-the-spot coverage of bona fide news events. Congress carved out the exemptions to protect broadcasters' ability to provide the public with coverage of political candidates in traditional newsworthy context.[17]

Noncommercial Broadcasting & Political Speech

The Public Broadcasting Act of 1967 created the Corporation of Public Broadcasting (CPB) and authorized it to fund local noncommercial broadcast licensees. Under the Public Broadcasting Act Section 496 [47 U.S.C. 396], the corporation is mandated to obtain content "with the strict adherence to objectivity and balance in all programs or series of programs of a controversial nature" and "addresses the needs of unserved and underserved audiences." Under Section 398 of the Communications Act, Congress intended that the FCC have no jurisdiction over the CPB, the D.C. Circuit affirmed in *Accuracy in Media, Inc. v. FCC*, 521 F.2d 288 (1975). The FCC, however, does exercise some authority over the CPB by virtue of its licensing process. The FCC licenses FM radio and TV stations as commercial or noncommercial educational, and AM radio stations are licensed as commercial operations.

Additionally, Section 399 of the Public Broadcasting Act of 1967 once provided that "no noncommercial educational broadcast station may engage in editorializing or may support or oppose any candidate for political office." But in *FCC v. League of Women Voters*, 468 U.S. 363 (1982), the U.S. Supreme Court, 5–4, struck down the ban on editorializing by PBS stations as unconstitutional. In its ruling, the Court applied intermediate-level scrutiny, asking whether the government showed that Section 399 was necessary to achieve a substantial or important governmental interest, and that the section was narrowly tailored to that interest. The government argued that Section 399 was necessary to protect public television from being coerced by politicians because it relied on Congressional approval for funding, and to prevent the public from assuming that editorials sponsored by private concerns represented official government views. The Court, however, said the ban went far beyond traditional fairness mandates because "in sharp contrast to the restrictions upheld in *Red Lion* or in *CBS, Inc. v. FCC*, which left room for editorial discretion and simply required broadcast editors to grant others access to the microphone, § 399 directly prohibits the broadcaster from speaking out on public issues even in a balanced and fair manner."[18]

Access

Neither the Fairness Doctrine nor the First Amendment requires broadcast licensees to sell time to individuals or groups wishing to run editorial advertisements addressing public issues, the Court ruled in *CBS v. Democratic National Committee (DNC)*, 412 U.S. 94 (1973). *CBS v. DNC* is the Court's most vigorous defense of broadcaster licensees' editorial autonomy. The ruling also is notable for the Court's rejection of an expansive theory of the public's right of access to the press, championed by legal scholar Jerome Barron in his seminal work, "Access to the Press—A New First Amendment Right," published in 1967.[19] Barron argued that one of the core purposes of the First Amendment is to promote democratic discourse, and, to that end, news media were obligated to guarantee that the public could voice their views via the corporate-owned media. In effect, the personal attack, political editorial, equal time rules, and Fairness Doctrine are narrow applications of Barron's access theory. But in *CBS v. DNC*, 412 U.S. 94 (1973), the Court declined to recognize a public right of access to include paid political editorials.[20] Similarly, no form of mandatory access to print outlets can be tolerated under the First Amendment, the Court ruled in *Miami Herald Publishing Co. v. Tornillo*, 418 U.S. 241 (1974).

> SUMMARY: There is no requirement that commercial broadcasters present fair and balanced reporting now that the FCC no longer enforces the Fairness Doctrine or the personal attack and political editorial rules. The Equal Opportunities for Political Candidates, or Equal Time, rule is still in effect, though. It's not the same for noncommercial public television. Under the Public Broadcasting Act Section 496, the public broadcasting corporation is mandated to obtain content "with the strict adherence to objectivity and balance in all programs or series of programs of a controversial nature" and "addresses the needs of unserved and underserved audiences." But the government may not prevent broadcasting stations from taking editorial positions on public issues.

Broadcast News Distortion

The FCC's *Report on Editorializing by Broadcast Licensees* also spawned the Commission's little-known— and seldom-invoked—Broadcast News Distortion rule and prohibition on news hoaxes, or knowingly broadcasting false information.[21] Though the FCC has never formally adopted these provisions, the U.S. Court of Appeals for the D.C. Circuit has twice upheld the FCC's authority to enforce them.

In *Galloway v. FCC*, 778 F.2d 16 (D.C. Cir. 1985), the U.S. Court of Appeals for the D.C. Circuit ruled against Carl Galloway, who claimed that a CBS News broadcast had violated the personal attack rule and the news distortion policy. The appeals court, however, upheld the FCC's policy against rigging, staging, or distorting the news: "The key elements of this standard are, first, that the distortion or staging be deliberately intended to slant or mislead…Second, the distortion must involve a significant event and not merely a minor or incidental aspect of the news report."[22]

In *Serafyn v. FCC*, 149 F.3d 1213 (1998), the D.C. Circuit ruled against a petitioner who sought the revocation of CBS's license because it had aired a news program in which it intentionally distorted the situation in Ukraine by claiming that most Ukrainians are anti-Semitic, though the court still affirmed the legitimacy of the news distortion rule: "As we noted in *Galloway*, the Commission's policy makes its investigation of an allegation of news distortion extremely limited [in] scope. But within the constraints of the Constitution, Congress and the Commission may set the scope of broadcast regulation; it is not the role of this court to question the wisdom of their policy choices."[23]

Payola and Plugola

Sponsorship Identification rules—found in Sections 317 and 507 of the Communications Act of 1934, and Sections 73.1212 and 76.1615 of the FCC's rules—target payola, the undisclosed acceptance of money, gifts, or service in exchange for airplay. The rules also cover the airing of video news releases (VNR), a practice that surfaced in 2005 when the FCC learned that television stations aired Bush administration-produced and corporate-produced videos indistinguishable from legitimate news reports. The rules demand that broadcasters and companies, operating as cable programming originators, "inform the audience, at the time of airing: (1) that such matter is sponsored, paid for or furnished, either in whole or in part; and, (2) by whom or on whose behalf such consideration was supplied."[24] In 2007, the FCC fined Comcast, a cable program originator, $4,000 for airing a VNR that promoted a nonprescriptive sleep aid without disclosing its corporate source.

Children's Television Act

Pursuant to its public interest authority, the FCC issued a *Children's Television Report and Policy Statement*, 50 FCC 2d, 15 (1974), declaring that broadcasters have a special obligation to serve children. The D.C. Circuit upheld the authority of the FCC to require programming to meet the needs of children in *ACT v. FCC*, 564 F.2d 458, 465 (D.C. Cir. 1977), saying, "It seems to us that the use of television to further the educational and cultural development of America's children bears a direct relationship to the licensee's obligations under the Communications Act to operate in the 'public interest.'"

Free marketplace advocate and FCC Chairman Fowler and the Republican-dominated FCC did not see it that way, and repealed the 1974 statement in 1984, leading to radical changes in advertisers' efforts targeting children. The development of programs solely for the purposes of selling toys was the most controversial of these marketing schemes. Soon, a backlash ensued and Congress enacted The Children's Television Act of 1990 (CTA) to rein in children's toy advertising and children's programming. The CTA has three main components: (i) it sets time limits on advertising during children's programming, (ii) it obligates broadcasters to endeavor to air programming beneficial to children, and (iii) it puts licensees on notice that compliance with the limits and obligations will be weighed at license renewal time. In 1996, the FCC issued *In the Matter of Policies and Rules Concerning Children's Television Programming*, FCC 96–335 (1996), to clarify its children's programming rules. Its revised rules and restrictions included a requirement that broadcasters fulfill their children's programming obligations by providing "core programming," content that "serves the educational and informational needs of children as a significant purpose," and such programming must air between a regularly scheduled, weekly program of at least 30 minutes, aired between 7:00 a.m. and 10:00 p.m., and be identified as educational and informational.[25]

SUMMARY: The FCC's Broadcast News Distortion policy, Sponsorship Identification rules, and the Children's Television Act are policies, rules, and laws that allow the FCC to regulate broadcasting content in ways that would constitute an impermissible infringement upon a publisher's editorial autonomy in the print, cinema, and Internet media.

Obscene, Indecent, and Profane Speech

Under U.S. Code 18 U.S.C. § 1464, "Broadcasting Obscene Language," the FCC has the authority to regulate obscene, indecent, and profane speech. Though the terms are related in meaning, a substantial legal gulf separates obscenity from indecency and profanity, and obscenity is rarely an issue that comes before the FCC. In contrast, few issues have generated more controversy for the FCC than its interpretation and enforcement of indecency and profanity, which, during the last 40 years, has placed it in a position of refereeing culture war scuffles between religious and social conservatives and their Congressional allies, and shock jocks, broadcaster owners, and their listeners. The FCC notes that in "2004 alone," it "took action in 12 cases, involving hundreds of thousands of complaints, assessing penalties and voluntary payments totaling approximately $8,000,000."[26]

Meanwhile, First Amendment advocates and broadcasters argued that the FCC's definition of indecent and profane speech was unconstitutionally vague, meaning that the definition offers little guidance for broadcast licensees to avoid fines for airing indecent and profane words and images. Increasingly, more observers are adopting the free market position that indecency enforcement should end because the scarcity doctrine that props it up no longer reflects the scope of the diverse media marketplace and our technological capabilities. They also argue that the other reason for regulating broadcast—its pervasive presence and unique accessibility to children—cannot be justified now that there exists a rating system tied to a technology that allows parents to block unwanted programming. Yet, at the same time, some of those who back the current FCC indecency regime urge the Commission to expand its reach to include cable and satellite television and to regulate violent content as well.

A judge or a jury determines whether speech that describes sexual conduct in a patently offensive way is obscene. The U.S. Supreme Court has established a a three-prong test for obscenity: (1) an average person, applying contemporary community standards, must find that the material, as a whole, appeals to the prurient interest (i.e., material having a tendency to excite lustful thoughts); (2) the material must depict or describe, in a patently offensive way, sexual conduct specifically defined by applicable law; and (3) the material, taken as a whole, must lack serious literary, artistic, political, or scientific value. (See Chapter 12.) Once speech is found to be obscene, it is illegal. It falls outside the scope of First Amendment protection and cannot be aired.

Indecent and profane speech is partly defined by what it is not; it is not obscenity. Thus, it enjoys some First Amendment protection and cannot be banned from the airways. Accordingly, with court approval, the FCC limits the airing of indecent and profane speech from 6 a.m. to 10 p.m., local time to protect children. From 10 p.m. to 6 a.m. are deemed "safe harbor" hours for broadcasters to air such speech without fear of financial penalty.

Unlike obscenity, indecent language and images have serious literary, artistic, political, or scientific value and lack prurient appeal. More specifically, indecent content, according to the FCC, "depicts or describes sexual or excretory organs or activities in terms patently offensive as measured by contemporary community standards for the broadcast medium...In our assessment of whether material is "patently offensive," context is critical. The FCC looks at three primary factors when analyzing broadcast material: (1) "whether the description or depiction is explicit or graphic; (2) whether the material dwells on or repeats at length descriptions or depictions of sexual or excretory organs; and (3) whether the material appears to pander or is used to titillate or shock. No single factor is determinative. The FCC weighs and balances these factors because each case presents its own mix of these, and possibly other, factors."[27]

Profane language includes words that are highly offensive such as the F-word—depending on the context—and they are words that are akin to a nuisance, meaning that others find the content disagreeable, excessive, unhealthy, and unacceptable when disseminated during the wrong time or place.

The FCC derives its authority to regulate indecency under 47 U.S.C. § 303 (g), which requires the Commission to "encourage the larger and more effective use of radio in the public interest," and 18 U.S.C. § 1464. The language for U.S. Code 18 U.S.C. § 1464, "Broadcasting Obscene Language," was originally language found in the Communications Act, § 326. It wasn't until the late 1960s, however, that the FCC became seriously involved with addressing indecency and profanity, and not until *Eastern Education Radio*, 24 F.C.C. 2d 409 (1970) did it explicitly adopt a definition of indecency. The U.S. Supreme Court's 5–4 ruling, *FCC v. Pacifica Foundation*, 438 U.S. 726 (1978), serves as the landmark decision in defining indecency.

In *Pacifica*, the Court ruled that the FCC had authority to regulate broadcasts that are indecent but not obscene, and such regulatory authority is not a form of censorship forbidden by § 326 of the Communications Act or the First Amendment. *Pacifica* involved a 12-minute monologue, "Filthy Words," or "Seven Words You Can Never Say on Television." It was delivered by satirist George Carlin and aired at about 2 p.m. on WBAI-FM, a New York-based radio station owned by Pacifica Foundation. The case stemmed from the complaint of one man who said he heard the broadcast while driving with his young son. Pacifica explained that the monologue had been played during a program about contemporary society's attitude toward language, that immediately before its broadcast, listeners had been advised that it included language that might offend and that Carlin was a significant satirist. That explanation proved unpersuasive.

In *Pacifica*, the Court also adopted two core rationales for allowing government to regulate indecent speech on the airwaves—pervasiveness and broadcasting's unique accessibility to children. The nature of broadcasting and the technology the audience uses to access content on radio and television means that the "audience is constantly tuning in and out, prior warnings cannot completely protect the listener or viewer from unexpected program content" thus making it "pervasive," the Court said.[28] Broadcasting is "uniquely accessible to children," the Court said, because it comes directly into their homes and government has an interest in the well-being of children and supporting parent's ability to safeguard them from indecent content.[29] The Court rejected the contention that "one may avoid further offense by turning off the radio when he hears indecent language," comparing it to "saying that the remedy for an assault is to run away after the first blow."[30]

From 1978 until 1987, the FCC did not penalize a single broadcaster for airing indecent words or images.[31] Broadcasters' avoidance of the "seven dirty words" had a great deal to do with the commission not issuing fines for those 10 years. But the factions stoking the culture wars, primarily the Religious Right and Congress, pressured the FCC to announce a test for patent offensiveness that covered sexual innuendo in *Public Notice, New Indecency Enforcement Standards To Be Applied to All Broadcast and Amateur Radio Licensees*, 2 FCC Rcd 2726 (1987). Legal scholar Lilli Levi observed that from that year to about 2004, the FCC's "'send-a-message' cases…put broadcasters on notice that crass shock-jocks, boundary-crossing college radio stations, and programs targeting particular groups (such as gay men) could all be found to have aired actionable indecency even if they did not use any of the forbidden words."[32]

Also in 1987, the FCC came to the conclusion that the indecency standard it employed was unduly narrow and offered further clarification in *Infinity Broadcasting Corporation of Pennsylvania (Indecency Policy Consideration)*, 3 F.C.C. Rcd. 930 (1987). The FCC announced it: (i) would judge indecency and profanity from the view of "an average broadcast viewer"—a national standard, instead of a local one; (ii) rejected the argument that its approach impermissibly intruded on the editorial decisions of broadcasters; (iii) declined a ban on some sexually explicit material as impermissible under the First Amendment; (iv) suggested a midnight to 6 a.m. safe harbor; (v) declined to define "patently offensive"; and (vi) declined to exempt material with serious literary, artistic, political or scientific value.

Commercial broadcasting networks, public broadcasting entities, licensees, associations of broadcasters and journalists, program suppliers, and public interest groups challenged the Commission's revisions. They argued that the expanded indecency standard was unconstitutionally vague and the Commission's safe harbor approach was unconstitutionally overbroad, meaning that it limited adults to seeing and hearing content fit only for children. They also argued that the decision making was arbitrary and capricious because the FCC failed to offer reasoned analysis for its revisions.

In *Action for Children's Television v. FCC (ACT I)*, 852 F.2d 1331 (D.C. Cir. 1988), the appeals court said that *Pacifica* precluded lower courts from ruling on the petitioner's vagueness challenge and rejected the overbreadth argument because the safe harbor approach was a legitimate balancing of parents, government, broadcasters, and adult listeners' rights. The appeals court, however, did find that part of the FCC's decision was arbitrary and capricious—the times the Commission had chosen for the safe harbor hours were inadequately supported by factual data—and remanded the matter to the Commission for reconsideration.

Later that year, Congress entered the fray by passing the Congressional Ban on Indecent Speech, Pub. L. No. 100–459, 608, 102 Stat. 2186, 2228 (1988), a 24-hour ban. In compliance, the FCC adopted the full ban. The ban was challenged. The appeals court remanded the case to the FCC to conduct a hearing on the matter. In 1990, the FCC adopted a report supporting the full ban. Its decision was challenged in *Action for Children's Television v. FCC (ACT II)*, 932 F.2d 1504 (D.C. Cir. 1991). The Court reversed the FCC's action, essentially turning the clock back to *ACT I*.

Again, Congress acted. It passed the Public Telecommunications Act of 1992 which required, among other things, that the FCC allow commercial broadcast to air indecent programming from midnight to 6 a.m., and to allow public broadcast to air indecent content between 10 p.m. and midnight in some cases. Broadcasters challenged the new rules, the full D.C. Circuit (en banc) reviewed the ban in *Action for Children's Television v. FCC (ACT III)*, 58 F.3d 654 (1995) and found that the government had a compelling interest in protecting children under the age of 18 from exposure to indecent broadcasts and sent the matter to the FCC with instructions to permit the broadcasting of indecent content between the 10 p.m. and 6 a.m. Today, that period remains as the constitutionally valid.

In 2001, the FCC issued a policy statement, *In re Industry Guidance on Commission's Case Law Interpreting 18 U. S. C. § 1464 and Enforcement Policies Regarding Broadcast Indecency*, 16 FCC Rcd. 7999. The document emphasized that "whether the material dwells on or repeats at length descriptions of sexual or excretory organs or activities" was one of three significant factors in determining what it considered patently offensive. Moreover, the document cited examples of descriptions of sexual or excretory organs or activities that the FCC found permissible because it was fleeting and isolated.

"Fleeting Expletives"

Three years later, the FCC issued a substantial revision of its indecency policy, *In the Matter of Complaints Against Various Broadcast Licensees Regarding their Airing of the "Golden Globe Awards" Program*, F.C.C. Rcd. 4975 (2004), declaring that fleeting and isolated indecent and profane language could be found indecent under the law. This revision, the Court would later note in *FCC v. Fox*, came after the FCC had issued fines for incidents occurring in 2002 and 2003, soon after it had issued its 2001 statement saying that fleeting and isolated statements would not be considered indecent. Responding to complaints about U2 lead singer Bono's exclamation, "This is really, really, f—ing brilliant," upon receiving an award during a live broadcast, the FCC announced that it would hold broadcasters responsible for scripted and even unscripted use of the F-word or other expletives. Such use, the Commission argued, is offensive based on a national standard of the average viewer because the F-word is "one of the most vulgar, graphic and explicit descriptions of sexual activity in the English language. Its use invariably invokes a coarse sexual image...The use of the 'F-Word' here, on a nationally telecast awards ceremony, was shocking and gratuitous."[33] The FCC added other swear words to the list such as shit and "bullshitter." In *Complaints Regarding Various Television Broadcasts Between February 2, 2002 and March 8, 2005*, 21 F.C.C. Rcd, (2006), the Commission later reversed itself on the use of "bullshitter" because it was uttered during a "bona fide news interview." The Commission's rapidly changing position on what words fell under its "fleeting expletives" ban made it difficult for broadcasters to predict which words and images might be indecent. In 2006, Fox Television Stations, along with other broadcast networks and numerous amici, challenged the FCC's fleeting expletive policy.

The question went before the U.S. Court of Appeals for the Second Circuit in *Fox Television Stations, Inc. v. FCC*, 489 F.3d 444 (2007), which held that the "fleeting expletives" policy was a significant departure from the Commission's earlier policy and was arbitrary and capricious under the federal Administrative Procedure Act. Under the act, agency action is arbitrary and capricious "if the agency has relied on factors which Congress has not intended it to consider, entirely failed to consider an important aspect of the problem, offered an explanation for its decision that runs counter to the evidence before the agency, or is so implausible that it could not be ascribed to a difference in view or the product of agency expertise."[34]

The FCC appealed to the Supreme Court. The Court, 5–4, ruled only on the procedural matter and reversed the Second Circuit, in *FCC v. Fox Television Stations, Inc.*, 129 S. Ct. 1800 (2009). On remand, the Second Circuit addressed the First Amendment question in *Fox Television Stations, Inc., v. FCC*, 613 F.3d 317 (2d Cir. 2010). It ruled that the FCC's policy violated the First Amendment because it was unconstitutionally vague:

> The first problem arises in the FCC's determination as to which words or expressions are patently offensive. For instance, while the FCC concluded that 'bullshit' in a 'NYPD Blue' episode was patently offensive, it concluded that 'dick' and 'dickhead' were not...Other expletives such as 'pissed off,' 'up yours,' 'kiss my ass,' and 'wiping his ass' were also not found to be patently offensive...This hardly gives broadcasters notice of how the Commission will apply the factors in the future.[35]

The Commission's crackdown on indecency also targeted "fleeting images." In 2004, it imposed a record $550,000 fine on CBS for the half-second exposure of singer Janet Jackson's nipple during the halftime show of the Super Bowl XXVIII broadcast in what has been coined a "wardrobe malfunction." The U.S. Court of Appeals for the Third Circuit voided the FCC's fine in *CBS Corp. v. FCC*,

535 F.2d 167 (3d Cir. 2008). In *FCC v. CBS Corp.*, 08–653 (2009), the U.S. Supreme Court, however, granted review, vacated the judgment, and sent the case back to the Third Circuit for reconsideration in light of its ruling in *FCC v. Fox Television Stations, Inc.*, 129 S. Ct. 1800 (2009). The Third Circuit, however, stuck with its initial analysis—the FCC's enforcement actions were arbitrary and capricious.[36] In 2012, the Court declined to review the "wardrobe malfunction" case because its ruling in *Fox Television Stations, Inc.* had addressed the question.[37]

When the Court placed *Fox Television Stations, Inc.* on its fall 2011 calendar for oral arguments, it was reasonable to believe that the validity of *Red Lion*'s scarcity doctrine and *Pacifica*'s indecency doctrine were at stake. In *Fox Television Stations, Inc., v. FCC*, the Second Circuit, for example, took note of the many media technologies or outlets available today that did not exist when *Pacifica* was handed down in 1978: Cable TV was in its infancy, the Internet was merely a government-run project, and there was no YouTube, Facebook, or Twitter. The Second Circuit also noted that the V-chip, available in every "television, 13 inches or larger, sold in the United States since January 2000…allows parents to block programs based on a standardized rating system."[38] The Second Circuit drew a parallel to the U.S. Supreme Court's ruling in *U.S. v. Playboy Entertainment Group*, 523 U.S. 803 (2000), in which the Court struck down a provision of the Telecommunications Act of 1996 that prohibited cable television operators from broadcasting sexual content during certain hours because cable systems have the capacity to block unwanted channels on a household-by-household basis. V-chip technology performs a similar function—provides the capacity to block unwanted programming on a household-by-household basis—the Second Circuit noted. The Second Circuit, however, said precedent "regardless of whether it reflects today's realities" bound it, so it could not overturn *Pacifica*.

Precedent does not bind U.S. Supreme Court judges as tightly. Associate Justice Clarence Thomas had signaled that he was prepared to abolish the spectrum scarcity doctrine and the related notion of broadcast as a uniquely pervasive medium. Thomas said in his concurring opinion in *FCC v. Fox*, "The extant facts that drove this Court to subject broadcasters to unique disfavor under the First Amendment simply do not exist today…These dramatic changes in factual circumstances might well support a departure from precedent under the prevailing approach to stare decisis…For all these reasons, I am open to reconsideration of *Red Lion* and *Pacifica* in the proper case."[39]

The Court in an 8–0 decision, however, struck down the fleeting expletive rule as vague on Fifth Amendment due process grounds. Specifically, the Court found that broadcasters could not have known that they would be punished for fleeting expletives and images when the FCC had said that such words and images were not actionable in its 2001 policy statement. Yet, between 2002 and 2004, before the FCC had officially announced its change in policy, broadcasters were punished for such speech. In effect, it upheld the Second Circuit, which struck down the rule as vague, but on First Amendment grounds.

Though Justice Ruth Bader Ginsburg signed on to the majority ruling, she said she was prepared to strike down traditional and fleeting indecency as unconstitutional: "In my view, the Court's decision in *FCC v. Pacifica Foundation*, 438 U. S. 726 (1978), was wrong when it issued. Time, technological advances, and the Commission's untenable rulings in the cases now before the Court show why *Pacifica* bears reconsideration."[40]

Nevertheless, the indecency standard is still good law; the ruling only affected the broadcasters who were previously sanctioned. Now broadcasters are subject to fines for airing indecent and profane broadcasts whether they are repeated, prolonged, or fleeting. In his concurrence of the denial of review of the "Wardrobe Malfunction" ruling, issued nine days after *Fox Television Stations, Inc.*, Chief Justice John Roberts observed, "It is now clear that the brevity of an indecent broadcast—be it word or image—cannot immunize it from FCC censure."[41] As of July 2012, the FCC had a backlog of 1.5 million indecency complaints involving 9,700 TV broadcasts.[42]

Violent programming. In 2007, the FCC released a report, *In the Matter of Violent Television Programming and Its Impact on Children*, 22 F.C.C. Rcd. 79299 (2007). Among its findings, it identified "strong evidence that exposure to violence in the media can increase aggressive behavior in children, at least in the short term."[43] But in the aftermath of Justice Antonin Scalia's ruling in *Brown v. Entertainment Merchant Association*, 08–1448 (2011), it's unlikely that the Court will uphold restrictions on violent content. *Brown v. Entertainment Merchant Association* involved a California statute restricting minors' access to violent video games. In striking down the statute, Scalia noted that there has been no longstanding tradition in the U.S. of "specially restricting children's access to depictions of violence," and he rejected nearly all the studies that purported to show a causal link between video game playing and violent behavior in children as methodologically flawed, showing at best a correlation between video game playing and violence in children.

SUMMARY: In *FCC v. Pacifica*, 438 U.S. 726 (1978), the U.S. Supreme Court upheld FCC authority to protect children from sexually indecent and profane broadcast programming based on the rationale that over-the-air broadcasting is a pervasive medium and is uniquely accessible to children. It is pervasive because "prior warnings cannot completely protect the listener or viewer from unexpected" programming. It is uniquely accessible to children because it comes directly into homes. Thus, the FCC may impose fines on broadcasters who air sexually indecent and profane content from 6 a.m. to 10 p.m., though not between 10 p.m. and 6 a.m. because indecent and profane content enjoys some First Amendment protection. Obscene broadcasts, however, are prohibited altogether.

What is indecent programming? It has been defined as patently offensive sexual or excretory material that does not rise to the level of obscenity. In 2004, the FCC revised its definition of indecency to include fleeting expletives, which are indecent or profane comments or images that may be as brief as a phrase or an image lasting merely seconds.

In *FCC v. Fox Television Stations*, 132 S. Ct. 2307 (2012), the Court threw out FCC-imposed fines against three broadcasters—Fox, ABC and, in the related case *CBS Corp. v. FCC*, 663 F. 3d 122 (3d. Cir. 2011), CBS—for airing fleeting expletives only because the FCC had not given fair notice about the new fleeting expletives policy. Now, the FCC may police the airways for repeated, prolonged, and fleeting indecent content.

Media Ownership Rules

Pursuant to its licensing authority as provided in Section 309 [47 U.S.C.A. § 309], the Commission has sought to limit the number of stations a licensee may own nationwide and locally and the types of affiliations the licensee forges with other media businesses since the late 1930s. The FCC has been concerned that concentration of ownership in the hands of a small number of entities would undermine its public interest objectives of protecting local news and public affairs coverage, and promoting the airing of diverse programming and views, business competition, and innovation in the media marketplace. Meanwhile, courts, most recently the U.S. Supreme Court in 2012, have rebuffed arguments that the FCC's authority to regulate the number of broadcasting and print outlets a licensee may own violates the free speech rights of media companies.

The FCC first applied local ownership restrictions to radio in *Genesee Radio Corp.*, Flint MI., 5 F.C.C. 183 (1938), creating what has become known as the duopoly rule. Under the rule, the Commission would not allow one entity to own two broadcast stations in the same local market.

The Commission, however, relaxed that restriction in *Radio Multiple Ownership Rules*, 7 F.C.C. Rcd 2755 (1992), allowing owners to own more stations in a designated market area (DMA). Later, it relaxed a television duopoly rule and modified a one-to-one market rule that prevented one owner from owning a radio and VHF-TV station in the same local market. The Commission promulgated a National Television Station Ownership (NTSO) rule in the 1940s. The rule banned common ownership of more than three television stations. That number was increased to 12 stations in 1984 under the Amendment of Multiple Ownership Rules, Report & Order, 100 F.C.C.2d 17, ¶¶ 14, 16, 1984 WL 251222 (1984). As discussed earlier in this chapter, the Court affirmed the FCC's authority to regulate the relationship between licensees and networks in *NBC v. U.S.* in 1943.

The Court upheld the Commission's *Rules and Regulations Relating to Multiple Ownership*, 18 F.C.C. 288 (1953), in *U.S. v. Storer Broadcasting Co.*, 351 U.S. 192 (1956). Those rules provided that licenses for broadcasting stations would not be granted if the applicant, directly or indirectly, had an interest in other stations beyond a limited number. The Court affirmed the Commission's limits on one entity owning a newspaper and a broadcast station in the same community (cross-ownership) in *FCC v. National Citizens Committee for Broadcasting*, 436 U.S. 775 (1978). More important, the Court ruled in *NCCB* that the cross-ownership limits need only to meet the **rational basis** judicial scrutiny test. Courts apply this minimal standard of review, asking whether the government's method is a rational way to achieve its stated goals. The FCC also reviews mergers involving media corporations. The Federal Trade Commission and the U.S. Justice Department also may reject or approve such business agreements on antitrust grounds.

The 1980s and 1990s saw an aggressive campaign to deregulate media industries and the Telecommunications Act of 1996 provided extensive deregulatory provisions coupled with relaxed restrictions on the concentration of media ownership. Heeding its mandate to review its media owner rules biennially, the FCC began a review in 1998 but soon after found itself before the D.C. Circuit, after deciding to neither repeal nor modify its NTSO and the cable/broadcast cross-ownership rules.

At the time, the NTSO Rule prohibited any entity from controlling television stations with a potential audience reach exceeding 35% of the television households in the U.S. The 1970 cable/broadcast cross-ownership rule prohibited a cable television system from carrying the signal of any television broadcast station if the system owned a broadcast station in the same local market.

In response Fox, NBC, CBS, and others challenged the decision as a violation of the Telecommunications Act of 1996, the First Amendment, and on administrative law grounds. In *Fox Television Stations, Inc., v. FCC*, 280 F.3d 1027 (D.C. Cir. 2002), the D.C. Circuit said the decision was arbitrary and capricious. It vacated the cable/broadcast cross-ownership rule and ordered the Commission to further evaluate the NTSO rule. Later that year, in *Sinclair Broadcast Group, Inc. v. FCC*, 284 F. 148 (D.C. Cir. 2002), the D.C. Circuit sent the local television duopoly rule back to the FCC demanding that it adequately explain its decision.

Following its mandate to review its broadcast ownership rules every four years the FCC announced in 2002 it was reviewing six rules : the NTSO's 35% cap, local television duopoly, newspaper/broadcast cross-ownership, local radio multiple ownership, dual network ownership, and cable/broadcasting cross-ownership. After conducting one public hearing, soliciting twelve studies on media ownership, and receiving two million letters, postcards, emails, and petitions opposing further relaxation of the rules, the FCC, 3–2, released its revisions, a "new, comprehensive framework for broadcast ownership regulation," on June 2, 2003.[45] Here are how the rules changed:

- Dual Network Rule. Under the dual network rule, a television station may affiliate with more than one network except that it may not affiliate with more than one of the four largest networks, ABC, CBS, Fox, and NBC. The FCC let it stand as it was.
- Local television duopoly. In effect, the existing rule precluded duopolies in most markets. The revision would have "allowed triopolies in the nine largest DMAs, which represent 25.2% of the population. Duopolies could exist under the new rule in the largest 162 markets, representing 95.4% of the nation's population."[46]
- Local Radio Ownership. The FCC retained its sliding-scale numeral limits on radio ownership but adopted a different way of determining the size of a local radio market. Opponents, however, had previously challenged the numerical limits imposed under the existing rules as arbitrary. Newspaper/Broadcast and Radio/Television Cross-ownership. Under the newspaper/broadcast cross-ownership rule, no entity could own a newspaper and a television station serving the same local community. The Radio/Television Cross-ownership rule set limits on the number of broadcast stations that could be owned based on the size of the market. The Commission created one Cross-media limit, restricting cross-ownership based on the market size with the exemption of the largest markets where there would be not restriction.
- National Television Station Ownership. The FCC increased the NTSO cap to 45% from 35%.

The FCC's Republican majority argued that easing the ownership restrictions was necessary because the old rules did not reflect the 21st-century media landscape where Internet, satellite broadcasts, and cable television programming offered the public numerous and diverse resources for entertainment, news, and information. They argued that the new rules would promote greater competition and innovation among media companies, and consumers would benefit because increased competition would lower prices. The FCC's move to eliminate a number of ownership limits was sought by major media companies such as News Corp., owner of the Fox network, and Viacom, the parent company of CBS and UPN.

Opponents of FCC's media ownership revisions were in great number and politically diverse from the ultra-conservative National Rifle Association and then-U.S. Senator Trent Lott (R-Miss.), to small broadcasters and the Consumers Union, to the media political economists and reformers on the Left such as media scholar Robert W. McChesney and his advocacy organization Freepress. Consumer advocacy and media reformers, among the opposition groups, argued that more than two decades of free-market deregulatory policies and laws had led to consolidation of the media, resulting in the airing of less diverse programming and opinions, and higher prices for consumers.

The NTSO 45% cap and the cross-ownership rules drew the most flak. In 2004, Congress passed a bill reducing the ownership cap to 39%, which had the not-so-coincidental effect of allowing Viacom/CBS and News Corp/FOX to keep all of the stations they owned at the time.

By 2011, after two rulings by the U.S. Court of Appeals for the Third Circuit, only the Congressionally created NTSO 39% cap had survived judicial scrutiny, and several of the rules in place before the 2003 revisions were reinstated. In its first ruling, *Prometheus Radio Project v. FCC*, 373 F.3d

372 (3d Cir. 2004), the court sent the numerical caps for cross-media ownership and the revisions of the local television and radio limits back to the FCC, demanding greater details justifying the changes. In its second ruling, *Prometheus Radio Project v. FCC*, 652 F.3d 431 (3d Cir. 2011), the Third Circuit vacated the revised newspaper/broadcast cross ownership rule adopted by the FCC in 2008. It also upheld the FCC's decision in 2007 to reinstate the radio/television cross-ownership rule, local television ownership rule, local radio ownership rule, dual network rule and the failed station solicitation rule that were in place before 2003.

Additionally, the Third Circuit rejected, as it did in the 2004 ruling, a constitutional challenge to the ownership rules. Broadcasters argued that because media scarcity no longer existed there was no justification for applying the rational basis test. The strict scrutiny must be applied to test the constitutionality of the ownership rules. The Third Circuit, citing *Ruggiero v. FCC*, 278 F.3d 1323, 1325 (D.C. Cir. 2002),[47] said the airwaves were still scarce:

> Even were we not constrained by Supreme Court precedent, we would not accept the…contention that the expansion of media outlets has rendered the broadcast spectrum less scarce. In *NCCB*, the Court referred to the 'physical scarcity' of the spectrum—the fact that many more people would like access to it than can be accommodated. The abundance of non-broadcast media does not render the broadcast spectrum any less scarce.[48]

In 2012, the Court rejected without comment three challenges to the media ownership rules stemming from *Prometheus Radio Project*. It rejected an appeal by Media General Inc., a company that owns newspapers, broadcast television stations, websites, and other digital platforms. Media General argued that the Newspaper/Broadcast and Radio/Television Cross-ownership restrictions should be subject to strict scrutiny and that the Court should overturn *Prometheus Radio Project* and *NCCB*.[49] The Tribune Company, which owns newspapers, radio and television outlets, argued that the Court should overturn the scarcity doctrine of *Red Lion*, the media ownership rules, and that Newspaper/Broadcast and Radio/Television Cross-ownership rules violated the First and Fifth Amendment of newspapers.[50] The National Association of Broadcasters filed a petition arguing that the rulings in the Third Circuit's *Prometheus Radio Project* and D.C. Circuit's *Sinclair Broadcast Group* were inconsistent and that the Third Circuit in effect overruled the D.C. Circuit.[51]

SUMMARY: Under its authority to license broadcasters in the public interest, the FCC sets limits on the number of broadcast stations an entity can own, as well as limits on the common ownership of broadcast stations and newspapers. The FCC's media ownership rules, which the FCC must review every four years, are a battleground for advocates of media regulation and deregulation. Courts have rejected several lawsuits brought by media companies contending that the rules violate their First Amendment rights and that they cannot be justified under the spectrum scarcity doctrine and are illogical in an era of media convergence.

Cable Television and the First Amendment

The "must-carry" provisions of the Cable Television Consumer Protection and Competition Act (1992 Cable Act) require cable television operators to carry the signals of certain local TV stations operating in a cable company's market. In a landmark ruling, *Turner Broadcasting System v. FCC*, 520 U.S. 180 (1997) II, the U.S. Supreme Court held that the provisions did not violate cable operators' First Amendment rights. Without the must-carry obligations, the Court said, cable operators would wield "bottleneck" or "gatekeeper control" over local programming. In other words, if operators choose to reject certain programming from their systems, Americans who receive broadcast television programming via cable, the overwhelming majority, would not receive that programming. The act also provides market modification provisions that authorize the FCC to exclude or include communities from a cable system's market to better serve viewers' local programming needs.

When the FCC ordered Cablevision Systems Corp. to carry WRNN, a Kingston, New York, signal to its Long Island subscribers, Cablevision balked and sued. The cable operator asked, among other questions: What important local programming needs were served by forcing it to carry a predominately home-shopping network channel from a broadcaster based more than 100 miles away from Long Island's Nassau and Suffolk counties? It didn't get the answer it wanted to hear. The U.S. Court of Appeals for the Second Circuit rejected Cablevision's arguments in *Cablevision Systems Corp. v. FCC*, 570 F.3d 83 (2009). The following year, without comment, the U.S. Supreme Court denied Cablevision's request for review in *Cablevision Systems Corp. v. FCC*, 130 S. Ct. 3275 (2010).

Cable's Route toward Regulation

The cable television industry, or community antenna television systems (CATV), emerged in the late 1940s. Then, cable functioned merely as a retransmission medium for communities located too far away from an antenna, or blocked by mountains, to receive TV signals. Cable served as a passive carrier for television signals. Accordingly, a cable operator could reasonably have been regulated as a common carrier. But in *Frontier Broadcasting v. Collier*, 24 FCC 251 (1958), the FCC ruled that cable was not a common carrier and the Commission had no authority to regulate the industry. By the early 1960s, the FCC, noting that cable operators had the potential to transmit their own content as well as television-produced content, started to create a regulatory framework that was partly common carrier and broadcast, a hybrid system.

What had changed? At first, CATV relied solely on coaxial cable to carry television signals from an antenna where the reception was good to subscribers in outlying communities whose home antennas could not pick up television signals. Eventually, many operators started to use a microwave-to-cable system to reach subscribers in those communities. By the early 1960s, the industry had taken on a regional scope with the promise of national transmission. Small market broadcasters, fearful that CATV would draw away viewers and advertisers, turned to Congress and the FCC for help. Congressional action stalled, but broadcasters won relief in the courts.

The FCC Expands Its Reach

In *Carter Mountain Transmission Corp. v. FCC*, 321 F.2d 359 (D.C. Cir. 1963), a federal appeals court upheld the FCC's authority to deny a license to a microwave company that planned to service a CATV system. The FCC said the company's plan to bring in outside programs for the CATV system would put a local TV broadcaster out of business, leaving much of the community that chose not to pay or could not afford to pay monthly fees without access to free over-the-air broadcast service. So *Carter Mountain Transmission* provided the FCC with a precedent to justify its authority to regulate cable television operations. The FCC established rules in 1965 for cable systems that received signals by microwave antennas, and in 1966, rules for systems using cable and microwave.

The FCC's restriction of a cable operator's transmission of Los Angeles TV broadcasting signals into San Diego led to a U.S. Supreme Court landmark ruling, *U.S. v. Southwestern Cable*, 392 U.S. 157 (1968). Southwestern Cable argued, among other theories, that "CATV, with certain of the characteristics both of broadcasting and of common carriers, but with all of the characteristics of neither, eludes altogether" the grasp of the 1934 Communications Act.[52] The Court, however, held that the FCC had authority to regulate CATV systems because, under the 1934 Communications Act:

> The Commission has been charged with broad responsibilities for the orderly development of an appropriate system of local television broadcasting. The significance of its efforts can scarcely be exaggerated, for broadcasting is demonstrably a principal source of information and entertainment for a great part of the Nation's population…We have elsewhere held that we may not, 'in the absence of compelling evidence that such was Congress' intention…prohibit administrative action imperative for the achievement of an agency's ultimate purposes'…There is no such evidence here, and we therefore hold that the Commission's authority over 'all interstate…communication by wire or radio' permits the regulation of CATV systems."[53]

Communications Policy Act of 1984

By the early 1980s, as the cable television industry spread to large suburban and urban communities, the FCC and municipalities vied over regulatory control of the industry. Typically, large municipalities had leverage over cable companies because installation of cable on public property in well-populated communities often limited service to one company. Local regulators could and did demand content and rate limitations, and deny renewal.

Congress, however, intervened and amended the Communications Act of 1934 with the Communications Policy Act of 1984 to establish uniformed municipal franchise procedures and standards. The 1984 law bans anyone from operating a cable system without a franchise, sets a cap on franchise fees, and imposes a must-carry provision requiring cable operators to set aside public access channels for use by local individuals or groups. It was "the first comprehensive federal statute regulating the cable television industry. A stated primary purpose of the legislation was 'to assure that cable communications provide and are encouraged to provide the widest possible diversity of information sources and services to the public.'"[54]

City of Los Angeles vs. Preferred Communications Inc., 476 U.S. 488 (1986)

Even with the national franchise procedures and standards in place, Preferred Communications Inc. brought a First Amendment and antitrust challenge against Los Angeles for denial of a cable television franchise and refusal to give them access to underground power line conduits. In essence, the company argued that the city was unfairly discriminating against one speaker in favor of another by allowing only one cable TV company to operate in Los Angeles when the city had sufficient space to accommodate more than one cable system. The city countered that even though there was enough physical capacity to accommodate another system, the installation of more than one system would overly burden the city's utility structures and public streets causing traffic jams and marring the city's esthetics. Also, the city argued there was insufficient economic demand to justify two systems. The Supreme Court did not resolve the controversy; it remanded the case to the lower court, allowing the parties to develop a thorough record on the disputed facts of the case.

City of Los Angeles v. Preferred is seminal because the Court recognized that cable TV operators' First Amendment rights are implicated by municipality franchise award decisions. Applying First Amendment media-specific analysis, the Court noted that, like newspapers and magazines, cable television is in the business of providing news, information, entertainment, and space for the public to air their views. Also, some cable TV operators provide their own content and all exercise editorial discretion about which networks and programs to offer subscribers: "Cable television partakes of some of the aspects of speech and the communication of ideas as do the traditional enterprises of newspaper and book publishers, public speakers, and pamphleteers."[55]

What level of scrutiny should a court apply when balancing an operator's First Amendment interests against a community's interests in controlling its public thoroughfares and utilities? The Court answered that question in the first of two rulings on a constitutional challenge brought by the Turner Broadcasting System (TBS).

Turner Broadcasting System v. FCC, *512 U.S. 622 (1994) and Intermediate Scrutiny*

Before *Turner*, Congress passed the Cable Television Consumer Protection and Competition Act of 1992. The act, imposed, among other things, revised must-carry obligations that gave cable system broadcasters, operating within the same television market, the privilege to demand to be carried or retransmitted, and authorized the FCC to regulate cable rates for the basic tier where cable companies had no "effective" competition. Broadcasters opting for retransmission may negotiate for compensation from a cable operator in lieu of carriage. The act also provides that once every three years, broadcast stations may elect between must-carry and retransmission consent. Congress feared that without the must-carry provisions there would be a substantial likelihood that cable operators would not carry the local broadcast station signals. As noted earlier in this chapter, Congress feared that cable operators would exercise bottleneck or gatekeeper control over local TV broadcasters. Soon after the act became law, Turner Broadcasting System sued the FCC, arguing that the must-carry provisions infringed on its First Amendment right of editorial autonomy.

In *Turner*, the Court recognized that must-carry provisions burden cable operators' free speech rights because the "rules reduce the number of channels over which cable operators exercise unfettered control, and they render it more difficult for cable programmers to compete for carriage on the limited channels remaining."[56] The Court, however, recognized that the provisions served three "important" interests: (i) preserving the benefits of free, over-the-air local broadcast television, (ii) promoting the widespread dissemination of information from a multiplicity of sources, and (iii) promoting fair competition in the market for television programming. The challenge then was to determine the appropriate level of judicial scrutiny to apply when testing the provisions' constitutionality.

The Court rejected TBS's argument that the must-carry provisions should undergo strict scrutiny analysis. First, the Court said the must-carry provisions were not a content-based regulation because they were "not designed to favor or disadvantage speech of any particular content. Rather, they are meant to protect broadcast television from what Congress determined to be unfair competition by cable systems."[57] The Court also rejected TBS's arguments that strict scrutiny must be applied because the provisions "(1) compel speech by cable operators, (2) favor broadcast programmers over cable programmers, and (3) single out certain members of the press for disfavored treatment."[58]

The Court ruled that the content-neutral provisions must be subjected to intermediate scrutiny; it must be shown that the provisions promote an important or substantial governmental interest that would be achieved less effectively absent the government regulation. Because there were genuine issues about the facts of the case still in dispute, the Court remanded the case for further proceedings.

Three years later, the parties returned to the Court in *Turner Broadcasting System v. FCC*, 520 U.S. 180 (1997) II. A majority of the Court reaffirmed that intermediate scrutiny was the appropriate test and ruled that the must-carry provisions furthered important governmental interests and did not burden speech substantially more than necessary to promote those interests.

Is Must-Carry Still Necessary?

The cable TV industry has not made peace with the must-carry provisions. It would like to see *Turner I & II* overturned, or modified to have strict scrutiny applied to must-carry because it says the rules ignore the marketplace realities of the 21st century. According to the industry, cable TV doesn't have the market power it once did. The "bottleneck" or "gatekeeper" conditions that undergirded the *Turner* Court's rationale for applying intermediate scrutiny barely exist in the 21st century, the industry contends. Direct Broadcast Satellite (DBS), the Internet, and telephone companies now compete with cable TV operators to bring multichannel video programming to viewers. Consequently, cable TV operators stand to lose subscribers when they drop popular broadcast signals because consumers have options that did not exist in the mid-1990s, the industry argues. Additionally, the industry argues that must-carry often does not promote its core goals of preserving the benefits of free, over-the-air local broadcast television, promoting the widespread dissemination of information from a multiplicity of sources, and promoting fair competition in the market for television programming.

C-SPAN, the cable network that provides public affairs coverage, is a self-described "consistent and active opponent of the must-carry statute that infringes its First Amendment rights as a speaker."[59] In its amicus curiae brief supporting Cablevision, it noted that because of must-carry "between June 1993 and the end of the 1990s, 12 million cable homes lost all or some access to C-SPAN's public service programming as cable operators were forced to make room on their systems to carry hundreds of additional broadcast stations."[60] WRNN is a perfect example of what is wrong with the must-carry regime, the amici and Cablevision argue, because as a predominately home shopping network, it did not provide the type of "quality local programming" *Turner I* sought to protect.

In *Cablevision v. FCC*, Cablevision attacked the 1992 Cable Act market modification provision as a content-specific regulation that required strict scrutiny. The provision allows the FCC to add or exclude communities from a broadcaster's market to better promote the act's local programming goals. When a community is excluded from the market, a cable operator does not have to carry the broadcaster to that community. Conversely, when the FCC adds a community to a broadcaster's market, the operator must-carry that broadcaster. But the modification criteria the FCC weighs includes consideration of whether a television station provides local news and service coverage.

Cablevision argued that because the FCC granted carriage rights to WRNN based on the part of broadcaster's programming that targeted Long Island, the FCC's order was content-specific and, thus, subject to strict scrutiny analysis. The Second Circuit, however, ruled that the FCC modification order was content neutral, deserving of intermediate scrutiny. That was so, the court said, because "WRNN's local programming was an inconsequential factor in the FCC's ultimate decision."[61] But it recognized the possibility that the *Turner* rulings "do not foreclose the possibility of a successful as-applied First Amendment challenge to the 1992 Cable Act's market modification provisions" brought in future cases in which the facts favor a cable operator.[62]

Cablevision also contended the FCC's decision awarded "gamemanship" on WRNN's part. Kingston-based WRNN moved its transmitter closer to Long Island and modified its programming simply to take advantage of the statute's privilege to demand that Cablevision carry its signal to Long Island. But the statute was designed to protect existing, local-based broadcasters, not carpetbaggers, Cablevision contended. The Second Circuit, however, said the changes WRNN undertook were consistent with "a central premise of the regulatory scheme that a regulated entity will change its conduct in socially desirable ways to achieve a regulatory benefit."[63]

Full First Amendment Protection for Cable?

In *U.S. v. Playboy Entertainment Group, Inc.*, 529 U.S. 803 (2000), a majority of the Court declared that, at least with respect to the regulation of programming on cable television, strict First Amendment scrutiny applies. The majority rejected the government's argument that the intermediate scrutiny was appropriate to test the constitutionality of Section 505 of the Telecommunications Act of 1996 (or Communications Decency Act) that required cable TV operators to scramble or block channels offering sexually-explicit programming. Unlike over-the-air viewers, cable subscribers can choose "targeted blocking" of unwanted channels. With such technology, placing the burden on the operators was not the least restrictive way to prevent children from watching pornography, the Court reasoned.

But the precedent *Playboy Entertainment* set does not directly bolster cable operators' efforts to unburden themselves of must-carry. That is because the Court construed Section 505 to be a content-based regulation—it singled out sexually explicit programming content and their programmers—and the Court's precedents demanded that it test the constitutionality of a content-based regulation with strict scrutiny. In contrast, courts have ruled that the must-carry provisions do not single out a particular type of content or programmer.

SUMMARY: When cable TV was a fledgling industry, the FCC issued an administrative ruling in *Frontier Broadcasting v. Collier*, 24 FCC 251 (1958), in which it declared it had no authority over the new medium. As the industry expanded and threatened the existence of local broadcasting stations, the FCC changed its mind. In *U.S. v. Southwestern Cable*, 392 U.S. 157 (1968), the Court upheld the FCC's right to regulate cable TV systems to protect local broadcasting, pursuant to powers of interstate wire and radio communication regulation conferred on it in the 1934 Communications Act.

As the cable TV service moved from small outlying rural communities to big suburban and urban ones, Congress adopted the Communications Policy Act of 1984 to establish uniform municipal franchise procedures and standards. A First Amendment challenge to community franchise authority led to *City of Los Angeles v. Preferred Communications Inc.*, 476 U.S. 488 (1986), in which the Court recognized that "cable television partakes of some of the aspects of speech and the communication of ideas as do the traditional enterprises of newspaper and book publishers, public speakers, and pamphleteers."

The two *Turner* rulings—*Turner Broadcasting System v. FCC*, 512 U.S. 622 (1994) I, and *Turner Broadcasting System v. FCC*, 520 U.S. 180 (1997) II—established that intermediate scrutiny was the appropriate analysis to test the constitutionality of content-neutral laws regulating cable. Applying that standard, the *Turner II* Court ruled that the must-carry provisions of the Cable Television Consumer Protection and Competition Act of 1992 promote important governmental interests and do not burden substantially more speech than necessary to promote those interests.

So far, the cable industry's continuing efforts to unburden itself of must-carry obligations have been dashed by the courts. The courts decline to apply strict scrutiny to the content-neutral provision. But content-based laws that burden cable TV are subject to strict scrutiny, the Court held in *U.S. v. Playboy Entertainment Group, Inc.*, 529 U.S. 803 (2000).

ONLINE RESOURCES

1. Federal Communications Commission, http://www.FCC.gov
2. "Obscenity, Indecency and Profanity," Federal Communications Commission, http://www.fcc.gov/guides/obscenity-indecency-and-profanity
3. "The FCC's Regulation of Indecency," http://www.firstamendmentcenter.org/madison/wp-content/uploads/2011/03/FirstReport.Indecency.Levi_.final_.pdf
4. "The Public Interest Standard in Television Broadcasting," http://govinfo.library.unt.edu/piac/novmtg/pubint.htm
5. "Program Content Regulations," Federal Communications Commission, http://www.fcc.gov/guides/program-content-regulations
6. "Review of the Broadcast Ownership Rules," Federal Communications Commission, http://www.fcc.gov/guides/review-broadcast-ownership-rules
7. "Evolution of Cable Television," Federal Communications Commission, http://www.fcc.gov/encyclopedia/evolution-cable-television
8. "FAQs—Television and Cable," Federal Communications Commission, http://www.fcc.gov/encyclopedia/faqs-television-and-cable
10. "United States: Cable Television," http://www.museum.tv/eotvsection.php?entrycode=unitedstatesc

QUESTIONS

1. In October 2004, politically conservative Sinclair Broadcasting, a corporation that controls more television broadcast licenses than any other, had planned to force its 62 stations to pre-empt prime-time programming to air *Stolen Honor: Wounds That Never Heal*, a blatantly one-sided documentary opposed to the Democratic presidential candidate, John Kerry. Reacting to reports that Sinclair was to air *Stolen Honor* shortly before the election, members of the United States Congress asked the FCC to consider the legality of the planned broadcast. The Democratic National Committee filed a complaint with the Federal Election Commission. As this controversy made the news, with a num-

ber of Sinclair advertisers pulling their ads and Sinclair stock dropping 17% in eleven days, Sinclair announced that it had never intended to air *Stolen Honor* in an hour slot in the first place, indicating that it might instead show clips of the video in a discussion panel format. Ultimately, Sinclair did not broadcast any such show. Do you think the Sinclair controversy shows the need to have the Fairness Doctrine, or does it show how broadcast companies like Sinclair are responsive to public opinion and thus there is no need for a Fairness Doctrine?

2. According to the findings of a study published in the *Journal of Law and Economics* in 2008, a ban on fast food television advertisements during children's programming would reduce the number of overweight children ages 3–11 by 18%, while also lowering the number of overweight adolescents ages 12–18 by 14%. Could the FCC justify such a ban under its public interest standard and the provisions of the Children's Television Act of 1990? Do you think such a ban would survive judicial scrutiny?

3. Commercial Advertisement Loudness Mitigation (CALM) Act (HR 6209), http://www.opencongress.org/bill/111-h1084/text. Under the act, the FCC has the authority to regulate the volume on TV ads, ensuring the sound on commercials does not overly exceed the decibel level during the program. It is clear that under the First Amendment, Congress could not tell newspapers, magazines, or websites to limit the brightness of the colors used in the ads they carry or limit the size of their ads. Do you think the proposed law violates broadcasters' First Amendment rights?

4. Generally, the policy behind our mass media laws has been to promote the free flow of a wide diversity of ideas, information, and opinion with the aim of stimulating civic participation, individual autonomy, national cohesion, and cultural and technological innovation. Congress imposed must-carry provisions on cable operators with the goal of furthering many of those societal interests on a local level. Do you think the FCC's decision to order Cablevision to carry the Kingston, New York,. television signal in *Cablevision v. FCC* is consistent with the FCC's core media policy?

5. In *U.S. v. Southwestern Cable*, 392 U.S. 157 (1968), the U.S. Supreme Court ruled that the FCC had authority to regulate cable TV to protect local broadcast stations mostly because "broadcasting is demonstrably a principal source of information and entertainment for a great part of the Nation's population." Do Americans' changing media consumption patterns give us reason to question one of the core justifications for FCC's regulatory authority over cable TV? See, for example, the findings of the Pew Center Project for Excellence in Journalism's State of the News Media 2011 report at http://stateofthemedia.org/2011/overview-2/key-findings.

ENDNOTES

1. See David Houska. "Indecent Exposure: *FCC v. Fox* and the End of an Era," 7 *Duke Journal of Constitutional Law & Public Policy Sidebar* 193–210(2012); L. A. Powe Jr. "Red Lion and Pacifica: Are They Relics?" 36 *Pepperdine Law Review* 445–462 (2009), http://digitalcommons.pepperdine.edu/plr/vol36/iss2/10; Adam D. Thierer. "Why Regulate Broadcasting? Toward a Consistent First Amendment Standard for the Information Age," 15 *CommLaw Conspectus-Journal of Communications Law and Policy* 431–482 (2008), http://ssrn.com/abstract=1092137; Christopher S. Yoo. "Technologies of Control and the Future of the First Amendment," 53 *William & Mary Law Review* 747 (2011).

2. See Chapter 2 discussion of "The Broadcast Model and the Federal Communication Commission."

3. "A fundamental and longstanding principle of judicial restraint requires that courts avoid reaching constitutional questions in advance of the necessity of deciding them." *Lyng v. Northwest. Indian Cemetery Protective Association*, 485 U.S. 439 (1988).

4. Justice Sonia Sotomayor did not participate because of her involvement with the case when she was a U.S. Second Circuit Court of Appeals judge in New York.

5. *Miami Herald Publishing Co. v. Tornillo*, 418 U.S. 241 (1974).

6. *NBC v. U.S.*, 319 U.S. 190, 211–212 (1943).

7. Commercial Advertisement Loudness Mitigation (CALM) Act (HR 6209).

8. Proceedings of the Fourth National Radio Conference and Recommendations for Regulation of Radio 7 (Nov. 9–11, 1925). Government Printing Office (1926).

9. 47 U.S.C Chapter 4, Radio Act of 1927.

10. *Great Lakes Broadcasting Co.*, 3 FRC Ann. Rep. 32, 33 (1929), affirmed in part and reversed in part, 37 F.2d 993 (D.C. Cir.), certiorari. dismissed, 281 U.S. 706 (1930).

11. *NBC v. U.S.*, 319 U.S. 190, 213 (1943).

12. Ibid. 216–217.

13. Ibid. 226.

14. Stephen Clark. "Conservatives Raise Alarm about Fairness Doctrine in 'Different Garb,'" FoxNews.com, September 2, 2011, http://www.foxnews.com/politics/2011/09/02/conservatives-raise-alarms-about-fairness-doctrine-in-different-garb/

15. *Red Lion Broadcasting v. FCC*, 395 U.S. 367, 385 (1969).

16. Ibid. 393.

17. *Branch v. FCC*, 824 F. 2d 37, 46 (D.C. 1987).

18. *FCC v. League of Women Voters*, 468 U.S. 363, 385 (1982).

19. Jerome Barron. "Access to the Press—A New First Amendment Right," 80 *Harvard Law Review* 1641 (June 1967).

20. *CBS v. DNC*, 412 U. S. 94, 126 (1973).

21. The Media Bureau. "Broadcast Programming: Basic Law and Policy," *The Public and Broadcasting: How to Get the Most from Your Local Station* (July 2008), http://www.fcc.gov/mb/audio/decdoc/public_and_broadcasting.html#_Toc202587539

22. *Galloway v. FCC*, 778 F.2d 16, 20 (D.C. Cir. 1985).

23. *Serafyn v. FCC*, 149 F.3d 1213, 1217 (1998).

24. Request for Comments on the Use of Video News Releases by Broadcast Licensees and Cable Operators, May 11, 2005, MB Docket No. 05–171; FCC 05–84, http://edocket.access.gpo.gov/2005/05–9105.htm

25. *In the Matter of Policies and Rules Concerning Children's Television Programming*, FCC 96–335, ¶4, (1996).

26. "Regulation of Obscenity, Indecency and Profanity," Federal Communications Commission (March 1, 2011), http://www.fcc.gov/eb/oip/

27. See "Obscenity, Indecency & Profanity—Frequently Asked Questions," Federal Communications Commission, http://www.fcc.gov/guides/obscenity-indecency-and-profanity

28. *FCC v. Pacifica Foundation*, 438 U.S. 726, 749–750 (1978).

29. Ibid. 750.

30. Ibid. 748–749.

31. *Action for Children's Television v. FCC (ACT II)*, 932 F.2d 1504, 1506 (D.C. Cir. 1991).

32. Lilli Levi. "First Report: The FCC's Regulation of Indecency," University of Miami Legal Studies Research Paper No. 2007–14 (August 6, 2007), 2, http://ssrn.com/abstract=1023822

33. In the Matter of Complaints Against Various Licensees Regarding their Airing of the "Golden Globe Awards" Program, EB-03- IH-0110, (March 3, 2004) http://transition.fcc.gov/eb/Orders/2004/FCC-04–43A1.html

34. *Fox Television Stations, Inc. v. FCC*, 489 F.3d 444, 455 (2007), quoting *SEC v. Chenery Corp.*, 332 U.S. 194, 196, (1947).

35. *Fox Television Stations, Inc., v. FCC*, 613 F.3d 317, 330 (2d Cir. 2010).

36. *CBS Corp. v. FCC*, 663 F.3d 122 (3d Cir. 2011).

37. *CBS Corp. v. FCC*, 663 F.3d 122 (3d. Cir. 2011) cert. denied, 132 S.Ct. 2677 (2012). http://www.supremecourt.gov/orders/courtorders/062912zr4f6k.pdf

38. *Fox Television Stations, Inc. v. FCC*, 613 F.3d at 326 (2d Cir. 2010).

39. *FCC v. Fox*, 129 S. Ct. 1800, 1822 (2009).

40. *FCC v. Fox Television Stations*, 132 S. Ct. 2307, 2321 (2012).

41. *CBS Corp. v. FCC*, 663 F.3d 122 (3d. Cir. 2011) cert. denied, 132 S.Ct. 2677 (2012).

42. Dave Seyler. "Commissioners Weigh in on Supreme Court Indecency Ruling," *Radio & Television Business Report* (June 21, 2012), http://rbr.com/commissioners-weigh-in-on-supreme-court-indecency-ruling/

43. *In the Matter of Violent Television Programming and Its Impact on Children*, 22 F.C.C. Rcd. 79299 (2007),¶ 45, http://fjallfoss.fcc.gov/edocs_public/attachmatch/FCC-07-50A1.pdf

44. "FCC Biennial Regulatory Review 1998," Federal Communications Commission (March 9, 2001), http://www.fcc.gov/biennial/1998.html

45. *Prometheus Radio Project v. FCC*, 373 F.3d 372, 387 (3d Cir. 2004).

46. Ibid. 387.

47. The FCC said in *Ruggiero v. FCC*, 278 F.3d 1323, 1325 (D.C. Cir. 2002) that "[n]ow…radio service is widely available throughout the country and very little spectrum remains available for new full-powered stations."

48. *Prometheus Radio Project v. FCC*, 652 F.3d 431, 464 (3d Cir. 2011).

49. *Media General v. FCC*, No. 11–691 (2012).

50. *Tribune Co v. FCC*, No. 11–696 (2012).

51. *National Association of Broadcasters v. FCC*, 11–698 (2012).

52. *U.S. v. Southwestern Cable*, 392 U.S. 157, 172 (1968).

53. Ibid. 178.

54. *Caprotti v. Woodstock*, 94 N.Y.2d 73, 76 (N.Y. Ct. App. 1999).

55. *City of Los Angeles v. Preferred*, 476 U.S. 488, 494 (1986).

56. *Turner Broadcasting System v. FCC*, 512 U.S. 622, 637 (1994).

57. Ibid. 652.

58. Ibid. 653.

59. Brief for C-Span as Amicus Curiae Supporting Petitioner, *Cablevision Systems Corp v. FCC*, 570 F.3d 83 (February 23, 2010) (No. 09–901), *2.

60. Ibid. 7.

61. *Cablevision Systems Corporation v. FCC*, 570 F.3d 83, 97 (2009).

62. Ibid.

63. Ibid. 95.

CHAPTER TWELVE

Sexual Expression
& the First Amendment

CONTROVERSY: Had authorities arrested Dwight Edwin Whorley between April 17, 2002, and April 30, 2003, for possession of sexually explicit Japanese anime, chances are he would be a free man today. Anime, or manga, are hand-drawn or computer-animated cartoons featuring characters with highly stylized facial expressions. A variety of the illustrative form exists that features adults having sex with minors. On March 30, 2004, a woman spotted Whorley downloading such images from a computer at the Virginia Employment Office.[1] Whorley had used the Virginia Employment Office computer room, which is often monitored, to access pornography without incident many times before.[2] Whorley believed the cartoons, though sexually explicit, were legal because they did not depict actual children. That defense would have worked under the Child Pornography Prevention Act of 1996 (CPPA). That's because the U.S. Supreme Court ruled in *Ashcroft v. Free Speech Coalition*, 535 U.S. 234 (2002) that sections of CPPA were unconstitutionally overbroad because they would allow the government to ban sexual depictions of minors where no minors were used, such as by computer imaging, or when adult actors were made to look like teenagers. But the federal child pornography law changed. Under The PROTECT Act of 2003 ("Prosecutorial Remedies and Other Tools to end the Exploitation of Children Today"[3]), depictions of minors engaged in sexual explicit conduct can be obscene whether actors are really underaged, digitally created, or drawn using no models. Whorley's text-only emails also were used against him. His conviction was affirmed by the U.S. Court of Appeals for the Fourth Circuit in *U.S. v. Dwight Edwin Whorley*, 550 F.3d 326 (4th Cir. 2008). In 2010, the U.S. Supreme Court rejected Whorley's petition for review.[4]

Chapter's Focus

Few can sympathize with an individual like Whorley, obsessed with communicating and consuming media content about minors engaged in sexual activity. But *Whorley* raises questions about the right of individuals to engage in freedom of thought and expression, and society's interest in policing immoral behavior. Courts in this nation have wrestled with this effort to control such behavior since moral crusader Andrew Comstock's New York Society for Suppression of Vice campaign led to the first federal antipornography law, the Comstock Act, in 1873. The two inconsistent current definitions of child pornography are emblematic of the difficulty courts and legislatures have had for more than 100 years, and the U.S. Supreme Court for nearly 50, in defining obscenity. As U.S. Court of Appeals for the Fourth Circuit Court Judge Roger L. Gregory noted in his dissent in *Whorley*, "The Supreme Court's attempts to define obscenity for over half a century, including its enunciation of differing standards for obscenity and child pornography, reveal one truth: a material's obscenity, or lack thereof, ultimately depends on the subjective view of at least five individuals."[5]

In this chapter we consider the leading cases in the U.S. involving the clash between freedom of expression and society's interest in policing alleged pornography-linked harm and antisocial conduct. This chapter will discuss the societal drive to censor offensiveness that led to the adoption of the *Hicklin* rule in the 1860s and its demise starting in the 1930s; the development of the *Miller* doctrine in the 1970s; the rejection of pornography as a violation of women's civil rights in the 1980s; and finally, the effort to reign in actual and virtual child pornography starting in the 1980s. Note that Chapter 3 covers related material, specifically the 15-year congressional effort to censor the Internet by targeting sexually explicit content starting with *Reno v. ACLU*, 521 U.S. 844 (1997), and tapering off with *Mukasey v. ACLU*, 129 S. Ct. 1032 (2009).

"Comstockery"[6]: When the First Amendment Did Not Matter.

For more than a century, antipornographers have argued that exposure to sexually explicit content causes harm—harm to the emotional and moral stability of those that consume it, harm to the objects of the porn driven to perform depraved acts, and harm to the moral fabric of society. In the post-Civil War era, Comstock identified the contraceptive trade as promoters of immorality and the eponymous federal law criminalized production, distribution, and possession of contraceptive devices and information about them, and much more. The Comstock Act "outlawed any material that a jury believed might offend the sensibilities of the most vulnerable segments of society" leading to the ban of "classic works by such authors as D.H. Lawrence, Theodore Dreiser, Edmund Wilson and James Joyce…Other targets of the Society's crusades included such literary giants as Tolstoy and Balzac."[7] It was easy for a prosecutor to win an obscenity conviction in the post-Civil War era. American courts borrowed a test from the British case *Regina v. Hicklin*, Q.B. 360 (1868), which required a jury to find obscenity when a few passages of a text had a tendency "to deprave the minds of those open to such influences and into whose hands a publication of this character might come."[8]

The Demise of Comstockery and Hicklin

Hicklin remained the leading test of obscenity until U.S. Judge John Woosley's ruling in *U.S. v. One Book Called* Ulysses, 5.Supp. 182 (S.D.N.Y.1933). Woosley created a new obscenity test. In contrast to the *Hicklin* test, an alleged obscene work had to be judged as a whole and not solely on a few offending passages. The work's tendency for arousal must be judged based on the mind of an individual with average sexual instincts, rather than a mind open to immoral influences such as abnormal adults and children. In affirming Woosley's ruling declaring James Joyce's *Ulysses* not obscene, the U.S. Court of Appeals for the Second Circuit made note of the threat obscenity laws pose to artistic creativity:

> Art certainly cannot advance under compulsion to traditional forms, and nothing in such a field is more stifling to progress than limitation of the right to experiment with a new technique. The foolish judgments of Lord Eldon about one hundred years ago, proscribing the works of Byron and Southey, and the finding by the jury under a charge by Lord Denman that the publication of Shelley's 'Queen Mab' was an indictable offense are a warning to all who have to determine the limits of the field within which authors may exercise themselves.[9]

> SUMMARY: After 1868, courts applied the *Hicklin* rule to determine whether sexual and nonsexual materials were obscene. The rule required a trier of fact to hand down a verdict of obscenity based on a few passages of a book if they had a tendency "to deprave the minds of those open to such influences and into whose hands a publication of this character might come." The First Amendment was not a defense and many leading literary works were deemed obscene. A federal judge's ruling in *U.S. v. One Book Called* Ulysses, 5. Supp. 182 (S.D.N.Y.1933), marked a turning point because it departed from the *Hicklin* rule by requiring that a sexually explicit work be judged in its entirety and for its effect on the mind of an individual with average sexual instincts, rather than for the impact a handful of passages might have on a mind open to immoral influences such as abnormal adults and children.

The First Amendment & Sexually Explicit Speech

Under the current First Amendment approach to obscenity, offensiveness to societal norms, not harm, is the chief concern. As U.S. Court of Appeals for the Seventh Circuit Judge Richard Posner declared in *American Amusement Machine Association v. Kendrick*, 244 F.3d 572, 575 (2001), "No proof that obscenity is harmful is required either to defend an obscenity statute against being invalidated on constitutional grounds or to uphold a prosecution for obscenity. Offensiveness is the offense." In 1959, the U.S. Supreme Court handed down its first opinion on obscenity in *U.S. v. Roth*, 354 U.S. 476 (1957), establishing a nationwide standard: "Whether to the average person, applying contemporary standards, the dominant theme of the material taken as a whole appeals to prurient interest." Brennan also declared that obscenity enjoys no protection under the law because it is "utterly without redeeming social importance."

Over the course of the following 16 years, the Court wrestled with its definition of obscenity until it reached a consensus in *Miller v. California*, which rejected the "utterly without redeeming social importance" criterion. Under the *Miller* guidelines, a trier of fact must weigh: (a) "whether the average person, applying contemporary community standards" would find that the work, taken as a whole, appeals to the prurient interest; (b) the work depicts or describes, in a patently offensive way, sexual conduct specifically defined by the applicable state law; and (c) whether the work, taken as a whole, lacks serious literary, artistic, political, or scientific value.

Miller further explained that the contemporary community standards criterion is intended to make certain that the material "will be judged by its impact on an average person, rather than a particularly susceptible or sensitive person—or indeed a totally insensitive one."[10] "Community" is the geographic locale in which the communication is received or where it originates. Soon after, in *Hamling v. U.S.*, 418 U.S. 87, 104 (1974), a case involving obscene material sent via mail, the Court explained that for federal obscenity laws, a juror "is entitled to draw on his own knowledge of the views of the average person in the community or vicinage from which he comes" to determine contemporary community standards.

Contemporary Community Standards in Cyberspace

The *Miller* definition of community standards stems from the characteristics of certain distribution modes—vehicles and the mail system—that allow a publisher to control the destination of its message. In contrast, many Internet-based modes of distribution such as blogging, websites, and message boards do not allow such control. Therefore, many types of Internet publishers cannot tailor their message to avoid the least-tolerant communities. Should the original definition of community standards apply to Internet communications or be redefined? Many defendants and legal scholars have asked that question. In the first such challenge, *U.S. v. Thomas*, 74 F.3d 701, 712 (6thCir. 1996), the defendants argued that a computer bulletin board system, which included email, chat threads, and public messages, required "a new definition of community, i.e., one that is based on the broad-ranging connections among people in cyberspace rather than the geographic locale of the federal judicial district of the criminal trial." But the court ruled that there was no need to develop a new definition to judge the case because the bulletin board operator had knowledge and control over the physical jurisdictions where materials were distributed for downloading or printing. In *Ashcroft v. ACLU*, 535 U.S. 564 (2002), the Court failed to reach a consensus on the appropriate geographic definition of contemporary community standards to be applied for Internet communications. At the same time, a majority of the *Ashcroft* Court held the Child Online Protection Act (COPA)'s use of community standards to identify materials harmful to minors did not offend the First Amendment.

Consequently, the pre-cyberspace definition of "community standards" controls. For example, in *U.S. v. Kilbride*, 584 F.3d 1240, 1255 (9th Cir. 2009), a three-judge panel said, "a national community standard must be applied in regulating obscene speech on the Internet, including obscenity disseminated via email." But it held that the lower court's failure to apply a national community standard was not sufficient reason to reverse the defendant's conviction because "the relevant law in this area was highly unsettled with the extremely fractured opinion in *Ashcroft* providing the best guidance," the court ruled.

In *U.S. v. Stagliano*, 693 F. Supp. 2d 25 (Dist. Ct., Dist. of Columbia, 2010), a federal judge rejected an overbreadth challenge to the application of community standards to charges stemming from sending an obscene movie trailer over the Internet in a way that minors could access it. Citing *Ashcroft v. ACLU*, the judge ruled, "If COPA's incorporation of community standards did not *by itself* render that statute substantially overbroad, then the obscenity statutes' incorporation of community standards does not—standing alone—render those statutes substantially overbroad."[11]

Obscenity Defined as Speech Subordinating Women

In the wake of *American Booksellers v. Hudnut*, 771 F.2d 323 (7th Cir. 1985), a ruling affirmed by the U.S. Supreme Court, a crusade to win women the right to sue publishers for pornography-linked violence against women was mortally wounded. According to its feminist advocates, led by attorney Catherine MacKinnon and author Andrea Dworkin, pornography, as opposed to erotica, is a form of hate speech that perpetuates the subordination of women and violence against them, including rape. So, MacKinnon and Dworkin campaigned to get lawmakers to adopt a law providing civil remedies for actresses harmed in the making of pornography, or women harmed by men who were supposedly influenced by exposure to pornography, including monetary damages and publication bans for provable harm. They drafted such a law for Minneapolis, Minnesota. The Minneapolis mayor vetoed it. The Indianapolis City Council passed a similar ordinance. The Seventh Circuit struck it down because it allowed government to choose a preferred viewpoint: "Speech treating women in the approved way—in sexual encounters 'premised on equality'...is lawful no matter how sexually explicit. Speech treating women in the disapproved way—as submissive in matters sexual or as enjoying humiliation—is unlawful no matter how significant the literary, artistic, or political qualities of the work taken as a whole...The Constitution forbids the state to declare one perspective right and silence opponents."[12]

> SUMMARY: *Miller v. California*, 413 U.S. 15 (1973), established the current test for obscenity: (a) whether "the average person, applying contemporary community standards" would find that the work, taken as a whole, appeals to the prurient interest; (b) whether the work depicts or describes, in a patently offensive way, sexual conduct specifically defined by the applicable state law; and (c) whether the work, taken as a whole, lacks serious literary, artistic, political, or scientific value. Many, however, question whether "the average person, applying contemporary community standards" prong of the test should be applied to Internet modes of communication such as blogging, websites, and message boards that do not allow a publisher to send its message selectively to avoid sexually conservative and intolerant communities. In *Ashcroft v. ACLU*, 535 U.S.564 (2002), a majority held that the Child Online Protection Act (COPA)'s use of community standards to identify materials harmful to minors did not offend the First Amendment. Consequently, the *Miller* community standards definition still applies to the Internet—obscenity may be judged by the standards of the community where the message originated or where it was received. Meanwhile, feminist efforts to redefine obscenity as a way to win women the right to sue publishers for pornography-linked violence against women was rejected in *American Booksellers v. Hudnut*.

Child Pornography as a Separate Category of Unprotected Speech

Starting with *New York v. Ferber*, 458 U.S. 747 (1982), the Court recognized an exception to the rule that sexually explicit speech is legal until deemed obscene. The exception is child pornography, which was initially defined as sexually explicit visual depictions in which actual minors are used as models or actors. In *Ferber*, the court said the justification for the exception is that government has a compelling interest in protecting minors from sexual abuse. Thus, under *Ferber*, a defendant merely in possession of child pornography, distinct from the distribution, may face prison time. In contrast, government may not criminalize the mere possession of obscene materials depicting adults, the Court ruled in *Osborne v. Ohio*, 495 U.S. 103 (1990).

Ferber placed the production, sale, and possession of child pornography outside the First Amendment's protection. As the *Ferber* Court noted, New York's child pornography ban was part of a nationwide trend, as "the Federal Government and 47 States…sought to combat the problem with statutes specifically directed at the production of child pornography."[13] The *Ferber* Court justified its departure from *Miller* based on (i) a state's compelling interest in protecting minors; (ii) the "intrinsic" link between child pornography and the exploitation of children used in the production of the materials; (iii) the negligible artistic and literary value of child pornography; (iv) precedent that allows the Court to classify certain kinds of speech as unprotected; and (v) elimination of an economic motive for child pornography.

Here is how the *Ferber* child pornography test differs from *Miller*'s. Under *Ferber*, "[a] trier of fact need not find that the material appeals to the prurient interest of the average person; it is not required that sexual conduct portrayed be done so in a patently offensive manner; and the material at issue need not be considered as a whole."[14] The Court, however, said that child pornography was "limited to works that *visually* depict sexual conduct by children below a specified age."[15]

Child pornography can be treated differently under the law than any other sexually explicit content because of the state's interest in protecting minors from exploitation when used as models, the Ferber court explained. But the Child Pornography Prevention Act of 1996 (CPPA) extended the federal child pornography ban to prohibit, under § 2256(8)(B), "any visual depiction, including any photograph, film, video, picture, or computer or computer-generated image or picture," and under §2256(8)(D) "is, or appears to be, of a minor engaging in sexually explicit conduct." The Free Speech Coalition, the trade association for the adult entertainment industry, and others, challenged CPPA. The statute's reach was too broad, they contended, because it would, for example, allow juries to convict if they believed a porn actor appeared to be a minor.

As noted at the outset of this chapter, the Court in *Free Speech Coalition* struck down § 2256(8)(B) and §2256(8)(D) of the CPPA as unconstitutionally overbroad. The Court identified a number of historical and contemporary literary works that deal with teenage sexual activity and the sexual abuse of children, among them the play *Romeo and Juliet* and the film *American Beauty*, which could be banned under the CPPA provisions: "The CPPA prohibits speech despite its serious literary, artistic, political, or scientific value. The statute proscribes the visual depiction of an idea—that of teenagers engaging in sexual activity—that is a fact of modern society and has been a theme in art and literature throughout the ages."[16] The Court found that government could only criminalize the receipt, possession, and distribution of images that were obscene and involving actual minors.

After *Free Speech Coalition*, Congress produced The PROTECT Act of 2003, which targets material "that reflects the belief, or that is intended to cause another to believe" that the material is "an obscene visual depiction of a minor engaging in sexually explicit conduct; or a visual depiction of an actual minor engaging in sexually explicit conduct." No real adults are required. Under the act, it is sufficient that the material depicts minors engaging in sexually explicit conduct and that the depictions are obscene. The PROTECT Act also amended a portion of the CPPA, 18 U.S.C § 2252A, to provide that any person who either "knowingly possesses, or knowingly accesses with intent to view any book, magazine, periodical, film, videotape, computer disk, or any other material that contains an image of child pornography" is subject to criminal penalties.

Dwight Edwin Whorley, convicted for receiving and possessing sexual explicit cartoon depictions of children, made three unsuccessful arguments challenging the act's constitutionality. He contended that based on *Ferber* and *Free Speech Coalition*, visual depictions of minors have to be of actual minors. But the Fourth Circuit rejected his argument with rather dubious logic: "Thus, regardless of whether § 1466A(a)(1) requires an actual minor, it is nonetheless a valid restriction on *obscene speech* under *Miller,* not a restriction on non-obscene pornography of the type permitted by *Ferber.*"[17]

Whorley argued that the act's use of the word "receive" was impermissibly vague because it would ensnare innocent recipients of obscene emails and pop-up ads. The court acknowledged that possibility, but said that a trier would have to determine what constituted "knowing" receipt. Finally, the court rejected his contention that email texts are not visual depictions and therefore are not covered by the act. Citing *Miller,* the court said, "Obscenity can, of course, manifest itself in conduct, in the pictorial representation of conduct, or in the written and oral description of conduct."[18]

In *U.S. v. Williams,* 128 S. Ct. 1830, 1837 (2008), the Court ruled that the PROTECT Act's soliciting and pandering provision did not violate the First Amendment partly because the "emergence of new technology and the repeated retransmission of picture files over the Internet could make it nearly impossible to prove that a particular image was produced using real children . . ." The Court in *U.S. v. Williams* ruled that criminalizing offers to sell fake child pornography was not impermissibly overboard or vague. Thus, "offers to provide or requests to obtain child pornography" fall outside the First Amendment's protection.[19] But dissenting judges David Souter and Ruth Bader Ginsburg voiced a view held by many: The PROTECT Act and the majority's sanction of it undermine *Ferber* and *Free Speech Coalition*'s protection of virtual or fake child pornography by allowing the government to criminalize propositions to buy and sell such images rather than ban the images themselves.

Within three months of *U.S. v. Williams,* a defendant, Christopher Handley, charged under the act for receipt, possession, and mailing of books of manga children sex cartoons, sought to have the charges dropped based on a First Amendment defense. A federal judge dismissed only one of the charges brought against Handley, ruling that the PROTECT Act Sections 1466A(a)(2) and (b)(2) failed to require a finding of obscenity based on the *Miller* test.[20] Other subsections of the act, however, did make such a requirement, and in 2010 Handley, who pleaded guilty, was sentenced to serve six months in prison. Despite the PROTECT Act's departure from the limitations imposed by *Ferber* and *Free Speech Coalition,* by mid-2012 no federal appeals court had strayed from *Williams.*[21]

"Receiving and Possessing." In an apparently novel but narrow ruling, the New York Court of Appeals said individuals in New York State can view still or moving images of child pornography just as long as they do not download, print, or distribute them. In *People v. James D. Kent,* 2012 NY Slip Op 03572 (N.Y. Ct. App. May 8, 2012), the state's highest court held that the mere viewing of child pornography on a computer is insufficient evidence to convict under the state's Promoting a Sexual Performance by a Child Possessing a Sexual Performance by a Child law. The ruling reversed the conviction of James Kent, a former professor at Marist College whose computer was found to contain pornographic images in 2007, on the two counts of obtaining the material, but upheld 133 counts of possessing child pornography. Evidence showed that he might have been searching the Web for child pornography for a possible research project. Kent won reversal on those two counts because the only evidence to show that he had visited a particular child porn site was contained in his computer's cache function. A web browser automatically saves the contents of visited webpages, and stores them in a cache, so the pages load faster when revisited. The court held that files stored in a computer cache function may constitute evidence of viewing, but to establish "possession" under the state law, a defendant's conduct must exceed mere viewing.

The ruling's effect on the interpretation of the PROTECT Act was expected to be marginal. That is because the New York court interpreted the reach of a New York state child pornography statute, passed before the advent of the Web. The statute did not have language comparable to the amended

18 U.S.C. § 2252A's "knowingly *accesses* with *intent to view* [emphasis added] any book, magazine, periodical, film, videotape, computer disk, or any other material that contains an image of child pornography." Such language criminalizes viewing child pornography via the Web regardless of whether the viewer downloads, prints, or distributes the material. In contrast, the New York statute criminalized "possession" and "control" of child pornography.

Moreover, as of mid-2012, four federal circuits upheld convictions for the viewing of child pornography stored in temporary Internet files pursuant to the 2008 amended version of the law: *U.S. v. Ramos*, No. 10–4802-cr (July 2, 2012); *U.S. v. Pruitt*, 638 F.3d 763 (11th Cir. 2011); *U.S. v. Kain*, 589 F.3d 945 (8th Cir. 2009); and *U.S. v. Bass*, 411 F.3d 1198 (10th Cir. 2005). The courts said that such viewing of child pornography amounted to knowingly receiving and possessing child pornography under 18 U.S.C. §2252A.

Ex-professor Kent claimed he was conducting research, but he did not make the argument that viewing child pornography for the purpose of producing a literary or nonfiction work should be a defense against a charge of receiving or possessing child pornography. Others have, and judges have rejected such a defense. One theory claims that such research is protected under the *Miller* standard of "serious literary works." Under *Miller*, "serious literary works" cannot be obscene. Citing *U.S. v. Matthews*, 209 F.3d 338 (2000), a federal judge in Maryland ruled that "the Fourth Circuit has…firmly established, in accordance with the Supreme Court, that the First Amendment affords no protection to child pornography offenses, regardless of the motivations of the possessor."[22]

The other theory is motive; that merely investigating child pornography is a good motive and a defense against such a charge. But a three-judge panel in *U.S. v. Fox*, 248 F.3d 394, 408 (5th Cir. 2001), ruled that such an argument "seriously mischaracterizes the statute's scienter element: The government must prove that the defendant *knowingly*, i.e., voluntarily and intentionally, received child pornography, not that he had some degree of *mens rea.*"

Decriminalizing Sexting. Under state or federal law, a child pornography conviction exacts a tough penalty. Those convicted under § 2252A(a)(3)(B) of the PROTECT Act face a minimum sentence of five years imprisonment and a maximum of 20 years. Also, those convicted of possession, sale, and distribution of child pornography under federal and state laws typically are branded as sexual offenders, subject to tracking by sexual offender registries.

What about minors engaging in sexting, who send sexually explicit images of themselves to others? Should a minor who sends nude images of herself via cell phone or over the Internet and the minor or who receives the image serve prison time? Should the minor have to wear the mark of "sexual offender" for 20 years, a status that anyone in the world can learn about via the Web? Consider Phillip Alpert's case.

A search for "Phillip Alpert sex offender," for example, leads to a page that shows Alpert's photo and offense.[23] He was convicted as a minor for transmitting child pornography under Florida law in 2008. He didn't have to serve five years in prison; he was sentenced to five years of probation. He is, however, a registered sex offender, a status he carries until age 43.

Here is Albert's crime. For a while, his romantic relationship with a sixteen-year-old was going fine. He was 18. She sent him nude photos of herself. But then the relationship soured and they broke up. He became so angry over the breakup that he sent the nude photos to more than 70 people, including adults and her parents.

> It was 3:28 in the morning, I think it was, and I got up and I went to my computer, and I sent a couple of pictures that she had sent to me to her contact list. And I went back to sleep…I was barely awake when I

did it and I didn't even remember and…then a few days later, my mother called and says, 'Why are there police officers at the house?' I went—'Oh no!' And it came back the same way a dream does.[24]

Surveys have found that as little as 7% or as many as 20% of U.S. teenagers have received nude or semi-nude photographs of other teenagers.[25] But many believe that foolish and impulsive minors should not be treated like pedophiles and pornographers, who share or profit from child pornography. Besides, where is the exploitation of children by adults when a teenager sends his or her own nude image to other teenagers? Increasingly, state legislatures have decided that sexting does not necessarily equal child pornography and have passed laws to shield sexting minors from punishment imposed under child pornography laws. As of July 2012, 19 states, including Florida, have passed laws to address youth sexting.[26]

Unfortunately, Albert will not be able to benefit from Florida 847.0141, a statute that decriminalizes youthful sexting. Under the bill, passed in 2011, sexting by minors is a misdemeanor and first time offenders can be sentenced to eight hours of community service, or a $60 fine, and possibly training and instruction. The second sexting offense, a first degree misdemeanor, is punishable by a jail term of not more than one year and may include a fine of not more than $1,000. The third such offense, a third degree felony, is punishable by imprisonment not exceeding five years and may include a fine not exceeding $5,000.

SUMMARY: In *New York v. Ferber*, 458 U.S. 747 (1982), the Court carved out an exception from *Miller* by allowing states to pass laws banning the possession and sale of depictions of actual minors engaged in sexual acts without having to find such materials obscene. The New York law in question was premised on stopping the sexual exploitation of children used in the child porn trade. Consistent with that standard, the Court struck down a federal child porn ban—Child Pornography Prevention Act of 1996 (CPPA)—in *Ashcroft v. Free Speech Coalition*, 535 U.S. 234 (2002), as unconstitutionally overbroad because it allowed the government to ban sexual depictions of minors where no minors were used, such as by computer imaging, or when adult actors were made to look like teenagers. The Court, however, upheld Congress's response—The PROTECT Act of 2003—in *U.S. v. Williams*, 128 S. Ct. 1830, 1837 (2008). The PROTECT Act criminalizes the possession, sale, distribution, and receipt of "virtual child porn"—depictions and text-only emails, according to *U.S. v. Dwight Edwin Whorley*, 550 F.3d 326 (2008)—of minors engaged in sexual acts *regardless* of whether actual human beings are used as models or actors when the material also is found to be obscene by a judge or jury.

U.S. Supreme Court: "Violence Is Not Obscenity"

Over the years, legal scholars have argued that the First Amendment should not protect depictions of violence. Michigan State University College of Law Professor Kevin W. Saunders, the author of *Violence as Obscenity* and *Saving Our Children from the First Amendment*, is a leading voice of the violence-is-obscenity movement. "Our focus on language with a possible sexual connotation or with body parts has diverted our attention," Saunders told the *New York Times*.[27] "It is a regular media diet of murder and mayhem that harms children. It makes them believe the world is a more dangerous place than it is and, according to the leading organizations of health professionals, leads to real world violence. But that seems to raise little concern on the part of most."

Karen E. Dill is one of the health professionals arguing that certain types of extreme depictions of violence should be deemed obscene. Social psychologist Dill testified before Congress on media violence in 2000 and was one of a dozen pediatricians and psychologists who filed an amicus brief in *Brown v. Entertainment Merchant Association*, 131 S. Ct. 2729 (2011), in support of California's position that the First Amendment allowed it to ban the sale of violent video games to minors. "[I]s there any level of violence that you would consider obscene?" Dill asked rhetorically in a *Psychology Today* opinion piece.[28] She continues, "For me, the answer to those questions is easy. The answer is yes. If you cannot imagine a violent video game that is too extreme to sell to children, I refer you to…the game RapeLay—a game that glorifies the crime of rape as well as psychological torture."[29]

Several states have sought to limit access to violent content without success. In *Video Software Dealers Association v. Weber*, 968 F.2d 684 (8th Cir. 1992), the U.S. Court of Appeals for the Eighth Circuit struck down a Missouri statute that prohibited the rental or sale of violent videos to minors and required video dealers to display or maintain the videos in a separate area within their stores. The court said the state had to show that the statute met strict scrutiny, that it was narrowly drawn to advance a compelling governmental interest, and that its means were carefully tailored to achieve that purpose. The court also rejected the argument that violence is obscene: "Material that contains violence but not depictions or descriptions of sexual conduct cannot be obscene."[30]

In *Davis-Kidd Booksellers, Inc. v. McWhorter*, 866 S.W.2d 520 (Tenn. Sup. Ct. 1993), the Tennessee Supreme Court ruled the term "excessive violence" in a law regulating distribution and display of materials allegedly harmful to minors was unconstitutionally vague.

The Sixth Circuit declined "to extend [its] obscenity jurisprudence to violent, instead of sexually explicit, material," in *James v. Meow Media, Inc.*, 300 F.3d 683, 698 (6th Cir. 2002).

In *American Amusement Machine Association v. Kendrick*, 244 F.3d 572, 574–75 (7th Cir. 2001), cert. denied, 534 U.S. 994 (2001), the Seventh Circuit imposed a preliminary injunction on an Indianapolis ordinance that sought to limit minors' access to video games that depict violence. "The notion of forbidding not violence itself, but pictures of violence, is a novelty, whereas concern with pictures of graphic sexual conduct is of the essence of the traditional concern with obscenity,"[31] the court said.

As the recitation above indicates, state, and federal courts have rejected the argument that depictions or descriptions of violence can be banned under an obscenity theory. Precedent binds these courts; consequently, their reluctance to create new law is not surprising.

The U.S. Supreme Court struck down as vague a New York criminal statute banning "any book, pamphlet, magazine, newspaper or other printed paper devoted to the publication, and principally made up of criminal news, police reports, or accounts of criminal deeds, or pictures, or stories of deeds of bloodshed, lust or crime" as obscene in *Winters v. New York*, 333 U.S. 507, 508 (1948).

The *Winters v. New York* ruling, however, predates about a half-century of rulings in which the Court established categories of speech unprotected by the First Amendment: fighting words, in *Chaplinsky v. New Hampshire*, 315 U.S. 568 (1942); true threats, in *Watts v. U.S.*, 394 U.S. 705 (1969); incitement, in *Brandenburg v. Ohio*, 395 U.S. 444 (1969); obscenity, in *U.S. v. Roth*, 354 U.S. 476 (1957); child pornography, in *New York v. Ferber*, 458 U.S. 747 (1982); and "offers to provide or requests to obtain child pornography," in *U.S. v. Williams*, 128 S. Ct. 1830, 1842 (2008). Thus, it would seem that the Court had established grounds for recognizing new categories of unprotected speech.

That is what the U.S. government contended when it argued in *U.S. v. Stevens*, 130 S. Ct. 1577, 1585 (2010) that, "'depictions of animal cruelty' should be added to the list...depictions of 'illegal acts of animal cruelty' that are 'made, sold, or possessed for commercial gain' necessarily 'lack expressive value,' and may accordingly 'be regulated as *unprotected* speech.'" *U.S. v. Stevens* stemmed from the conviction of Robert Stevens for selling videos of illegal dog fighting under 18 U.S.C. Section 48, which criminalizes the commercial creation, sale, or possession of certain depictions of animal cruelty.

But Chief Justice John Roberts, writing for the majority, rejected the government's argument. First Amendment doctrine does not, Roberts said, allow the Court to create categories of unprotected speech based solely on a finding that the speech lacks expressive value and avoid the heightened scrutiny to which content-based regulation is ordinarily subject under the First Amendment. He used *New York v. Ferber* as an example: "*Ferber* thus grounded its analysis in a previously recognized, long-established category of unprotected speech, and our subsequent decisions have shared this understanding."[32]

Now, it would appear that *Brown v. Entertainment Merchants Association*, 131 S. Ct. 2729 (2011) has derailed further attempts to persuade the Court that some types of depictions and descriptions of violence should be treated under the First Amendment exactly like some types of depictions and descriptions of sex. In its 7–2 ruling, the Court struck down a California law that banned the sale or rental of violent games to minors. Video games qualify for First Amendment protection, as does violent content, the Court ruled. Consequently, the California statute, which imposed a restriction on content of protected speech, had to pass strict scrutiny. It failed to do so because California could not show a "direct causal link between violent video games and harm to minors."[33]

Writing for the majority, Justice Antonin Scalia, citing *U.S. v. Stevens* as controlling, emphatically stated, "speech about violence is not obscene."[34] He elaborated:

> Certainly the *books* we give children to read—or read to them when they are younger—contain no shortage of gore. Grimm's Fairy Tales, for example, are grim indeed. As her just deserts for trying to poison Snow White, the wicked queen is made to dance in red hot slippers 'till she fell dead on the floor, a sad example of envy and jealousy...' Cinderella's evil stepsisters have their eyes pecked out by doves...And Hansel and Gretel (children!) kill their captor by baking her in an oven...High-school reading lists are full of similar fare. Homer's Odysseus blinds Polyphemus the Cyclops by grinding out his eye with a heated stake...('Even so did we seize the fiery-pointed brand and whirled it round in his eye, and the blood flowed about the heated bar. And the breath of the flame singed his eyelids and brows all about, as the ball of the eye burnt away, and the roots thereof crackled in the flame'). In the *Inferno*, Dante and Virgil watch corrupt politicians struggle to stay submerged beneath a lake of boiling pitch, lest they be skewered by devils above the surface...And Golding's *Lord of the Flies* recounts how a schoolboy called Piggy is savagely murdered *by other children* while marooned on an island.[35]

Scalia also discounted the significance of the findings of Craig Anderson and, by implication, his co-author Karen E. Dill:

> They do not prove that violent video games *cause* minors to *act* aggressively (which would at least be a beginning). Instead, '[n]early all of the research is based on correlation, not evidence of causation, and most of the studies suffer from significant, admitted flaws in methodology'...They show at best some correlation between exposure to violent entertainment and minuscule real-world effects, such as children's feeling more aggressive or making louder noises in the few minutes after playing a violent game than after playing a nonviolent game.[36]

The Court may never allow states to relegate violent content to the ashbin of unprotected speech. But in his concurrence, Justice Alito left open the possibility that a properly drawn statute limiting minors' access to extremely violent video games could pass Constitutional scrutiny:

> …I would hold only that the particular law at issue here fails to provide the clear notice that the Constitution requires. I would not squelch legislative efforts to deal with what is perceived by some to be a significant and developing social problem. If differently framed statutes are enacted by the States or by the Federal Government, we can consider the constitutionality of those laws when cases challenging them are presented to us.[37]

Meanwhile, the results of a national telephone poll of registered voters conducted by the Fairleigh Dickinson University's PublicMind™ soon after *Brown v. Entertainment Merchants*, revealed support for states regulating the sale of violent video games to minors. Four of seven voters (57%) said states should have the right to protect individuals under 18 from violent video content, just as states now have the right to prevent minors from buying cigarettes, alcohol, and pornography. Thirty-nine percent, however, said states should leave such decisions up to parents.[38]

SUMMARY: According to the Media Education Foundation, the average 18-year-old American will have watched 200,000 acts of violence and 16,000 murders on television. About 90% of U.S. kids ages 8 to 16 spend about 13 hours a week playing video games, and at least one study shows that those children are more aggressive than their peers who do not play video games. Such statistics have spurred social behaviorists, legal scholars, children's advocacy groups, and legislators to support legislation that treats extreme violence as obscenity, that is, speech unprotected by the First Amendment. But state and lower federal courts have consistently rejected that concept, as did the U.S. Supreme Court in *U.S. v. Stevens* in 2010 and *Brown v. Entertainment Merchants* in 2011. Justice Scalia said it succinctly in *Brown v. Entertainment Merchants*, "speech about violence is not obscene."

ONLINE RESOURCES

1. "Fact Sheet on Sex and Censorship," The Free Expression Policy Project, http://www.fep project.org/factsheets/sexandcensorship.html
2. "Issues—Violence in the Media," The Free Expression Policy Project, http://www.fep-project.org/issues/violence.html
3. "Media Violence," National Center for Children Exposed to Violence, http://www.nccev.org/violence/media.html
4. "Selected U.S. Supreme Court Obscenity Decisions," http://www.findlaw.com/01topics/06constitutional/cases.html
5. "A Conversation with Catherine MacKinnon," Think Tank, http://www.pbs.org/think-tank/transcript215.html

QUESTIONS

1. The 2–1 ruling in *U.S. v. Dwight Edwin Whorley*, 550 F.3d 326, 330 (2008), held that the PROTECT Act covered text-only emails. Does it follow that the novel *Lolita* could be

banned as child pornography under the PROTECT Act? What about the movie version? Read the transcript and hear the oral argument[39] before the Court in *U.S. v. Williams*, No. 06–694 (2007), where such questions were raised.

2. Whorley was searching for cartoon depictions of children engaged in sexual acts to satisfy his fantasy. Did the law violate his right to freedom of thought? Consider that the Court in *Stanley v. Georgia*, 394 U.S. 557, 566 (1969), said, government "cannot constitutionally premise legislation on the desirability of controlling a person's private thoughts." In his dissent in *Whorley*, Judge Gregory said, "Today, under the guise of suppressing obscenity—whatever meaning that term may encompass—we have provided the government with the power to roll back our previously inviolable right to use our imaginations to create fantasies. It is precisely this unencumbered ability to fantasize that has allowed this nation to reap the benefits of great literary insight and scientific invention."

3. Based on *U.S. v. Thomas*, 74 F.3d 701, 712 (6th Cir. 1996), discussed above, do you think Facebook users require a new definition of community standards, i.e., one that is based on the "broad-ranging connections among people in cyberspace rather than the geographic locale of the federal judicial district of the criminal trial"?

4. One of the reasons attempts such as the antiporn feminist crusade and the violence-as-obscenity argument failed to pass constitutional scrutiny is that under current obscenity doctrine "offensiveness is the offense," as Judge Posner said when he struck down an Indianapolis ordinance that sought to limit the access of minors to video games that depict graphic violence to protect them from harm in *American Amusement Machine Association v. Kendrick*, 244 F.3d 572, 575 (2001). Even if the Court were to consider weighing the harm sexually explicit content or graphic violence in the media might cause, is there definitive scientific data to support such a link? See, for example, "The Effects of Pornography: An International Perspective," by Milton Diamond.[40]

5. Are videos featuring the intentional torture and killing of helpless animals, including cats, dogs, monkeys, mice, and hamsters, analogous to videos showing minors engaged in sexual activities? The latter are not protected under the First Amendment and criminalized under the PROTECT Act. The U.S. Supreme Court, however, declined to rule on "whether a statute limited to crush videos or other depictions of extreme animal cruelty would be constitutional" and, instead, struck down the statute as substantially overbroad in *U.S. v. Stevens*, 130 S. Ct. 1577, 1592 (2010).

ENDNOTES

1. *U.S. v. Dwight Edwin Whorley*, 550 F.3d 326, 330 (2008).
2. Ibid.
3. The PROTECT Act of 2003, Pub.L. No. 108–21, § 504, 117 Stat. 650, 680–82 (2003), criminalizes the possession, sale, distribution, and receipt of specific sexually explicit visual representations of minors.
4. *Whorley v. U.S.*, 130 S. Ct. 1052 (2010).
5. *U.S. v. Whorley*, 550 F.3d at 346.
6. "The term 'Comstockery,' coined by George Bernard Shaw, refers to overzealous moralizing like that of Anthony Comstock, whose Society for the Suppression of Vice censored literature in America for more than sixty years." RobertCorn-Revere. "New Age Comstockery."4 *The Catholic University of America Commlaw Conspectus* 173 (Summer, 1996).
7. Ibid.
8. *U.S. v. One Book Entitled* Ulysses, 72 F.2d 705, 708 (2d Cir. 1934).

9. Ibid.

10. *Miller v. California*, 413 U.S. at 33.

11. *U.S. v. Stagliano*, 693 F. Supp. 2d 25, 32 (Dist. Ct., Dist. of Columbia, 2010).

12. *American Booksellers v. Hudnut*, 771 F.2d 323, 325 (7th Cir. 1985).

13. *N.Y. v. Ferber*, 458 U.S. 747, 749 (1982).

14. Ibid. at 764.

15. Ibid.

16. *Ashcroft v. Free Speech Coalition*, 535 U.S. 234, 246–247 (2002).

17. *U.S. v. Dwight Edwin Whorley*, 550 F.3d at 337.

18. Ibid, 335.

19. *U.S. v. Williams*, 128 S. Ct. 1830, 1842 (2008).

20. *U.S. v. Handley*, 564 F. Supp. 2d 996 (2008).

21. See: *U.S. v. Handley* 564 F. Supp. 2d 996 (2008); *U.S. v. Hotaling*, No. 09–3935-cr. (2d Cir. Feb. 2011); *U.S. v. Furman*, No. 09–16133 (11th Cir. March 16, 2011).

22. *U.S. v. Charles Johnson*, No. AW-11-552 (Dist. Court, D, Md. 2012.)

23. "Phillip Michael Alper," Florida Department of Law Enforcement, http://offender.fdle.state.fl.us/offender/flyer.do?personId=60516

24. Vicki Mabrey and David Perozzi. "'Sexting': Should Child Pornography Laws Apply?" ABC *Nightline*, (April 1, 2010), http://abcnews.go.com/Nightline/phillip-alpert-sexting-teen-child-porn/story?id=10252790#.T_xhnXZQono

25. Kim Painter. "Sexting among Teens Lower Than Thought," *USA Today* (December 5, 2011), http://www.usatoday.com/news/health/wellness/teen-ya/story/2011–12–05/Sexting-numbers-among-teens-lower-than-thought/51643910/1

26. National Conference of State Legislatures. "2012 *Sexting* Legislation," (July 9, 2012), http://www.ncsl.org/issues-research/telecom/sexting-legislation-2012.aspx

27. Kevin W. Saunders. "It's the Violence!" *New York Times* (July 27, 2010), http://www.nytimes.com/roomfordebate/2010/7/18/decency-rules-on-network-tv-versus-cable/the-fcc-should-shield-children-from-violence. See also Kevin W. Saunders. "Media Violence and the Obscenity Exception to the First Amendment," 3 *William & Mary Bill of Rights Journal* 107 (1994), http://scholarship.law.wm.edu/wmborj/vol3/iss1/4

28. Karen E. Dill. "Sex Is Too Obscene for Kids, but Violence Isn't? *Brown v. Entertainment Merchants*," *Psychology Today* (June 27, 2011), http://www.psychologytoday.com/blog/how-fantasy-becomes-reality/201106/sex-is-too-obscene-kids-violence-isnt-brown-v-entertainment

29. Ibid.

30. *Video Software Dealers Association v. Webster*, 968 F.2d 684, 688 (8th Cir. 1992).

31. *American Amusement Machine Association v. Kendrick*, 244 F.3d 572, 575–576 (7th Cir. 2001).

32. *U.S. v. Stevens*, 130 S. Ct. 1577, 1585, 1586 (2010).

33. *Brown v. Entertainment Merchants Association*, 131 S. Ct. 2729, 2738 (2011).

34. Ibid. at 2735.

35. Ibid. at 2736–2737.

36. Ibid. at 2739.

37. Ibid. at 2751.

38. "U.S. Public Says Regulate Violent Video Games, the Focus of *Brown v. Entertainment Merchants*," [Press release] Fairleigh Dickinson University's PublicMind™ Poll (June 6, 2011), http://publicmind.fdu.edu/2011/vmerchants/final.pdf

39. *U.S. v. Williams*, No. 06–694 (2007), Transcript and Oral Arguments, http://www.oyez.org/cases/2000–2009/2007/2007_06_694/argument

40. Milton Diamond. The Effects of Pornography: An International Perspective," http://www2.hu-berlin.de/sexology/BIB/DIAM/effects_pornography.htm

CHAPTER THIRTEEN

Copyright Law

CONTROVERSY: Do superheroes really have super powers? Yes, if you consider making tons of money a super feat. Marvel Entertainment, the company that created Spider-Man, the Fantastic 4, the X-Men, and Iron Man, is worth about $4 billion. Now, imagine if your dad co-created many of those comic-book-heroes-turned-Hollywood-box-office-stars, and Marvel didn't cut your father a share of the blockbuster profits. Would you need a super weapon to get the money due your father? No, just everyday copyright law.

In 2010, the heirs of comic book artist Jack Kirby sued Marvel and Disney, its owner, in federal court in Los Angeles. They wanted to regain copyrights to some of Kirby's artistic creations that helped make the comic book company a pop culture phenomenon by turning its print-based fictional characters to big screen stars. The family wanted about 88% of Marvel's big screen earnings. Pop culture fans know that Kirby was a creative force at Marvel. That's not disputed. The case turns on Kirby's employment status. Was he an independent contractor, as his heirs claim, or merely a freelancer as Marvel argues? Under the Copyright Act's "works made for hire" provision, the Kirbys will lose their lawsuit if a judge rules that their father was a freelancer.

In July 2011, a federal judge in New York ruled for Marvel. But the Kirbys have intellectual property lawyer Marc Toberoff in their corner, the so-called legal man of steel who won copyright battles for the heirs of Superman creators Joe Shuster and Jerry Siegel. The Kirbys were expected to appeal the summary judgment ruling to the U.S. Court of Appeals for the Second Circuit in New York.

Chapter's Scope

This chapter examines the key sections of Title 17 of the U.S. Code covering copyright holder's rights, including the right to bring an infringement claim, and the court-made merger and substantial similarity doctrines that are used to determine whether impermissible copying has occurred. The major defenses, or limitations on a holder's exclusive rights, are discussed, with particular emphasis on the fair use doctrine . Fair use is one of the most important checks on a copyright holder's right to stop others from using copyrighted material. It allows unauthorized use of copyrighted material based on the belief that everyone should be able to discuss and criticize copyrighted materials and quote from them or use portions of the content.

Courts have also applied the fair use doctrine to allow the use of new copying technologies that threaten a copyright holder's ability to prevent others from making copies of portions of or entire works. For example, in *Sony Corp. of America v. Universal City Studios, Inc.*, 464 U.S. 417 (1984), the U.S. Supreme Court ruled that Sony's Betamax video tape recording device, which allowed anyone to make a complete copy of a television show, was a fair use. But the Betamax device was analog technology, and nothing copies quite as well as digital copy technologies.

Consequently, the advent of digital technologies in the 21st century—DVRs, MP3 audio devices, Google's search engines and Google Books project, and YouTube—has led to a flood of infringement cases in which the fair use doctrine proved pivotal, or promises to. Chapter 14 continues this discussion of copyright law, focusing on the efforts by the courts and Congress to resolve conflicts over new technologies that facilitate copying, existing copyright laws, and the fair use doctrine.

Copyright's Importance

You were introduced to copyright law in Chapter 2. There, you learned about its origins, how the idea that the law should protect an author's right to control the copying of his expression is nearly a thousand-years-old. You learned that the Constitution's framers wrote Article I, § 8, the Copyright Clause, of the U.S. Constitution, which authorizes Congress to "promote the Progress of Science and useful Arts, by securing for limited Times to Authors and Inventors the exclusive Right to their respective Writings and Discoveries."[1] The clause, often referred to as the Copyright Clause, also covers patent law. What did the framers seek to achieve by incorporating this property right in the highest law of the land? Scholars believe the framers sought to encourage a wide flow of information and knowledge for the public good by providing economic incentives for authors to share their works and creations with the public.

Also in Chapter 2, you learned that copyright law has tended to be—and many legal scholars expect it to be—responsive to technological change. The expectation is that Congress and judges should know when, and when not, to extend copyright's control to emerging media technologies that allow others to infringe—to copy without permission—on a copyrighted content. In other words, copyright law seeks to strike a balance between the economic interests of the author/owner, on one hand, the educational, cultural, creative, and informational interests of the public, including other authors and artists, on the other.

Copyright law protects a copyright holder's right to control creativity fixed in a tangible form for a limited period of time. Creative expression that captures the imagination of hundreds of millions of consumers is not easy to come by and is not cheap. Marvel superheroes and their storylines are a successful entertainment formula that have captivated Baby Boomers, Generation X, and the

Millennial consumers of comic books, television programs, movies, DVDs, and video games. Why spend the money to create new profit-making characters, storylines, and patterns of action, when the old ones still draw blockbuster audiences? So there's a great deal of money to be made in retelling the stories of Wolverine, Spider Man, the Hulk, and Iron Man in other mass media. That is why Kirby's heirs sued Marvel. The superheroes and story lines Kirby helped to create in the 1950s and 1960s for comic books selling at as little as 10 cents a copy are now recycled for the big screen for as much as $15 a ticket, then redistributed for cable television and DVD. Hundreds of millions of dollars are at stake.

17 U.S.C. § 102. Subject Matter and Scope of Copyright: Criteria for Qualifying for Copyright Protection

"Copyright protection subsists…in *original* works of *authorship fixed* in any *tangible medium of expression* [emphasis added], now known or later developed, from which they can be perceived, reproduced, or otherwise communicated, either directly or with the aid of a machine or device. Works of authorship include the following categories: (1) literary works; (2) musical works, including any accompanying words; (3) dramatic works, including any accompanying music; (4) pantomimes and choreographic works; (5) pictorial, graphic, and sculptural works; (6) motion pictures and other audiovisual works; (7) sound recordings; and (8) architectural works. (9) In no case does copyright protection for an original work of authorship extend to any idea, procedure, process, system, method of operation, concept, principle, or discovery, regardless of the form in which it is described, explained, illustrated, or embodied in such work."

What Is an Original Work?

In copyright law, the bar for originality is quite low, a slight amount of creativity will suffice; novelty is not required. In *Feist Publications, Inc. v. Rural Telephone Service Co., Inc.*, 499 U.S. 340, 345 (1991), U.S. Supreme Court Justice Sandra Day O'Connor explained that originality "means only that the work was independently created by the author…The vast majority of works make the grade quite easily, as they possess some creative spark, 'no matter how crude, humble or obvious' it might be."[2] At issue in *Feist* was the copyrightability of a telephone directory. Feist Publications copied Rural Telephone Service's directories after it refused to give Feist a license to do so. The Court ruled in Feist's favor, concluding that Rural's directory was an alphabetical listing of names—mere facts—void of even a slight amount of creativity, and thus not protected under copyright law. Facts, then, are not copyrightable, but copyright law does cover compilations, which typically depend on editorial decision making as to format and content, the "creative spark" necessary for satisfying the originality requirement.

How Is "Authorship" Defined?

The Court defined "authorship" more than 125 years ago in *Burrow-Giles Lithographic Co. v. Sarony*, 111 U.S. 53 (1884). The case pitted a lithographic company, the defendant, against a photographer, Sarony, the plaintiff. The defendant argued that a photograph—a then-emerging technology—was not writing, nor the work of an author, and thus not protected under copyright law. The Court, however, ruled that photography was indeed the work of an author, defined as "'he to whom anything owes its origin; originator; maker; one who completes a work of science or literature'...By writings in that clause is meant the literary productions of those authors, and Congress very properly has declared these to include all forms of writing, printing, engraving, etching...by which the ideas in the mind of the author are given visible expression."[3]

Works Made for Hire

Marvel Entertainment responded to the lawsuit brought by Kirby's heirs by arguing that the authorship of the copyrighted superheroes are not shared by Kirby because he was merely an employee, and, consequently, his stories and drawings are "works made for hire" under 17 U.S.C. 101. Section 101 defines works made for hire as "(1) a work prepared by an employee within the scope of his or her employment, or (2) a work specially ordered or commissioned for use as a contribution to a collective work, as a part of a motion picture or other audiovisual work, as a translation, as a supplementary work, as a compilation, as an instructional text, as a test, as answer material for a test, or as an atlas, if the parties expressly agree in a written instrument signed by them that the work shall be considered a work made for hire."

Since Kirby's works were published between 1958 and 1963, the Copyright Act of 1909 controlled. The earlier act is considered not to be as artist-friendly as the 1976 Copyright Act. In *Marvel v. Kirby*, 2011 U.S. Dist. LEXIS 82868 (2011), a federal judge applied the Second Circuit's "instance and expense" test to determine whether a work is a made for hire under the 1909 Act. Under the test, copyright belongs to the individual at whose instance and expense the work was created. The instance prong looks at whether the employer was the motivating agent in producing the work, or had the right to control or supervise the work. Kirby, the judge concluded, did not create the comic book characters until Stan Lee, Marvel editor and president, or others at the company, assigned or approved them. The expense requirement looks to determine which party bore the risk that the work would not sell. The judge ruled that though Kirby's contribution to the comic books was critical, Marvel bore the risk. Jack Kirby's estate has filed an appeal of the U.S. District Court ruling to the Second Circuit.

What Is a Work Fixed in a Tangible Medium of Expression?

According to a congressional report on the legislative history of the Copyright Act of 1976, the medium doesn't matter. The medium "may be one 'now known or later developed,' and the fixation is sufficient if the work 'can be perceived, reproduced, or otherwise communicated, either directly or with the aid of a machine or device.'"[4] The act clarified whether live broadcasts are fixed in a tangible medium. In its explanation of fixation and live broadcasts, the congressional report further clarified the distinction between authorship and fixation. Television coverage of a football game constitutes authorship because cameramen and editors decide what images will be sent out over the air. When the game is recorded before transmission, or simultaneously recorded and shown live, the transmission is fixed and protected under copyright law. Thus, fixation is met when a work is (i) embodied in a medium that can be perceived or reproduced, and (ii) embodied for "so fleetingly that it cannot be copied." For computers and cyberspace, fixation occurs when a photograph is stored on a hard disk, or other storage devices.[5] Also, a website, including its screen displays and computer code, may constitute a fixed tangible medium for purposes of copyright law.[6]

What Works of Authorship Are Protected?

In addition to the works listed in § 102, websites, computer software, maps, and architectural plans are protected.

Unprotected Works

Unprotected works include unrecorded or unnoted choreographic works, improvisational speeches or performances, titles, names, domain names, short phrases, symbols, slogans, designs, typographic ornamentation, lettering, coloring, listing of ingredients or contents. Copyright law has been interpreted to make a distinction between ideas and the expression of the idea, the former not protected under the law. Expression, which is protected, is the author's *execution* of an idea, which may be as common as a statute of a nude male. The more creativity, originality, and skill a sculptor brings to carving out a male figure from stone, the more the scope of copyright protection increases.[7] Accordingly, procedures, methods, systems, processes, concepts, principles, discoveries, devices, calendars, height and weight charts, tape measures and rules, and lists or tables taken from public documents or other public sources are not protected under copyright law.

Securing Copyright

When your work is original and fixed in a tangible medium of expression, it automatically gains copyright protection. Under the act, you no longer have to publish with notice of copyright or register your work with the U.S. Copyright Office to gain protection. There are, however, advantages to registration. One being that registration of a work of U.S. origin is a prerequisite to bringing an infringement lawsuit in courts here.

17 U.S.C. § 106. Exclusive Rights to Copyrighted Works.

Copyright holders enjoy six exclusive rights to their works, subject to limitations such as the fair use exception discussed later in this chapter. To claim infringement, a copyright holder must show ownership and that one of the exclusive rights has been violated.

1. The Right "To Reproduce the Copyrighted Work in Copies or Phonorecords"

It is unlikely that a copyright holder will be able to reap the full benefit of his or her work if unauthorized copying is allowed. Thus, a copyright holder may seek legal remedies against anyone who makes an unauthorized copy of his or her original work. Phonorecords are media on which sound may be recorded such as audiocassette tapes and CDs, but not media that record both sound and images, such as videotape. Phonorecords are not "sound recordings." Sound recordings are not copies of a recording, but the actual or first recording of a song or musical composition, typically produced and owned by a record company.

2. The Right "To Prepare Derivative Works Based upon the Copyrighted Work"

Many artists, particularly satirists, create new art by tapping into the symbolism of pop cultural icons. But some adaptations are mere exploitations of iconic characters and narratives. Such works may be derivative. According to 17 U.S.C. § 101, a derivative work is based on one or more existing works. Such works include translations, musical arrangements, dramatizations, fictionalizations, motion picture versions, sound recordings, art reproductions, abridgments, condensations, or any other forms in which a work may be recast, transformed, or adapted. They also include any work "consisting of editorial revisions, annotations, elaborations, or other modifications, which, as a whole, represent an original work of authorship." A copyright holder may give permission to someone else to use the original content, or sell a license for its use. There is, however, a great deal of money to be made from adapting highly popular characters and plots to new mediums, as noted above in the discussion of the Kirby infringement action against Marvel Entertainment.

3. The Right "To Distribute Copies or Phonorecords of the Copyrighted Work to the Public By Sale or Other Transfer of Ownership, or By Rental, Lease, or Lending"

The "public distribution" provision gives the copyright owner the right to control the first sale, rental, or free transfer of authorized copies. Keep in mind, however, that the routine practices of borrowing, renting, and resale conducted at libraries, used book stores, and movie and video game rental franchises that we take for granted would be severely limited if this provision were not checked by 17 U.S.C. § 109, or the "first sale" doctrine. In other words, under § 109, the copyright holder's distribution rights end with the first buyer, and the owner of the copy can resell it or give it away.[8] The first sale doctrine, however, does not provide a defense for the first buyer who makes copies from the copy he or she bought.[9]

Conversely, buyers of sound recordings and phonorecords—audiocassette tapes and CDs—may not sell or give their copies away under § 109 (b) (1) (A), which codifies the Record Rental Amendment of 1984. But the first sale doctrine does apply to "books on tapes," the Court of Appeals for the Sixth Circuit ruled in *Brilliance Audio v. Haights Cross Communications*, 474 F.3d 365 (2007). Congress revised § 109 (b) in its Computer Software Rental Amendments of 1990 to allow copyright holders of software to authorize or prohibit the rental of copies after the first sale. In June 2010, The Universal Music Group (UMG) went before a federal appeals court in Seattle to appeal a ruling in *UMG Recordings, Inc. v. Augusto*, 558 F. Supp. 2d 1055 (Dist. Ct. CD. California, 2008), in which a judge said that labeling a CD "for promotional use only, not for sale" did not prevent an eBay seller's first sale doctrine right to auction such a CD. Meanwhile, other copyright holders pursued similar action against other eBay sellers.

4. The Right "In the Case of Literary, Musical, Dramatic, and Choreographic Works, Pantomimes, and Motion Pictures and Other Audiovisual Works, To Perform the Copyrighted Work Publicly"

Under this provision, performances of copyrighted work in even semipublic venues "such as clubs, lodges, factories, summer camps, and schools are 'public performances' subject to copyright control." But what about in cyberspace? As of 2011, the U.S. Supreme Court had not ruled on the matter. A federal trial court in New York, however, ruled in 2007 that digital downloads of music were not considered performance.[10] In 2009, another federal court judge in New York ruled that Verizon's transmission of a ringtone to a customer did not constitute a public performance.[11]

5. The Right "In The Case of Literary, Musical, Dramatic, and Choreographic Works, Pantomimes, and Pictorial, Graphic, or Sculptural Works, Including the Individual Images of a Motion Picture or Other Audiovisual Work, To Display the Copyrighted Work Publicly"

Under this provision, the copyright holder controls the right to display his or her work *publicly*, and display includes the transmission of an image by radio and television waves, cable lines, or "similar viewing apparatus connected with any sort of information storage and retrieval system." Websites are included. In *Perfect 10, Inc. v. Amazon, Inc.*, 487 F.3d 701(9th Cir 2007), the U.S. Nineth Circuit Court of Appeals, however, ruled that the responses provided by Google's image search service—which only provide HTML instructions directing a user's browser to access others' websites and not the image itself—did not constitute display or distribution under the statute.

6. The Right "In The Case of Sound Recordings, To Perform the Copyrighted Work Publicly by Means of a Digital Audio Transmission"

This provision codifies the Digital Performance Right in Sound Recordings Act of 1995, Congress's response to the advent of digital audio transmissions and satellite-radio direct transmission that allow subscribers to listen to the recorded songs when they so desire. Recording companies and artists were concerned that such subscribers would no longer have the need to buy their products recorded on audiotapes and CDs.

Additionally, the Visual Rights Act of 1990 (VARA) grants certain rights—called "moral rights"—to a work's creator to prevent the "revision, alteration, or distortion" of his or her work even when they no longer hold the copyright to it. The act, codified in § 106 (A)—"Rights of certain authors to attribution and integrity"—covers paintings, drawings, prints, sculptures, and photographs, existing in a single copy or a limited edition of 200 signed and numbered copies or fewer. A photograph must have been taken for exhibition purposes only and works must be of "recognized stature" to qualify under the statute. The statute does not allow creators of books, magazines, or other print media, broadcast programs, and or motion pictures to invoke moral rights. Congress passed the law because the international copyright treaty, the Berne Convention, to which the U.S. is a party, requires such protection.

International Copyright

Even before the Internet made content globally accessible, copyright holders were vulnerable to unauthorized copying performed in other countries. For most of the 19th century, Americans pirated European works, as their copyright laws had no authority here. But after about 100 years of weighing whether to become a signatory of the Berne Convention for the Protection of Literary and Artistic Work, which European states adopted in 1886, the U.S. signed on in 1989. The reality that 20th-century U.S. copyright holders had become the targets of pirates from abroad played a role in changing our attitude about the value of international copyright protection for our authors. Today, some 147 nations, from Albania to Zimbabwe, including communist China, Cuba, North Korea, and Vietnam, are signatories. Other countries belong to the Universal Copyright Convention, as does the U.S. Consequently, in addition to the recognition of "moral rights," U.S. copyright holders can protect their works abroad as soon as the works exist because the Berne Convention provides that notice is no longer required to protect foreign works published after March 1, 1989.

17 U.S.C. §§ 302–305. Duration of Copyright

Recall the trade-off sought by the Constitution framers in drafting the Copyright Clause. The law grants authors a monopoly over their works to allow them to reap the economic benefit from their labors, but only for "limited times." When that period expires, such works are said to be in the "public domain." At that point, anyone may publish new editions of the works or adapt the works without obtaining permission from or paying fees to the copyright holder. By limiting copyright holder's monopoly over their works, the society as a whole benefits because other creative individuals can freely build on existing works. And artists have produced surprisingly creative and commercially successful works—sometimes masterpieces—by reshaping public domain works. William Shakespeare borrowed heavily from contemporary works. *Romeo and Juliet* (1591), for example, is a reworking of Arthur Brooke's poem *Romeus and Juliet*, published 29 years earlier. Almost 400 years after, Arthur Laurents, Leonard Bernstein, and Stephen Sondheim created the highly successful Broadway musical, *West Side Story*, a reworking of the earlier play and poem. Directors have reworked Shakespeare's plays in numerous ways such as remaking Macbeth as a fascist dictator, Hamlet as a rebel, and Prospero as an imperialist.

Consequently, getting the balance right between the author's exclusive control and unlimited dissemination is a significant debate that "is as old as the oldest copyright statute and will doubtless continue as long as there is a copyright law."[12] The debate flared again most recently when Congress passed the Sonny Bono Copyright Term Extension Act (CTEA), now codified in § 302, which extended the duration of copyrights set forth in the 1976 Act. The CTEA extended the copyright term from 50 years to 70 years following the author's death for works created after January 1, 1978. An author's heirs are most likely to benefit from the extension. The duration of the copyright for anonymous and pseudonymous works and "works for hire" increased from 75 years to 95 years. Typically, media entertainment companies own "works for hire" copyright. The term of works created before 1978 are protected for 95 years from the date of the first copyright. Media companies stand to benefit most by this extension.

The statute's detractors dubbed it the Mickey Mouse Protection Act because Disney and other corporate copyright holders lobbied Congress to protect their copyrights that were about to expire. For instance, the first animated cartoon featuring the now iconic Mickey Mouse was copyrighted in 1928. Under the copyright law before the CTEA, Disney's copyright was due to expire in 1998, casting Mickey Mouse into the public domain. Under the CTEA, however, Disney's control of the lucrative cartoon mouse expires 95 years from the date of publication, or 2023.

The debate reached the U.S. Supreme Court in *Eldred v. Ashcroft* 537 U.S. 186 (2003). The lead plaintiff Eric Eldred—a retired computer programmer who scanned and posted public domain works such as Nathaniel Hawthorne's *Scarlett Letter* on a free public library website he created—could not do the same with a collection of Robert Frost's poetry that had been scheduled to enter the public domain in 1998. Under the CTEA, he would have to wait until 2019. Eldred's lawyers argued that the framers expected the copyright term to be short and Congress had exceeded its authority beyond constitutional restraint by repeatedly extending the terms of existing copyrights—eleven times since the 1960s. They also contended that as a content-neutral law, the CTEA violated First Amendment free speech guarantees because under the intermediate scrutiny test, the law failed to advance an important government interest.[13]

The plaintiffs lost. The Court said the framers did not interpret the Copyright Clause language "limited times" to mean that the copyright period had to be forever fixed at its original limit. It said it deferred to Congress's authority to define the scope of the limited monopoly and the revised law was a rational exercise of congressional authority: "Guided by text, history, and precedent, we cannot agree with petitioners' submission that extending the duration of existing copyrights is categorically beyond Congress' authority under the Copyright Clause."[14]

Just as important, the Court rejected the plaintiff's First Amendment arguments: "The Copyright Clause and First Amendment were adopted close in time. This proximity indicates that, in the Framers' view, copyright's limited monopolies are compatible with free speech principles. Indeed, copyright's purpose is to *promote* the creation and publication of free expression."[15]

17 U.S.C. § 501 (A). Elements of an Infringement Claim

This section provides that a copyright holder may bring a lawsuit claiming infringement against anyone who violates his or her exclusive rights "or who imports copies or phonorecords into the United States in violation of [17 U.S.C. § 602]." Note, however, that 17 U.S.C. § 412 makes formal registration a prerequisite for an award of damages or attorney's fee. But the act does not tell a plaintiff what he or she must establish to present a prima facie case—one that a judge will allow to go to trial. Judges, however, have. Over the years, judges have settled upon two requirements for a prima facie case: (i) prove ownership of a valid copyright and (ii) establish that the defendant "copied" the copyrighted material or violated the copyright holder's other exclusive rights. A plaintiff may prove such misconduct with direct evidence, such as the defendant's admission to seeing or hearing the work, or witnesses testifying that they knew the defendant had access to the work. But, as the courts have noted, direct evidence is rarely available.

Consequently, in the vast majority of infringement actions, plaintiffs have relied on indirect evidence: (i) They must show that the defendant had access to the work and (ii) that a substantial similarity exists between the defendant's work and the protectable elements of the plaintiff's.[16] Ultimately, the plaintiff will also have to show that the copying was illegal. For example, a defendant can legitimately copy facts and ideas. Only original expression is protected, and the amount of copying must be more than de minimis.

Courts do not take the defendant's intent—whether he or she intended to copy—into consideration when determining infringement. For instance, in *ABKCO Music, Inc. v. Harrisongs Music, Ltd,* 722 F.2d 988 (2d Cir. 1983), a court found the late George Harrison, the ex-Beatle, liable for copyright infringement of an earlier rock-and-roll hit, "He's So Fine," even though he unconsciously copied the tune while writing "My Sweet Lord." A judge, however, may consider the defendant's innocent intentions when awarding damages and other remedies.[17]

(i) PROVING OWNERSHIP

The plaintiff must establish that he or she owns the copyright to the work. In situations where a copyright owner may transfer or assign some or all of his or her exclusive rights, proving ownership may not be as straightforward as one might think:

> In other words, exclusive rights may be chopped up and owned separately, and each separate owner of a subdivided exclusive right may sue to enforce that owned portion of an exclusive right, no matter how small. For instance, A may own the copyright in a book, while B may own the right to develop the book into a

screenplay. A may sue an infringer of the book; B may sue an infringer of the screenplay. But only owners of an exclusive right in a copyright may sue. For instance, neither A nor B in the example above could assign an accrued claim for copyright infringement to C if C had no legal or beneficial interest in the copyright.[18]

(ii) ESTABLISH THAT THE DEFENDANT COPIED THE WORK

In the absence of direct evidence of copying, a plaintiff must prove access, that the defendant had a "reasonable opportunity" or that there was a "reasonable possibility" that the defendant reviewed the plaintiff's work.[19] That's an easy task when a work is well known such as a highly popular song that has become a standard, or one that was once a hit during the defendant's life. In the absence of such evidence, plaintiffs may show that the defendant had dealings with a songwriter, recording company, publisher, or other entity that had possession of the work.

Substantial Similarity: What Constitutes Wrongful Copying?

The co-authors of *Substantial Similarity in Copyright Law*, a text for copyright litigators, tell us that the legal standard of substantial similarity is the essential prerequisite of a copyright infringement lawsuit: "It is that part of an infringement claim that addresses the question: What constitutes wrongful copying? Yet despite substantial similarity's importance…it remains one of the most elusive concepts in copyright law."[20]

At first glance, it should be easy to identify a copy; it looks exactly like the original. But copyright cases seldom involve identical works. Rather, they typically involve copies that borrow some elements of an original work mixed with new elements such as two songs that appear to share the same riffs or note patterns but the lyrics have nothing in common. Or infringement cases ask judges or juries to distinguish between works created in different media. Additionally, a determination has to be made about what shared elements are protected and which shared elements are not. Generally, if the works of the plaintiff and the defendant share substantially similar copyright-protected elements, the plaintiff should prevail.

For about 140 years, copyright in the U.S. protected a copyright holder against only literal copying—word for word, note for note, scene for scene—and not shared similarities of construction, such as plot, or general characteristics, such as characters and their roles. But in *Nichols v. Universal Pictures, Corp.*, 45 F.2d 119, 121 (2d Cir. 1930), federal appeals court Judge Learned Hand devised the "abstraction test," allowing similarities of construction and general characteristics to be weighed. The case involved a playwright who sued a movie producer claiming that the movie, *The Cohens and the Kelleys*, was taken from her play *Abie's Irish Rose*. Both works centered round a Jewish New York family whose daughter is romantically involved with an Irish Catholic. Under the abstraction tests, Hand said that in a play "the controversy chiefly centers upon the characters and sequence of incident."[21] In 1971, U.S. Court of Appeals for the Ninth Circuit explained that the abstraction test suggests that the difference between unprotected ideas and protected expression is "really one of degree" and the "guiding consideration in drawing the line is the preservation of the balance between competition and protection reflected in…copyright laws."[22]

Judge Hand also gave the Second Circuit U.S. Court of Appeals the "ordinary observer test" in *Peter Pan Fabrics, Inc. v. Martin Weiner Corp.*, 274 F.2d, 487, 489 (1960), which provides that, "In deciding [similar substantiality] one should consider the uses for which the design is intended, especially the scrutiny that observers will give to it as used." Under the ordinary observer test, a judge typically ignores expert testimony. The First, Third, Fifth and Seventh circuits use the ordinary observer test. If the work in question is used by experts, or is particularly complex, some courts have found that substantial similarity should be viewed from the perspective of an expert, the intended audience.[23]

In many jurisdictions, once a court identifies the appropriate audience, it applies one of several substantial similarity tests: abstraction, fragmented literal similarity, comprehensive nonliteral similarity, subtractive, extrinsic/intrinsic, totality, analytic dissection of similarities, and abstraction-filtration-comparison. All these tests stem from the effort by judges to distinguish shared ideas from shared expressions of the ideas. Under copyright law, only an author's particular expression of an idea, and not the idea itself, is protected. But it is often difficult to determine where an idea ends and the expression of the idea starts.

Quantitative-Qualitative Test

Learned Hand's contemporary successors on the Second Circuit U.S. Court of Appeals apply a substantial similarity test that requires that copying be "quantitative" and "qualitative." Generally, "quantitative" means the amount of copyrighted work that is copied amounts to more than de minimis. Next, courts look at the value of the copied material to the plaintiff's work because copyright protects copyright holders from unauthorized works that diminish the value of their works, and to prevent plagiarists from arguing that the portion they took was of small value to the new work and therefore not infringement.[24]

The Second Circuit, for example, applied the quantitative-qualitative test to determine whether the *Sienfeld Aptitude Trivia* quiz book infringed the copyrighted *Sienfeld* television series in *Castle Rock Entertainment v. Carol Publishing Group* 150 F.3d 132 (2d Cir. 1998). Finding for the plaintiff, the court first determined that the amount of copying far exceeded a minimal amount and analyzed the aggregate amount copied from 84 Seinfeld episodes.[25] The Second Circuit, however, declined to apply Learned Hand's ordinary observer test "[b]ecause in the instant case the original and secondary works are of different genres and to a lesser extent because they are in different media, tests for substantial similarity other than the quantitative/qualitative approach are not particularly helpful to our analysis."[26]

The Second Circuit devised a substantial similarity test to compare computer programs in *Computer Associates International, Inc. v. Altai, Inc.*, 982 F.2d 693 (2d Cir. 1992):

> A court would first break down the allegedly infringed program into its constituent structural parts. Then, by examining each of these parts for such things as incorporated ideas, expression that is necessarily incidental to those ideas, and elements that are taken from the public domain, a court would then be able to sift out all non-protectable material. Left with a kernel, or possible kernels, of creative expression after following this process of elimination, the court's last step would be to compare this material with the structure of an allegedly infringing program. The result of this comparison will determine whether the protectable elements of the programs at issue are substantially similar so as to warrant a finding of infringement.[27]

Extrinsic-Intrinsic Test & Scenes-A-Faire Doctrine

The extrinsic-intrinsic test weighs the objectively and subjectively considered elements of two works. The extrinsic test often requires analytical testimony from experts about the type of work, and the ideas and materials involved in each work—"breaking down works into their constituent parts to determine whether similarities between the works are attributable to unprotected elements (such as idea/expression merger, public domain, *scene a faire*, etc.)"[28] For books, plays, films, for example, experts testify about plot, theme, dialogue, mood, setting, pace, characters and sequence of events. For songs, experts testify about use of the rhythms, pitch, cadence of the title hook phrase, and verse/chorus relationship.

The scenes-a-faire doctrine recognizes that certain genres and works share common themes, settings, or plots and, as a result, those elements might be covered by copyright. It can also be used as a defense. Honda Motor Co. unsuccessfully pursued a scenes-a-faire defense when James Bond moviemakers Metro-Goldwyn-Mayer Inc. claimed a Honda commercial copied scenes from its Bond movies. "Based on Plaintiffs' experts' greater familiarity with the James Bond films, as well as a review of Plaintiffs' James Bond montage and defense expert Needham's video montage of the 'action/spy' genre films, it is clear that James Bond films are unique in their expression of the spy thriller idea," a federal court in California said. The court continued, "A filmmaker could produce a helicopter chase scene in practically an indefinite number of ways, but only James Bond films bring the various elements Casper describes together in a unique and original way."[29]

Even so, when a defendant strings together scenes-a-faire elements, ideas, or public domain work elements in a combination similar to the plaintiff's work, the plaintiff's combination of unprotected elements may be copyrightable and the extrinsic test met. In *Metcalf v. Bochco*, 294 F.3d 1069 (9th Cir. 2002), the court held that "the particular sequence in which an author strings a significant number of unprotectable elements can itself be a protectable element. Each note in a scale, for example, is not protectable, but a pattern of notes in a tune may earn copyright protection. A common 'pattern [that] is sufficiently concrete...warrant[s] a finding of substantial similarity.'"[30]

The intrinsic test relies on the subjective evaluation of a reasonable person about the total concept and feel of a work. Expert testimony is not considered in this portion of the test. And, under certain circumstances, a court may decide to use only one part of the test, as the U.S. Court of Appeals for the Ninth Circuit did in *Sid & Marty Krofft Television v. McDonald Corp.*, 562 F.2d 1157 (9th Cir. 1977), relying only on the intrinsic portion. The court rejected McDonald's use of the extrinsic portion of the test to show that, though it had copied merely the *idea* of the Pufnstuf fantasyland television series, it did not copy the expression of it in its commercials. The court said reliance on expert analysis as required under the extrinsic test was inappropriate: "the present case demands an even more intrinsic determination because both plaintiffs' and defendants' works are directed to an audience of children. This raises the particular factual issue of the impact of the respective works upon the minds and imaginations of young people."[31]

Substantially Similar: Media And Genre

As noted earlier, courts focus on plot, theme, dialogue, mood, setting, pace, characters and sequence of events for fictional works when judging substantial similarity. For nonfiction works, generally a higher quantity of copying is required to support a finding of substantial similarity than in fictional works.[32] Generally, courts look at the compilation of elements in unscripted television shows such as game shows and cooking shows.[33] For songs, courts have found substantial similarity in either the lyrics or the arrangement of notes, or both. For the recently developed television subgenre of reality television, courts apply the principles used in assessing literary works.[34] For audiovisual works—movies, music videos, television programs, computer games—courts may compare the audiovisual elements in cases involving adaptations of literary works, or they may compare audiovisual elements in cases involving two audiovisual works. For computer programs, similarities may be found in the source code,[35] or the structure, sequence and organization of a computer program.[36]

Keep in mind that there is no universally accepted definition of the substantial similarity test. It really depends on the facts of the case and the jurisdiction, and some courts have avoided defining the term. According to co-authors of *Substantial Similarity in Copyright Law*, "Ultimately, the question whether two works are substantially similar boils down to whether there is enough similarity between the defendant's work and the original elements of the plaintiff's work to convince a jury that the defendant wrongfully took something of significance from the plaintiff."[37]

SUMMARY OF AN INFRINGEMENT CLAIM: A copyright plaintiff must prove (i) ownership of the copyright, and (ii) infringement, that is, that the defendant copied protected elements of the plaintiff's work. Absent direct evidence of copying, proof of infringement involves fact-based showings that the defendant had access to the plaintiff's work and that the two works are substantially similar. Proof of access requires evidence of a reasonable possibility of viewing the plaintiff's work, not a bare possibility.

Proof of infringement is often highly circumstantial. Circumstantial evidence of reasonable access is proven in one of two ways: (i) a particular chain of events is established between the plaintiff's work and the defendant's access to that work (such as through dealings with a publisher or record company), or (ii) the plaintiff's work has been widely disseminated.

In the absence of proof of ownership or access of the copyrighted material, a copyright plaintiff can still make out a case of infringement by showing that the works were substantially similar. The legal standard of substantial similarity is the essential prerequisite of a copyright infringement lawsuit: "It is that part of an infringement claim that addresses the question: What constitutes wrongful copying?"

In determining substantial similarity, several jurisdictions apply "the ordinary observer test" to judge works that are consumed by lay people. Several jurisdictions apply expert observer tests for works that require special knowledge and skill to operate or appreciate. Additionally, jurisdictions apply one of several substantial similarity tests: abstraction, fragmented literal similarity, comprehensive nonliteral similarity, subtractive, extrinsic/intrinsic, totality, analytic dissection of similarities, and abstraction-filtration-comparison. The scenes-a-faire doctrine recognizes that certain genres and works share common themes, settings, or plot. Thus, those shared elements might be found unprotected under copyright law.

Defenses to an Infringement Claim

A target of an infringement lawsuit may assert several defenses: (I) Independent creation: A defendant may show that he or she created a second work with no knowledge of the copyrighted work. (II) De minimis: A defendant may show that the amount of work copied was so trivial as to preclude trial, to warrant a substantial similarity inquiry, or a de minimis finding may be considered relevant in a fair use defense.[38] (III) As discussed earlier under "What is an original work?" a defendant may rely on the idea/expression dichotomy and show that he or she has copied only the idea and other unprotected elements and items such as facts, titles, short phrases, concepts, lists, or tables. Here, defendants also can rely upon the merger or scenes-a-faire doctrines. The merger doctrine provides that when an idea and the way to express it are closely tied, there may be extremely limited ways to express it, and, thus, no way to copyright the expression.

17 U.S.C. § 107. Limitations on Exclusive Rights: Fair Use

A defendant may also seek protection under the fair use exceptions. The judicial doctrine of fair use is "one of the most important and well-established limitations on the exclusive right of copyright owners…given express statutory recognition for the first time in section 107."[39]

The fair use doctrine maintains that, "notwithstanding the provisions of sections 106 and 106A, the fair use of a copyrighted work, including such use by reproduction in copies or phonorecords or by any other means specified by that section, for purposes such as criticism, comment, news reporting, teaching (including multiple copies for classroom use), scholarship, or research, is not an infringement of copyright. In determining whether the use made of a work in any particular case is a fair use the factors to be considered shall include: (i) the purpose and character of the use, including whether such use is of a commercial nature or is for nonprofit educational purposes; (ii) the nature of the copyrighted work; (iii) the amount and substantiality of the portion used in relation to the copyrighted work as a whole; and (iv) the effect of the use upon the potential market for or value of the copyrighted work." The fact that a work is unpublished shall not itself bar a finding of fair use if such finding is made upon consideration of all the above factors.

Section 107 codifies a more than two-hundred-year-old Anglo-Saxon legal doctrine—that to debate the value of an idea one must be able to quote a work. A copyright holder may benefit from others quoting his or her work in published reviews, research studies, news accounts, and classroom discussion. Book and movie reviews, for instance, often promote sales. Yes, a bad review can hurt sales, but as the U.S. Supreme Court pointed out in *Campbell v. Acuff-Rose Music, Inc.*, 510 U.S. 509 (1994), such criticism "does not produce a harm cognizable under the Copyright Act."[40] In turn, public discussions and critiques add to our cultural and intellectual development.

But who is likely to pay to see a movie, or buy a CD or book, when all or most of the compelling and illuminating parts have been publicly disclosed? For judges then, the challenge is to identify the point at which the amount of quoting undermines the economic value of the copyright holder's property.

In *Folsom v. Marsh*, 9 F. Cas. 342, 348 (C.C.D. Mass. 1841), Justice Joseph Story fashioned a test now codified in Section 107: "In short, we must often, in deciding questions of this sort look to the nature and objects of the selections made, the quantity and value of the materials used, and the degree in which the use may prejudice the sale, or diminish the profits, or supersede the objects, of the original work." It is important to note that Section 107's four factors are guidelines; they do not define fair use. They are factors, among others, that judges weigh. Consequently, judges are free to adapt the fair use doctrine on a case-by-case basis, and they have.

1. The Purpose and Character of the Use: The Transformative Factor

In *Campbell v. Acuff-Rose Music, Inc.*, the U.S. Supreme Court identified the "purpose and character of the use" inquiry as the key gauge of fair use, stressing that whether the new work was "transformative" often is determinative. "The goal of copyright, to promote science and the arts, is generally furthered by the creation of transformative works," the Court said. Consequently, one should ask whether a new work adds "something new, with a further purpose or different character, altering the first with new expression, meaning, or message."[41] In an earlier ruling, *Harper & Row v. The Nation*,

471 U.S. 539 (1985), the Court singled out Section 107(4) as the most important of the four factors, as discussed below. But the Court in *Campbell v. Acuff-Rose* said that all of the fair use factors should be weighed against each other, though the more transformative a work is, "the less will be the significance of other factors, like commercialism, that may weigh against a finding of fair use."[42]

For the parties in *Campbell v. Acuff-Rose Music*, the transformative inquiry led to a ruling that a rap song "Pretty Woman" performed by 2 Live Crew, a rap group led by Luther R. Campbell, was protected as a parody that gave new expression and meaning to the 1960s' rock-and-roll hit "Oh, Pretty Woman" by Roy Orbison. The Court recognized that parody, a form of criticism, works only when it mimics the original work, when the audience can recognize the original work in the parody. Therefore, it must share some key similarities with the original work:

> While we might not assign a high rank to the parodic element here, we think it fair to say that 2 Live Crew's song reasonably could be perceived as commenting on the original or criticizing it, to some degree. 2 Live Crew juxtaposes the romantic musings of a man whose fantasy comes true, with degrading taunts, a bawdy demand for sex, and a sigh of relief from paternal responsibility. The later words can be taken as a comment on the naivete of the original of an earlier day, as a rejection of its sentiment that ignores the ugliness of street life and the debasement that it signifies. It is this joinder of reference and ridicule that marks off the author's choice of parody from the other types of comment and criticism that traditionally have had a claim to fair use protection as transformative works.[43]

Simply, converting or transmitting a work into another medium is not enough to make it transformative. According to the U.S. Court of Appeals for the Ninth Circuit in *A&M Records, Inc. v. Napster, Inc.*, 239 F.3d 1004, 1014 (9th Cir. 2001), downloading MP3 files, retransmitting radio broadcast over telephone lines, or reproducing an audio CD into MP3 format does not render the work transformative. To be transformative, a work has to do more than recast, transform, or adapt an original work because it would be little more than a derivative work otherwise.[44]

Generally, when analyzing whether nonparodic copies are transformative, courts ask whether the copy's use differs from the protected work, and does not supplant the need for the original work. For example, a copy used for informational purposes is not likely to supplant an original creative work, and, therefore, more likely to be deemed transformative, the Ninth Circuit explained in *Kelly v. Arriba Soft Corp.*, 336 F.3d 811 (9th Cir. 2003).

2. The Nature of the Copyrighted Work

This factor recognizes that nonfiction works are more likely to gain fair use protection than fictional works. Again, a defendant is highly unlikely to prevail if a fair use defense is based *solely* on the copying of information, instruction, news, or other nonfiction material, as the Court emphasized in *Harper & Row v. The Nation*, 471 U.S. 539 (1985) when it ruled that *The Nation*, a news and public affairs magazine, did not have a fair use defense to publish excerpts from former President Gerald Ford's yet-to-be published memoirs. The fact that news reporting was the general purpose of *The Nation*'s use was just one of the factors to consider, the Court said, because, "*The Nation* went beyond simply reporting uncopyrightable information and actively sought to exploit the headline value of its infringement, making a 'news event' out of its unauthorized first publication of a noted figure's copyrighted expression."[45] *Harper & Row v. The Nation* adopted positions on two other important propositions: (i) neither First Amendment free speech protections nor the fair use doctrine include a public figure exception to copyright, and (ii) unlicensed disclosure of unpublished works are not likely to be held fair.

3. The Amount and Substantiality of the Portion Used in Relation to the Copyrighted Work as a Whole

Under common law, before fair use was codified in Section 107, it was "almost unanimously accepted that a scholar could make a handwritten copy of an entire copyrighted article for his own use, and in the era before photoduplication it was not uncommon (and not seriously questioned) that he could have his secretary make a typed copy for his personal use and files.."[46] The *Sony Corp. of America v. Universal City Studies, Inc.* 464 U.S. 417 (1984) ruling allows the videotaping of entire television shows for noncommercial use. Additionally, courts have noted that, "wholesale copying does not preclude fair use per se."[47] As a rule, however, the more you copy from an original work, the less likely a court will grant fair use protection. There is no consensus on a word-count limit for a written work or an element count for a visual work.

There also is the qualitative standard of substantiality, determining whether the defendant copied "the heart of the work," the portions that are most interesting or compelling to an audience. When former-President Ford brought his infringement action before the Second Circuit, that court found that *The Nation* copied 300 words, merely "a meager, indeed an infinitesimal amount of Ford's original language."[48] In reversing the Second Circuit ruling, the U.S. Supreme Court found that the magazine had copied the "heart of the book," noting that its editor had published quotes that were "among the most powerful passages."[49] Parody, as the Court pointed out in *Campbell v. Acuff-Rose Music,* is an exception to the rule that copying will not be a fair use when the portion that is copied constitutes "the heart of the work."

4. The Effect of the Use upon the Potential Market for or Value of the Copyrighted Work

The U.S. Supreme Court has said that Section 107(4) is the most important of the four factors.[50] And when a defendant's copying is shown to do economic harm to the copyright owner—to impair the marketability of the work in current and future markets—judges are likely to favor the copyright owner. But determining whether the copyright owner has or will suffer economic harm from the unauthorized copying is often not easy. Sometimes, for example, the distribution of unauthorized copies might gain a copyright owner new paying customers. Additionally, courts seek to strike a balance between "the benefit the public will derive if the use is permitted and the personal gain the copyright owner will receive if the use is denied."[51]

For example, Mattel Inc., the makers of the iconic Barbie doll, lost two infringement cases against artists who used the doll in rather unflattering creations. In both cases, courts found no evidence that the rival dolls threatened or were likely to threaten sales of, or licensing fees from, Mattel's Barbie. An artist dressed up Barbie dolls in sadomasochistic garb and placed them in similarly themed situations in *Mattel v. Pitt.* 229 F. Supp. 2d 315, 321–22 (S.D.N.Y.2002). In *Mattel v. Walking Mountain Productions*, 353 F.3d 792 (9th Cir. 2003), the defendant's photos portrayed a nude Barbie as the target of vicious household appliances. The *Walking Mountain* court said the photos posed no threat to Mattel because it assumed the company had no plans to compete with the photographer for customers in the adult-oriented photographic market. The public benefit? "It is not in the public's interest to allow Mattel complete control over the kinds of artistic works that use Barbie as a reference for criticism and comment," the U.S. Court of Appeals for the Ninth Circuit said.[52]

SUMMARY OF INFRINGEMENT DEFENSES: A defendant may show that (i) he or she created a second work with no knowledge of the copyrighted work; (ii) argue that the amount of work copied was de minimis, so trivial as to preclude trial or a substantial similarity inquiry; (iii) rely on the idea/expression dichotomy and show that he or she has copied only the idea and other unprotected elements such as facts, titles, short phrases, concepts, list or tables; or (iv) invoke the merger or scenes-a-faire doctrines.

A defendant may also invoke the fair use provisions of the Copyright Act Section 107 which requires a case-by-case determination whether a particular use is fair. The statute notes four nonexclusive factors to be considered: (i) The purpose and character of the use, including whether such use is of a commercial nature or is for nonprofit educational purposes; (ii) the nature of the copyrighted work; (iii) the amount and substantiality of the portion used in relation to the copyrighted work as a whole; and (iv) the effect of the use upon the potential market for or value of the copyrighted work. A finding of de minimis use also may be considered relevant in a fair use defense.

ONLINE RESOURCES

1. "Copyright & Fair Use," http://fairuse.stanford.edu/
2. *"My Sweet Lord v. He's So Fine,"* http://www.youtube.com/watch?v=sYiEesMbe2I
3. "Questions about Copyright," https://www.eff.org/issues/bloggers/legal/liability/IP
4. "Ten Famous Intellectual Property Disputes," http://www.smithsonianmag.com/history-archaeology/Ten-Famous-Intellectual-Property-Disputes.html?c=y&page=2
5. U.S. Copyright Office, http://www.copyright.gov/

QUESTIONS

1. The *Associated Press* and artist Shepard Fairey settled their copyright dispute over Fairey's Barack Obama "Hope" poster. Fairey based his poster on an AP photograph of Obama. In both renditions, the tilt of Obama's head and expression are similar. But the parties—who, based on the settlement, now share the rights to make the poster and related merchandise—did not resolve the infringement issue. You be the judge. Search the Internet to find the poster and the photograph, and related commentary, to determine whether the poster is a fair use.

2.

   Above, are the four notes that are played twice at the start of Beethoven's 5th Symphony. The four-note motif has been used in many songs, including a disco hit. But what if Beethoven's estate, or anyone else, still owned copyright to his song? Would the use, or sampling, of the four-note motif be de minimis or infringement?

3. Vincent Peters sued rapper Kanye West for copyright infringement, claiming substantial similarity in *Peters v. West*, 776 F. Supp. 2d 742 (N.D. Ill, 2011). Peters, however,

appealed the federal district court ruling dismissing the claim. Here are some of the key lyrics at issue. Are they substantially similar? Peters's hook is: "What don't kill me make me stronger/The more I blow up the more you wronger/You coped my CD you can feel my hunger/The wait is over couldn't wait no longer." West's hook: "N-N-N-now th-th-that don't kill me/Can only make me stronger/I need you to hurry up now/Cause I can't wait much longer/I know I got to be right now/Cause I can't get much wronger/Man I've been waitin' all night now/That's how long I've been on ya."

ENDNOTES

1. U.S. Constitution, Art. I, § 8.cl . 8.
2. *Feist Publications, Inc. v. Rural Telephone Service Co., Inc.,* 499 U.S. 340, 345 (1991).
3. *Burrow-Giles Lithographic Co. v. Sarony,* 111 U.S. 53, 58 (1884).
4. H.R. Rep. No. 94–1476, 94th Cong. 2d Session.52 (1976).
5. *MAI Systems. Corp. v. Peak Computer, Inc.* 991 F.2d 511, 517–518 (9th Circ. 1993).
6. *Integrative Nutrition, Inc. v. Academy of Healing Nutrition,* 476 F. Supp. 2d 291, 296 (S.D.N.Y.2007).
7. See *Sid & Marty Krofft Television v. McDonald Corp.,* 562 F.2d 1157, 1168 (9th Cir. 1977).
8. *Bobbs-Merrill Co. v. Straus,* 210 U.S. 339 (1908).
9. *U.S. v. Wise,* 550 F.2d 1180, 1187 (9th Cir. 1977).
10. *U. S. v. American Society of Composers, Authors and Publishers,* 485 F. Supp. 2d 438, 441–42 (S.D.N.Y. 2007).
11. *In Re Cellco Partnership* (doing business as Verizon Wireless), 663 F. Supp. 2d 363 (S.D.N.Y 2009).
12. "Historical and Revision Notes." H.R. Rep. No. 94–1476, 94th Cong. 2d Sess. 133 (1976), http://uscode.house.gov/download/pls/17C3.txt
13. Brief for Petitioner, *Eldred v. Ashcroft,* 537 U.S. 186 (No. 01–618, *10), http://cyber.law.harvard.edu/openlaw/eldredvashcroft/supct/opening-brief.pdf
14. *Eldred v. Ashcroft,* 537 U.S. 186, 204 (2003).
15. Ibid. 219.
16. *Ellis v. Diffie,* 177 F.3d 503, 506 (6th Cir. 1999); *Computer Associates Intern., v. Altai, Inc.,* 982 F.2d 693, 710 (2d Circ. 1992).
17. *ABKCO Music, Inc. v. Harrisongs Music, Ltd,* 722 F.2d 988, 999 (2d Cir. 1983); *See* 17 U.S.C. § 504(c).
18. *Silvers v. Sony Pictures Entertainment, Inc.,* 402 F.3d 881, 887 (9th Cir. 2005) (en banc).
19. Melville B. Nimmer & David Nimmer, *Nimmer on Copyright,* § 13.02[A], at 13–19 (1999); *Jason v. Fonda,* 526 F. Supp. 774, 775 (C.D. Cal. 1981), affirmed, 698 F.2d 966 (9th Cir. 1983).
20. Robert C. Osterberg and Eric C. Osterberg. *Substantial Similarity in Copyright Law.* New York: Practising Law Institute (2009), p. xxi.
21. *Nichols v. Universal Pictures, Corp.,* 45 F.2d 119, 121 (2d Cir. 1930).
22. *Herbert Rosenthal Jewelry Corp. v. Kalpakian,* 446 F.2d 738, 742 (9th Cir. 1971).
23. *Dawson v. Hinshaw Music, Inc.,* 905 F.2d 731, 733 (4th Cir.1990); *Kohus v. Mariol,* 328 F.3d 848 (6th Cir. 2003).
24. Osterberg at Section 2, 19.
25. *Castle Rock Entertainment v. Carol Publishing Group,* 150 F.3d 132, 138 (2d Cir. 1998).
26. Ibid. 139.
27. *Computer Associates International, Inc. v. Altai, Inc.,* 982 F.2d 693, 706 (2d Cir. 1992).
28. Osterberg at Section 3, 23.
29. *Metro-Goldwyn-Mayer, Inc. v. American Honda Motor Co.,* 900 F. Supp. 1287, 1295 (C.D. Cal. 1995).
30. *Metcalf v. Bochco,* 294 F.3d 1069, 1074 (9th Cir. 2002).
31. *Sid & Marty Krofft Television v. McDonald Corp.,* 562 F.2d 1157, 1166 (9th Cir. 1977).
32. *Landsberg v. Scrabble Crossword Game Players, Inc.,* 736 F.2d 485, 288 (9th Cir. 1984).
33. *Barris/Fraser Enterprise, Ltd. v. Goodson-Todman Entertainment, Ltd.,* 638 F. Supp. 292 (S.D.N.Y. 1988).
34. *Rodriguez, et al. v. Hiedi Klum Co. et al.,* 05-CV-102318 (S.D.N.Y. Jan. 8, 2009).
35. *Apple Computer, Inc. v. Franklin Computer Corp,* 714 F.2d 1240 (3d Cir. 1983).

36. *Kepner-Tregoe, Inc. v. Leadership Software, Inc.*, 12 F.3d 527, (5th Cir. 1994), cert. denied, 513 U.S. 820 (1994).

37. Osterberg at Section 1, 4.

38. See *Ringold v. Black Entertainment Television, Inc.* 126 F.3d 70 (2d Cir. 1997).

39. H. R. Rep. No. 94–1476, 94th Cong., 2d Sess. 65–66 (1976).

40. *Campbell v. Acuff-Rose Music, Inc.*, 510 U.S. 509, 592 (1994).

41. Ibid. 579.

42. Ibid.

43. Ibid. 583.

44. *Salinger v. Colting*, 641 E. Supp. 2d 250, 262 (S.D.N.Y 2009).

45. *Harper & Row v. The Nation*, 471 U.S. 539, 541 (1985).

46. *Williams & Wilkins Co. v. U.S.*, 487 F.2d 1345, 1350 (Ct. Claims, 1973) affirmed by U.S. Supreme, 420 U.S. 376 (1975).

47. *Hustler Magazine, Inc. v. Moral Majority, Inc.*, 796 F.2d 1148, 1155 (9th Cir.1986).

48. *Harper & Row v. The Nation*, 471 U.S. at 566.

49. Ibid.

50. Ibid.

51. *Mattel Inc. v. Walking Mountain Productions*, 353 F.3d 792, 805 (9th Cir. 2003).

52. Ibid. 806.

CHAPTER FOURTEEN

Copyright, New Technologies & Trademark

CONTROVERSY: In 2004, Google Inc. launched a campaign to scan all the books in the world and make them available on the Web via its search engine. Google has plans to create the largest library ever—or bookstore, some argued. University of Michigan President Mary Sue Coleman said the project, now known as Google Books, "can, and will, change the world" because it takes "the corpus of human knowledge and puts it in the hands of anyone who wants it."[1] But the reality of copyright law soon intruded. In 2005, the Authors Guild and the Association of American Publishers brought a class action lawsuit against Google, charging it with massive copyright infringement. Google was scanning and uploading the content of books from libraries without getting permission from authors, including books known as "orphan works." Orphan works—they number in the millions—are out-of-print copyrighted works whose copyright holders cannot be located or are unknown. Yet, under copyright law, such holders retain their rights until their copyrights expire. Under the terms of a settlement between the Guild and Google announced in 2008, orphan works copyright holders would lose their rights if they failed to opt out of the settlement.

In 2011, a federal judge rejected the settlement on a number of grounds, including a concern about Google's copying of orphan and other copyrighted works. The settlement's terms deprive millions of authors of their basic right of control, the judge ruled.[2] Yet, the project would allow scholars, educators, students, bibliophiles, and disadvantage peoples worldwide to access the wealth of human knowledge, preserve old books in digital form, and give authors of out-of-print books new readers. Those benefits seem consistent with copyright law's core purpose, as expressly stated in the Constitution: to promote the progress of knowledge and learning. Why, then, let traditional notions of copyright law stand in the way of progress?

Chapter's Focus

New copying technologies that facilitate infringement have always raised concerns about the usefulness of copyright laws created to address older technologies. In the past, judicial interpretation of the fair use doctrine or congressional legislation, or a combination of the two, has reasonably resolved the tension between existing copyright law and new copying technologies. A thorough examination of this judicial and legislative dynamic is beyond the scope of this work. This chapter, however, provides some insight into that process by examining the leading judicial and legislative responses to photocopying machines, videotaping devices, and digital technologies such as MP3 peer-to-peer file sharing, search engines, and YouTube that have occurred since the 1970s. The Google Book settlement is the outlier approach to this judicial/legislative dynamic; it co-opts the authority of Congress to establish copyright law policy and sidesteps a fair-use analysis. Yet, many, including Google, believed the company has a strong fair-use defense. Perhaps, by the time you read this chapter, Congress would have stepped in to address the orphan works issue, or a court would have addressed the fair-use issue.[3]

The second part of this chapter covers trademark law. Under federal law, trademarks are protected under the Lanham (Trademark) Act, pursuant to Congress's authority to regulate interstate commerce provided by the Constitution's commerce clause, Article 1, Section 8, clause 3. But state statutes and common law also control trademarks used in connection with products and services within intrastate commerce. The third kind of intellectual property, patents, also is protected under Article I, Section 8, clause 8 of the U.S. Constitution. Patent law, however, does not directly affect communication and media use. Patent law covers inventions. Trademark and copyright law, however, control intellectual property that directly affects expression. Thus, our discussion of intellectual property is limited to trademark and copyright law because they affect media use and communication.

Fair Use & Photocopying

Is there a college student who has not received a photocopied article as part of his or her course reading materials? Probably not. Many teachers distribute "coursepacks or packets," bound copies of several articles and book excerpts. Are your professors violating copyright law? Or, does such photocopying fall under fair-use protections?

Today, the law provides straightforward answers about academic photocopying and fair use. The circumstances were different about 50 years ago, during the start of the "reprographic revolution"[4] spurred by Xerox's marketing of Chester Carlson's xerography invention in 1959. The then-controlling Copyright Act of 1909 did not provide fair-use protection, and its framers did not contemplate reprographic technology. Absent clear congressional guidance, the U.S. Court of Claims applied the judicially created fair use[5] doctrine in *Williams & Wilkins Co. v. United States*, 487 F.2d 1345 (Ct. Cl. 1973), the first case involving an infringement claim stemming from the use of a Xerox copier. In this case, affirmed by the U.S. Supreme Court,[6] the Court of Claims ruled that the photocopying of 100,000 articles of a publisher's medical journals by the National Institutes of Health and the National Library of Medicine was a fair use. The court found for the U.S. government because the publisher could not prove that the photocopying resulted in a loss of subscriptions, and the government expert showed that the distribution of the photocopies might have actually helped the publisher.[7]

The Copyright Act of 1976 codifies the four fair-use factors. The act, however, did not take a firm position on photocopying and fair use. It lists the reproduction of copies for classroom teaching purposes as a *possible* fair use. But the "Agreement on Guidelines for Classroom Copying in Not-for-Profit Educational Institutions with Respect to Books and Periodicals (Classroom Guideline)" published in the House of Representatives 1976 report imposes restrictions, including limits on the amount and frequency a teacher may copy, and says copying "shall not be used to create or to replace or substitute for anthologies, compilations or collective works."[8]

The 1976 Copyright Act and the agreement guidelines' deterrent effects were minimal. The tension between academic use of xerographic copying technology and author's exclusive rights under copyright law has been addressed through a case-by-case basis. By 1982, book publishers were fed up with the widespread, unauthorized photocopying of their books for classroom use. Led by the American Association of Publishers, publishers sued New York University for infringement. NYU settled, agreeing to enforce the Classroom Guidelines. Apparently, Kinko's Graphic Corporation ignored the warning signaled by the action against NYU. In 1989, several major New York-based publishing houses sued Kinko's for creating copy packets for distribution at New York City-based colleges and universities. Kinko's fair-use defense failed, a federal judge ruled in *Basic Books, Inc. v. Kinko's Graphics Corp.*, because its purpose and use were merely repackaging for commercial use. The materials were nonfiction, weighing in Kinko's favor, but the portions copied were the heart of the copyrighted material and the copies unfavorably affected the sales of the plaintiffs' books and permission fee revenue. The judge ordered Kinko's to pay $500,000 in damages to the publishers and issued an order forbidding it to prepare course packets without securing permission from and prepaying fees to the appropriate publishers.[9]

In 1996, the U.S. Court of Appeals for the Sixth Circuit took up the infringement issue in *Princeton University Press v. Michigan Document Services, Inc.* 99 F.3d 1381 (6th Cir. 1996) (en banc), cert. denied, 520 U.S. 1156 (1997). Publisher Princeton University Press sued Michigan Document Services, a photocopy shop, for photocopying and binding copies of various readings assigned by professors for students. The copy shop declined to pay fees to the publisher, arguing that the course-packs it created were fair use. The Sixth Circuit, however, weighed the fair-use factors and found that the activity was not a fair use. The court found that "the purpose and character of the use" was commercial, that "the nature of the copyrighted work" was creative, "the amount and substantiality of the portion used" was considerable, going well beyond the "Classroom Guidelines" limits, and the copying could "only have a deleterious effect upon the incentive to publish academic writings."[10]

In sum, because a photocopy machine allows users to make an unlimited number of copies for commercial use, the fair use of the device is limited to making copies of small portions of copyrighted materials for research and educational purposes. Photocopy makers continue to thrive, and unauthorized copying by professors and photocopy shops persists. During the last decade, publishers filed infringement lawsuits against copy stores serving the University of Florida in Gainesville, University of Texas in Austin, Northeastern University in Boston, University of Massachusetts in Amherst, and University of Michigan.

Fair Use & Videotaping

When Sony Corporation introduced its Betamax videotape recording device in 1975, Universal Studios and Walt Disney Production saw a threat. The home video recording device allowed anyone to make a copy of a television show. Universal and Disney feared that Betamax would limit their ability to gain revenues from syndicating and licensing their content to television stations and networks, and from sales of their content on videotapes and videodiscs. So the filmmakers sued Sony for infringement in 1976. Sony argued, among other defenses, fair use; that Betamax allowed consumers to time-shift programming, to record a television program for noncommercial use while watching another channel.

In 1984, the U.S. Supreme Court handed down a landmark 5–4 copyright ruling, *Sony Corp. of America v. Universal City Studios, Inc.* In *Sony*, the Court said, "home time-shifting is fair use."[11] The *Sony* Court created a "safe harbor"—a legal provision limiting a party's liability—from infringement liability for makers and sellers of copying equipment when "a *significant* portion of the product's use is *non-infringing*...If virtually all of the product's use, however, is to infringe, contributory liability may be imposed; if no one would buy the product for non-infringing purposes alone, it is clear that the manufacturer is purposely profiting from the infringement, and that liability is appropriately imposed."[12] In sum, because a significant portion of a video recording device's use consists of allowing customers to make a copy of a television program for home use, merely to shift the time that viewers watch copyrighted programming, that constitutes a fair-use, noninfringing activity.

Fair Use & the Internet

Sony set the stage for continuing courtroom battles pitting entertainment and information industry plaintiffs against peer-to-peer file-sharing software producers such as Napster and their end-user defendants, leading to the passage of the Digital Millennium Copyright Act (DCMA) of 1998. Here is why. Digital rights, free-culture advocates, and many other legal scholars who argued that copyright law should be interpreted to favor technological innovation, sought to extend the *Betamax* defense to emerging digital technologies. They contended that the Betamax defense should cover makers of software and other digital innovations who sell or distribute to the public a product that is capable of substantial noninfringing uses, though some individuals may use the technology to infringe. Like the Betamax technology in *Sony*, the sale or distribution of such products should not constitute contributory infringement, advocates argued.

The entertainment and information industries, however, sought to persuade judges that the *Sony* ruling should not control in cases in which the technology allows end users to make multiple copies for other users as opposed to one copy for an individual's home use. Courts also should take into account whether the technology maker or distributor is secondarily liable. In other words, when manufacturers and distributors engage in activities that encourage users to download and share copyrighted material, they should be subject to secondary infringement liability. That was the winning argument in *A&M Records, Inc. v. Napster, Inc.*, 239 F.3d 1004 (9th Cir. 2001). Today, music lovers who download songs from the Internet from Apple iTunes and Amazon MP3 expect to pay a fee for the service. But at first, in June 1999, end users were able to get downloads for free thanks to Napster Inc.'s MusicShare software. That all changed after the U.S. Court of Appeals for the Ninth Circuit sided with the 18 members of the Recording Industry Association of America in its 2001 ruling in *A&M Records, Inc. v. Napster, Inc.*, a landmark copyright case.

Napster's MP3 peer-to-peer (P2P) music files allowed individuals to use computers to receive and upload data, downloading copies of the contents of an MP3 file from one computer to another over the Internet. An individual searching to download a song accessed Napster's song title database and Napster linked that searcher to another end user's computer where the song was stored. Consequently, music lovers could access all or some songs of a copyrighted CD without paying the copyright holder, typically artists, songwriters, or recording companies.

To cyber utopians, creative commons and digital rights advocates, and many music consumers, the company's software was ushering in a revolution. Napster, they argued, created a highly decentralized Internet in which individuals linked their computers to each other without a corporate-owned central server. Music lovers—and potentially all consumers of creative content and information—could free themselves from the "tyranny" of the recording industry's overpriced CDs. Even some rock artists cheered the arrival of Napster, arguing that free distribution of their songs might expose more consumers to their music. The recording industry, however, argued that Napster's facilitating of the mass sharing of unauthorized copies threatened their current content distribution and display system—e.g., CDs, radio and live forum play, and music stores—and their ability to move into the emerging digital market.

But those are policy arguments. In federal district court in California, Napster's legal defense was that its users did not engage in infringement because their sharing was fair use: "sampling, where users make temporary copies of a work before purchasing; space-shifting, where users access a sound recording through the Napster system that they already own in audio CD format; and permissive distribution of recordings by both new and established artists."[13] The court, however, disagreed, and issued an injunction against Napster, concluding that the plaintiffs had a strong case against Napster as a contributory infringer. The Ninth Circuit upheld the lower court ruling. Napster users' activities were not fair use because the purpose and use were not transformative; rather they were commercial, "demonstrated by a showing that repeated and exploitative unauthorized copies of copyrighted works were made to save the expense of purchasing authorized copies."[14] The nature of the use of music is creative, factor two in determining infringement, favored the plaintiffs. Because file sharing involves copying of an entire work, Napster users' wholesale copying also favored the plaintiffs' argument. Finally, among the evidence showing Napster's impact on the potential market was a finding that "Napster use harms the market for plaintiffs' copyrighted musical compositions and sound recordings by reducing CD sales among college students."[15]

The court also said that "space-shifting"—the cyber analog to time-shifting—was not a fair-use defense that could be applied to Napster users because the technology was used for far more than home use. In an earlier ruling, *Recording Industry Association of America. v. Diamond Multimedia Systems, Inc.*, 180 F.3d 1072 (9th Cir. 1999), the Ninth Circuit said that Rio, a device with headphones that allows a user to download MP3 audio files from a computer and to listen to them elsewhere, merely shifted space for home use.

Conduct That Renders the Sony Fair-Use Defense Irrelevant

Within eight months of the *Napster* ruling, twenty-eight entertainment companies filed an infringement lawsuit against Groskter, Ltd. and SteamCast Networks in October 2001. Grokster, Ltd. and StreamCast Networks had been distributing free space-shifting software, enabling end users to download and share music and video. A federal trial court judge found for the defendants on summary judgment under a *Sony* defense because the defendants did not provide sites or otherwise facilitate direct infringement as Napster had done.[16] The defendants won on the federal appeals court level, too, where they did not rely on a fair-use defense.[17]

Ultimately, the defendants lost in *Metro-Goldwyn-Mayer Studios, Inc. v. Grokster, Ltd*, 545 U.S. 913 (2005), when the U.S. Supreme Court held that, "One who distributes a device with the object of promoting its use to infringe copyright, as shown by clear expression or other affirmative steps taken to foster infringement, going beyond mere distribution with knowledge of third-party action, is liable for the resulting acts of infringement by third parties using the device, regardless of the device's lawful uses."[18]

In *Grokster* the Court said the lower courts had misapplied the *Sony* rule. Liability for distributing a product capable of infringing and noninfringing uses did not require that the defendant knew users were misusing the product, or that upon learning of the misuse the defendant failed to stop or report it, the Court said. Rather, it was enough that the defendant encouraged others to use the product in a way that would infringe. The *Grokster* Court created a new copyright legal theory for secondary liability: inducement.

Previously under the law, a plaintiff who wished to sue a party for allegedly facilitating others' infringement argued contributory or vicarious infringement. To prove contributory infringement, a plaintiff must show that the defendant had knowledge of the direct infringer's activities and induced, caused, or materially contributed to the direct infringers conduct.[19] To prove vicarious liability, a plaintiff must show that the defendant—typically an employer—has the right and ability to control the direct infringer's acts and receives a direct financial benefit from the infringement, and the secondary infringer need not have knowledge of the infringement.[20]

Under the *Grokster* inducement test, a plaintiff must show (i) direct infringement, (ii) evidence of the intent of the alleged inducer to take affirmative steps to promote, advertise, or persuade users to commit infringement, and (iii) evidence of such promotional activities. Under the inducement theory, the plaintiff *does not have to show that the defendant knows* that others are using the product in an illegal way. Typically, inducement is an easier standard for a plaintiff to meet than a contributory liability standard because a contributory infringer *must know* that others are using the product to infringe. The vicarious liability theory is not likely to apply to P2P file sharing providers because such providers typically do not have a legal right to control the infringer's actions and P2P files are offered free of charge.

Meanwhile, the music industry targeted end users. The activities of one such end user, Cecilia Gonzalez, who downloaded more than 1,000 copyrighted songs, led to a ruling by the Seventh Circuit in *BMG Music v. Gonzalez*, 430 F.3d 888 (7th Cir. 2005) rejecting the fair-use contention that "downloading on a try-before-you-buy basis is good advertising for copyright proprietors."[21]

In contrast, in *Perfect 10, Inc. v. Amazon.com, Inc.*, 508 F.3d 1146 (2007), Google and Amazon, relying on the *Sony* fair-use defense, were able to persuade the Ninth Circuit to lift a temporary injunction in an infringement suit brought by Perfect 10, a pay-for-access website featuring nudes. Perfect 10 claimed that the Google search engine's embedding technology—using an HTML line linked to another site allowing you to display a thumbnail version of a large photograph or image from another site—infringed its display and distribution rights. But the federal appeals court said that embedding was transformative because Google used its technology to allow the public to easily find images on the Internet, "a significant social benefit," and a use that is fundamentally different from Perfect 10's use of its images.[22]

But the court found that Google could be secondarily liable under a *Grokster* inducement test— though the court called it "contributory infringement"—and remanded the case back to the lower court to decide. Though much of the discussion focused on Google, Amazon's A9.com and Alexa.com search sites were also under attack. In February 2010, Amazon reached a settlement with Perfect 10. Perfect 10's action against Google had not been resolved when this book went to press.

Some, such as intellectual property legal scholar and free-culture advocate Larry Lessig, said *Groskter* would intimidate digital technological startup operations because it was unclear how such operations could avoid infringement lawsuits under a *Grokster* liability standard. "It might take 10 years of litigation to get a clear sense of this," Lessig told *Businessweek* in 2005. He continued, "That's 10 years of chilled innovation. That's really quite costly."[23]

By July 2009, a study by Peter S. Menell, director of the Berkeley Center for Law & Technology, found that *Groskter* had not had the effect Lessing predicted: "Each month brings new digital technologies—iPod, image search engines, MySpace, YouTube, Facebook, Google's Book Search, BitTorrent, iPhone, Twitter, Kindle 2.0—many of which could be (and have been) portrayed as facilitating copyright infringement. The development and commercialization of these technologies suggest that the cloud of liability has not throttled the digital innovation pipeline."[24]

Still, Menell's findings may be premature. As of early 2012, an objective viewer might reasonably conclude that the results were mixed. Viacom's infringement action brought against YouTube and Google, its owner, filed in 2007, continued to wind through the courts. Viacom alleges that YouTube violates the Digital Millennium Copyright Act (DMCA), discussed below, by allowing thousands to upload Viacom's television content. The defendants won a summary judgment against Viacom in 2010, only to have it reversed by the Second Circuit in *Viacom International, Inc. v. YouTube, Inc.*, 10–3270-cv (2d Cir. April 5, 2012). Though a federal judge rejected the Google Books settlement in *Authors Guild v. Google*, 05 CV 8136 (March 22, 11 2011, S.D.N.Y), the case was still scheduled for trial in 2012. A federal judge in California in *Columbia Pictures Industries, Inc. v. Fung*, 2:06-cv- 05578-SVW-JC (C.D. Cal. Dec. 21, 2009) found inducement and ordered BitTorrent file-sharing network's search engine Isohunt to remove all infringing content in December 2009. In July 2009, about the same time Menell published his study, the U.S. Supreme Court declined to review the U.S. Court of Appeals for the Second Circuit's ruling in *The Cartoon Network and Cable News Network v. CSC Holdings, Inc., et al.*, 536 F.3d 121 (2008), cert denied 129 S. Ct. 2890 (2009). To the disappointment of the cable television networks, the federal appeals panel said that the distribution and use of RS-DVR technology (TiVo) did not constitute infringement. And in May 2010, a federal judge in New York granted a summary judgment in favor of the music industry that brought infringement claims against LimeWire, a company that operated a file-sharing service in *Arista Records LLC v. Lime Group LLC*, No. 06 CV 5936 (KMW) (S.D.N.Y. May 11, 2010).

The Digital Millennium Copyright Act (DMCA) of 1998, 17 U.S.C. § 1201

The *Sony* creation of a fair-use safe harbor in 1984 helped to spur Congress to pass the DMCA. The DMCA provides civil and criminal penalties for anyone—there are exemptions—providing devices or tools that help others circumvent technology that protects copyrighted devices, commonly known as digital rights management (DRM). What's the connection? Recall that under the *Sony* fair-use safe harbor, a producer or distributor of copying technology will not be secondarily liable for infringement so long as the technology is merely capable of substantial noninfringing uses. The problem for copyright holders is that some circumvention devices and antilocking technology are also capable of substantial noninfringing uses. Under such circumstances, the *Sony* exception shielded the makers and distributors of such devices from copyright infringement lawsuits, making copyright owners of digital and Internet content vulnerable to piracy.

And courts, in fact, did allow the sale and distribution of technology that unlocked DRM devices. *Vault Corp. v. Quaid Software*, 847 F.2d 255 (5th Cir. 1988), is one such ruling. Vault made computer diskettes designed to prevent unauthorized duplication of programs placed on its diskettes. But Quaid produced a diskette that unlocked Vault's protective measures. Vault sued Quaid for infringement, among other claims. Quaid argued its diskette served the legitimate purpose of allowing buyers of programs recorded on Vault's diskettes to make archival copies, copying that constituted a substantial noninfringing use under U.S. 17 § 117 (a)(2). Finding for Quaid, the Fifth Circuit reasoned that, "Because § 117(2) permits the making of fully functional archival copies, it follows that [Quaid's diskette] is capable of substantial non-infringing uses."[25]

The DMCA's § 1201 (a)(2)(b) eliminates the *Sony* fair-use defense for antilocking technology because the statute bans the "manufacture, import, offer to the public…or otherwise traffic in any technology, product, service, device, component, or part thereof, that is primarily designed for the purpose of circumventing protection afforded by a technological measure that effectively protects a right of a copyright owner" and doesn't allow for weighing whether the technology is capable of substantial noninfringing use.

Under the DMCA, consumers who use such technology may face civil and criminal penalties. Section 1201 however, carves out exceptions for law enforcement, intelligence agencies and other government activities, nonprofit library, archive and educational institutions, reverse engineering—"for the sole purpose of identifying and analyzing elements of the program necessary to achieve interoperability with other programs"—encryption, protection of minors, personal privacy, and security testing.

Self-described free hackers—"enthusiastic computer programmers who share their work with others"—are fond of sharing their novel software that often contains circumvention codes by posting them on the web. And many users post other individual and corporation's copyrighted video and images on social networking and video-sharing sites. Section 512 (d) of the DMCA attempts to thwart hackers and other infringers by targeting the owners of websites with a carrot-and-stick approach. Site owners, Internet service providers, or hosting companies get immunity from infringement liability when they respond "expeditiously" to "take down or block access to material" in response to a copyright owner's notification, do not gain financially from the infringing activity, and did not know about the infringing activity before notification by the copyright owner.

The DMCA's § 1201(c)(1) provides that nothing in § 1201 affects defenses to copyright, including fair use. A host of critics take issue with that assertion. So-called digital rights advocates such as the Electronic Frontier Foundation and others say as more and more content becomes digitalized, the legal authority the DMCA gives copyright holders to fight pirating of copyrighted material threatens to eliminate the public's fair-use rights. They also say that corporations are abusing the DMCA by filing takedown notices against legitimate fair-use material and activity.[26]

In Bad Faith?

Critics say the arbitrary use by copyright holders of takedown notices and the interpretation of § 512's misrepresentation and "good faith" provisions allows copyright holders to censor speech on the Internet and deprive individuals of exercising fair use. When a copyright owner suspects his or her copyright is being infringed, the owner must follow the notice and takedown provisions set forth in § 512(c)(3) of the DMCA and the copyright owner must have "*a good faith belief* that use of the material in the manner complained of is not authorized by the copyright owner, its agent, or the law," according to § 512(c)(3)(A)(v).

Section 512 of the DCMA provides that anyone who files a takedown notice and knowingly misrepresents that the material or activity is infringing may be subject to liability. Courts, however, have interpreted the misrepresentation and good faith provisions to favor copyright holders. The Ninth Circuit's ruling in *Rossi v. Motion Picture Association of America (MPAA)*, 391 F.3d 1000 (9th Cir. 2002), illustrates the difficulty defendants in such cases face, largely because the complaining copyright owner does not have to make a showing that the posting is not likely to be a fair use.

In *Rossi v. Motion Picture Association of American,* defendant Michael J. Rossi owned Internet Movies.com, a directory of websites containing information about movies. Though Internet Movies.com claimed it had downloadable movies, users, in fact, could not download movies from the site: "Rossi contends that if the MPAA had conducted such an investigation, it would have inevitably concluded that Rossi's website could not possibly have been providing a source for downloading movies."[27] Rossi asked the court to impose an objective standard of review for determining the reasonableness of MPAA's takedown notice issued to Ross. Showing that the copyright holder actually knew—the subjective standard—is a more difficult standard to meet than showing that a reasonable copyright holder would have attempted to download the materials to determine if infringement was even possible. The Ninth Circuit, however, rejected the objective standard, finding that Congress did not incorporate an objective standard into the DMCA.[28]

DMCA critics hope that courts will adopt the *Lenz v. Universal Music Corp.*, 572 F. Supp. 2d 1150 (2008), approach to interpreting the misrepresentation and good faith provisions. *Lenz* is a case of first impression because no previous case had actually adjudicated whether fair use qualifies as a defense in connection with a takedown notice under the DMCA. In *Lenz,* Stephanie Lenz posted a video on YouTube of her daughter dancing in a kitchen with 20 seconds of Prince's hit, "Let's Go Crazy," playing in the background. Universal owns the copyright, and Prince demanded that the music not be played on the Internet. ABC Television News dubbed the case, "The Home Video Prince Doesn't Want You to See: Pa. Mom Fights Back with Lawsuit Against Movie Company." Universal sent YouTube a takedown notice. Lenz eventually filed a suit against Universal alleging misrepresentation under 7 U.S.C. § 512(f). The federal judge sitting in California refused to dismiss Lenz's case. He said that even under *Rossi's* subjective standard, copyright holders such as Universal are required to apply the four factors of fair use—the purpose and character of the use, the nature of the copyrighted work, the amount and substantiality of the portion used, and the effect of the use upon the potential market for or value of the copyrighted work—before issuing a takedown notice.[29]

By 2012, *Lenz v. Universal Music Corp.* was still in court, several legal experts had weighed in on the matter in law review articles, but no other court had adopted the *Lenz* fair-use determination requirement. Meanwhile, some copyright owners who filed takedown notices had backed down once defendants countersued alleging fair use and other defenses. One such case involves a removal notice sent by Apple Inc. to a wiki site known as Bluwiki, alleging that site users' online discussions about how Apple iPods and iPhones interoperate with software other than Apple's own iTunes violated the DMCA. OdioWorks, the owners of Bluwiki, filed a lawsuit in federal court in San Francisco seeking a declaratory judgment that the discussions did not violate the DMCA's anticircumvention provisions nor infringe Apple's copyrights.[30] OdioWorks argued that the discussions were protected by fair use, and "the computer code posted on the iTunesDB pages constitutes a small portion of the iTunes software, relates to common functions used in virtually all computer code, and is not original creative expression owned by Apple."[31] According to Electronic Frontier Foundation lawyers, Apple withdrew its takedown notice and legal threats in July 2009.

Meanwhile, congressional efforts to blunt DMCA's impact on fair-use activities have stalled. The Benefit Authors without Limiting Advancement or Net Consumer Expectations (BALANCE) Act of 2003, revised in 2005, would protect, among other things, end users who use lawfully obtained digital works for archival and private purposes, who sell or give away their lawfully obtained copy of digital works (first sale doctrine), and who employ circumvention devises for noninfringing purposes. The Digital Media Consumers' Rights Act, or H.R. 1201, introduced in 2003 and revised in 2005, provides, among other reforms, that it is not a violation of the DMCA to circumvent a device to gain access to or use a work if circumvention does not result in infringement.

Despite these efforts, the DMCA remains unchanged. In defense of the DMCA, *Wired* magazine staffer David Kravets wrote an article entitled, "10 Years Later, Misunderstood DMCA is the Law That Saved the Web." Kravets argued that § 512(d) immunity for webspace providers proved crucial to the Web 2.0 explosion in interactive websites because the shield gave such providers a way to deal with infringement claims against users without having to go to court. "Blogs, search engines, e-commerce sites, video and social-networking portals are thriving today thanks in large part to the notice-and-take-down regime ushered in by the much-maligned copyright overhaul," Kravets contended.[32]

SUMMARY: In the 1980s, courts invoked the fair use doctrine to strike a balance between the consumers' use of new copying technologies and copyright holders' right to protect their property. Because a photocopy machine allows users to make an unlimited number of copies, the fair use of the device is limited to making copies of limited portions of copyrighted materials for research and educational purposes. The U.S. Supreme Court's ruling in *Sony Corp. of America v. Universal City Studios, Inc.*, carved out a fair-use exception for the Betamax video recording device that television production companies viewed as a threat. The court ruled that a significant portion of consumers used video recorders solely for home use. The device, the Court said, merely shifted the time that viewers viewed copyrighted programming and did not harm content makers' financial interest. Thus, the video recording is used primarily for noninfringing activity, a fair use.

By the early 21st century, courts were confronted with infringement actions brought against digital technologies. In the landmark *A&M Records, Inc. v. Napster, Inc.*, 239 F.3d 1004 (9th Cir. 2001), a federal appeals court ruled that MP3 peer-to-peer file sharing technology that allows users to distribute copies among an unlimited number of individuals rather than for an individual's home use was not a fair-use technology.

Makers and distributors of software that enables end users to infringe copyright-protected content are not protected under fair use when they induce others to use the devices to infringe, the Court ruled in *Metro-Goldwyn-Mayer Studios, Inc. v. Grokster, Ltd.*, 545 U.S. 913 (2005). Copyright holders can sue the makers and distributors under a theory of inducement: the maker or distributor encouraged others to use the product in a way that would infringe. Consequently, when a maker or distributor has induced others to infringe, the *Sony* fair-use defense doesn't apply.

The Digital Millennium Copyright Act (1998) provides civil and criminal penalties for anyone—there are exemptions—providing devices or tools that help others circumvent digital rights management (DRM) or anticircumvention devices. It targets technologies that allow users to circumvent measures that protect online copyrighted content. Consequently, it eliminates the *Sony* fair-use and substantially noninfringing defense for circumvention technologies.

The DMCA also authorizes copyright holders to demand that a website take down a device or content that a copyright holder says is infringing. Critics say the courts' interpretation of the statute's takedown provisions allow copyright holders to undermine the fair use doctrine and free expression by pressuring Internet service providers and website operators to remove users' posted content that is used in noninfringing ways.

Trademark Law

As noted in Chapter 13, copyright law does not protect titles, names, domain names, short phrases, symbols, slogans, designs, typographic ornamentation, lettering, coloring, or listing of ingredients. Producers and sellers, however, can seek protection for such designations, and sounds, fragrances, packaging (trade dress), and other indicia, under trademark and unfair competition laws. These laws include the federal Lanham (Trademark) Act, state statutes, and common law. The Lanham (Trademark) Act, however, provides the primary source of trademark protection.

Trademark and unfair competition laws are closely related, as the former is a subspecies of the latter.[33] Unfair competition law provides legal actions in law and equity—a body of law that addresses concerns of fairness outside the boundaries of common law—that allow an individual or corporation to stop dishonest or fraudulent competition in trade and commerce. Unfair competition and trademark share the goal of protecting consumers from confusion.

Trademark law, however, only protects marks that identify commercial products and services. A trademark is a word, phrase, or symbol that is used to identify a manufacturer or sponsor of a good or the provider of a service. It gives a trademark holder the exclusive right to stop those that would use the holder's identifying marks to exploit the good will associated with the holder's services or products.[34] Simply put, a trademark—a familiar brand logo or container color design, for example—signals to a customer that the package of coffee he or she just picked off the shelf is, in fact, the one that the customer prefers and not an inferior or different-tasting brand of coffee.

To qualify as a trademark, an identifying mark must be used in "commerce." Under the Lanham (Trademark) Act, an identifying mark is deemed to be used in commerce when: (i) the mark is placed in any manner on goods, their containers, their displays, on the goods' tags or labels and, in certain cases, on documents associated with the goods or their sale; and (ii) the goods are sold or transported in interstate commerce. For all practical purposes, a service mark is the same as a trademark except that trademarks promote products while service marks promote services. Some familiar service marks include McDonalds, Pepsi, Google, Walmart, and Microsoft.

Trademark law's purpose, the U.S. Supreme Court explained in *Qualitex Co. v. Jacobson Products, Co. Inc.*, 514 U.S. 159, 163–164 (1995), is to protect trademark holders and customers. If you're Nike, for example, you do not want other competitors using your famous swoosh logo. Nike has the exclusive right to use the swoosh logo and can sue for trademark infringement to stop others from using the same or similar mark, thereby preventing consumers from being confused or misled about who made the sneaker or related apparel. Though some might be willing to pay $25 for a knock-off Nike sneaker, no reasonable consumer knowingly wants to pay Nike-like prices for a fake Nike sneaker.

Because Nike's swoosh is known worldwide, the company can also sue under federal and state trademark dilution law.[35] A trademark owner can seek remedies under dilution to stop competitors from using a mark similar to its famous mark to sell unrelated goods or service. Trademark dilution law protects an owner's investment in its mark. Dilution comes in two forms: blurring and tarnishing. Blurring arises when a mark creates "the possibility that the mark will lose its ability to serve as a unique identifier of the plaintiff's product."[36] Tarnishing, however, results "when a famous mark is improperly associated with an inferior or offensive product or service."[37]

A trademark owner may also bring additional trademark-related actions under state unfair competition laws such as misappropriation, passing or palming off, contributory passing off, and reverse passing off. In misappropriation, a defendant co-opts his rival's intangible trade value as if it were his own to the plaintiff's disadvantage. The doctrine was established in *International News Service v.*

Associated Press, 248 U.S. 215 (1918). Nearly a century later, Associated Press (AP), the defendant accused of misappropriating International News Services' "hot news" stories, is suing Meltwater U.S. Holdings, a news clipping service, for copyright infringement and misappropriation. According to AP, Meltwater misappropriates AP's news stories because Meltwater sells its excerpts of AP stories to subscribers while incurring "no expense to create or license the content it delivers, allowing it to reap substantial subscription fees with minimal expenses while undercutting its competitors—including the AP, and other entities who have paid valuable consideration to AP for licenses to distribute its content."[38]

The tort of passing or palming off, a subspecies of fraud, developed in the 19th century and is the seed that grew into unfair competition and trademark law.[39] Under this doctrine, liability is imposed when a defendant passes off its product as the plaintiff's product.

Not All Marks Are Equal. Under the Lanham (Trademark) Act, a mark must be distinctive in consumers' minds, not merely descriptive, and consumers must associate the mark with the seller or producer of a specific product. A descriptive mark, however, may be accepted as distinctive by "proof of substantially exclusive and continuous use of the mark applied to the applicant's goods for five years preceding the application."[40]

Whether the mark is protectable is the threshold issue in trademark infringement cases.[41] To determine whether a mark is protectable, the courts place the mark in one of four categories: generic, merely descriptive, suggestive, and arbitrary and fanciful. Generic marks receive no protection. The other categories "almost automatically tell a customer that they refer to a brand."[42] Keep in mind, however, that the "categories, like the tones in a spectrum, tend to blur at the edges and merge together. The labels are more advisory than definitional, more like guidelines than pigeonholes."[43]

Typically, cases in which the generic status of a trademark is in dispute involve a name that the public identifies with the type of product, but not a particular company. Once a court deems the term generic, the former trademark holder cannot prevent competitors from using the term to identify their products. Generic terms "can *never* be trademarks. Examples of brand names held to be generic terms are Convenient store retail store, Dry Ice solid carbon dioxide, Light Beer ale-type beverages, and, in a case where a once-fanciful mark had, over time, been assimilated into the language, Thermos vacuum-insulated bottles."[44] In *Abercrombie & Fitch Co. v. Hunting World, Inc.*, 537 F.2d 4 (2d Cir. 1976), the Second Circuit ruled that "safari" could not be used as a trademark with enforceable rights because it had come to represent a generic type of product.

Descriptive marks do not distinguish a producer or seller's goods from anyone else's; they merely identify a characteristic or quality of an article or service typical of merchants marketing similar goods or services. Typically, courts have resorted to a number of tests to classify a mark as descriptive: dictionary definitions, the "imagination test," "whether competitors would be likely to need the terms used in the trademark in describing their products," and "the extent to which a term actually has been used by others marketing a similar service or product."[45]

Courts do not grant rights to descriptive marks unless such marks have acquired "secondary meaning." As the Court in *Kellogg Co. v. National Biscuit Co.*, 305 U.S. 111, 118–119 (1938) established, a descriptive mark acquires secondary meaning when "the primary significance of the term in the minds of the consuming public is not the product but the producer." The emphasis is on the primary meaning of the term in the public's mind. A subordinate meaning is insufficient to establish secondary meaning. In *Kellogg v. National Biscuit*, for example, the Court ruled that National Biscuit did not have a trademark on "shredded wheat," because, in part, even though for "a long period in which the plaintiff or its predecessor was the only manufacturer of the product, many people have come to associate the product, and as a consequence the name by which the product is generally known, with the plaintiff's factory at Niagara Falls." As a result, "The showing which it has made does not entitle it to the exclusive use of the term shredded wheat but merely entitles it to require that the defendant use reasonable care to inform the public of the source of its product."[46]

To determine whether secondary meaning has been created, courts typically look at: survey evidence, consumer testimony, manner, and duration of use of the mark, sales volumes, number of customers, and amount and manner of advertising. It must be remembered, however, that, "the question is not the extent of the promotional efforts, but their effectiveness in altering the meaning of [the term] to the consuming public."[47]

Generally, a suggestive mark warrants trademark protection without proof of secondary meaning. A term is suggestive if it invokes a characteristic of the underlying product or service, is related to the underlying product or service, but requires imagination, thought and perception to reach a conclusion as to the nature of goods.[48] The Second Circuit's ruling in *Hasbro, Inc. v. Lanard Toys, Ltd.*, 858 F.2d 70, 75 (2d Cir. 1988), is illustrative. There, the court ruled toymaker Hasbro should be awarded a preliminary injunction to stop a rival from using use its unregistered mark of "Gung-Ho" because the term was suggestive: "Connecting the fantasy personality to the toy action figure requires imagination. And, quite simply, it is this need to resort to imagination that renders 'GUNG-HO' suggestive rather than descriptive. Thus, we hold that 'GUNG-HO' as used by Hasbro on its marine action figure as part of the 'G.I. JOE' line is a suggestive mark."

An arbitrary or fanciful mark is inherently distinctive and accorded a high degree of protection because it does not describe the underlying product or is mismatched with the type of product in dispute. For example, Xerox and Kodak "are fanciful [names], having been completely fabricated by the trademark holders"[49] and have no inherent relationship with electronic copiers or photo cameras. Apple, when used as a trademark for computer products is mismatched, and thus "arbitrary." Use it as a term associated with an apple grower's products, then the mark is generic, deserving of no protection.

Acquiring trademark rights. If a trademark is arbitrary, fanciful, suggestive, or descriptive with second meaning, an individual or corporation can acquire trademark rights in one of two ways: (i) by being the first to use the mark in commerce; or (ii) by being the first to register the mark with the U.S. Patent and Trademark Office (PTO).

Under common law, the first to use a mark in a particular geographic market in connection with sales of a particular product or service acquires trademark rights in that market area, and the courts may consider "pre-sales publicity or sales solicitation using the mark with intent to continue use, without actual sales…to establish rights."[50] Under common law or state statutes, unlike Lanham (Trademark) Act protection, a trademark holder's rights are limited to a geographical market.

Registration. A party does not have to register a mark to get protection under the Lanham (Trademark) Act, but doing so has its benefits: exclusive nationwide use of the mark with the presumption that the mark is not generic;[51] the right to go to federal courts to resolve infringement actions;[52] enhanced ability to block imported infringing goods;[53] potential to recover treble damages, attorneys' fees, and other remedies not available to unregistered trademark owners;[54] and "incontestability" after a five-year period of registration.[55] Incontestability gives the registrant conclusive evidence of the exclusive right to use the registered mark. Consequently, in an infringement action, the other party cannot argue that the mark should not have been registered, is similar to another mark, or not inherently distinctive. An incontestable trademark, however, can be challenged as abandoned, that it has lapsed into a generic status, or that registration was fraudulent.

Trademark Infringement. The Lanham (Trademark) Act and common law allow parties to sue for infringement and seek enjoinment, illegal profits, attorney, and court fees. In such an action, a plaintiff argues that the infringing party used a similar or identical mark in connection with the sale of goods or services, raising the likelihood of confusion among consumers about the source of the goods or services. Generally, a plaintiff must show that (i) it possesses a valid and enforceable mark and a right of priority over the defendant to use that mark; and (ii) that the defendant used the mark in connection with goods or services at issue in the case in a way that is likely to confuse consumers about the true source of the goods or services.

Courts have identified several factors to determine likelihood of confusion. The Fourth Circuit, for example, weighs "(a) the strength or distinctiveness of the mark; (b) the similarity of the two marks; (c) the similarity of the goods/services the marks identify; (d) the similarity of the facilities the two parties use in their businesses; (e) the similarity of the advertising used by the two parties; (f) the defendant's intent; (g) actual confusion."[56] The Ninth Circuit weighs: "(1) the similarity of the marks; (2) the relatedness of the parties' goods; (3) the similarity of trade or marketing channels; (4) the strength of the plaintiffs marks; (5) defendant's intent; (6) evidence of actual confusion; (7) the degree of care exercised by the average purchaser; and (8) the likelihood of expansion into other markets."[57]

Trademark Dilution. In 2006, the federal Trademark Dilution Revision Act became effective. The act overturned the U.S. Supreme Court's ruling in *Moseley v. Secret Catalogue, Inc.*, 537 U.S. 418 (2003). In that controversy, the Victoria's Secret lingerie company sued Victor and Cathy Moseley's Kentucky strip mall shop, "Victor's Little Secret," under a claim of dilution. The Court ruled that Victoria's Secret had to prove actual dilution, not merely the likelihood that the small company's play on the name Victoria's Secret would dilute or tarnish the distinctive quality of the Victoria's Secret trademark. Now, under the 2006 revision, a plaintiff has to show that a defendant's mark is *likely* to dilute the plaintiff's mark. Unlike a trademark infringement case, the likelihood of consumer confusion is not at issue in dilution cases.

Earlier in this chapter, we identified Nike as an owner of a distinct and famous trademark, and that the famous status of the trademark allowed it to bring a trademark dilution action. The Trademark Dilution Revision Act, which amends 15 U.S.C. § 1125(c), requires a plaintiff to show: (i) its mark is famous; (ii) its mark is distinctive; (iii) the defendant began using its mark or trade name after the plaintiff's mark became famous; (iv) the defendant's use of his mark is in commerce; and (v) the defendant's mark must be likely to cause dilution to the plaintiff's mark.[58]

Typically, state statutory law provides for trademark dilution actions. Though the elements for a trademark dilution cause of action vary from state to state, the New York statute has its counterparts in at least twenty other states, and, thus, is illustrative to a large degree. Under the New York statute, a plaintiff is required to show that (i) the mark has a distinctive quality capable of dilution and (ii) show a likelihood of dilution.[59] Courts interpreting state statutes have defined distinctiveness in several ways, including the trademark's conceptual strength or uniqueness. Courts have also defined distinctiveness as having "secondary meaning"; that the mark "has become so associated in the mind of the public with that entity or its product that it identifies the goods sold by that entity and distinguishes them from goods sold by others."[60]

Defenses: Matters of public concern, parody, and fair use. Conceptually, trademark and First Amendment free expression laws are in conflict. That is because trademark law gives someone the right to prevent others from using a specific word, phrase, or symbol for commercial purposes. The two doctrines do not come into conflict when an alleged infringer or diluter uses someone else's trademark for commercial purposes because the First Amendment does not protect commercial speech that is misleading or deceptive. But can news reporters, politicians, critics, satirists, and artists fend off infringement and dilution actions based on free speech concerns?

Trademark Infringement & News. Neither the courts nor the Lanham (Trademark) Act recognize a non-commercial speech exemption for news reporting and commentary in infringement cases. Nevertheless, those who use trademarks in news accounts or in public affairs discussions generally have a defense against infringement. Courts consider the noncommercial aspect of news reporting and political speech when determining consumer confusion—whether the defendant used the mark in connection with goods or services at issue in the case in a way that is likely to confuse consumers about the true source of the goods or services. Consider, for example, the Ronald Reagan administration, politicians, scientists, and news media's use of the phrase "star wars" to describe the administration's Strategic Defense Initiative (SDI) program in the mid-1980s. Did they infringe Lucasfilms, Ltd.'s trademark of the term Star Wars? George Lucas thought so. He argued that associating the movie title Star Wars with the political controversy would injure the goodwill he achieved with the Star Wars movie series. He sued for trademark infringement and other claims. A federal district court judge, however, rejected his claim in *Lucasfilms, Ltd. v. High Frontier*, 622 F. Supp. 931, 934–935 (D.D.C. 1985):

> [Trademark and unfair competition] laws do not reach into the realm of public discourse to regulate the use of terms used outside the context of trade. Defendants' use of the phrase star wars to persuade the public of their viewpoint through television messages is not an infringing use…When politicians, newspapers, and the public generally use the phrase star wars for convenience, in parody or descriptively to further a communication of their views on SDI, plaintiff has no rights as owner of the mark to prevent this use of STAR WARS…Trademark laws regulate unfair competition, not the parallel development of new dictionary meanings in the everyday give and take of human discourse.

Trademark Infringement, Parody, and Artistic Expression. Perhaps, the Ninth Circuit best explained the effectiveness of parody as a defense in *Dr. Seuss Enterprises, LP v. Penguin Books*, 109 F.3d 1394, 1405 (9th Cir. 1997), by quoting *McCarthy on Trademarks and Unfair Competition*: "Some parodies will constitute an infringement, some will not. But the cry of 'parody!' does not magically fend off otherwise legitimate claims of trademark infringement or dilution. There are confusing parodies and non-confusing parodies. All they have in common is an attempt at humor through the use of someone else's trademark. A non-infringing parody is merely amusing, not confusing."

According to the Fourth Circuit, under trademark law, parody is (i) "a 'simple form of entertainment conveyed by juxtaposing the irreverent representation of the trademark with the idealized image created by the mark's owner;' (ii) that must 'convey two simultaneous—and contradictory—messages: that it is the original, but also that it is *not* the original and is instead a parody.'"[61] If the parody conveys only the trademark's message "it is not only a poor parody but also vulnerable under trademark law, since the customer will be confused. While a parody necessarily must engender some initial confusion, an effective parody will diminish the risk of consumer confusion 'by conveying [only] just enough of the original design to allow the consumer to appreciate the point of parody.'"[62]

Only a handful of courts—most notably the Ninth and Sixth federal appeals courts—recognize a blanket First Amendment exemption for trademarks used in parodies and artistic works. *In Mattel, Inc. v. MCA Records, Inc.*, 296 F.3d 894, 900 (9th Cir. 2002), the Ninth Circuit said, "Simply put, the trademark owner does not have the right to control public discourse whenever the public imbues his mark with a meaning beyond its source-identifying function."[63]

Many other courts rely on the Second Circuit's *Rogers v. Grimaldi*, 875 F.2d 994 (2d Cir. 1989), balancing test of First Amendment free expression and avoiding consumer confusion. In *Rogers v. Grimaldi*, the court held that the Lanham (Trademark) Act will normally not support a finding of infringement when the use of the mark is artistically relevant and does not explicitly mislead consumers as to the source of the work.

Dilution Defenses. Courts take a different approach to trademark dilution. That is because the Trademark Dilution Revision Act of 2006, 15 U.S.C. § 1125(c)(3)(B), bars dilution claims for news reporting, criticism, commentary, and parody. Nevertheless, when others use a famous or distinctive trademark in reporting, criticism, commentary, or parody, the use must not be commercial; that is, it must not be in connection with the promotion or sales of a good or service that competes with the plaintiff's business. Therefore, for example, the Second Circuit ruled that Wolfe's Borough Coffee's "Charbucks"—a play on "Starbucks" to identify the Wolfe line of coffee that was darker than Starbucks coffee—was not the kind of parody that protected against Starbucks' dilution action. That was because, the court said, "Charbucks parody is promoted not as a satire or irreverent commentary of Starbucks but, rather, as a beacon to identify Charbucks as a coffee that competes at the same level and quality as Starbucks in producing dark-roasted coffees."[64]

In contrast, Walmart critic Charles Smith's designs and slogans that were variations of his "Walocaust," and "Wal-Qaeda" phrases were protected criticism and parodies even though he sought to make money from mugs, underwear, camisoles, teddy bears, bumper stickers, bibs and t-shirts bearing the phrases, a federal court in Georgia ruled in *Smith v. Wal-Mart*, 537 F. Supp. 2d 1302, 1340 (N.D. Ga. 2008). The judge said a reasonable jury could only find that Smith "primarily intended to express himself with his Walocaust and Wal-Qaeda concepts and that commercial success was a secondary motive at most."

The Trademark Dilution Act also provides a fair-use exemption, and there are two kinds: descriptive and nominative. A mark is descriptive if it identifies a characteristic or quality of an article or service, such as its color, odor, function, dimensions, or ingredients. The fair-use defense applies when the descriptive mark is used in good faith for its primary meaning and consumer confusion is unlikely.[65]

Under the nominative use theory, a trademark holder cannot prevent someone from using a famous mark when the mark is the only way to reasonably refer to trademarked product or service. The Ninth Circuit established the test for nominative use in *New Kids on the Block v. News America Publishing, Inc.*, 971 F.2d 302, 308 (9th Cir. 1992): "First, the product or service in question must be one not readily identifiable without use of the trademark; second, only so much of the mark or marks may be used as is reasonably necessary to identify the product or service; and third, the user must do nothing that would, in conjunction with the mark, suggest sponsorship or endorsement by the trademark holder."[66]

Anticybersquatting Consumer Protection Act of 1999. ACPA amends the Lanham (Trademark) Act, 15 U.S.C. § 1125(d)(1)(A), by allowing a trademark holder to sue a person who uses a mark as a domain name that is "identical or confusingly similar to" the holder's distinctive or famous mark in "a bad faith intent to profit from that mark." Courts may employ the statute's nine factors or others to determine bad faith.[67] Thus, to win a cybersquatting claim, a plaintiff must show (i) that its trademark, is distinctive at the time of registration of the domain name, (ii) that the domain names registered by the defendant are identical or confusingly similar to the trademark, and (iii) that the defendant used or registered the domain names with a bad faith intent to profit.

SUMMARY: Trademark law enables an individual, group, or corporation to protect its commercial interest in a mark, which tells customers that the source of the products and services they buy, is, indeed, the one that they have come to trust. If someone uses another's trademark or a similar-looking one without permission, the true trademark holder is deprived of the good will and money he or she has invested in a product or service. Just as important, consumers may be misled or deceived by the similar or copied trademark into buying a different or inferior product.

Trademarks are a form of communication: words, slogans, logos, packaging, graphic signals, symbols, under certain conditions colors, and other communicative shorthand that signal to a consumer the true source of the product or service. In the U.S., under trademark law—whether under the federal Lanham (Trademark) Act or state statues—such marks do not qualify as trademarks until they are used in commerce; that is, they must be affixed to the goods or related documents, transported, promoted, advertised, or sold. Under the Lanham (Trademark) Act, the goods must be transported, promoted, advertised, or sold in interstate commerce.

The law provides a trademark holder with two primary legal actions: infringement and dilution. In an infringement action, a plaintiff argues that another party has used a similar or identical mark in connection with the sale of goods or services, raising the likelihood of confusion among consumers about the source of the goods or services. In a dilution action, the holder of a distinct or famous trademark must show that a party is tarnishing or blurring the owner's ability to use the mark as a unique identifier of its product or service. Defendants, however, may defeat infringement or dilution claims, arguing that their use of a mark was for reporting news, commentary, criticism, parody, or a fair use.

ONLINE RESOURCES

1. Google Book Settlement, http://www.googlebooksettlement.com/agreement.html
2. U.S. Copyright Office Summary of the Digital Millennium Act of 1998, http://www.copyright.gov/legislation/dmca.pdf
3. Copyright Timeline: A History of Copyright in the United States, http://www.arl.org/pp/ppcopyright/copyresources/copytimeline.shtml#18C
4. Overview of Trademark Law, http://cyber.law.harvard.edu/metaschool/fisher/domain/tm.htm
5 Trademark Infringement Primer, http://www.pillsburylaw.com/siteFiles/Publications/25A0E7B0FA655AD2336C8C937472C3C8.pdf

QUESTIONS

Metamorphosis is a new and amazing technology. It looks and works something like a scanner but does far more than produce a digital copy of an analog work. If you place a copy of a novel, for example, onto the Metamorphosis's screen and push one button, Metamorphosis will transform it into a video version of the book, with the similar characters, plots, and descriptions depicted in moving images. Push another button and Metamorphosis will produce statuettes of the characters, places, and things similar to those described in the novel. Insert a music CD, push another button and Metamorphosis creates a short story on paper based on the CD's lyrics, or a music video with characters and plot based on the lyrics and using the music. It also can change genres as well as mediums. For example, it can change a work of fiction into to a nonfictional account. Metamorphosis has another feature called idiosyncrasy, and Metamorphosis can't operate without it. A user must download personal data about his or her personality, personal creative skills and tendencies, and aesthetic standards. Each new work created by Metamorphosis is reshaped to fit the user's idiosyncratic creative vision. For example, if a user's ability to paint is limited to stick fingers and finger painting, those limits will be reflected in the Metamorphosis copy. If the user is comical and clever, a Metamorphosis-produced copy can turn a serious work into a comedy. Metamorphosis cannot create identical copies, only similar, but idiosyncratic, works. Also, Metamorphosis can only create one new idiosyncratic work from a copyrighted or non-copyrighted work.

1. Would a work made by Metamorphosis create a derivative work?
2. Assuming Metamorphosis makes derivative works, a plaintiff brings an infringement action. The defendant argues that he or she has created an "original work" with Metamorphosis. What do you think? Does Metamorphosis create original works?
3. Assuming Metamorphosis makes derivative works, a plaintiff brings an infringement action. The defendant argues that his new work is a fair use. Is it? Apply the four-part criteria to decide.
4. Is the maker and distributor of Metamorphosis likely to be protected under the *Sony Corp. of America v. Universal City Studies, Inc.*, 464 U.S. 417 (1981) ruling? In other words, is Metamorphosis a "dual-use" technology, "capable of substantially noninfringing uses"?
5. Do you think the maker and distributor of Metamorphosis is vulnerable to a charge of vicarious liability? (See discussion of *Marvel Entertainment, Inc. v. NCSoft Corp.*, No. 04 CV 9253 RGK (PLAx) (C.D. Cal. Mar. 9, 2005), and vicarious liability above.)

ENDNOTES

1. Kevin Bergquist. "Google Book Project Promotes Public Good," *The University of Michigan Record Online*, February 13, 2006, http://www.ur.umich.edu/0506/Feb13_06/02.shtml
2. *Authors Guild v. Google, Inc.*, 770 F. Supp. 2d 666, 682 (2011).
3. *See HathiTrust Statement on Authors Guild, Inc. et al. v. HathiTrust et al.*, 11 CIV 6351, (S.D.N.Y., Sept. 21, 2011), http://www.authorsguild.org/advocacy/articles/authors-3.attachment/authors-v-hathitrust-9834/Authors%20v.%20HathiTrust%20Complaint.pdf
4. Reprography is the reproduction of graphics through mechanical or electrical means, such as photography or xerography.
5. *Folsom v. Marsh*, 9 F. Cas. 342, 348 (C.C.D. Mass. 1841).
6. *Williams & Wilkins Co. v. United States*, 420 U.S. 376 (1975).
7. *Williams & Wilkins Co. v. United States*, 487 F.2d 1345, 1359 (Ct. Cl. 1973).
8. "Notes on 17 U.S.C. § 107: U.S. Code Notes," House Report No. 94–1476, http://codes.lp.findlaw.com/uscode/17/1/107/notes
9. *Basic Books, Inc. v. Kinko's Graphics Corp*, 758 F. Supp. 1522 (1991).
10. *Princeton University Press v. Michigan Document Services, Inc.*, 99 F.3d 1381 (6th Cir. 1996) (en banc).
11. *Sony Corp. of America v. Universal City Studios, Inc.*, 464 U.S. 417, 455, (1984).
12. Ibid. 492.
13. *A&M Records, Inc. v. Napster, Inc.*, 239 F.3d 1004, 1014 (2001).

14. Ibid. 1015.
15. Ibid. at1017.
16. *Metro-Goldwyn-Mayer Studios, Inc. v. Grokster, Ltd.*, 259 F. Supp. 2d 1029, (Dist. Court, CD California 2003).
17. *Metro-Goldwyn-Mayer Studios, Inc. v. Grokster, Ltd.*, 380 F.3d 1154 (9th Cir. 2004).
18. *Metro-Goldwyn-Mayer Studios, Inc. v. Grokster, Ltd.*, 545 U.S. 913, 919 (2005).
19. *Apple Computer, Inc. v. Microsoft Corp.*, 35 F.3d 1435 (9th Cir. 1994).
20. *Shapiro, Bernstein & Co. v. H.L. Green Co.*, 316 F.2d 304, 306 (2d Cir.1963).
21. *BMG Music v. Gonzalez*, 430 F.3d 888, 890 (7th Cir. 2005).
22. *Perfect 10, Inc. v. Amazon.com, Inc.*, 508 F.3d 1146, 1168 (2007).
23. Larry Lessig. "Ten Years of Chilled Litigation," Bloomberg Businessweek (June 29, 2005), http://www.businessweek.com/technology/content/jun2005/tc20050629_2928_tc057.htm
24. Peter S. Menell. "Chilled Innovation v. Balanced Evolution: Reflecting on Indirect Copyright Liability in the Digital Age," *The Media Institute* (July 24, 2009), http://www.mediainstitute.org/IPI/2009/072409_Chilled Innovations.php
25. *Vault Corp. v. Quaid Software*, 847 F.2d 255, 267 (5th Cir. 1988).
26. "Unintended Consequences: Twelve Years under the DMCA," Electronic Frontier Foundation (March 2010), https://www.eff.org/wp/unintended-consequences-under-dmca
27. *Rossi v. Motion Picture Association of America*, 391 F.3d 1000, 1003–1004, (9th Cir. 2002).
28. Ibid. 1004–1005.
29. *Lenz v. Universal Music Corp.*, 572 F. Supp. 2d 1150, 1155–1156 (2008).
30. *OdioWorks, LLC v. Apple, Inc.*, CV 09 1818 (April 27, 2009, NDCA), http://www.citmedialaw.org/threats/apple-v-odioworks
31. Ibid. 8.
32. David Kravets. "10 Years Later, Misunderstood DMCA is the Law That Saved the Web," Wired (October 27, 2008), http://www.wired.com/threatlevel/2008/10/ten-years-later/
33. *Dell Publishing Co. v. Stanley Publications, Inc.*, 9 N.Y.2d 126 (1961).
34. See *Safeway Stores, Inc. v. Safeway Properties, Inc.*, 307 F.2d 495, 497–498 (2d Cir. 1962); *Yale Electric Corp. v. Robertson*, 26 F.2d 972, 973, 974 (2 Cir. 1928).
35. See *Nike, Inc. v. Nikepal Int'l, Inc.*, 2007 WL 2782030 (E.D. Cal. Sept. 18, 2007).
36. *Panavision International, L.P. v. Toeppen*, 141 F.3d 1316, 1326 n. 7 (9th Cir.1998).
37. Ibid.
38. *Associated Press v. Meltwater U.S. Holdings, Inc., et al.*, No. 12 Civ. 1087 (S.D.N.Y.), http://www.wired.com/images_blogs/threatlevel/2012/02/meltwater.pdf
39. See *Keaton & Keaton v. Keaton*, 842 N.E.2d 816 (2006).
40. *Abercrombie & Fitch Co. v. Hunting World, Inc.*, 537 F.2d 4, 10 (2d Cir.1976).
41. *Zatarains, Inc. v. Oak Grove Smokehouse, Inc.*, 698 F.2d 786, 790 (5th Cir. 1983).
42. *Abercrombie & Fitch Co. v. Hunting World*, 537 F.2d at 9–10.
43. *Zatarains, Inc. v. Oak Grove Smokehouse*, 698 F.2d at 790.
44. *Sara Lee Corp. v. Kayser-Roth Corp.*, 81 F.3d 455, 464 (4th Cir. 1996).
45. *Zatarain's, Inc. v. Oak Grove Smokehouse*, 698 F.2d at 793.
46. *Kellogg Co. v. National Biscuit Co.*, 305 U.S. 111, 119 (1938).
47. *Aloe Creme Laboratories, Inc. v. Milsan, Inc.*, 423 F.2d 845, 850 (5th Cir. 1970).
48. *Stix Products, Inc. v. United Merchants & Manufacturers, Inc.*, 295 F. Supp. 479, 488 (S.D.N.Y.1968).
49. *Kellogg Co. v. National Biscuit Co.*, 305 U.S. at 624.
50. *SODIMA v. International Yogurt Co.*, 662 F. Supp. 662, 853 (D. Or. 1987).
51. *Coca-Cola Co. v. Overland, Inc.*, 692 F.2d 1250, 1254 (9th Cir. 1982)
52. 15 U.S.C. § 1121.
53. 15 U.S.C. § 1124.
54. 15 U.S.C. § 1116, 1117.
55. 15 U.S.C. § 1065.

56. *Lamparello v. Falwell*, 420 F.3d 309,314–315 (4th Cir. 2005).

57. *Adidas-America, Inc. v. Payless Shoesource, Inc.*, 546 F. Supp. 2d 1029, 1052 (D. Oregon, 2008).

58. *General Motors Co. v. Urban Gorilla, LLC*, 2010 U.S. Dist. LEXIS 136711 *14, (D. Utah, 2010); See also *National Pork Board and National Pork Producers Council v. Supreme Lobster and Seafood Co.*, 96 U.S.P.Q.2d 1479 *44–45 (TTAB 2010), http://ttabvue.uspto.gov/ttabvue/ttabvue-91166701-OPP-99.pdf

59. *Mead Data Central, Inc. v. Toyota Motor Sales, U.S.A., Inc.*, 875 F.2d 1026, 1030 (2d Cir. 1989).

60. Ibid. 1031.

61. *People for the Ethical Treatment of Animals v. Doughney ("PETA")*, 263 F.3d 359, 366 (4th Cir. 2001).

62. Ibid.

63. See also *ETW Corp. v. Jireh Publishing, Inc.*, 332 F.3d 915, 927–28 (6th Cir. 2003); *E.S.S. Entm't 2000, Inc. v. Rock Star Videos, Inc.*, 444 F. Supp. 2d 1012 (C.D. Cal. 2006), *appeal docketed*, No. 06–56237 (Sept. 8, 2006).

64. *Starbucks v. Wolfe's Borough Coffee, Inc.*, 588 F.3d 97, 113 (2d Cir. 2009).

65. *Zatarain's, Inc. v. Oak Grove Smokehouse, Inc.*, 698 F.2d 786 (5th Cir. 1983).

66. See also *Universal Communication Systems, Inc. v. Lycos, Inc.*, 478 F.3d 413, 424 (1st Cir. 2007); *PACCAR Inc. v. Telescan Technologies, L.L.C.*, 319 F.3d 243, 256 (6th Cir. 2003).

67. *Sporty's Farm, LLC v. Sportsman's Market, Inc.*, 202 F.3d 489,498 (2d Cir. 2000).

CHAPTER FIFTEEN

Commercial Speech

CONTROVERSY: If a business sells a legal product or activity, can government stop it from advertising that product or activity? What if it is widely accepted that the legal product or activity is a "vice," such as liquor, alcohol, or gambling? What if the product were sex? In 11 counties in Nevada, customers are allowed to buy the services of prostitutes employed at state-regulated brothels. But the state severely restricts advertising for paid sex in the 11 counties and bans it in the rest of the state.

High Desert Advocate and *Las Vegas City Life*, owned by Coyote Publishing, and the Shady Lady Ranch brothel, challenged the Nevada advertising ban on First Amendment free speech grounds in a lawsuit filed in 2006. They won at the federal trial level. But the publisher and brothel owner lost in March 2010 before the U.S. Court of Appeals for the Ninth Circuit in *Coyote Publishing, Inc. v. Miller*, 598 F.3d 592 (9th Cir. 2010). In a 3–0 ruling, the court upheld the ban. That ruling is consistent with the U.S. Supreme Court's widely criticized ruling on the constitutionality of bans on advertising of "vice" products and activities in *Posadas de Puerto Rico Associates v. Tourism Co. of PR*, 478 U.S. 328 (1986). But *Posadas* is a wobbly precedent. In *Posadas*, a majority of the Court held that, "the greater power to completely ban casino gambling necessarily includes the lesser power to ban advertising of casino gambling." The Court's later rulings, however, severely limited *Posadas'* authority. Now, a four-part intermediate scrutiny test established in *Central Hudson Gas & Electric Corp. v. Public Service Commission*, 447 U.S. 557 (1980), and revised in *Board of Trustees of State University of New York v. Fox*, 492 U.S. 469 (1989), and in *44 Liquormart, Inc. v. Rhode Island*, 517, U.S. 484 (1996), is at the core of the commercial speech doctrine.

Chapter's Scope

The comparatively new commercial speech doctrine seeks to strike a balance between the free expression rights of advertisers, marketers, and consumers with the state's interest in protecting consumers from false, deceptive, or misleading advertising, and those promoting unlawful activities and vice. The bulk of this chapter describes the Court's development of the commercial speech doctrine, and the application of its *Central Hudson* test to laws restricting the advertising of vice products such as alcoholic beverages, tobacco, and, as adjudicated for the first time in *Coyote Publishing, Inc. v. Miller*, prostitution.

Our examination of the commercial speech doctrine is followed by a look at the corporate speech doctrine, which calls into question the logic of the commercial speech doctrine, some contend. Corporate speech may come in the form of advertising and public relations campaigns, yet it is considered political speech, noncommercial, and deserving of strict scrutiny protection. But why should corporate-produced advertising have less expressive value than corporate-produced noncommercial speech?

We also look at the compelled commercial speech and government speech doctrines. Under the compelled commercial speech doctrine, a business may be forced to subsidize industry-wide organized generic advertising and public relations campaigns promoting the products they sell, such as milk or vegetables. Similarly, the government speech doctrine gives the government authority to force businesses to subsidize government advertising and public relations campaigns promoting products and produce. The chapter concludes with another example of commercial speech's diminished First Amendment protection—Federal Trade Commission (FTC) regulatory authority.

The Commercial Speech Doctrine Evolves

For all of the 19th century and most of the 20th, the First Amendment did not protect words, images, and sounds conveyed for generating profit. The First Amendment protected only political speech—the dissemination of facts, opinions, and ideas about public political, economic, social, and religious matters. As discussed in Chapter 2, the U.S. Supreme Court's restricted view of First Amendment-protected speech led to its ruling in *Mutual Film Corporation v. Industrial Commission of Ohio*, 236 U.S. 230, 244 (1915), depriving cinema of First Amendment protection because, it reasoned, that "the exhibition of moving pictures is a business, pure and simple, originated and conducted for profit, like other spectacles, not to be regarded, nor intended to be regarded by the Ohio Constitution, we think, as part of the press of the country, or as organs of public opinion."

Accordingly, the Court declined to confer First Amendment protection to advertising in *Valentine v. Chrestensen*, 316 U.S. 52 (1942). *Valentine v. Chrestensen* stemmed from efforts by New York City to restrict the distribution of commercial speech on its public streets. During the subsequent four decades, the Court vastly broadened individuals' right to dissent and news outlets' protection against government censorship, and in turn, expanded its definition of protected speech. In the 1950s and 1960s, the Court set a foundation for altering its position that speech concerning commercial transactions did not enjoy First Amendment protection when it extended the First Amendment's scope to include cinema, sexual expression, newspaper operations, and defamation.

In *Burstyn v. Wilson*, 343 U.S. 495 (1952), the Court addressed the First Amendment status of cinema under its then 30-year-old First Amendment doctrine. In doing so, it rejected the principle it expressed in *Mutual Film Corporation* that speech concerned solely with profit was not protected under the First Amendment.

The Court's expansion of protection for sexual expression in its landmark ruling in *Roth v. U.S.* 354 U.S. 476 (1957) provided it with yet another logical foundation for bringing commercial speech into the First Amendment's ambit. In other words, if the Court could find First Amendment value in sexual expression, why could it not find that advertising conveyed ideas, information, and commentary concerning civic affairs? Then, in *Smith v. California*, 361 U.S. 147 (1959), and *Ginzburg v. United States*, 383 U.S. 463, 474 (1966), the Court ruled that a newspaper's profit motive did not exclude it from enjoying First Amendment protection.

The Court took its next big step toward developing its commercial speech doctrine in *New York Times v. Sullivan*, its landmark libel ruling. As discussed in Chapter 5, the 1964 ruling stemmed from the *Times'* publication of a paid political advertisement. The Court distinguished the handbills in *Valentine v. Chrestensen* from the political ad in *Sullivan*, saying that the handbills were purely commercial advertising, while the ad in *Sullivan* communicated complaints, opinion, and information about civic affairs. The Court said the fact that the *Times* was paid to run the ad was irrelevant; the ad deserved First Amendment protection.

SUMMARY: The Court entered the 1970s with two essential principles to allow it to extend First Amendment protection to commercial speech: (i) disseminating speech for pay or profit does not deprive the speaker of First Amendment protection and (ii) non-political content is capable of expressing information, ideas, and opinion about civic affairs.

Commercial Speech & Intermediate Scrutiny

In *Pittsburgh Press Co. v. Pittsburgh Commission on Human Relations*, 413 U.S. 376 (1973), a Pittsburgh newspaper lost its argument that the First Amendment gave it the right to publish help-wanted ads designated by gender. Such ads promoted an illegal activity—hiring on the basis of gender—the Court said. The Court suggested that had the ad dealt with a legal activity, the First Amendment might have protected the newspaper's right to publish it: "Any First Amendment interest which might be served by advertising an ordinary commercial proposal and which might arguably outweigh the governmental interest supporting the regulation is altogether absent when the commercial activity itself is illegal and the restriction on advertising is incidental to a valid limitation on economic activity."[1] The Court also acknowledged that government had to do more that rely on *Valentine* to successfully challenge a government restriction on advertising.

In *Bigelow v. Virginia*, 421 U.S. 809, 818 (1975), the Court, citing *Pittsburgh Press* and *Sullivan*, said that no one should assume that "First Amendment guarantees of speech and press are inapplicable to paid commercial advertisements. Our cases, however, clearly establish that speech is not stripped of First Amendment protection merely because it appears in that form." The case dealt with a newspaper ad publicizing abortion services that were legal in New York, but illegal in Virginia at the time. The Court ruled that the state law against advertising abortion services could not be applied to an ad that solicited patients to travel to a state where abortion was legal without infringing on the newspaper's First Amendment rights.

With its ruling in *Bigelow v. Virginia* the Court stood poised to leave *Chrestensen*, yet not quite pre-pared to articulate a First Amendment test to protect commercial speech. The Court, however, estab-lished one core principle for its commercial speech doctrine in *Virginia State Pharmacy Board v. Virginia Citizens Consumer Council*, 425 U.S. 748 (1976). The Court rejected paternalistic regulations. It said adults must be allowed to make choices between buying lower-priced drugs versus higher-priced, possibly supe-rior ones, so long as the lower-priced drugs are lawful and not harmful. Otherwise, the state embarks on "a highly paternalistic approach" that generally should be avoided in a democratic republic predicated on informed citizens making their own choices, Justice Harry Blackmun said. But the Court limited its holding to the type of restriction and commercial speech at issue in the case—a ban on truthful infor-mation about lawful activity for the purpose of protecting pharmacists and customers:

> Advertising, however tasteless and excessive it sometimes may seem, is nonetheless dissemination of informa-tion as to who is producing and selling what product, for what reason, and at what price. So long as we pre-serve a predominantly free enterprise economy, the allocation of our resources in large measure will be made through numerous private economic decisions. It is a matter of public interest that those decisions, in the aggre-gate, be intelligent and well informed. To this end, the free flow of commercial information is indispensable.[2]

During the remainder of the late 1970s, the Court built on *Virginia Pharmacy* in striking down New York statutes banning nonprescriptive contraceptive ads, real estate ads, and a state bar associ-ation's ban on lawyers advertising. Finally, in *Central Hudson Gas & Electric Corp. v. Public Service Commission*, 447 U.S. 557 (1980), the Court developed its initial balancing test for commercial speech, a four-step analysis later modified in *Board of Trustees of State University of New York v. Fox*, 492 U.S. 469 (1989). The goal of the analysis is to achieve a proper balance between the First Amendment rights of an advertiser and the government's attempt to protect and promote important social, economic, and political policies.

The first prong of the *Central Hudson Gas* intermediate scrutiny test requires that when a restric-tion on commercial speech is challenged on First Amendment grounds, a court must determine whether the commercial speech is protected by the First Amendment. For commercial speech to come within that provision, it must concern lawful activity and not be misleading. The Court seeks to con-fer qualified First Amendment protection on commercial speech to protect its informational value. Then, under the second part, if the speech is protected, a court must ask whether the purpose the gov-ernment seeks to protect is substantial.

If the speech is protected and the government's purpose is substantial, a court must determine, under part three of the test, whether the restriction directly advances the substantial interest the government seeks to protect. Finally, a court must determine whether the restriction is not more extensive than is nec-essary to serve that substantial government interest. As discussed below, the Court later revised the fourth prong of the test.[3]

Central Hudson Gas stemmed from a dispute between the New York State Public Service Commission, which had imposed a ban on advertisements promoting electrical use during a nationwide energy crisis in the early 1970s. Central Hudson Gas & Electric Corporation had opposed the ban on First Amendment grounds. Applying that test in *Central Hudson Gas*, the Court struck down the regulation.

Board of Trustees v. Fox, 492 U.S. 469 (1989) and the "Reasonable Fit" Prong

In a 6–3 ruling, the Court held that the "least-restrictive-means" prong of its four-part intermedi-ate scrutiny analysis should not apply to commercial speech cases. Writing for the majority, Justice

Antonin Scalia reasoned the *Central Hudson Gas* intermediate analysis test created logical inconsistencies in First Amendment doctrine. The Court originally crafted the intermediate analysis formula to test the constitutionality of political speech in *U.S. v. O'Brien*, 391 U.S. 367 (1968). There is no least-restrictive means prong under O'Brien. Applying one to commercial speech restrictions would mean that the Court believed that commercial speech was constitutionally superior to political speech. The Court, however, had consistently said that "'commercial speech [enjoys] a limited measure of protection, commensurate with its subordinate position in the scale of First Amendment values,' and is subject to 'modes of regulation that might be impermissible in the realm of noncommercial expression,'" Scalia noted.[4]

The Court, Scalia pointed out, also applies a time, place, and manner analysis to commercial speech restrictions, as noted earlier in this chapter, and has said that it is "substantially similar" to the intermediate scrutiny test. Yet, Scalia said, "we have specifically held [that the time, place and manner test] does not require least restrictive means."[5] Under the time, place, and manner doctrine, government may regulate when, where, and how speech is expressed in a public setting to protect public peace and safety.

To maintain logical consistency, the Court replaced the fourth prong—"least restrictive means"—with a "reasonable fit" standard. Now, the government has to show that there is a reasonable fit between the government's goals and the means it chooses to reach such goals: "A fit that is not necessarily perfect, but reasonable; that represents not necessarily the single best disposition but one whose scope is 'in proportion to the interest served'…that employs not necessarily the least restrictive means but, as we have put it in the other contexts discussed above, a means narrowly tailored to achieve the desired objective."[6] Under the *Fox* revision, a restriction can be more extensive than necessary as long as it is not unreasonably so.

Defining Commercial Speech

The Court has offered two definitions of commercial speech. As Justice John Paul Stevens noted in *Central Hudson Gas*, the Court has defined commercial speech as (i) "expression related solely to the economic interests of the speaker and its audience"[7] and (ii) as "speech proposing a commercial transaction."[8] Stevens, however, found neither definition adequate. The former definition is too broad, covering speech that is clearly not commercial advertising such as "a labor leader's exhortation to strike…an economist's dissertation on the money supply…even Shakespeare may have been motivated by the prospect of pecuniary reward."[9] The latter definition should not include all promotional advertising, Stevens said, but a "salesman's solicitation, a broker's offer, and a manufacturer's publication of a price list or the terms of his standard warranty would unquestionably fit within this concept."[10]

Those shortcomings aside, the Court provided in *Pittsburgh Press* what is now the most widely held and succinct definition of commercial speech: Commercial speech is speech that does "no more than propose a commercial transaction."[11] Typically, commercial speech takes the form of broadcast commercials, billboards, in-store displays, telemarketing, product labels, handbills, and other print advertisements. Nevertheless, the Court generally uses the terms "commercial speech" and "advertising" interchangeably.

SUMMARY: Under *Virginia State Board of Pharmacy v. Virginia Citizens Consumer Council*, paternalistic laws that prevent individuals from making choices between products that are lawful and harmless should be avoided. The *Central Hudson/Fox* intermediate scrutiny test for commercial speech considers the following four prongs: (I) When a restriction on commercial speech is challenged on First Amendment grounds, a court must determine whether the commercial speech is protected by the First Amendment. For commercial speech to come within that provision, it must concern lawful activity and not be misleading. The Court seeks to confer qualified First Amendment protection on commercial speech to protect its informational value. (II) If the speech is protected, a court must ask whether the purpose the government seeks to protect is substantial. (III) If the speech is protected and the government's purpose is substantial, a court must determine whether the restriction directly advances the substantial interest the government seeks to protect. (IV) There must be a reasonable fit between the means and the goals.

The Court's revision in *Board of Trustees v. Fox* did not go far enough in remedying what several justices, other judges, and scholars see as major shortcomings in the commercial speech test. Critics say parts two and three of the test—whether the purpose the government seeks to protect is substantial and whether the restriction directly advances the substantial interest—allow judges too much latitude to insert their subjective assessments. Consequently, the test provides little guidance for government and advertisers, critics say. Some commentators argue that the "reasonable fit" test is too deferential to government and, thus, insufficiently protective of free speech interests.

Advertising Legal Vices

Government efforts to regulate vice products and activities have been a hotly contested area of the commercial speech doctrine since the 1980s. Typically, legislators have targeted the promotion of tobacco, liquor, casino gambling, and lotteries motivated by concern that the misuse of such legal products and activities can lead to physical, moral, and financial ruin. Commercial-speech advocates, however, contend that the government should not suppress information about legal vice products and activities used by adult consumers. Such laws, they argue, stem from a paternalism that the Court said should be avoided in *Virginia State Pharmacy Board*.

Nevertheless, ten years after *Virginia State Pharmacy Board*, the Court upheld a ban on advertising the vice of casino gambling by applying the *Central Hudson* test. The ruling was *Posadas de Puerto Rico Associates v. Tourism Co. of PR*, 478 U.S. 328 (1986). In *Posadas*, 5–4, the Court upheld Puerto Rico's Games of Chance Act of 1948, which banned advertising of casino gambling aimed at the residents of Puerto Rico, even though gambling was legal in Puerto Rico, and the government there allowed advertising to attract tourists to gamble at the same casinos. As noted in the chapter's introduction, the majority of the Court came to question the validity of *Posadas*.

In *44 Liquormart, Inc. v. Rhode Island*, 517 U.S. 484 (1996), the Court invalidated a Rhode Island ban on advertisements that provided the public with accurate information about retail prices of alcoholic beverages. In doing so, the justices produced four separate opinions on the application of the *Posadas* and the *Central Hudson* tests.

Justices John Paul Stevens, Ruth Bader Ginsberg, and Anthony Kennedy argued that full bans on truthful or nonmisleading commercial speech require courts to apply strict scrutiny analysis.

Justices Anthony Kennedy, John Paul Stevens, and David Souter, however, argued for the Court to return to the analysis it applied in *Virginia State Board of Pharmacy* (1976) and allow consumers to make choices about the merits of advertisements promoting lawful products and activities. They said the *Central Hudson* test allows judges to assign a preference to either free expression or other societal values by considering the individual circumstances of each case. In other words, the test allows judges to engage in ad hoc balancing.

Four justices—Stevens, Ginsburg, Kennedy, and Thomas—overruled *Posadas*. Another four—O'Connor, Rehnquist, Breyer, and Souter—acknowledged that the Court had long since stopped relying on the *Posadas* analysis. Though the Court as a whole has yet to overrule *Posadas*, because a majority of justices have not explicitly done so, it is nonetheless widely considered to have limited precedential value.

Under the Court's interpretation of the *Central Hudson* test in *Posadas*, the Court deferred to a legislative decision that a speech-repressive approach was no more extensive than necessary to protect Puerto Rican residents from the vices of legalized gambling. The majority rejected the argument that the legislature had an obvious alternative, one that the Court's "more speech doctrine" demanded. The government could have waged an antigambling advertising campaign. Justice Louis Brandeis articulated the "more speech" doctrine in *Whitney v. California*, 274 U.S. 357, 377 (1927): "If there be time to expose through discussion the falsehood and fallacies, to avert the evil by the processes of education, the remedy to be applied is more speech, not enforced silence. Only an emergency can justify repression." The Puerto Rican legislature was not faced with an emergency. Therefore, had the *Posadas* Court followed the "more speech" doctrine and the fourth-prong of the original test, or even the revised *Central Hudson* test, it would have invalidated the ban on gambling.

The *Posadas* Court also accepted the Puerto Rican government's rationale for the advertising ban without demanding that it provide evidence to support its claim of legalized gambling's ill effects on individuals.

Thus, it was logical for Rhode Island to argue in *44 Liquormart* that under *Posadas* judges were obligated to defer to a state's decision making because alcoholic beverages were "vice" products similar to gambling. Under *Posadas*, the "vice exception" holds that legislatures have greater authority to ban advertising of vice activities because they have the authority to regulate the activity. Consequently, such bans are not subject to *Central Hudson*'s intermediate scrutiny test, under *Posadas*.[12]

But a plurality of the justices in *44 Liquormart* rejected an exception that allowed legislatures to ban speech promoting legal activities that government deemed harmful to health or morality without a showing that there was a reasonable fit between the law and the purpose. Writing for the plurality, Justice Stevens reasoned that defining the "vice" exception's scope would be nearly impossible and he voiced concern that the exception provides legislatures with too much unchecked power:

> Almost any product that poses some threat to public health or public morals might reasonably be characterized by a state legislature as relating to 'vice activity.' Such characterization, however, is anomalous when applied to products such as alcoholic beverages, lottery tickets, or playing cards, that may be lawfully purchased on the open market. The recognition of such an exception would also have the unfortunate consequence of either allowing state legislatures to justify censorship by the simple expedient of placing the 'vice' label on selected lawful activities, or requiring the federal courts to establish a federal common law of vice. For these reasons, a 'vice' label that is unaccompanied by a corresponding prohibition against the commercial behavior at issue fails to provide a principled justification for the regulation of commercial speech about that activity.[13]

Justice O'Connor wrote a concurrence in which Rehnquist, Souter, and Breyer joined, finding that the Rhode Island ban was not a reasonable fit between the government's goal and the approach. Rhode Island said it banned the advertising of competitive alcoholic beverages prices to keep the public from consuming too much alcohol. But Rhode Island had alternatives to discourage consumers from buying low-priced alcoholic beverages: establish minimum prices or increase sales taxes on alcoholic beverages. The Court wrote,

> The fit between Rhode Island's method and this particular goal is not reasonable. If the target is simply higher prices generally to discourage consumption, the regulation imposes too great, and unnecessary, a prohibition on speech in order to achieve it. The State has other methods at its disposal—methods that would more directly accomplish this stated goal without intruding on sellers' ability to provide truthful, nonmisleading information to customers.[14]

SUMMARY: According to *44 Liquormart*:

- The *Central Hudson* test requires judges not to defer to legislature judgment.
- Four justices required a state to show a statute directly advances the state's asserted interest to meet the third prong of the test.
- Three justices declined to adopt the above interpretation of the third prong.
- Consequently, *44 Liquormart* did not clarify the amount of proof required to show that a commercial speech restriction directly advances the state's interest.
- There was near unanimity, however, about the fourth prong of the *Central Hudson* test. When government bans speech promoting legal activity, it must show that alternative non-speech-related measures would not more directly achieve its goals. Thus, *44 Liquormart* made the "reasonable fit" prong more protective of free speech.
- Courts must apply the more free-speech-protective strict scrutiny analysis, when government bans "truthful, nonmisleading commercial messages for reasons unrelated" to consumer protection. Accordingly, the government must show that the ban furthers a compelling state interest and is narrowly tailored to achieve that interest.[15]

Applying 44 Liquormart

Meanwhile, as *44 Liquormart* made its way to the U.S. Supreme Court, federal appeals courts ruled on similar cases involving restrictions on liquor, cigarette, and gambling advertising. The Court ordered lower federal courts to reconsider such rulings by applying the *44 Liquormart* standards.

The U.S. Court of Appeals for the Fourth Circuit upheld the city of Baltimore's restrictions on billboards advertising cigarettes and alcoholic drinks in *Anheuser-Busch, Inc. v. Schmoke*, 101 F.3d 325 (4th Cir. 1995). The Fourth Circuit found that a reasonable fit between the restrictions and Baltimore's interest in protecting children from a constant barrage of advertising encouraging them to drink alcohol and smoke tobacco products. Applying the *44 Liquormart* standards, the Fourth Circuit still found Baltimore's ordinance constitutionally valid, noting that the law did not ban alcohol and tobacco advertising from all areas of the city. Rather, Baltimore restricted such billboards to the city's commercial and industrial zones, and banned them in areas where children were likely to frequent. "Although no ordinance of this kind could be so perfectly tailored as to all and only those areas to which children are daily exposed, Baltimore's efforts to tailor the ordinance by exempting commercial and industrial zones from its effort renders it not more extensive than is necessary to serve the governmental interest under consideration," the Fourth Circuit said.[16]

The Supreme Court also remanded *Greater New Orleans Broadcasting Association v. U.S.*, 519 U.S. 801 (1996), to the U.S. Court of Appeals for the Fifth Circuit. The matter before the Fifth Circuit was the constitutionality of a federal statute (18 U.S.C. § 1304) prohibiting the broadcast of radio and television advertisements for casino gambling. The Fifth Circuit concluded that the federal ban on broadcast advertisements of casino gambling failed to satisfy *Central Hudson*'s requirements. When the Fifth Circuit applied the *44 Liquormart* interpretation of the fourth prong of the *Central Hudson* test, it reached a 2–1 decision upholding the ban in *Greater New Orleans Broadcasting Association v. U.S.*, 149 F.3d 334 (5th Cir. 1998).

Yet the Supreme Court ruled to the contrary in *Greater New Orleans Broadcasting Association, Inc. v. U.S.*, 527 U.S. 173, 176 (1999). It said that the federal ban on broadcasting advertisements promoting casino gambling "may not be applied to advertisements of private casino gambling that are broadcast by radio or television stations located in Louisiana, where such gambling is legal."

The 8–1 *Greater New Orleans Broadcasting* majority noted that the four prongs of the *Central Hudson* test are interrelated. Accordingly, the Court reasoned that the substantiality of the government's purpose for banning broadcast advertisements of private casino gambling was dubious because the federal government had, for example, sanctioned casino gambling owned by Indian tribes and allowed states to run lotteries. The Court asked how could a ban on advertising promoting private casino gambling could protect those in states against gambling addiction when the government approved and engaged in activities that undermined that effort:

> While it is no doubt fair to assume that more advertising would have some impact on overall demand for gambling, it is also reasonable to assume that much of that advertising would merely channel gamblers to one casino rather than another. More important, any measure of the effectiveness of the Government's attempt to minimize the social costs of gambling cannot ignore Congress' simultaneous encouragement of tribal casino gambling, which may well be growing at a rate exceeding any increase in gambling or compulsive gambling that private casino advertising could produce. And, as the Court of Appeals recognized, the Government fails to 'connect casino gambling and compulsive gambling with broadcast advertising for casinos'—let alone broadcast advertising for non-Indian commercial casinos.[17]

In *Greater New Orleans Broadcasting Association*, the Court also declined to abandon its *Central Hudson* four-prong analysis in spite of the urgings to do so by judges and scholars, and petitioners who filed amici curiae briefs in that case.

As noted above, Justice Stevens reasoned that, "a 'vice' label that is unaccompanied by a corresponding prohibition against the commercial behavior at issue fails to provide a principled justification for the regulation of commercial speech about that activity."[18] It would seem that in *Coyote Publishing, Inc. v. Miller*, the case discussed in the chapter's introduction, the Ninth Circuit made an unprincipled ruling. In Nevada counties where prostitution is legal, brothels cannot advertise in public theaters, or on public streets and highways. The Ninth Circuit however, said it was not applying a *Posadas*-like "vice exception" to protections accorded commercial speech. Instead, the panel said, it was carving out an exception for the sale of sexual services under a novel "commodification" theory. Under the Ninth Circuit's novel commodification theory, there are strong historical, cultural and moral justifications why the sale of sexual services should be treated differently than other advertising bans on vice products and activities, the panel said. Nevada's advertising restrictions, the court reasoned, directly advanced the asserted substantial governmental interest to prevent the spread of the commodification of sex, and is not more extensive than is necessary to serve that interest.

No appeal was filed. Professor Lyrissa C. Barnett Lidsky, of the University of Florida Levin College of Law, however, is certain the court reached the wrong decision: "If the state isn't willing to ban the commodification of sex, why should it be allowed to ban its citizens from receiving information about a lawful commodity? The Ninth Circuit seemed to assume that banning speech about brothels was a lesser evil than banning brothels. It was wrong."[19]

Tobacco Advertising and Federal Statutes

The Court's decision not to review *Anheuser-Busch, Inc. v. Schmoke* gave a green light to state and city efforts targeting tobacco advertising near schools and areas where children played, and where tobacco products were sold. Meanwhile, the four largest tobacco companies in the U.S. and attorney generals of 46 states adopted a settlement in November 1998, the Tobacco Master Settlement Agreement (MSA). The terms of the agreement included confirmation of the Federal Drug Administration's authority to regulate tobacco products under the Food, Drug and Cosmetic Act, a ban on all outdoor tobacco advertising, and the elimination of cartoon characters and human figures, such as Joe Camel and the Marlboro Man, both deemed attractive to young people.[20]

That settlement, however, did not discourage Massachusetts from passing a law banning outdoor advertising of smokeless tobacco or cigar products within a 1,000-foot radius of a school or playground, and requiring store owners to place indoor tobacco ads no lower than five feet from the floor. Lorillard Tobacco Company's challenge of that ban made its way up to the U.S. Supreme Court in *Lorillard Tobacco Co. v. Reilly*, 533 U.S. 525 (2001). The Court ruled in the tobacco company's favor, striking down the billboard ban on free speech grounds.

Writing for the majority, Justice O'Connor said the billboard ban failed the fourth prong of the *Central Hudson* test because it was an unreasonable way to protect children from the harms of cigarettes. The 1,000-foot zone had the actual effect of banning such billboards in just about all parts of some areas, she said. Consequently, the ban infringed on the free-speech rights of adults and tobacco companies and retailers. "We must consider that tobacco retailers and manufacturers have an interest in conveying truthful information about their products to adults, and adults have a corresponding interest in receiving truthful information about tobacco products," O'Connor said.[21]

The majority also found that the point-of-sale advertising restriction, placing a height limit on indoor display ads, did not directly advance the substantial interest Massachusetts sought to protect nor was the restriction a reasonable way to achieve the objective. O'Connor noted that, "the State's goal is to prevent minors from using tobacco products and to curb demand for that activity by limiting youth exposure to advertising. The 5-foot rule does not seem to advance that goal. Not all children are less than 5 feet tall, and those who are certainly have the ability to look up and take in their surroundings."[22]

The majority also ruled that the FDA's authority to regulate cigarettes, but not cigars and chewing tobacco, under the 1965 Federal Cigarette Labeling and Advertising Act (FCLAA), pre-empted states' authority to ban or restrict cigarette advertising. The FCLAA bans cigarette advertising on any medium of electronic communication, and requires cigarette packaging, advertisements, and billboards to carry "Surgeon General's Warnings." Exercising its authority under the act, the FDA ordered Madison Square Garden to remove a Marlboro sign from a courtside location during televised New York Knicks basketball games.[23] The agency also ordered Philip Morris Incorporated to remove prominent Marlboro billboards from professional baseball, football, basketball, and hockey stadiums and arenas around the country.[24]

The FCLAA also provides pre-emption language that prohibits states from imposing any "requirement or prohibition based on smoking and health…with respect to the advertising or promotion of…cigarettes." In *Lorillard*, the Court held that the FCLAA pre-empts only state regulations targeting cigarette advertising. Justice Sandra Day O'Connor explained that, "Congress pre-empted state cigarette advertising regulations…because they would upset federal legislative choices to require specific warnings and to impose the ban on cigarette advertising in electronic media in order to address concerns about smoking and health."[25]

In 2009, Congress passed the Family Smoking Prevention and Tobacco Control Act. The act gives the FDA regulatory authority over the tobacco industry. The act includes, among other requirements and restrictions, that tobacco companies print new government warnings on the top 50% of both sides of all cigarette packaging with messages such as, "Cigarettes cause cancer." The statute also requires that the warning must be in 17-point font and include color graphics depicting the negative health consequences of smoking. Any labeling or advertising for cigarettes or smokeless tobacco must use only black text on a white background. The act also bans all outdoor cigarette and smokeless tobacco advertising within 1,000 feet of the perimeter of any public playground, playground area in a public park, elementary school, or secondary school. Under the act, Congress also directed the FDA to reissue regulations that ban tobacco brand-name sponsorship of athletic, social, and cultural events.

Most state restrictions of tobacco advertising are pre-empted now, and federal laws restricting tobacco advertising remain subject to the *Central Hudson* analysis, as was demonstrated in *Commonwealth Brands, Inc. v. US*, 678 F. Supp. 2d 512 (2010). In *Commonwealth Brands, Inc. v. U.S.*, six tobacco companies challenged the Family Smoking Prevention and Tobacco Control Act on First Amendment and Fifth Amendment due process grounds. The companies won a partial victory in *Commonwealth Brands* as U.S. District Judge Joseph H. McKinley Jr. upheld most of the statute's advertising and marketing restrictions, including the requirement that warning labels cover the top 50% of both sides of all cigarette packaging. The judge, however, struck down the black-text-on-a-white-background only requirement. He said that, contrary to the government's contention, some uses of color communicate important commercial information about a product and its maker. Therefore, color was protected speech in this context. Applying the third prong of the *Central Hudson* test, McKinley ruled that the color and graphic ban did not directly advance the substantial interest the government sought to protect. The FCLAA went into effect in June 2010. The tobacco companies did not file additional challenges.

Broadcasting and Tobacco Advertising

In *Capital Broadcasting Co. v. John Mitchell, Attorney General of the U.S.*, 333 F. Supp. 582 (1971), the U.S. District Court ruled that Section 6 of the Public Health Cigarette Smoking Act of 1969 did not violate the Fifth nor First Amendment rights of broadcasters. Section 6 of the Act provides that, "After January 1, 1971, it shall be unlawful to advertise cigarettes on any medium of electronic communication subject to the jurisdiction of the Federal Communications Commission." The court reasoned that banning tobacco ads from television and radio did not deprive broadcasting licensees of their ability to use their airways for discussion of the sale and use of tobacco products. The Court said, "It is dispositive that the Act has no substantial effect on the exercise of petitioners' First Amendment rights. Even assuming that loss of revenue from cigarette advertisements affects petitioners with sufficient First Amendment interest, petitioners, themselves, have lost no right to speak—they have only lost an ability to collect revenue from others for broadcasting their commercial messages."[26]

SUMMARY: The Family Smoking Prevention and Tobacco Control Act of 2009 gives the FDA regulatory authority over the tobacco industry. The Central Hudson/Fox test, however, still controls.

Corporate Speech vs. Commercial Speech

In *First National Bank of Boston v. Bellotti*, 435 U.S. 765 (1978), the Court ruled that, under the First Amendment, a corporation had the right to spend money to publicize its views on a proposed revision of a Massachusetts constitutional amendment. It said that speech concerning self-governance and civic ideas should not be designated as commercial speech simply because it is conveyed in the form of an ad or is communicated by profit-motivated entities. Accordingly, the Court has characterized the following as "noncommercial speech": corporate advertising of views on public policy, such as the promotion of one form of energy compared to another as environmentally beneficial;[27] and "charitable appeals for funds, on the street or door to door."[28] In other words, corporate speech is corporate-generated or profit-related speech that conveys ideas about political matters or addresses controversial public policy issues, and, arguably, laws that restrict corporate speech should be subjected to strict scrutiny analysis.

The Court, however, has not offered a bright-line definition to distinguish commercial speech from noncommercial corporate speech. A case involving Nike, the sports shoe company, presented such an opportunity. But the Court declined to review the California Supreme Court's ruling in *Kasky v. Nike*, 45 P.3d 243 (Cal. Supreme 2002), and the parties in the case reached an out-of-court settlement. Consequently, the authority of the California Supreme Court's novel test to distinguish commercial speech from corporate speech is limited to that state.

Kasky stemmed from a lawsuit brought by California community activist Marc Kasky. He claimed that Nike issued a number of false statements or material omissions of fact in its press releases and letters to editors and university presidents as part of its public relations campaign responding to allegations that it was mistreating and underpaying workers at its foreign facilities. Kasky invoked California's Unfair Competition Law. Nike argued that its communications were "corporate speech," deserving of strict scrutiny First Amendment protection, and, thus, not subject to the state law.

In response, the California Supreme Court departed from the *Central Hudson* test and created what it referred to as a "limited-purpose test…to distinguish commercial from noncommercial speech under the First Amendment" which weighed "three elements: the speaker, the intended audience, and the content of the message."[29] Applying those elements, the California Supreme Court ruled for Kasky, finding that Nike's messages were merely commercial speech because "the messages in question were directed by a commercial speaker to a commercial audience, and because they made representations of fact about the speaker's own business operations for the purpose of promoting sales of its products."[30]

The U.S. Supreme Court agreed to hear oral arguments on *Kasky v. Nike*, but ultimately dismissed the case because the lower court in California had not entered a final judgment, among other reasons. In their dissent, Justices Breyer and O'Connor said they were prepared to confer the highest form of constitutional protection—strict scrutiny—to the type of speech Nike engaged in to defend its public image against charges that it was illegally exploiting foreign workers. The two Justices described Nike's press releases and letters as "not purely commercial in nature. They are better characterized as involving a mixture of commercial and noncommercial (public-issue-oriented) elements."[31]

For now, the Court still defines commercial speech as speech that does "no more than propose a commercial transaction." It remains to be seen, however, whether the Court's 5–4 landmark ruling in *Citizens United v. the Federal Election Commission* is a signal that it is prepared to confer full First Amendment protection to commercial speech, and end the unclear distinction between corporate and commercial speech. In *Citizens United*, the Court held that, under the First Amendment, corporate funding of independent political broadcasts in candidate elections cannot be restricted. Citing a long list of rulings in which the Court recognized that First Amendment protection extends to corporations, the majority said, "We find no basis for the proposition that, in the context of political speech, the Government may impose restrictions on certain disfavored speakers."[32] The Court also "rejected the argument that political speech of corporations or other associations should be treated differently under the First Amendment simply because such associations are not 'natural persons.'"[33]

In a law review article, "Citizen United and the Threat to the Regulatory State," Tamara R. Piety, a law professor at University of Tulsa College of Law, argues that *Citizens United* signals the Court's inclination to confer full First Amendment protection on commercial speech: "[*Citizens United*] suggest that with the proper case, there is an increased likelihood the Supreme Court will either do away with the commercial speech doctrine altogether and declare that commercial speech should be treated as fully protected speech, or it will nominally retain the doctrine but apply strict scrutiny review."[34]

Justice Anthony Kennedy wrote the *Citizen's United* opinion and in the following year, 2011, penned the majority opinion in *Sorrell v. IMS Health, Inc.* Tea-leaf-reading Court watchers have interpreted the Court's ruling in *Sorrell v. IMS Health, Inc.* as yet another step toward the demise of *Central Hudson*. In a 6–3 ruling, the Court held that Vermont's Prescription Confidentiality Law, which restricted the sale, disclosure, and use for marketing purposes of pharmacy records that reveal the prescribing practices of individual doctors, was subject to strict scrutiny review because it imposed content- and speaker-based burdens on protected expression. Vermont had argued that strict scrutiny review was unwarranted because, among other reasons, prescriber-identifying information is a mere commodity. Kennedy, however, said, "Speech in aid of pharmaceutical marketing, however, is a form of expression protected by the Free Speech Clause of the First Amendment. As a consequence, Vermont's statute must be subjected to heightened judicial scrutiny."[35]

SUMMARY: On the scale of First Amendment-protected speech, advertising falls below political speech because, arguably, it has less expressive value than political speech. But should a corporation-issued political ad or press release concerning public affairs issues be designated political or commercial? Should there be a distinction? Some legal thinkers say the distinction is false. In 2003, the U.S. Supreme Court seemed poised to resolve the matter in *Kasky v. Nike*, but made no substantive ruling. Two recent rulings—*Citizens United v. the Federal Election Commission*, 130 S. Ct. 876 (2010) and *Sorrell v. IMS Health, Inc.*, 131 S. Ct. 2653 (2011)—may be signaling that a majority of the Court is prepared to grant commercial speech strict scrutiny protection.

Compelled Commercial Speech

In a line of rulings starting with *West Virginia Board of Education v. Barnette*, 319 U.S. 624 (1943), the Court established that government has no right to compel individuals to say something, or to not say something—at least with regard to "political speech." In other words, the government has no authority to make you salute the American flag, adhere to a political belief, or endorse a religion. As this chapter has established, commercial speech enjoys limited protection under the First Amendment. Thus, it should not come as a surprise that government *does* have authority under the First Amendment to force certain kinds of businesses to endorse statements about commercial matters.

The Court has said that two kinds of compelled funding, or economic regulations, do not infringe the First Amendment rights of agricultural producers. One kind of economic regulation compels agricultural producers to fund their industry's advertising and marketing schemes. Another kind compels agricultural producers to fund government advertising and marketing schemes that stimulate demand for their industry's products.

Compelled Funding of Industry Ad Campaigns

The California Milk Advisory Board's "Got Milk" campaign is one of the more memorable—and effective—private industry-compelled speech efforts. It was also the target of a lawsuit—*Gallo Cattle Co. v. California Milk Advisory Board*, 185 F.3d 969 (9th Cir. 1999)—in which the milk producer unsuccessfully challenged the board's compulsory payments for the promotion and advertising of California's dairy products.

The precedent for private industry-compelled funding cases relied upon in *Gallo Cattle* is *Glickman v. Wileman Brothers & Elliot*, 521 U.S. 457 (1997). In *Glickman*, 5–4, the Court rejected a First Amendment challenge to a series of agricultural marketing orders that required certain California tree fruit producers to pay assessments for product advertising. The Court stressed that compelled funding cases were not to be analyzed under the *Central Hudson* test. Instead, courts must ask: Does the funding order prevent a producer or distributor from communicating their own messages to any audience; does it force anyone to engage in any actual or symbolic speech; and does the order force producers to endorse or finance a political or ideological view that is not germane to the advertising campaign?

Compelled Funding of Government Ad Campaigns

Compelled funding cases in which the government requires companies to subsidize the government's commercial messages are controlled by the "government-speech doctrine." Courts developed the government-speech doctrine in the 1990s. Under the doctrine, government speech is free of First Amendment restrictions based on the reasoning that the First Amendment says nothing about the free-speech rights of the federal government. The government did not use the doctrine to challenge this type of compelled funding schemes until *Johanns v. Livestock Marketing Association*, 544 U.S. 550 (2005).

Consequently, as Justice Antonin Scalia ruled in *Johanns v. Livestock Marketing Association*, 544 U.S. 550, 562 (2005), when "the government sets the overall message to be communicated and approves every word that is disseminated, it is not precluded from relying on the government-speech doctrine merely because it solicits assistance from nongovernmental sources in developing specific messages."

Menus and Packaging Disclosure: The Rational Basis Test

Compelled commercial speech laws also come in the form of regulations requiring packaging and, most recently, restaurant menus, to disclose certain information. In *Zauderer v. Office of Disciplinary Council of the Supreme Court of Ohio*, 471 U.S. 626 (1985), the U.S. Supreme Court iterated its position on laws requiring private concerns to disclose factual and noncontroversial information. It said that such requirements affect advertisers' interests "more narrowly…than do flat prohibitions on speech" because they "dissipate the possibility of consumer confusion or deception."[36] The Court said that, "an advertiser's rights are adequately protected as long as disclosure requirements are reasonably related to the State's interest in preventing deception of consumers."[37]

Consequently, judges subject labeling and menu disclosure laws to the rational basis test. Courts apply this minimal standard of review, asking whether the state's method is a rational way to achieve its stated goals. Applying the rational basis test, the Second Circuit upheld the constitutionality of New York City's pioneering calorie labeling law in *New York State Restaurant v. New York*, 556 F.3d 114 (2009). The city's law, effective July 2008, required chain restaurants such as McDonald's, Burger King and Kentucky Fried Chicken to post calorie content information on their menus and menu display boards. The restaurant association argued that the law violated the First Amendment rights of the fast food establishments, as one of its claims, and the court should apply intermediate scrutiny. The appeals court, however, applied the rational basis analysis, finding that there was a rational connection between the state's goal of fighting an obesity epidemic by reducing consumer confusion and deception and promoting informed consumer decision making.

> SUMMARY: Under the compelled commercial speech doctrine, government may compel businesses to subsidize industry- and government-sponsored ad campaigns, and include factual and noncontroversial information on product labels and in menus.

Federal Trade Commission

For about a year, from fall 2008 to fall 2009, Nestlé HealthCare Nutrition Inc. boasted that its BOOST Kid Essentials tasted great and prevented colds and the flu. Now Nestlé's claims for its nutritional drink are far more conventional: "The taste they love, the nutrition they need." The Federal Trade Commission (FTC) reined in the beverage and chocolate company. In July 2010, as part of the terms of a settlement of false advertising charges brought by the FTC, Nestlé agreed to stop making bold flu and cold prevention claims about BOOST Kid Essentials unless it had the scientific evidence to support them.[38]

The FTC brought the charges under Section 5 of the FTC Act (15 U.S.C. § 45(a)). Under Section 5 of the FTC Act, the FTC's Division of Advertising Practices may bring administrative lawsuits in federal court to stop unfair and deceptive advertising. According to the FTC Policy Statement on Deception,[39] an ad is deceptive if it includes material information that is false or that is likely to mislead a consumer acting reasonably under the circumstances; or if it omits material information that is likely to mislead a consumer acting reasonably under the circumstances. Proof that an ad caused harm is not important. It does not matter whether the deception or falsity was a mistake and the advertiser's intentions are irrelevant.

Federal and state laws regulate advertising that is deceptive, misleading, or false. But the FTC is the main federal agency that takes action against unlawful advertising. The FTC can pursue a number of actions to make an advertiser comply: cease-and-desist orders, civil lawsuits, court-ordered injunctions, or orders that require the advertiser to run corrective ads. FTC orders that require marketers to stop making false or unsubstantiated statements do not infringe upon First Amendment rights.

Under Section 42(a) of the federal Lanham (Trademark) Act of 1946, individuals may bring private actions against false advertising claims. To prevail on a false advertising claim under the Lanham Act, the plaintiff must show that: (i) the advertiser made a false or misleading statement of fact; (ii) the statement deceived or had the capacity to deceive a substantial segment of the audience; (iii) the deception was likely to influence the purchasing decision; (iv) the advertiser must have caused its goods to enter interstate commerce; and (v) the false or misleading statement injured or was likely to injure the plaintiff.

SUMMARY: Advertising's diminished expressive value allows it to be regulated under the First Amendment. The Federal Trade Commission can sue to stop deceptive and unfair ads and impose fines on advertisers. Under the Lanham Act, individuals may bring private actions against false advertising claims.

ONLINE RESOURCES

1. "Advertising and the First Amendment: Overview," First Amendment Center, http://archive.firstamendmentcenter.org/Speech/advertising/overview.aspx
2. "Advertising Guidelines," Federal Trade Commission, http://www.ftc.gov/bcp/guides/guides.shtm
3. "Government Regulations of Commercial Speech," Exploring Constitutional Conflicts, http://law2.umkc.edu/faculty/projects/ftrials/conlaw/commercial.htm

QUESTIONS

1. In states such as Colorado, California, and Montana, where use of marijuana for health purposes is legal, newspapers are running ads from businesses with names like Mile High Mike's, Happy Buddha, and the Healthy Connections. Would a law restricting ads promoting marijuana clinics in those states survive a *Central Hudson* analysis?

2. Is it commercial or noncommercial speech? The U.S. Supreme Court has not offered a bright-line definition to distinguish commercial speech from noncommercial corporate speech—corporate-generated or profit-related speech that conveys ideas about political matters or addresses controversial public policy issues. But the California Supreme Court's ruling in *Kasky v. Nike*, 45 P. 3d 243 (Cal. Supreme 2002), did create such a test: a "limited-purpose test…to distinguish commercial from noncommercial speech under the First Amendment" which weighed "three elements: the speaker, the intended audience, and the content of the message." Apply the limited-purpose test to the following facts.

> A representative of a private university, in a speech to a class of high school seniors, touts the academic and athletic curricula of the university in an effort to offset declining enrollment and thereby fill the university's coffers.

> The CEO of an American automobile corporation urges consumers to "buy American" because the purchase is patriotic and the buying of foreign autos helps to put Americans out of work.

3. In January 2010, three Stanford University researchers published, "Calorie Posting in Chain Restaurants," a study of the impact of New York's City's pioneering calorie labeling law that went into effect July 2008. According to the study's findings, the average calorie count per transaction at Starbucks stores decreased 6% over a 10-month period. In contrast, the findings of a study by New York University and Yale professors published in October 2009, "Calorie Labeling and Food Choices: A First Look at the Effects on Low-Income People in New York City," showed that 28% of the customers at fast-food chains in poor neighborhoods of New York City who said they were aware of the calorie information ordered slightly more calories than the typical customer had before the labeling law went into effect.

   Do the conflicting findings support or undermine the ruling in *New York State Restaurant Association v. New York*, 556 F.3d 114 (2d Cir. 2009) in which the U.S. Court of Appeals for the Second Circuit said that there was a rational connection between the state's goal of fighting an obesity epidemic by reducing consumer confusion and deception and promoting informed consumer decision making?

ENDNOTES

1. *Pittsburgh Press Co. v. Pittsburgh Commission on Human Relations,* 413 U.S. 376, 389 (1973).
2. *Virginia State Board of Pharmacy v. Virginia Citizens Consumer Council,* 425 U.S. 748, 765 (1976).
3. *Central Hudson Gas & Electric Corp. v. Public Service Commission,* 447 U.S. 557, 566 (1980).
4. *Board of Trustees v. Fox,* 492 U.S. 469, 477 (1989).
5. Ibid.
6. Ibid. 480.
7. *Central Hudson Gas,* 447 U.S. at 562.
8. Ibid. 580.
9. Ibid. 579–580.
10. Ibid. 580.
11. *Pittsburgh Press Co.,* 413 U.S. at 385.
12. *Posadas de Puerto Rico Associates v. Tourism Co. of PR,* 478 U.S. 328, 345–346 (1986).
13. *44 Liquormart, Inc. v. Rhode Island,* 517 U.S. 484, 514 (1996).
14. Ibid. 530.
15. Ibid. 501.
16. *Anheuser-Busch, Inc. v. Schmoke,* 101 F.3d 325, 328 (4th Cir. 1996).
17. *Greater New Orleans Broadcasting Association, Inc. v. United States,* 527 U.S. 173, 189 (1999).
18. *44 Liquormart, Inc.,* 517 U.S. at 514.
19. Lyrissa Lidsky. "Advertising Brothels: A Novel 'Commodification' Theory," [Web log post] (June 12, 2010), http://prawfsblawg.blogs.com/prawfsblawg/2010/06/advertising-prostitution.html
20. "Proposed tobacco industry settlement," (June 20, 1997), http://www.cnn.com/US/9705/tobacco/docs/proposal.html

21. *Lorillard Tobacco Co. v. Reilly,* 533 U.S. 525, 564 (2001).

22. Ibid. 566.

23. *U.S. v. Madison Square Garden,* L. P., No. 95–2228 (S.D.N.Y., April 7, 1995).

24. *U.S. v. Philip Morris, Inc.,* No. 95–1077 (D.D.C. June 6, 1995).

25. *Lorillard Tobacco,* 533 at 551.

26. *Capital Broadcasting Co. v. Mitchell,* 333 F. Supp. 582, 584 (Dist. Ct., Dist. of Columbia (1971).

27. Ibid. 56.

28. *Schaumburg v. Citizens for a Better Environment,* 444 U.S. 620, 632 (1980)

29. *Kasky v. Nike,* 45 P. 3d 243, 311 (Cal. Supreme 2002).

30. Ibid. 300–301.

31. *Nike, Inc. v. Kasky,* 539 U.S. 654, 676 (2003).

32. *Citizens United v. the Federal Election Commission,* 130 S. Ct. 876, 899 (2010).

33. Ibid. 900.

34. Tamara R. Piety. "Citizens United and the Threat to the Regulatory State," 109 University of Michigan First Impressions 16 (2010), http://www.michiganlawreview.org/assets/fi/109/piety.pdf

35. *Sorrell v. IMS Health, Inc.,* 131 S. Ct. 2653, 2659 (2011).

36. *Zauderer v. Office of Disciplinary Council of the Supreme Court of Ohio,* 471 U.S. 626, 651 (1985).

37. Ibid. 651.

38. *In the Matter of Nestlé HealthCare Nutrition, Inc., a corporation, Agreement Containing Consent Order,* FTC No. 092 3087 (July 14, 2010), http://www.ftc.gov/os/caselist/0923087/100714nestleorder.pdf

39. Federal Trade Commission, "FTC Policy Statement on Deception," Appended to Cliffdale Associates, Inc., 103 F.T.C. 110, 174 (1984), http://www.ftc.gov/bcp/policystmt/ad-decept.htm

Glossary

Actual malice. As used in libel, the term is part of the libel fault standard requiring public figures to show that a defendant made defamatory statements knowing they were false or with reckless disregard for the truth. According to *Harte-Hanks Communications, Inc. v. Connaughton*, 491 U.S. 657, 667, n. 7 (1989), juries may consider evidence concerning motive or care but "'[a]ctual malice may not be inferred alone from evidence of personal spite, ill will or intention to injure on the part of the writer.'"

Ad hoc balancing. Judges assign a preference to either free expression or other societal values by considering the individual circumstances of each case.

Areopagitica. Poet John Milton's appeal to Parliament to rescind their Licensing Order of June 16th, 1643, and a seminal work defending freedom of the press.

Amicus curiae brief. Individuals or groups with a strong interest in the outcome of an appeals case file "friend of the court" papers supporting the arguments of the petitioner or the respondent in the case.

Appropriation. A civil action in which a plaintiff argues that the defendant has used the plaintiff's name or likeness for his or her own benefit without permission.

Bootstrap. Courts will not allow the news media to "bootstrap" a private figure into a public one by relying on the coverage that triggered the libel lawsuit.

Burden of proof. An obligation placed on parties in criminal or civil actions to establish facts or make a prima facie showing, that is, evidence that the elements of a particular cause of action exist sufficient for a trial.

Categorical balancing. When courts disregard the individual circumstances of a case and place a free expression interest, or constitutionally protected one, into a class in which the balance tips in one direction, they are engaging in categorical balancing. For example, courts rate political speech the most deserving of protection, while obscenity warrants no protection.

Certiorari. Parties seeking review by the U.S. Supreme Court must file a writ of certiorari asking the court to review their case. The Court may either accept or deny certiorari.

Chilling Effect. The Court first used the term "chilling" in the free expression context to strike down McCarthy-era, government-imposed loyalty oaths. Such oaths indirectly infringed upon government employees' right of association protected under the First Amendment guarantees of speech, assembly, and petition. In a concurrence, in *Wieman v. Updegraff,* 344 U.S. 183, 195 (1952), Justice Felix Frankfurter noted that an Oklahoma loyalty requirement had "an unmistakable tendency to *chill* [emphasis added] that free play of the spirit which all teachers ought especially to cultivate and practice; it makes for caution and timidity in their associations by potential teachers."

Common carrier. A long-distance mass medium, such as a telephone system, the postal service, and direct broadcast satellite, that operates as a business to convey the content created by others.

Common law. Law created by judges as distinguished from statutory law, created by legislatures.

Communications Act of 1934. The federal statute that created the Federal Communications Commission, giving it authority to regulate long distance electronic communications. The Telecommunications Act of 1996 amended the Communications Act.

Compensatory (general) damages. Payment in a civil action to compensate an injured party for the injury sustained because of a breach of duty.

Concurrence. An opinion, written by a judge or judges on an appeals court panel, that agrees with the majority's opinion only in its result, and provides an alternative rationale and legal doctrine to reach the same conclusion.

Copyright. In the U.S., laws stemming from the Constitution's Article I, Section 8, known as the Copyright Clause, which authorized the Copyright Act of 1790. The act, which has been updated several times since 1790, protects a copyright holder's right to control creative works for a limited period.

Copyright infringement. Under 17 U.S.C. § 501 (A), a copyright holder may bring a lawsuit claiming infringement against anyone who violates his or her exclusive rights of ownership. To show infringement, the copyright holder must (i) prove ownership of a valid copyright and (ii) establish that the defendant "copied" the copyrighted material or violated the copyright holder's other exclusive rights. A plaintiff may prove such misconduct with direct evidence, such as the defendant's admission to seeing or hearing the work, or witnesses testifying that they knew the defendant had access to the work.

Cyber exceptionalism. A media policy that argues for the creation of new laws regulating Internet operation and use based on the technology's unique operational properties.

Defamation. A civil wrong against a reputational interest, and along with identification, publication, fault, and injury, comprises the five elements of a libel claim.

Doctrine. The rules and tests that judges create to resolve future legal disputes implicating the same statutes or substantive areas of law.

Equal Opportunities for Political Candidates or Equal Time Rule. Distinct from the Fairness rules, Section 315 of the Communications Act [47 U.S.C. § 315] "requires radio and television stations and cable systems which originate their own programming to treat legally qualified political candidates equally when it comes to selling or giving away air time."

En banc. Refers to when the "full bench"—all the members of the court—participate in ruling on a case when normally the court requires a smaller number of judges to do so. In the U.S. Circuit Court of Appeals, normally only a panel of three judges rule on a case. En banc hearings, which in the U.S. Court of Appeals for the Third Circuit consist of 15 judges, for example, are granted for rehearing complex cases or to resolve conflicting rulings by panels in the same circuit.

The Espionage Act, 18 U.S.C. § 798. The section of a federal law, originally passed in 1917, that provides criminal penalties for the knowing and willful unauthorized disclosure of federal classified documents.

Exacting Scrutiny. Applied mostly to test the constitutionality of election campaign spending disclosure laws, the analysis requires courts to uphold a stature only if it is narrowly tailored to serve and overriding state interest. The test is more protective of First Amendment and fundamental rights than the intermediate and rational basis tests but less protective than strict scrutiny.

Fairness Doctrine. Developed by the Federal Communications Commission in the 1940s, the now unenforced policy required that radio and television broadcasters devoted a reasonable portion of their broadcast time to the discussion and consideration of controversial issues of public importance and that they endeavored to make their facilities available for the expression of contrasting viewpoints. The FCC repealed the doctrine in 1987. No court, however, has declared the doctrine unconstitutional.

Fair Use Doctrine. Under copyright law, copyright holders enjoy the right to prevent or seek damages from others—infringers—who use their works such as books, movies, song lyrics, and photographs without permission. The Fair Use Doctrine, however, provides infringers with a defense against an infringement lawsuit based on the premise that certain types of unauthorized copying promote discourse beneficial to the public such as criticism, comment, news reporting, and classroom teaching, scholarship or research. The doctrine is codified in 17 U.S.C. § 107, which provides that the key factors in determining whether unauthorized copying are "(i) the purpose and character of the use, including whether such use is of a commercial nature or is for nonprofit educational purposes; (ii) the nature of the copyrighted work; (iii) the amount and substantiality of the portion used in relation to the copyrighted work as a whole; and (iv) the effect of the use upon the potential market for or value of the copyrighted work."

Federal Communications Commission. The federal agency that regulates interstate and international communications by radio, television, wire, satellite, and cable.

Federal Trade Commission. The federal agency, created in 1914, with authority to prevent unfair methods of commercial competition, including deceptive advertising.

Freedom of Information Act. Enacted in 1966, the FOIA requires federal agencies to make government records available to the public, subject to nine categories of exemptions.

Free expression. The right to exchange ideas and information for the purposes of self-governance, political dissent, self-fulfillment, commercial exchange, artistic creativity, and scientific development.

Incitement. Speech that is unprotected by the First Amendment and distinguishable from protected advocacy because it has an immediate and direct effect on provoking illegal conduct.

Intermediate scrutiny. Courts apply intermediate-level scrutiny to test the constitutionality of content-neutral restrictions on broadcast by asking, for example, (i) whether the limitation on free speech advances a substantial government interest, and (ii) whether it is narrowly tailored to achieve that interest. The Court originally crafted the intermediate analysis formula to test the constitutionality of incidental regulations of political speech in *U.S. v. O'Brien*, 391 U.S. 367 (1968). Strict scrutiny is the most speech protective. The rational basis test is the least protective of free speech.

Internet Corporation for Assigned Names and Numbers (ICANN). ICANN is a nonprofit private corporation contracted by the U.S. government to administer policy for the Internet name and address system. ICANN manages *the root*—"the beginning point in a long chain of contracts and cooperation governing how Internet service providers and end users acquire and utilize the addresses and names that make it possible for information to reach its destination . . . The security and stability of the root server system is critical to the viability of any service or function that relies on the Internet." In short, ICANN coordinates the Domain Name System (DNS), Internet Protocol (IP) addresses, space allocation, protocol identifier assignment, generic (gTLD) and country code (ccTLD) Top-Level Domain name system management, and root server system management functions.

Internet Engineering Task Force (IETF). The taskforce, founded in 1986, is a loosely self-organized international group of network designers, operators, and vendors, who contribute to the engineering and evolution of Internet technologies. It is the principal body engaged in the development of new Internet standard specifications and it sets the essential Transmission Control Protocol/Internet Protocol (TCP/IP) standards.

Interoperability. The policy requiring that technologies using the Internet have the capability of operating with existing and future technologies.

Jurisdiction. The geographical and subject-matter areas in which a court has authority.

Landmark ruling. A judicial ruling that substantially changes the interpretation of an area of law.

Libel. Libel is a false statement that injures reputation and is communicated in a fixed medium, traditionally print.

Marketplace of ideas. A First Amendment theory positing that society benefits when government allows all ideas to be exchanged among its citizenry because truth will emerge from the unfettered discussion.

Mass media policy. The general principles that governments use to guide them in establishing goals, methods, and laws affecting media ownership, technological development, and the public's use of media technologies.

Medium-specific First Amendment analysis. The U.S. Supreme Court confers full First Amendment protection to an emerging mass media technology when it operates like print, that is, it plays a major role in allowing citizens to share news and ideas, is not invasive, and is not a scarce commodity. Under the approach, the Court has given full First Amendment protection to print, cinema, the Internet, and video games.

Negligence. The failure to exercise the degree of care appropriate for the circumstance, or which a reasonable person with equal experience would have applied.

Network neutrality. The principle that companies providing broadband access to customers should not discriminate based on the applications, computers, or software consumers use, or the content other media companies provide via broadband.

Newsgathering tort. Recently developed civil causes of action and traditional privacy torts, such as intrusion and trespass, that plaintiffs pursue to hold news organizations liable for wrongdoing which occurs during the course of investigative and under-cover reporting.

Overbreadth doctrine. A legal doctrine that holds that a law is constitutionally invalid when it punishes protected as well as unprotected speech.

Prima facie case. In criminal and civil laws, those bringing formal accusations—prosecutors or plaintiffs—are required to provide a judge with the requisite elements of the particular charge to establish that they have a winnable case. The law, however, provides defendants with defenses and limitations against criminal or civil charges.

Personal Attack Rule. Under the personal attack rule [47 C.F.R. § 73.123], broadcasters had to give notice and free response time to individuals or groups whose honesty, character, or integrity were impugned "during the presentation of views on a controversial issue of pubic importance," whether the accusation was truthful or not. The rule, a corollary to the Fairness Doctrine, affected mostly radio and television talk shows. The rule, however, exempted accusations targeting public figures, foreign groups, or attacks made by political candidates or their authorized spokesperson during a political campaign. The rule also exempted commentary, interviews, interpretation, and analysis spoken in a newscast or news reporting. The FCC repealed the rule in 2000.

Policy arguments. Judges, legislators, and regulators justify the necessity of laws and regulations based on society's economic and social needs.

Political Editorial Rule. The FCC-imposed rule required broadcasters who aired editorials that endorsed or opposed a legally qualified candidate to provide other candidates for the same office a reasonable opportunity to respond. The FCC repealed the Political Editorial Rule and the Personal Attack Rule in 2000.

Precedent. An authoritative ruling for subsequent similar cases implicating the same legal questions.

Preferred balancing. Judges tip the scales toward free expression and place the burden of proof on government to show why its restriction is valid.

Prior restraint. A law, regulation, or policy that allows government to prevent publication, or provides harsh punishment after publication, and which ultimately discourages publication.

Public forum doctrine. The U.S. Supreme Court-created standards and tests determining when government-owned or -controlled space and services must be open to the public for free expression purposes such speechmaking, assembly, and accessing information. This doctrine includes the designated public forum and limited public forum doctrines. When government leases private property that it controls, such as a theater, it creates a designated public forum and it cannot prevent speakers from using the facility based on their political or religious views. Under the limited public forum doctrine, government may limit speech and access based on time, manner, and content in places such as municipal meetings and mailboxes.

Public interest. When media laws are written and applied with the goal of benefiting the public welfare. In the broadcasting context, the Federal Communications Commission operates to promote the "public interest, convenience or necessity," a phrase that currently means, for example, that media ownership rules are enforced to promote diversity, localism, and competition. In the privacy context, the newsworthiness defense can shield news outlets from intrusion, appropriation, and public disclosure of embarrassing private facts lawsuits.

Punitive damages. A civil damage award to punish a defendant for extreme carelessness or maliciousness.

Rational basis test. Courts apply this minimal standard of review in the hierarchy of judicial review that includes strict, exacting, and intermediate scrutiny, asking whether the state's method is a rational way to achieve its stated goals.

Section 230 of the Communications Decency Act. A federal law shielding Internet service providers from liability for the libelous and other tortious postings made by users.

Seditious libel. Communication that defames government officials and is subject to criminal penalties.

Slander is a spoken defamation, a false statement that injures.

Special damages. An award in a civil action based on evidence of economic loss.

Spectrum scarcity. Radio and television signals travel on the electromagnetic spectrum that has bandwidths capable of carrying only one signal at a time in a limited geographical area without causing frequency interference, which would make it impossible for any signal to be heard clearly. Thus, the U.S. Supreme Court has ruled, government must act as a public trustee by placing the broadcast spectrum in the public domain, and allocating its limited resources so that all may benefit.

Stare decisis. A legal term meaning "to stand by that which is decided." This core principle in Anglo-American common law jurisprudence requires judges to apply the same doctrines and tests to cases implicating the same areas of law and raising similar facts.

Strict scrutiny. Courts apply this most speech-protective analysis to test the constitutionality of laws that restrict content—the law must advance a compelling government interest and must be the least restrictive means of achieving that interest. The intermediate, exacting, and the rational basis tests are the less protective forms of judicial scrutiny. Courts also apply these tests to statutes that restrict other fundamental and constitution protections such as due process and equal protection.

Telecommunications. From the Greek word "tele," meaning distant or far off and the Latin word "communicare," for share or receive, telecommunications are media technologies that transmit words, sounds, images, or data in the form of electronic or electromagnetic signals or impulses over long distances. At first, there was mere telegraphy, long-distance communication such as smoke, flag or reflecting light systems. The development of man-made electricity enabled the development of electronic telecommunications—telegraph, telephone, radio, broadcast and cable television, fax machines, satellite, cellular phones, and the Internet.

Time, place, and manner restriction. The First Amendment allows government to regulate when, where and how speech takes place in public settings to maintain peace and safety as long as it does so without regard to the identity of the speaker or the speaker's message (content-neutral). Citing precedent in *Grayned v. City of Rockford*, 408 U.S. 104,116 (1972), the U.S. Supreme Court gave the following examples of reasons for imposing content-neutral time, place, and manner restrictions: "two parades cannot march on the same street simultaneously, and government may allow only one; a demonstration or parade on a large street during rush hour might put an intolerable burden on the essential flow of traffic, and for that reason could be prohibited; and "if overamplified loudspeakers assault the citizenry, government may turn them down."

Torts. Laws that provide a plaintiff with a right to bring an action in civil court alleging that a defendant failed to perform a legal duty and that the plaintiff suffered damages as a result of the defendant's breach of duty. Privacy and libel actions are a form of torts.

Universal service. A media policy concept requiring that a long-distance communication service should be affordable and available to even the most economical poor and geographically remote segments of a nation.

Vagueness doctrine. A law is constitutionally invalid when its language fails to make clear what is commanded or prohibited.

Subject Index

Cases Index